JAMES COLQUHOUN IRVINE

JAMES COLQUHOUN IRVINE

St Andrews' Second Founder

Julia Melvin

First published in Great Britain in 2011 by
John Donald, an imprint of Birlinn Ltd

West Newington House
10 Newington Road
Edinburgh
EH9 1QS

www.birlinn.co.uk

ISBN 978 1 906566 31 9

The publishers gratefully acknowledge the support of
The Pilgrim Trust, the Russell Trust,
the Strathmartine Trust and
the After Many Days Club of St Andrews Alumni
towards the publication of this book

British Library Cataloguing-in-Publication Data
A catalogue record for this book is available on request
from the British Library

Typeset in Minion by
Koinonia, Manchester
Printed and bound in Britain by
MPG Books, Bodmin, Cornwall

During the Second World War, in a sleepy backwater of suburban London, a little boy, kept home from school on account of the bombing, would have to amuse himself with pranks and ploys of his own. A distinguished elderly gentleman, after concluding his government business in London, would often make his way out to Hampton Wick to make a tea-time visit to his married daughter and small granddaughter. He was an object of fascination to the boy collecting conkers under the chestnut trees. Strolling back together afterwards towards the southern line railway station, the elder statesman and the little boy struck up a friendship. But who was this notable personage? Oh, said the boy's mother, that's Sir James Irvine. In the somewhat dowdy world of wartime London, his dapper appearance, in striped trousers, short black jacket, Homburg hat and spats over well-polished shoes, was bound to attract attention. The old gentleman was the very picture of a man upon whom wisdom and authority hung naturally. He was indeed the Grand Old Man of Education, the most senior vice-chancellor, the trusted servant of the Colonial Office, the scientific consultant par excellence in matters chemical and biochemical to a succession of governments, the intimate friend of the great pre-war philanthropists on both sides of the Atlantic, and a much lauded scholar and academic. To the little boy he was merry and interested. The union of innocence and experience, of master and pupil, was the cause that inspired Irvine's life.

I was the small granddaughter; the little boy became my husband. It is to him that I dedicate this book.

What is that end and aim of learning, as he conceived it? Learning, he says, is more than knowledge, however useful or ornamental; it is something which creates in us a benignity of mind, something which enables us to search for and seize opportunities to serve and to oblige. The test of education ... is found ultimately in goodwill and good breeding, in gentleness and a belief in the good intentions of those around us.

James Colquhoun Irvine recalling Benjamin Franklin on 'Learning'

Contents

Foreword

Every year, the University of St Andrews holds a service of thanksgiving in St Salvator's chapel at which we remember those men and women to whom, on an institutional and often individual level, we owe so much. The prayer in commemoration of our founders and benefactors speaks of 'all who by their learning, their goodwill, and their humble service have enriched this place'. We recall by name those men whose vision brought our university into being in the fifteenth century, and ensured its early survival and subsequent flourishing: Henry Wardlaw, James Kennedy, Alexander Stewart, John Hepburn, James Beaton and John Hamilton. Even today their legacy remains, and it is upon their shoulders that we stand and look out and engage with the world. It is from them that we have inherited our fundamental belief in the pursuit of truth, in the questioning of tired doctrines and in the important contribution made to society – both here in Scotland and on a national and international stage – by an academic community where intellectual debate flourishes, and where successive generations of students are encouraged to realise their own remarkable potential.

There can be few students who have realised that potential so successfully, or to the greater benefit of their alma mater, than James Colquhoun Irvine, who served as Principal and Vice-Chancellor of the University of St Andrews for over thirty years from 1921. 'Irvine of St Andrews', as he would become known in later life, first came to the university in 1895 as a lecture assistant. He subsequently matriculated as a student, and graduated with a BSc with special distinction in Chemistry and Natural Sciences in 1898. It was from such sure yet unremarkable beginnings that the foundations were laid for Irvine's career as a fine experimental chemist. Perhaps as importantly, it was surely during these formative years in St Andrews that his deep love of the university and the town was born.

After a spell of further study and research at the University of Leipzig, James Irvine returned to St Andrews as a junior lecturer. In addition to his considerable research skills, and his prowess as a popular and gifted teacher, it became increasingly clear as the years progressed that Irvine had an unusual and prodigious talent for administration. His appointment as Principal in 1921 heralded a period of previously unimaginable growth and development at the university. Under his careful and inspired leadership, University coffers were restored to health, student numbers were raised to a financially viable level, and the reputation of Scotland's oldest seat of learning was given a new lustre, which ensured that students and academics flocked to work and study here from near and, increasingly, far. Irvine was, by all accounts, a man of considerable charm, tact and diplomacy who had a great memory both for people and events. He never failed to use these gifts to further the university's cause, and worked tirelessly to realise his ambitions for St Andrews, particularly for the students, whose welfare was one of his greatest concerns.

This book is going to press as preparations gather pace for the celebration of the 600th anniversary of the foundation of the University. Such an historic milestone affords us an opportunity both to reflect with pride upon our rich past, and to plan for the future of the university. Principal Irvine was a man who left the institution he loved, and to which he devoted so many years of his life, strengthened and enriched by having passed through his hands. I am delighted that, through the publication of this biography, we have a fresh opportunity to give due recognition to the role that he played in the shaping of the university during a critical period in the twentieth century.

Dr Louise Richardson, FRSE,
Principal and Vice-Chancellor
of the University of St Andrews

List of Illustrations

Endpapers: two grisaille watercolours of the ruins of St Andrews Cathedral, painted by James Green, c. 1816. Courtesy of the author.

Plate section 1

1 The Irvine family's weaver's cottage at Ladycross, near Maybole, Ayrshire.
2 Mary Paton Colquhoun Irvine (1851–1923), James Colquhoun Irvine's mother, at the time of her marriage in 1874.
3 James Colquhoun Irvine, aged three years.
4 James Irvine at the Free Church Normal School, aged seven years.
5 James's father, John Irvine, in the garden of Heathfield, with James's brother Alec.
6 Springburn Harriers in the early 1890s.
7 James Irvine, October 1899, at the time of his award to an 1851 Exhibition Scholarship to study in Leipzig.
8 The microscope used in the St Andrews Chemical Research Institute by James Colquhoun Irvine.
9 Mabel Violet Williams, before her departure (1899) from Belfast to study violin and piano in Leipzig.
10 Mabel Violet Williams c.1900, as she was when 'Jim' first fell in love with her.
11 Irvine in the Erste Institut für Chemie in Leipzig.
12 James Colquhoun Irvine, DSc St Andrews, March 1903.
13 James Irvine (1904), when appointed to a lectureship in Chemistry in St Andrews. (University of St Andrews Collection: Read_366)
14 Irvine with Professor Purdie in the new Chemistry Research Laboratory, St Andrews, c.1905. (University of St Andrews Collection: Read_1754)
15 Irvine, 1909, at the time of his induction to the Chair of Chemistry in St Andrews.

Illustrations are from the collection of the author and Dr George Gandy, with the exception of Plates 13, 14, 17, 24, 29, 33-35, 40, 41, 43 and 44, which are from the University of St Andrews Photographic Collection and are reproduced with permission.

Acknowledgements

My greatest debt is to the wise and kindly support and encouragement of David Walker, Regius Professor Emeritus of Law at the University of Glasgow. My warmest thanks are extended to Professor Walker, who is James Colquhoun Irvine's nephew; he has read the whole text in draft and has contributed much valuable specialist information; and he undertook to write the index and correct the proofs for the publisher. His generosity and enthusiasm have helped to make this account of James Colquhoun Irvine's life.

I thank Dr Louise Richardson, FRSE, Principal and Vice-Chancellor of the University of St Andrews who, in the middle of a busy life, has found time to write the Foreword to this book.

This biography could never have been published without the generosity of a number of grant-giving trusts, and I remain deeply grateful for the interest of their trustees and for grants given towards its publication by The Pilgrim Trust, the Russell Trust, the Strathmartine Trust and the After Many Days Club of St Andrews alumni. Their support has honoured Irvine's name.

Many of my friends in Scotland have played a part in easing my path as I undertook the long research into the life of so busy a man as Irvine, and I would if I could thank them all by name, but I owe a great deal in particular to the friendship and professional advice of Dr Barbara Crawford of St Andrews and to her husband, Professor R. M. M. Crawford. I am deeply grateful to Barbara for having played a constant part in making sure that Irvine's Life was published.

I thank Dr Douglas Lloyd, Professor of Chemistry in the University of St Andrews, who has generously read the 'chemical' chapters for errors and who has given me specialist advice. I thank Dr Frank Quinault, who has read some chapters in draft and whose admiration for Irvine prompted him to urge me to write this Life. I acknowledge the assistance of the late

Dr Michael Barry for his conversations about pioneering carbohydrate research. I was received by Professor Dr Athanassios Giannis, the Direktor of the Institut für Organische Chemie in Leipzig, where I was also introduced to the archivist of the Institut. I thank Ana Rodrigez-Cano, whose father, John Oldham, was a favourite research student of Irvine's: Ana has passed on to me valuable source material concerning this period of Irvine's life.

I am grateful to Professor Roger Mason, Director of the St Andrews Institute for Scottish Historical Research, under the auspices of which this book has been published. I thank Professor Ian Carradice, Director of St Andrews University Museum Collections, for offering to hold an exhibition on the life of James Colquhoun Irvine in MUSA at the time of the launch of this book.

I thank Professor Michael Gardner, of the University of Bradford, for bringing to my attention the activities of the Hebridean Sporting Association.

I have spoken to and interviewed a selective number of people whose lives were touched by J.C. Irvine. Their views and experiences have done much to guide and inform this biography: these include firstly Irvine's elder daughter, my dear late mother, who enjoyed remembering all manner of interesting detail during her last years.

The late Dr John Fewster, the late Douglas Hamilton and the late Dr Kenneth Lowe each had an illuminating experience to recount.

I have enjoyed the discussion of details with Cecilia Irvine, the widow of Nigel Irvine.

Conversations with Professor Geoffrey Barrow, Jan Read, Betty Willsher and the Rev. Marie-Louise Moffett and her sister Ann Rose have contributed insight. John Stirling, of the Castle House Museum, at Dunoon, gave me much information concerning the Royal Clyde Yacht Club at Hunter's Quay, and I wish to thank him for his readiness to source obscure references for use in the writing of this book. Tam Dalyell was eager to recount his boyhood encounter with Irvine.

The primary sources for Irvine's life are considerable, but they are mainly of two types: his personal papers are still held by his family, and I am much indebted to the kindness of my brother Dr George Gandy for agreeing to their use for this purpose.

The other main source for this biography lies, of course, within the University of St Andrews and its library.

I acknowledge the professional support of the staff of the Special Collections of the University of St Andrews, with especial mention of Rachel Hart and Dr Norman Reid, to whom I owe more than I can well express. Their department conserves large sources for any study of James Colquhoun Irvine's life and of the history of the university during that life, and they have welcomed me to this resource almost as a colleague. I have used the Russell Papers in the university's Special Collections, and I am grateful to the trustees of the Russell family for according this use to researchers.

I wish to record my thanks to the staff of the photographic archive of St Andrews University, Marc Boulay and in particular Pam Cranston, whose respect for the subject of this book has helped me access some fine illustrations. I wish to acknowledge the generosity of the University of St Andrews in granting me permission to use photographs from the University's collection to illustrate this book. I also thank Marc Boulay, Photographic Archivist of the Photographic Collection at St Andrews, for his photograph of the Irvine window in the apse of St Salvator's College Chapel.

The copyright of Mabel Irvine's memoir, *The Avenue of Years*, from which I have quoted, rests with the University of St Andrews. I acknowledge the University's part in granting me this use.

In St Andrews also, I have been given enormous support by the Strathmartine Centre, and its Trust, the late Ronald Cant's gift for research into the history of St Andrews and of Scotland. The Centre's premises and library have become a home from home to me and I have become a grateful 'user'. The St Andrews Preservation Trust and John Matthews as its Chairman have been supportive of my research.

The forensic work of chasing up the details that should give a biography authenticity has led me to some wonderful libraries and their kindly staff.

I wish to acknowledge the assistance given by the following:

The staff of Glasgow University Archive Services; the archivists of the Special Collections of the Mitchell Library, Glasgow; the archivist of the Special Collections of Strathclyde University.

Alison Metcalfe, Manuscripts Curator at the National Library of Scotland, has put herself out to make my way easier. I am grateful to the trustees of the National Library of Scotland for granting me use of the Borthwick Papers, the Haldane Papers, the Cooper Papers and the autobiography of Major-General Douglas Wimberley.

I have been given valuable assistance by the staff of the National Archives of Scotland and the staff of the library of New College, Edinburgh.

I have used the resource of the Bibliothèque de l'Histoire de la Ville de Paris for information on the Exposition Universelle; readers in the Bibliothèque have the great pleasure of studying in a seventeenth-century *hôtel particulier.*

Angela Kenny, Archivist to the Royal Commission for the Exhibition of 1851, took a helpful interest in supporting the biography of a former scholar who became a commissioner.

The archivist of the Erste Institut für Chemie in Leipzig was most efficient in finding Irvine's matriculation papers for me.

I acknowledge the assistance of the Secretary of the Carnegie Trust for the Universities of Scotland, who gave me easy access to their records.

My path in tracing the paper trail whereby scientists were commissioned to work for the War Office during the First World War was made smooth by the staff of the library of the Royal Society. They accorded me the pleasant experience of working in their library, and made source material available to me with such ease.

I acknowledge my indebtedness to the trustees of the British Library for my use of the India Office Papers.

I have used the National Archives at Kew; the Special Collections Department of the library of University College, London, for the Moyne Papers in the Institute of Commonwealth Studies; also King's College London, the Liddell Hart Centre for Military Archives; and the Colindale Newspaper Library of the British Library.

I acknowledge the assistance of the trustees of the Bodleian Library in Oxford in making the papers of Clement Attlee and the papers of the Society for the Protection of Science and Learning available for my use; also the trustees of the Rhodes Trust, Oxford, for use of the papers of Margery Perham.

The staff of the Special Collections at the University of Sussex made the Rudyard Kipling Archive available to me, and in this respect I wish to acknowledge the kind permission of the National Trust to use the Rudyard Kipling Papers, which they own.

I am grateful for the help given me by Rupa Kundu and the British Science Association (formerly the British Association for the Advancement of Science), and for the help given me by David Allen, Keeper of the Library Collections of the Royal Society of Chemistry. I have also found the librarians of the Royal Institution helpful and interested.

My publishers, Birlinn Ltd, have been unerringly charming and easy, while remaining reassuringly businesslike. I am proud to have this biography of a great Scotsman published by such a fine press. I am particularly grateful to Hugh Andrew for his courtesy and to Mairi Sutherland, the Managing Editor of Birlinn's John Donald imprint, which has produced this book. Mairi has been always welcoming and helpful. I would also like to thank my copy-editor, who has been remarkably painstaking and patient and always ready with kind advice.

Lastly I thank my family: my two children, Lucy and Charles, who have looked on with amused approbation as my work took shape, and above all my endlessly patient husband, who has never ceased to believe that I would reach the summit. I do not deserve his admiration, but it has been essential to me. He is truly the chief patron of this book.

This biography is written for future generations, not only of Sir James Colquhoun Irvine's family, but of St Andrews University, of which he was a father figure.

Julia Melvin
Ascott and Paris

Introduction

James Colquhoun Irvine, KBE, DSc, FRS (1877–1952) was one of Scotland's great men of science; he was also an educationalist whose colourful attachment to the University of St Andrews formed the bedrock of a life devoted to the civilising force of education.

He earned an international reputation as a pioneering chemist during the first two decades of the twentieth century; the brilliance and drive that he brought to carbohydrate chemistry produced astounding results, and he and his small team synthesised and analysed in the laboratory in St Andrews an enormous corpus of over 700 sugars.

This was followed by a second career: throughout a period of thirty years, he was Principal and Vice-Chancellor of St Andrews University at its most significant point of development. Lastly, he devoted his skill and experience to furthering higher education all over the world. He will always be associated with the University of St Andrews: he was described as its second founder,[1] and in St Andrews he is something of a myth.

There are those today who have not forgotten his originality as a scientist, and who can aver that the chemical legacy of 'sugars Irvine' is alive. Others attest that his achievement as a university administrator still burns bright, while some will speak of him admiringly as an academic statesman operating at a time when the concept was new. Through the vehicle of education, he changed the lives of thousands of young men and women.

However, a further compelling reason why his story should live lies in a dimension of his personality that distinguished him from others: he was a deep romantic, whose sense of beauty and history bound him to a small university situated in a somewhat isolated position, far from the hub of metropolitan life. When still quite young but already known and admired as a university teacher who had most successfully turned Scottish Principal, larger wealthier institutions, even an Ivy League American university, looked enviously at St Andrews and tried to lure him away to more moneyed, more powerful posts, but always unsuccessfully. From his safe anchorage in the Trollopian world of Scotland's most ancient university, he pursued his vision on the world stage, at first on behalf of his beloved alma mater and then, in a far broader sense, on behalf of higher education wherever the map was coloured pink and wherever these countries needed his experience, support and vision. In the modern way, he lectured on his subject in America, and he attracted the support and friendship of the kindly American to the development of St Andrews University. He was to one and all 'Irvine of St Andrews'. If you go to the old cathedral burying ground, 'where the dew falls, and the rain and the wind and the sun, where the flowers and the leaves sink into the earth in winter,'[2] you will find his tombstone, carved by the Scottish sculptor, Hew Lorimer.[3] Read there, and you will be told: 'Remember James Colquhoun Irvine.'

Greatness is a quality that we can recognise in certain men and women of brilliance from Scotland's past. If we turn our minds to St Andrews, we are made aware that it nurtures a tradition of venerating the great men who formed its history. And now, today, St Andrews once again exerts a growing magnetism, and the world celebrates it not just for the golf but, with increasing justification, for its university, the most venerable in Scotland. It is now grown to maturity, while still miraculously maintaining the intimacy that Irvine knew and cherished a hundred years ago.

Scotland's heroes intrigue us today; there is a fascination with the psyche of the Scot. If we start to examine the giants on whose shoulders we stand, it is natural to think of the age of elegance and of the intellects that flourished in Scotland after the Treaty of Union of 1707. Those Scots who are associated with the Enlightenment undoubtedly bear an aura of glamour. The philosophers, economists, architects, inventors, scientists, lawyers, writers and churchmen of eighteenth-century Scotland put a stamp on western civilisation that was out of all proportion to the size and state of Scotland at that time.

Yet it could be argued that, as children of the twentieth century, we owe far more to a later group of men and women who belonged to the more complex culture of Scotland's mercantile success in the last quarter of the nineteenth century. This was a generation that was equipped to enter the new scientific age with confidence, but that was built out of the struggles and aspirations of earlier decades; this was a generation of professional men and women who became figureheads of our times. On the whole, none of these intelligent late Victorians would have said of themselves that what they had in common was being Scottish. They were British, and all conscious of distinguishing themselves for their nation in some wider way. However, if we look more closely at them we can see that they share the tension of a passionate love of their roots coupled with a strong sense of independence. James Colquhoun Irvine was one of these great men: determined, driven by self-belief, but visionary, they were the cornerstones of the modern age.

On his arrival in St Andrews in 1895, aged not quite twenty, he found a revered but antiquated institution with about 200 students and an impressive corpus of distinguished professors. From then on, he hardly left St Andrews. What is now known as the Irvine era was a period of unprecedented growth in numbers and prestige: it set a standard against which successive generations have tended to be measured. The Irvine era brought St Andrews to the notice of peoples all over the world, who unquestioningly admired and then emulated this tiny bastion of learning, seated on a northerly extremity of Europe. Distinguished visitors to the Principal's house – princes, poets, playwrights, actors and painters, as well as scholars – learned in Irvine's company to fall in love with the place. Soon in the drawing rooms, senior common rooms and gentlemen's clubs on both sides of the Atlantic, people would be talking of the spell they had fallen under in St Andrews as the guests of the enthusiastic Principal, and St Andrews benefited beyond measure from its new fame. The London newspapers became eager to publish news of the burgeoning, yet ancient, seat of learning in North Britain, as Scotland was still fashionably referred to.

James Irvine's life embraced many of the great ideals that had first taken root a generation earlier: ideals in secondary education as well as in higher education; in medical education and health; in the development of the colonies; and in philanthropy. Young Irvine was a Victorian, a man of strong Christian faith, holding fast to the virtues of serving God and empire. As an early twentieth-century scientist, he was not conscious of any conflict or compromise between his spiritual beliefs and his scientific training; he was, on the contrary, strengthened by a profound sense of the metaphysical.

The heroic early organic chemists whose lives he was able to record at first hand are also to be found in this book; they can be known and celebrated by us today through the eyes of their admiring young postulant. Janus-like, however, Irvine was of both the old century and the new. He was the very model of his age. The new scientific world that he inhabited in his early years had, like him, grown in large measure out of the manufacturing interests of Glasgow, but as a student in St Andrews he learned how to distance himself from industrial science. As a research chemist, he admitted to a sense of discovery comparable to that which had fired the Arctic explorers of his age, the botanists in the Himalayas and in South America, and the archeologists in Asia Minor. In his field he examined and defined the unknown.

Broadly, however, his life's work was education. His genial approach to his fellow man, and his belief that he was put on this earth to give his considerable talents to serve his country, rendered him a familiar figure far beyond St Andrews. On his gravestone, the belt round his personal coat of arms bears the words 'For God and the Empire': the motto of the Order of the British Empire, of which he was proud to be a member. His personal motto was *Ecce ego, mitte me*.[4] His young family colloquially translated this into 'Here am I, send me', rather in the manner of the Biblical Samuel, ministering to Eli. He would jokingly say that he should be described on his visiting card as 'Young Gentleman Travelling in Education'. 'Oh, there's Sir James,' cried Queen Elizabeth, later the Queen Mother,[5] on one occasion. 'My husband and I call him our unofficial ambassador.'

What is of far more interest than cataloguing his many achievements is to examine what shaped and formed him: what was his background; what were the features and even quirks of his character that sustained him along this relentless road; what cracks were there, perhaps, in the edifice? He gave to the chemical world solutions to some of the previously intractable problems of the past and produced insights into fields that had not previously been opened. Irvine liked to look back on the lives of his heroes, the Scottish chemists of the earlier centuries, whose number included Robert Murray, a foundation Fellow of the Royal Society. He could see that the Scottish character was often exemplified in these men: 'Industry and enthusiasm, Scotch caution and philosophic daring, dogged perseverance and certain disregard of public opinion'[6] were the qualities that he valued. We now have to admit that they can be discerned in him.

It was through the second stage of his life, while Principal and Vice-Chancellor of St Andrews, that he was finally called upon to give growth, vision and form to institutes of education all over the world. The Viceroy of India commissioned him to examine and report on the failings and future of the Indian Institute of Science in Bangalore. As chairman of the wartime Irvine Committee that reported on higher education in the West Indies[7] for the Asquith Commission, he became the founding father of the University of the West Indies. In his honour, it adopted a version of the St Andrews' scarlet gown in lightweight cloth, and named its first hall of residence Irvine

Hall. He was also sent on behalf of the Asquith Commission to further the development of Gordon College in Khartoum.

As for his beloved St Andrews, he left it soundly endowed, in many ways to the envy of its sister universities. St Andrews, which in his early days was marked by poverty, a paucity of students, a lack of proper buildings and equipment for the teaching of science, and neglect of the well-being of the student body, was once again brought to new life and promise. He had been a student himself at St Andrews when students moved from one lodging house to another. His great belief was in the corporate life that the residential system could provide, and the great change he wrought at St Andrews had at its heart the building of collegiate halls of residence, each a refined and civilised institution in its own right.

Irvine was a man of strong passions and deep affection towards young developing minds. There was something both intimate and awesome about this Buchanesque man, whose character had the stamp of high purpose but who never lost a lifelong and boyish sense of fun and adventure. He approached his lectures to the first-year chemistry students with barely suppressed excitement. With children, his games were inventive, conspiratorial and full of the joy of the moment. He did not suffer fools gladly, however, and he was quick to condemn the foolish, particularly when he found foolishness amongst those through whom he had to work. He was a dreamer of dreams, a charismatic Scot, who won over to his several causes the fortunes of many of the great philanthropists of the twentieth century. To most of those he encountered he was a most attractive personality, but he was also strongly disliked by some of his colleagues in St Andrews. It is arguable that his eventual disenchantment with his career in chemistry was exacerbated by his personality clash with his younger colleague, Norman Haworth[8] (later Sir Norman Haworth, FRS and Nobel Prize winner), who had joined his department as lecturer just before the outbreak of the First World War.

His autocratic command over the affairs of his alma mater was to him wise paternalism; to a few others it smacked of blind self-will. At the end of his life it was feared that his very personal nurturing of the University of St Andrews would be blown apart by the clamour of University College Dundee for greater self-government. He knew that St Andrews and Dundee needed each other. He had been in office in St Andrews for so long and had faced the problems of unity through many upheavals, but Dundee, Scotland's fourth city – some said third city – once the prosperous centre for jute, had been brought to bankruptcy by first the depression and then the Second World War. In a generation before the new universities of the Robbins Report, the city burghers of Dundee believed they could see a solution to the city's problems in the status it would be given if it were granted a university charter in its own right. When faced with this likelihood, Irvine could brook none of it, and opposed it with all the intellectual strength that he, by then a sick and elderly man, could muster. Was what he termed 'the Dundee fiasco' his Achilles heel? There is evidence to show that, had he lived, he would have fought the 1952 Royal Commission through its committee stage to garner some virtue out of necessity.

There is a relevance to us today in understanding the history of a brilliant Scot who, to such a pronounced degree, shaped his times. Such men do not come often. His life was enlivened by adventure, scientific innovation and even scientific espionage; it was sharpened by a youthful sense of competition and of discovery.

On his death, his fellow principal, Sir Hector Hetherington of Glasgow University,[9] wrote of him:

> Sir James Irvine will not be forgotten as long as the University of St Andrews endures. He was its Principal for more than thirty years; he is now one of the commanding figures of its long history. To him far more than to any other, the University owes the remarkable enlargement of its academic resources and the seemly beauty of its material estate. He loved St Andrews with all the strength of an eager and generous heart, and gave to it the full service of his powers.[10]

It is for the generation that lives at the time of the University's 600th year to remember the truth of these tributes, and to understand how the Irvine legacy was achieved.

ONE

The Power House of the Empire

James Colquhoun Irvine was born at 33 Bardowie Street, Possilpark, Glasgow in the district of Maryhill on 9 May 1877,[1] the second son of John and Mary Irvine. They were a family of Ayrshire weaving stock on the father's side and of seamen from the Western Highlands on Mary Irvine's side.

At times it has been claimed for James Irvine that he was that strange phenomenon found in some great Scotsmen: a 'lad o' pairts', a boy of lowly origins who struggled to rise from poverty to put his stamp upon the world. In fact this was not the case, and the truth about his roots is infinitely more interesting. James Irvine was a product of much of the best of late nineteenth-century Glasgow, and his Glasgow family background was immensely formative both of his abilities as an organic chemist and of his personality as a leader of twentieth-century higher educational reform. This was what he himself, in recounting Carnegie's life, called the 'first cause' that goes a long way in revealing the working of an adult mind.

On the surface, the Glasgow of young Irvine's childhood was a city that displayed considerable confidence in itself. It was entering what could be described as the third period of its industrial development: by the 1870s it had embraced a complex web of industries that had steadily grown from seeds sown in the previous century and now fed the growing expectations of the city's proud people. First, the large civil engineering works devoted to improving the Glasgow basin of the Clyde had made possible the move of the shipbuilding interest from Port Glasgow up into the city itself. Trade with the American colonies was the initial driving force. Fine classical buildings in ashlar-cut blonde sandstone housing the tobacco bonded warehouses, the customs house and exchange houses were built along the quaysides of the Clyde, symbolising the wealth of these first commercial activities. It was a wealth that was more anchored in the past, content at first with capitalising on imports from North America.

Daniel Defoe described early eighteenth-century Glasgow soon after the Treaty of Union of 1707 as 'the beautifullest little city I have seen in Britain; it stands deliciously on the banks of the river Clyde, over which there is a fair stone bridge of eight arches'.[2] Even in the first half of the nineteenth century, the city of Glasgow was still essentially a medieval town with an ancient university and a reputation for business. It was not yet the great port that in a generation it would become. In contrast were Port Glasgow, and the port of Irvine in Ayrshire, which served Scotland's hand-production of fine cotton. Until the end of the eighteenth century, Irvine town was known as the third port of Scotland. The mechanisation of the weaving industry brought the cotton mills to the city's southerly borders with Ayrshire and Renfrewshire. It was this industry that drove the early development of Glasgow as a manufacturing city, and it was to this industry that the Irvines belonged.

Glasgow's shipbuilding communities, whether in Port Glasgow or later on Clydeside, were attached to the south of the river: the north bank presented sandbanks even in the estuary. Irvine's mother's family, the Colquhouns, had settled in this community.

But the cotton mills and the shipbuilding were not enough alone to encourage Glasgow in her self-styled sobriquet, 'The Second City of the Empire'. The American War of Independence and later the American Civil War introduced major difficulties to the import of the raw cotton and the tobacco that Glasgow's elegant eighteenth-century quaysides had been designed to receive.

Nevertheless, the textile and chemical industries grew hand-in-hand. It is generally held that Scotland's Industrial Revolution can be attributed to this potent partnership: the invention of the steam-powered looms and the innovative development of the chemicals that served the cotton industry. The weaving mills south of the Clyde and the production of bleaching agents and dyes were the earliest of the noisome industries of Glasgow. From these beginnings, Glasgow grew into a hothouse of heavy engineering develop-ment and invention, coupled with the culture of keen business acumen. Throughout the nineteenth century, Glasgow helped to maintain Scotland's reputation for the machine weaving of fine cotton and the production of printed muslins, while the weaving communities of rural Ayrshire declined. It was Glasgow, not Manchester, where the finest cloth was still produced. Specialism was another of the ways whereby the old weaving traditions might be upheld and James Irvine's grandfather, Alexander Irvine, arrived in Glasgow as a specialist.

In its second period of expansion, Glasgow turned to large-scale manufacturing using cast iron. The Lanarkshire western lowlands on the north-eastern edge of the city offered the raw materials of iron and coal for smelting in a valuable and convenient form, the Lanarkshire coal being naturally banded with the blackband iron ore. Glasgow became the originator of heavy engineering and of railway stock of all kinds. Industry gradually moved up from around the river to the northerly greenfield sites of Springburn and the canal basins of Port Dundas, Glasgow's link with the Forth and Clyde Canal.

Throughout the United Kingdom it was the canal system that encouraged the growth of another iron-made product, ornamental cast iron. The use of cast-iron in buildings became an art form that embellished the builders' pattern books. By the 1870s of James Irvine's boyhood, Glasgow had successfully added the manufacture of cast-iron architectural goods to her well-balanced portfolio of industrial production. It was in the ornamental cast-iron industry that James Irvine's father prospered.

Many other industries and much invention followed in the wake of both the textile mills and the cast-iron factories. A new confluence of clever scientific minds with the availability of specific raw materials and a vast workforce were major contributors to the speed with which Glasgow was able to embrace the boom of the last quarter of the nineteenth century. No longer backward-looking and dependent on old trades, Glasgow above all cities in the United Kingdom based its success on its ability to shape and conceive an economy of the future.

The name Irvine, as well as belonging to Ayrshire, is found in Ulster; William Irvine, James Colquhoun Irvine's great-grandfather, was born in Ireland. Apart from this temporary lapse, these Irvines were resolutely Ayrshire men. A romance worthy of Sir Walter Scott's *Old Mortality* was the family belief that an Irvine ancestor had been a Covenanter and had been killed at the bloody skirmish of Airdsmoss in 1680, and thus came to be buried in Glasgow cathedral. If a generalisation can be made, the people of Ayrshire for centuries were a steely, independent race with a propensity towards high principles in matters of religion. The Irvines had in their blood the strength of character needed to rise above the modesty of their domestic lives. James Colquhoun Irvine's great-grandfather was the last to make his living in Ayrshire;[3] he worked the handloom and lived in a but-and-ben cottage at Ladycross near Maybole. The Irvines' small agricultural property at Ladycross suggests some social superiority from the weavers in the town of Maybole, whose cramped accommodation was for the most part 'tied' to their employment. The 1841 census shows that the three adult males of the Irvine family, including James Colquhoun Irvine's grandfather, Alexander, were all handloom weavers.[4] Men and women like this created Ayrshire's reputation for the production of fine cotton and muslin. It was, however, in large measure a cottage industry that complemented the farming activities of the heads of household. The Irvines, describing themselves as yeoman farmers with an interest in the weaving business, clung as long as they dared to a living that they had pursued for generations.

The effect of the slump in agriculture of the 1830s on these families was exacerbated by this failing local industry, which could not compete with the factory mills that were being opened up in the conurbation of Glasgow. The future for the Irvine family's domestic economy, so heavily dependent on artisan skills, was bleak. In these years Maybole became empty and decayed. The poor were in desperate straits and moral values were low.[5]

Round about the year 1850, James Colquhoun Irvine's grandfather brought his wife and young son to live in Glasgow, joining the large migration of those of working age from rural Scotland into the great city. Thousands were drawn there by the demand for labour offered by the new industries, but the Irish famine also brought unwelcome competition for factory jobs from across the Irish Channel. Leaving his farming interests behind, but with hope in his expertise in the printing of muslins, Alexander Irvine attempted to join this new workforce. Alexander must have carved out a livelihood for himself, for in 1874 he was to sign his eldest son's marriage certificate describing himself as 'journeyman muslin printer',[6] a prestigious occupation in the cotton industry. Like many Ayrshire men, he was progressive by nature, and he looked beyond the strictures of their life in Glasgow. He took himself down to London to view the 1851 Great Exhibition, to compare the techniques and designs in weaving machinery with those he knew in Scotland. He belonged to a generation that was transitional in the history of this great city. There is no doubt that, from about 1850, this family embraced the new age.

His son, John Irvine, the father of young James, was the only one of his siblings to have been born in Maybole before his parents abandoned their old way of life. He inherited an interest in technology from his father, Alexander, and he had a decidedly scientific bent. Glasgow offered a very appealing aspect to this rather serious-minded family, who were drawn to the wider possibilities for education to be obtained there. Glasgow held out to them the prospect of a better future. However, schooling provision was not universal until the Scottish Education Act of 1872, and although John Irvine's younger brother was encouraged to complete some schooling, the 1871 census shows that his elder sister, nineteen years old, already worked as a machinist in a book-producing factory. Even his younger sister, Anne Park Irvine, who was twelve in 1871, had what was probably a part-time job as a message girl. The little brother, Alexander, aged nine, is recorded as a 'scholar'.[7]

The two families, that of James Colquhoun Irvine's father and that of his mother, were alike to a considerable degree. The harsh reality that the sources of employment imposed on their households during the 1840s and 1850s defined the childhoods of both John Irvine and his wife Mary Paton Colquhoun. Both the Irvines and the Colquhouns were fiercely devout adherents to the tenets and way of life of the Free Church of Scotland. Two generations earlier, John Irvine's grandfather William, at Maybole, had been involved in the 1843 church schism in the Established Church of Scotland (known as the Disruption),[8] and had followed the new harsh ordinance of Free Church government and mission. Personal sacrifice and high ideals were demanded of these men, who had to make new provision for their ministers, for the building of churches and manses, for new schools and for the administration of the Church.

The Colquhouns also retained a keen consciousness of their family's past. Mary Irvine's father, Alexander Colquhoun, had similarly brought his family closer to the heart of Glasgow, in his case because of the rapidly diminishing demand for the family's traditional skills on the estuary of the Clyde. It was necessary for both families to be content with little, and to work hard. At the time of John and Mary's marriage, Mary was employed as a live-in housekeeper to a shipbroker.[9] Her elder brother, James, entered the merchant navy and got his master's ticket. They were perhaps less eager than the Irvines to leave their old ways behind, and they gave their two grandsons the conviction that they were all sailors at heart.

Mary's family had come to Port Glasgow from the western Highlands more than three generations earlier, but they continued to display many Highland characteristics. Her granddaughter remembered Mary as retaining to the end of her life a soft Highland voice and a gentle empathy with others. Even her appearance was Highland: lantern jaw, fine cheek-bones and soft sandy hair. Their background was in shipping and the sea. By the time James Irvine's parents met, Mary's father was a foreman sailmaker, though like his father he had served at sea in trading vessels under sail. Her grandfather had been master of a tea-clipper, the *Star of the*

East, and told the tale of being persuaded one day by a stranger to sail to St
Helena so that the man, a former prisoner of war, might dance a hornpipe
on Napoleon's grave. This would have been before 1840 and the emperor's
exhumation and re-interment in Les Invalides in Paris. The Colquhouns
were proud folk and good storytellers.

When James's maternal grandmother was born, the shipping lanes of Port
Glasgow were busy with vessels, their vast sails capable of bringing cargoes
of raw sugar and timber from North America. Floating timbers, some
fallen off the ships and some being seasoned in the salt water for use by the
shipwrights, lay in the navigation channels. These very imports produced
a demand for specialist local labour skills, but shipbuilding itself lay at the
heart of the eighteenth- and early nineteenth-century prosperity of Port
Glasgow. On the estuary of the Clyde, it looked towards the pretty wooded
northern shore, and behind it stretched the rolling hills of Renfrewshire. It
had grown up around the picturesque ruins of Newark Castle, a fifteenth-
century seat of the Maxwells. Eighteenth-century cottages survived from
the old village of Newark, jostling alongside newer terraces and tenements,
and even one or two fine public buildings in classical style. It had an importance in the eighteenth century as the customs port of Glasgow, and it
retained its own separate identity as a burgh right up until the end of the
nineteenth century. Ships sailed in from France and the Low Countries.
Their cargo then had to be transferred onto smaller boats with shallow
hulls in order to reach the then silted-up higher reaches of the Clyde in
Glasgow itself.

It is probable that John and Mary Irvine met through the church
and through relations of John Irvine living in the same street as
Mary Colquhoun's family: Clarence Street, in the heart of Clydeside's
shipbuilding district. On leaving Maybole, the Irvines had set up house
not far away in Bedford Street,[10] in the district that came to be known as
Laurieston just to the west of the Gorbals. In 1850, this was still a developing area of open lands: the tenements were newly built, and free from
the insanitary and degenerate conditions of life in the closes and wynds
of old Glasgow. Bedford Street overlooked orchards, parklands with
grazing sheep, and the mansion house of a Mr Pearson, a Clydeside rope-
maker. The adjacent canal served several local mills, including that of
the Port-Eglinton Spinning Company managed by David Stow,[11] the Free
Churchman who was the founding father of the educational system that
John and Mary Irvine's two sons would enter. Many in this community
were of the Free Church of Scotland, and they flocked to the church at

the corner of Bedford Lane, where the minister, Jonathan Anderson, was known for his fire-and-brimstone preaching.

John Irvine, James's father, took advantage of the movement for technical education that the Anderson Institute had pioneered, and at night school he acquired the tools of a business career, including the mastering of modern languages. He bought vocal scores of the oratorios of Handel, Haydn, and Mendelssohn, and sang in the choir of the great Glasgow Choral Union in its infancy. After an earlier, brief spell in a bank, he joined the firm of Walter MacFarlane, manufacturers of architectural cast-iron goods, in the heart of Glasgow and within walking distance of Bedford Street. He returned to night school for further training as an engineering draughtsman.

John and Mary Irvine moved soon after their marriage to the new culture of the city's north side: a brave venture. Mary's family was clannish, and the Colquhouns continued to remain in close kinship with the young Irvines of the north side in Possilpark. As the next generation grew up, they were in the habit of 'running over' to their Colquhoun grandparents' or to the households of their mother's two brothers, James and Archibald, who had both set up home on the south side. James Irvine was imbued with the spirit of self-improvement that was alive in the northerly district of the new Glasgow where he grew up, but his mother's family, living in the old burgh of Govan, gave him a sense of history. The past was always a romantic place to him.

In the 1871 census John Irvine is described as an ironfounder's clerk, a profession which served him well. In the second half of the nineteenth century, Walter MacFarlane's was recognised as the foremost firm for the architectural ironmongery trade, and it boomed. Just before John and Mary's marriage, Walter MacFarlane II took his father's foundry away from the congested streets of medieval Glasgow to be re-established on a new site on the estate lands of old Possil Park. The fine mansion house and its policies were soon swept away, all in the name of progress. The young couple's move to the hilly new suburb of Possilpark was entirely owing to John Irvine's employment as Walter MacFarlane's clerk, but the change to more salubrious surroundings cannot have been entirely unwelcome. The young parents steadily moved house, street by street, reaching further away from the industrial sprawl of Glasgow and into the old village on the edge of Possil Marsh, looking towards the Campsie Fells.

Walter MacFarlane had first set up his foundry close to the old Saracen's Head Inn in 1851, on the lands of Dovehill above the Gallowgate; the name was carried with it when the new Saracen Ironfoundry was developed in

Possilpark. The new premises were built, 1868–72, to the designs of James Boucher as a gigantic showcase for MacFarlane's products, complete with a huge glass-and-iron dome and with a selection of elaborate castings on its Gothic gateway. The Irvine children's father became the chief clerk, with many working under him turning out the necessary sectional drawings. Every screw in every size, every railing, every hopper head – an endless and inventive list – required the skill of a specialist draughtsman to draw in section, before the wooden moulds could be prepared to take the molten metal. John Irvine was a talented engineering draughtsman and a forward-looking businessman.

Glasgow's considerable and ever-increasing wealth prompted the growth in fine tenement and institutional building in the western and northern districts; development responded to the new housing needs not only of a growing middle class, but also of the more humble employees of Glasgow's business magnates. North Kelvinside, and even Possilpark, managed to remain good addresses. John and Mary Irvine's first son, Alexander, was born in Henderson Street, on the edge of North Kelvinside, but the family moved on before James was born. James and then Mary, the elder daughter, belonged for a few years to Bardowie Street.[12] The tenement flats of this private-enterprise development were situated for the most part above shops, but they were spacious, with wide bow windows looking to the front with country views. The first fifteen years of James's life were spent in Possilpark, first in Bardowie Street and then in Saracen Street, named after the transplanted foundry and therefore, even to the present day, associated with a folk myth of medieval Gallowgate's old coaching inn, the Saracen's Head. In Saracen Street, the family was completed with the birth of James's younger sister, Annie. In his young manhood James was close to his sister, Mary, who was clever, as they all were. She was given an exceptionally good education at Glasgow High School for Girls in Garnethill and was a prize-winning scholar, but in the old-fashioned way she was denied a university education and kept at home to help her mother. Annie, on the other hand, went to Glasgow University and then trained to be a schoolteacher.

On the other side of the railway tracks from the Irvine children's childhood home, it was a somewhat different story. In the nineteenth century and into the twentieth century, Springburn was the steam locomotive capital of the world and a fascinating example of Glasgow's pre-eminence in British heavy engineering. Beside the main line running through Springburn Station were the Hyde Park works of Neilson, Reid and Company, the seat of the Reid family's great wealth. Down Cowlairs Road, on the Glasgow to

Edinburgh main line, were the Cowlairs works of the North British Railway Company. The St Rollox railway engine works of the Caledonian Railway Company, south of Springburn Cross, were outstanding and became famous. In 1903 the three companies amalgamated and Sir Hugh Reid, as managing director, headed the largest manufactory of railway engines in Europe, employing at its peak over 8,000 skilled craftsmen. The company was a major contributor to the prosperity of Springburn and of Glasgow, and its activities dominated every aspect of life in this north Glasgow suburb.

Just as the locomotive companies defined Springburn, so Walter MacFarlane's foundry was the source of all that made up Possilpark: not only the extensive foundry premises themselves, but also the streets, houses, shops, a school and a church. Like so many magnates of his time, Walter MacFarlane became the developer of a whole suburb to serve his men and their families. He was lampooned as the Laird of Fossil Park, an allusion to the black deposit that soon encrusted every surface of his new development.

Although Possilpark was favoured by its green countrified aspect to the north, all who settled in the north-eastern districts of Glasgow cannot have escaped the ugliness of the contiguous urban landscape of south Springburn, with which it shared the all-important railway line that led to Queen Street Station at the centre of town. The heavy engineering of the railway works was not the only industrial activity there. Charles Tennant's bleach-manufacturing chemical works, which served the still-important textile industry, were the largest of their kind internationally, and the first industry to colonise this area, moving up to the north of Glasgow from their original location on the south side. 'Tennant's Stalk', a vast structure which at 455 feet was the tallest chimney in the world, belched out fumes on the busy thoroughfare of Springburn Road. These were but two of the causes of arguably the worst slum living in Glasgow's history.

If we want to know exactly what south Springburn looked like before the close of the nineteenth century there is no better picture than that given by Muirhead Bone, Glasgow's Gustav Doré. Muirhead Bone is remembered not only for his striking engravings of the landscape of the shipyards of Govan, but also for illustrations of the slum tenements and closes of Springburn and St Rollox that were home to the immigrant Irish foundry workers and their families. The Irish brought to Springburn an untidy way of life that irked the respectable, striving Calvinists, who were also for the most part competing with the incomers for employment. Irish goatherds sold goats' milk from the streets; children, goats and street vendors all thronged the thoroughfares in a picturesque manner unimaginable today. Unfortunately these Irish workers, many of whom were employed by MacFarlane's, fed a deepening prejudice amongst the Glasgow middle classes against Ireland and the Irish. This prejudice made itself felt later when James Irvine courted Mabel Williams, the daughter of an Ulster businessman who was, however, also a staunch Presbyterian.

Walter MacFarlane's Saracen works responded to the current awareness of the artistic possibilities of cast iron in the design of new products, besides the more prosaic hopper heads and down-water pipes. Architects began to design buildings with decorative railings, fanlights, canopies and staircases, all made in cast iron. MacFarlane's also played a major part in the development of a building technology that became increasingly daring through the use of cast-iron structures. Department stores and warehouses hid cathedrals of cast iron within their stone-clad exteriors, and as a result the Victorian development of commercial Glasgow also exhibited all that was new in architecture. The architect Alexander ('Greek') Thomson got MacFarlane's foundry to cast much of his ironwork, which was not only decorative but was an integral part of his commercial buildings, of which a rich example were the Egyptian Halls in Union Street. MacFarlane's commissioned Greek Thomson to design a wide variety of pieces for their standard range of merchandise. Large-scale demand for MacFarlane's decorative goods sprang from the spending power of the new rich, the burgeoning pride of civic authorities, and the growth of Victorian public philanthropy.

Balconies, bandstands, fountains, the structures of fashionable winter gardens, and then enormous and daring public buildings, such as greenhouses for botanic gardens, and even those of exhibition spaces, all featured in the capacious catalogues of Walter MacFarlane. Their trade catalogue,[13] first published in 1883, was 2,000 pages long, with 6,000 beautiful illustrations, each casting marked with full dimensions and meticulously drawn by John Irvine and his team of trained engineering clerks. At MacFarlane's apogee there were fifty of these draughtsmen. It became the largest firm making cast-iron architectural goods in the British empire, and with it John Irvine thrived. Today, MacFarlane's ornamental fountains are still to be found in parts of the world as far away as Brazil and Tasmania. In the late 1860s, when the Possil Estate was feued to Walter MacFarlane, it had ten inhabitants. Within ten years the inhabitants of Possilpark numbered 10,000, all drawn there to work in the foundry.

The Irvines were early members of Springburn North Free Church, which served an enormous congregation, and the growth of the Saracen

Foundry gave John Irvine plenty of opportunity to fulfill his obligations as a churchman. The circumstances of James Colquhoun Irvine's parents' own births had always required them to be prudent, but they were also philanthropic. The strong, plain faith of the Free Church of Scotland instilled in its members a social conscience.

John Irvine became an elder, and he was also the session clerk of the newly built church.[14] Their children, and the sense of serving God's purpose, were, without making too strong a point of it, the centre of their universe. With care, John Irvine soon provided his family with many of the comforts of aspirant Victorian society. This paterfamilias was bookish and, in an unassuming way, distinctly upwardly mobile. The books of his fairly conventional library were freely available to his children. Sets of the classics – Walter Scott, George Eliot, Jane Austen and Charles Dickens – fed the imaginations of the young Irvines. There were no locked bookcases, but 'never open a book without first washing your hands' was the dictum of the father, whom his sons called 'the governor'. Was this an indication of the grime that stuck even to the skin, as much as pious respect for a book? They stare out of the photographs, dressed in their best clothes, Mary erect and seemly, with some good jewellery.

Mary Irvine took on the responsibility for church sales of work and bazaars, and this brought her and her two daughters into the social circle of the wives of the railway barons. Her daughter, Mary, taught at the Sunday school. By the early 1890s the family had prospered, and their final move was to a handsome house in North Springburn, where their neighbours were the Reid family of Neilson, Reid and Company, the railway manufacturing conglomerate that became the North British Locomotive Company. Hugh Reid was the benefactor of the new church in North Springburn, built (1893–8) to replace the little corrugated-iron Free Church building of 1888. Mary Irvine found herself working for the great bazaar of 1893 in the St Andrews Halls, which in three days did so much to clear the debt of the 'foundry kirk'. Harry Lauder[15] was not yet the *succès fou* that he became on the London music halls, but, never slow to seize an opportunity for self-promotion, he offered to open the bazaar for her. The Irvines began to establish themselves in middle-class Glasgow society.

TWO

A Victorian Boyhood

John and Mary Irvine's second son, James, was not born with a silver spoon in his mouth. His baptismal gift, however, was a silver mug, brought for him from the Far East by his rather exotic uncle and namesake, Captain James Colquhoun, who served in the fleet of the Irawaddy Flotilla Company, the largest fleet of privately owned ships in the world. The example of this shipping company serves to demonstrate the thrust of commercial invention in Glasgow during the second half of the nineteenth century. It was the brainchild of the Denny Brothers, shipbuilders and shipowners, who started producing boats with wide, flat decks, steered simply from the prow and uniquely designed for navigating the estuaries of the rivers of Burma and other Far Eastern countries, with the intention of opening up a vast new trade. It was enormously successful, and fed the aesthetic movement's taste for Far Eastern art objects. At the time of James's birth, photographs of the sunburned Colquhoun uncle suggest a picture of someone eastern; his dark eyes twinkle beneath a broad-brimmed hat and he smokes cheroots. He was small-boned and recognisably a Scotsman, like our James Colquhoun Irvine, who took after his Highland forebears and whose skin acquired a deep tan in hot countries.

Enterprise and science were the driving forces of the new Glasgow, and the young James Irvine belonged to this world. He was born into a city that grew and changed before his very eyes, a city that was stirring and striving with endeavour, new hope and ambition, but which was also stinking with chemical effluent from factory and furnace, as well as being inescapably noisy. When James Irvine was born, Glasgow was failing to address the compound problems of poverty; overcrowding and a lack of sanitation encouraged widespread disease in working-class areas.

Possilpark, and Springburn with its shops and trams – the green trams – constituted the scene of James Colquhoun Irvine's early life. As a little boy, James's health had suffered because of a severe bout of measles; during the subsequent long convalescence, he was home-tutored by a Miss McClelland. It was on a transatlantic liner, more than forty years later, that he met her again, but this was characteristic of the odd encounters that often coloured his later life, when he was a public figure. At first he failed to recognise the good lady, whom he thought he should dismiss as nothing but a nuisance, but by the end of the voyage they were firm friends. All the Irvine children started in formal education at Possilpark Public School, a local school still in its infancy. The early development of Possilpark into a complete suburb coincided with the Scottish 1872 Education Act, and Possilpark was provided with a Board School. This handsome building stood overlooking land which remained undeveloped for a generation. This school awarded James his first prize, at the age of five and a half, for 'general progress and good behaviour'. These were attributes worthy of encouragement, but hardly indicative of academic brilliance. He soon moved on to the Free Church Normal School, which had been built and endowed by the Free Church of Scotland, and here he started to flourish.

The Normal School was independent in the sense that it was not state-financed: it was not, at that time, directly controlled by the Glasgow Board of Education. Like Allan Glen's School, to which James would move later, it was the product of an enlightened man's ideas. David Stow, who was arguably the most important figure in the history of modern secondary education, instituted the Free Church Normal School, together with the Normal School for the Training of Teachers, soon after the Disruption.[1] A fiercely principled Free Churchman, Stow clung to the integrity of his school, which practised his new philosophy of education, which was directed towards the development of the whole child. The school stood in a corner of Glasgow that has since been rebuilt but that the two Irvine brothers, Alexander and James, would have known in 1884 as lying adjacent to Dundas Vale and the canal basin. Close to Port Dundas, in an arcade between old Cowcaddens Street and the top of Hope Street, a large edifice in mixed Gothic and Tudor style and dating from 1846 provided for 800 pupils. It was a daunting prospect for a little boy of seven wending his way there from Possilpark, but in his first year in the Junior Department, he won first prize for English. This took the form of *Philip Farlow and his Friends*, an improving novel for little boys that extolled the virtues of 'courage, honesty and endurance'.

At the time of James Irvine's early schooling there are clues to the stimuli that might arouse the interest of any child. The popularisation of science, and of geology and astronomy in particular, encouraged general awareness of scientific developments. One day in the street an old gentleman tapped the young James on the shoulder. 'Look up there, young man,' he told the little boy. 'That's the transit of Venus. That will never again be seen in your lifetime.' The date was 6 December 1884, and James was seven years old. The old gentleman was quite correct: the next transit of Venus took place in 2004. He was perhaps the first to alert the little boy to a scientific habit of observation. In an address to the Workers' Educational Association in 1939, Irvine described this process as the hammer effect, a continual asking and answering of the questions 'whence, why and whither which mould the mind into a mechanism well designed for the conduct of human affairs'.[2] Later in life he realised that at seven years old he had been awakened to some of the questions of the universe.

James was a manly little boy and, although small of frame, he was starting to show something of the athleticism that remained with him throughout his adult life. He won school races as a sprinter, and thought he might try his hand at long-distance running. As James prepared to enter secondary school, Alexander suggested that his brother should join him in the Springburn Harriers. In his teens, James became quite a ringleader amongst his athletic friends, and on one occasion, after a run in Springburn Park, he persuaded his college friend to strip off with him and bathe in the inviting waters of the boating lake.[3] The fact that, if caught, they would have encountered the strong arm of the law as well the anger of his father seemed only to spur him on. Springburn Park was a genteel environment in the 1890s. It provided a place of leisure for the middle-class residents of north Springburn. The cricket matches and the tennis tournaments gave these boys and girls a social finish, and cricket and tennis came naturally to James, who needed these sports to relieve the headaches that frequently afflicted him, partly from a tendency to burn the midnight oil and partly from exposure to fumes in chemistry laboratories.

Long summer days spent at holiday places on the Firth of Clyde – little summer resorts such as Kilcreggan, a favourite with the Irvines – were the family's escape valve. From the moment they stepped onto the steamer at the Broomielaw, the Clyde steamer departure quay in the centre of town, they passionately relished these holidays. Like so many other Glasgow families of their class, they would take a house 'doon the watter' for a month in the summer, and summer after summer a band of family friends would be reunited, while the house in Glasgow was let. The Camerons of Kilcreggan, with boys the same age as the Irvine boys, were particular friends.

As the Irvine family sailed away from the shores of outer Glasgow, the scene unfolded to reveal a natural beauty of blue sea, rocky inlets and the wooded shore. Greenock, where the smell of the sea became more intense, marked the beginning of this magical contrast with the close urbanism of their everyday lives. James later recalled: 'In the old-fashioned days when the simplest method of transporting family and luggage for the annual holiday on the Firth of Clyde was to sail from the Broomielaw, Greenock marked for me the real beginning of that blessed period. You can imagine the rapture of the somewhat emotional boy as the view of the distant hills unfolds and as he feels again the fragrance of the sea.'[4] Here, on this sunny coastline, the boys could shake off the manacles of dirty Glasgow, and swim, fish and explore. Here the water was sweet and clean, clear of the effluent that poured into the river higher up. In 1876 it was noticed that: 'In April last, a large number of young salmon smolts were taken in baskets from the shallow water at Govan Ferry slip. It is thought the shoal was on its way to the sea, and that the fish were sickened by the poisonous waters in the harbour.'[5]

Best of all, their mother's brother, the seafaring uncle James Colquhoun, who had no children of his own, had by this time returned from the Far East a rich man, and had settled down in Glasgow. This favourite uncle was also a feature of these family summer holidays. He owned a racing yacht, was a member of the fashionable Royal Clyde Yacht Club, and mixed with a smart set of people spending the summer at Hunter's Quay, on the opposite shore from Kilcreggan. He taught Alexander and James to sail, and to crew for him in regattas in the Firth of Clyde. They sailed up and down the west coast, and even over to Ireland to compete in the Bangor Regatta races. The two boys then crewed for others: a Glasgow shipping family called Donaldson, who had Belfast connections, were also 'boaty', and Jim sailed on their yacht, the *Ysolde*, across to the regatta on Belfast Lough. This later impressed his future parents-in-law in Ireland. Sailing requires precision, a willingness to take commands and 'never to talk to the man at the wheel', which became, as a saying, almost a family joke. Irvine, looking back on his life, recognised this as a form of preparation for the exactitudes of the chemical laboratory.

Captain James Colquhoun had married Agnes McNeil, the girl who stood as witness at John and Mary's wedding in 1874. By the 1880s James Colquhoun was a pillar of respectability, a magistrate of the City of Glasgow, and a senior elder of the Free Church of Scotland.[6] He, with his wife and his brother-in-law Archibald McNeil, the headmaster of Govan's enormous Lambhill Street Board School (1,514 pupils), all lived together in considerable style at Dalmeny House, Ibroxholm. Ibroxholm, which today is near Ibrox Park, home of Glasgow Rangers Football Club, was then an exclusive enclave of detached villas built around an elliptical setpiece of early Victorian town planning not far from the old village of Govan. Archibald McNeil, Fellow of the Educational Institute of Scotland and a leading figure in education in Glasgow, was greatly loved by his young nephew by marriage, who was drawn to his powers as a dominie. Irvine in middle life credited his 'uncle' with having awoken in him the desire to teach; but, more than that, McNeil opened the boy's mind to the culture of the educated man, and to the fact that he could pursue a scientific career that was not in industrial science. As he told it later:

> The lesson was good for an impulsive boy already beginning in that age of the premature scientist to fall into that error from which some never escape that the universe can be translated in terms of atoms and molecules and that industrial science is the only outlet which is worth while; his wise counsel made me pause and reflect.[7]

The Irvine children's father was stern, clever and autocratic; their mother was gentle and a good home-maker. But, for all her sweetness, she was assiduous in ensuring that their children were industrious and God-fearing. It was a demanding household, although the two parents turned a blind eye to the four children's minor rebellions. The siblings were high-spirited and indulged in Victorian pranks. Surprise parties were a favourite amusement. These involved gathering on an unsuspecting neighbour's doorstep and, when the door opened, rushing inside, announcing that they had come for a surprise party, which their unwilling hosts then had to provide.

John Irvine, who played chess with Jim, tried hard to make companions of his two sons, referring until the end of his life to 'we three'. He was hoping, it may be supposed, to evoke the verse of Robert Burns' old ballad, 'We Twa' hae rin aboot the Braes'.[8] As the two boys grew older, John Irvine took them further from home. As an engineering draughtsman of ornamental cast iron in the 1890s, he needed to follow artistic developments in France and Belgium. Many commissions had already come from London, but stylistically Paris and Brussels were more advanced. Design in industry was fashionably celebrated in his generation by several great exhibitions that brought prosperity to these cities and prestige to their countries. James and Alec first visited Paris with their father for the Paris Exposition Universelle of 1889.[9] The 'Galerie des Machines' was prominently situated on the

Champ-de-Mars, and the structures in iron that it displayed attracted the attention of thousands of tourists and businessmen alike. In some measure the Paris exhibition had grown out of Glasgow's International Exhibition of 1888, at which Walter MacFarlane's foundry won several awards.[10] MacFarlane's enormous 1888 exhibit, a complex amalgam of almost everything featured in their catalogue, stood at the entrance to the Machinery Court, close to Dumbarton Road, in the new Kelvingrove building. Glasgow, aware that it had set itself up to compete with Manchester, Paris and Melbourne, constructed its first great exhibition on a world scale and demonstrated the internationalism of its trading interests. In 1897 it was Brussels' turn, and yet again 'we three' were visitors there; by 1900, Glasgow was preparing for another great exhibition. The Irvines were swept up in this fashionable social trend of considerable magnitude.

James was the more compliant of the two brothers. When still a young boy, he agreed to accompany his father with his remarkable friend, Henry Drummond, on geological expeditions on the Campsie Fells and in botanising out on Possil Marsh. As his own career as a chemist developed, James Irvine would admit to a sneaking preference for biology and botany, but at that date they seemed to offer neither the same prospects for professional success nor the beguiling prospect of work in a chemical laboratory with crucibles and crystals. The author of *Natural Law in the Spiritual World*,[11] Henry Drummond was a significant man in Glasgow at that time. He was professor of natural sciences at the Free Church Training College, which had followed in the wake of the Free Church school attended by James and Alexander. Drummond was one of those Victorians who tried to reconcile Darwinism and the current advance of scientific knowledge with the teachings of the Church. His friendship with John Irvine came through their joint work for the Free Church, and in founding with him the Possil 'Foundry Kirk' through the agency of the Renfrew Street Free Church Mission. Then came the innovative Foundry Boys Mission, which gave the young boys from MacFarlane's foundry some education on Sundays.

John Irvine was himself an amateur scientist with a deep interest in horticulture. He was proud to call Drummond his friend and to draw him into the warmth of the family circle. Drummond presented James with the telescope he had used on an expedition to Central Africa, and with a simple microscope. Sixty years later, James acknowledged that this interesting man was responsible for inducting him in the use of a tool central to his future métier; microscope work always held a certain romance for him after this. Perhaps this encounter was also responsible for James's choice to enter for a Foundation scholarship at Allan Glen's School. Or it may have been a boyhood visit to a chemical factory that triggered the wish to change from the school of his father's choice: 'It was a chance visit to a small chemical factory which decided my life's work, and I can still remember the thrill with which that small boy entered a laboratory for the first time and saw a few simple experiments. From that moment there was no turning back.'[12] His parents, who were becoming aware that their son was distinctly clever, encouraged his move from the school that they had chosen for him.

Allan Glen's was a pioneering school, established a generation earlier to offer 'a good practical education to about fifty boys, sons of tradesmen or persons in the industrial classes in Glasgow',[13] expressly designed to develop boys in the disciplines necessary for the industrial expansion of Glasgow. It was considered the leading school for science in the whole of the country. It specialised in the experimental sciences: chemistry and physics were taught at laboratory benches, and engineering drawing was added as a subject. The classics had been thrown out of the syllabus, although modern languages were included because of their usefulness to business careers. The school was situated in the centre of busy, commercial Glasgow, adjacent to Queen Street railway station, and it drew boys from all over the city. So it was that, aged thirteen and with his scholarship under his belt, James continued to cross Glasgow every morning to join the 700 or so boys, many of whom, like himself, would become leaders in their field. It was a competitive environment in which the boy flourished.

He developed a taste for team sports, and discovered that athletics opened the door to many friendships and a camaraderie that he enjoyed. Irvine was a self-confident boy, but at Allan Glen's under John Kerr, the prevailing gentlemanly values of fortitude and self-control were also pressed upon the boys: 'It was instilled into us that to take defeat gallantly was easier than to accept victory modestly,' Irvine recalled.[14] Kerr set about the business of humanising Allan Glen's: he forged a link with Queen's Park Football Club, so that the boys could play this new sport on their grounds, and in the classroom he introduced some Latin. It can only have been a sketchy Latin syllabus, because James always did have difficulty with the Latin orations of his later academic life. He retained a keen interest in playing football, however, and in following the game.

Hero-worship has been discredited by post-twentieth century society, but James made a hero out of headmaster John Kerr, who was a charismatic man by all accounts and the first of those several teachers whose fatherly influence was so important to Irvine. Kerr's opinion of young Irvine was that he would not be injured by early specialisation.[15] He was the only one of Jim's mentors who was not a scientist, but from his teaching Irvine learned much about the techniques of the teaching profession, and even the pleasures to be gained in developing young minds.

It was undoubtedly at Allan Glen's that James Irvine was allowed to think of himself as a specialist, beginning to think of chemistry as the dominating force in his life. Once, when invited to address the Andersonian Chemical Society, he looked back on the Glasgow of his youth, and recognised that it was in the laboratories of Allan Glen's school that he began to make a reality of boyhood ambition:

> With the continual reminder from the shipping of our river that raw materials come to this place from the uttermost ends of the earth, and that our heavy chemicals are distributed all over the world; with the ceaseless throb of machinery on every hand, the sky-line serrated with chimney stacks, the very atmosphere polluted with chemical fumes, the student of chemistry must feel that the interests of the community are largely dependent on his subject.[16]

By the early 1890s the Irvines' address was Heathfield, Springburn, a good semi-villa on the crest of Balgrayhill Road, with an outlook at the back over Springburn Park, which was ringed with the mansion houses of the railway barons. Sir Hugh Reid, the great magnate of Neilson Reid locomotives, their neighbour and friend, lived at Belmont on the same street. Heathfield had a large garden, in which John Irvine kept a glasshouse so that he could pursue his fascination with horticultural science; dahlias and the development of new strains were a particular interest. It was also a musical household, strongly observant of religion, and John bought a small organ for his house. He was formal about his dress; even his letter writing possessed a certain formality, and he wrote a beautiful, clerkly hand. His drawing skills were passed on to his elder son, Alec, and then to his grandson, Mary's son David. In James, who was quite a humourist, this talent came out in an Edwardian ability to produce caricature sketches of all manner of hilarious situations in which he found himself.

John Irvine was a remarkable example of a man whom Glasgow had made and who had in his turn helped to make Glasgow. He sent both of his boys to the Technical College, where Alec took classes in architectural and surveying draughtsmanship in support of his apprenticeship as a surveyor, and, in 1893, James was entered as an apprentice chemist. Although Allan

Glen's in the 1890s was no longer exclusively a science school, it remained a feeder to the Anderson Institute, or Glasgow and West of Scotland Technical College as it had become: school and college were amalgamated in 1887. It was a natural progression for James Irvine to move on from school to scientific studies under a professor. He had already obtained work in the laboratory of a consulting chemist, Dr Zinkeisen, and the records of the Technical College suggest that his apprenticeship indentured him to this chemist.[17] It would appear that the father envisaged his sons making lives for themselves in the industrial and mercantile milieu that had served him so well.

James's first professor was George Henderson, FRS, an organic chemist. From a degree in his native Glasgow, Henderson had completed his studies in Germany under Wislicenus in Leipzig during the summers of 1885 and 1886. He was already noted among chemists, and later held the chair of chemistry at Glasgow University. In 1893, however, he had not long been in post as Freeland Professor of Chemistry at the Technical College. The boy Irvine was excited by this figure who dared to permeate the teaching of the old classical chemistry with the new atomic chemistry of Ostwald and van't Hoff. There must have been something of the genius in a man who, without textbooks (there were none), introduced these novel ideas by means of lectures to a group of overgrown schoolboys who were being prepared to further the commercial life of Glasgow. Henderson's skill in holding his audience had something of the great preachers of the day. There were no research grants at that time, no Leverhulme awards, no Carnegie Fellowships. Alone and without a team, Henderson managed to develop his own original work, and to set an example to any lad who cared to notice. Irvine attached himself to him as a laboratory assistant. He progressed to demonstrator in chemistry to Professor Henderson, and stated that he had 'gained valuable experience in the management of the large classes in Practical Chemistry, which are so important a feature in the work of the College.'[18] The Technical College was recognized by the Institute of Chemistry as a qualifying institution for the training of professional chemists, and Henderson's duty was to train young chemists in the work of analysis and to forge links with industry, a role in which he was famously successful.

Irvine once described G.G. Henderson's personality in terms of examining a crystal:

> In imagination I turn the goniometer slowly; one by one the faces
> come into the field of vision and I see there are many things, among

them unsparing devotion to duty, unselfish perseverance, unflinching courage and (perhaps the most beautiful of all) unfailing love of country and of fellow-men. True it is that science and chemistry form the molecules of that bright crystal, but these are the faces presented to the world.[19]

Despite the difference in their ages, G.G. became Irvine's close friend later in life, both as a chemical colleague and on fishing expeditions in the western Highlands. Irvine was happy to reveal the roots of this friendship: 'Almost from boyhood's days I have given G.G. Henderson unstinted hero-worship. With the passage of the years this pardonable sin of youth has been transformed imperceptibly into an abiding friendship in which there still persists something of the relationship of father and son.' 'You know, you're my ain laddie,' were Henderson's reassuring words.[20]

But, in the meantime, for two years Irvine sat at Henderson's feet in the grim, unheated lecture rooms of the fine old institution. In all three of the professors who were to teach him chemistry, Jim sought and found this trusting, warm symbiotic friendship. Was it because his own father remained rather forbidding? Or was it because from boyhood he could never resist the charms of the educator? He was to write Henderson's entry in the *Dictionary of National Biography*, and wrote his obituary for the Chemical Society.[21] Henderson was in many ways Irvine's closest role model. Of medium height and athletic build, he presented a well-tailored appearance tempered by the charm of his manner. His humanity and gentleness were enlivened by a pawky and mordant sense of humour. His chief delight, apart from the well-being of his students and his department, was fishing in the lochs of the western Highlands, and the enjoyment of natural life that this afforded. One could almost have been describing Irvine.

At the Technical College his closest friend was John Rogers, who soon confided in James his boyhood affection for pretty Chrissie Colquhoun, a first cousin of the Irvine boys: James Irvine's social success at the College was now assured. Academically, John Rogers and James Irvine were neck and neck: they were examined *viva voce* for the same chemistry prizes, which it has to be admitted were not always won by Irvine. They were friends at sport as well as in the lecture room, and they gossiped intimately. John Rogers said that Irvine displayed a single-minded intensity about everything he did, including the preparation for a race. At the end of his second year James attained a first class certificate and prize in inorganic chemistry – although, ironically, he only won the second prize for organic chemistry.[22]

If he did not always win, the losing was faced with a sunny smile. He attributed this fortitude to the training he received from John Kerr.

When it was time to move on, both of the college friends explored the
possibility of employment in the research department of Nobel's explosives
factory at Ardeer, on the Clyde coast near Saltcoats, about fifty miles south-
west of Glasgow. The desolate site of Nobel's operations in Scotland was
eminently suitable for an explosives factory: it was conveniently situated on
the edge of Scotland's industrial belt, and the port of Irvine was commandeered for its purposes. However, Nobel himself commented that: 'Without
work the place would be intolerable.' Irvine spent time looking it all over,
and was offered a well-paid job as analyst in the chemical factory that
seemed a natural source of employment for someone of his background.
The early 1890s witnessed a vast expansion of the Ardeer complex of
Nobel's factories, and in the year that Jim Irvine and John Rogers visited it,
direct train access from Glasgow to a private railway station at the factory
was being constructed. Despite the fact that the research and test centre was
establishing a legendary reputation, Jim Irvine turned the job down. He
did, however, retain the memory, in minute detail, of every refinement of
the Ardeer research department: twenty years later he would return to the
factory to oversee the production of chemical warfare in the 1914–18 war.

John Rogers did decide to stay at Ardeer, and as time wore on he became
a captain of industry as chairman of Imperial Chemical Industries Ltd,
which grew out of the Nobel explosives factory. The friendship between
the two men never died, and the industrialist and the university vice-
chancellor found that they were mutually dependent: one in search of good
young chemistry graduates, the other in search of funding for university
development. Despite the long passage of years in which they never met,
the underlying closeness of their student friendship and their mutual roots
in Glasgow at its most exciting period of growth never left them.

Having considered work at Nobel's factory, Irvine came to the conclusion
that his attraction to chemical research would not be satisfied by work in
industry. He began to display the restlessness that was to drive him on until
it finally came to resolution in St Andrews on his appointment as Principal
and Vice-Chancellor of Scotland's oldest university. The 'well-paid' job at
Ardeer did not seem to offer the prospect of a leading position in research
chemistry: in fact, he he feared it might cauterise his advancement in a
research career. He felt incomplete, and knew that he had to enlarge his
understanding of the subject in a university. His chemical training with
Henderson had taught him something about chemical analysis; now he

needed to develop the finesse and precision that the original work of the research bench demanded. He yearned for more: for a deeper awareness of the problems of the fascinating new chemistry. Perhaps his father was right in showing his boys something of a world beyond Glasgow. On leaving the Technical College, James Irvine cast his eye about in several quarters for a job as a laboratory assistant in a university. Irvine's own first-hand account of the celebrated Glaswegian chemist, Sir William Ramsay, suggests that in 1895 he paid a visit to University College London, where Ramsay was in post and where in March 1895 he isolated helium. During the month of April 1895, Ramsay refined his calculation of the density of helium.[23]

> It is a poignant advantage of being able to conjure up the recollection of that arresting figure, to hear his voice, and to see the kindly eyes from which flashed in moments of exaltation the fire of genius.
>
> I have seen it, for I was with him on the day he calculated the density of helium . . . His isolation of the rare gases was not the only example of his discoveries which seemed to come most opportunely enabling the chemist to join forces with the physicist in the investigations on radioactivity which were soon to revolutionise the whole conception of atomic structure and the nature of the material universe.[24]

Henderson's standing among his peers was high, and he knew of Professor Thomas Purdie's particular working methods, which required a constant stream of chemical assistants. He suggested that James might apply to Purdie, professor of chemistry in St Andrews, for a job as an assistant in the teaching laboratory. Fortunately, when Irvine applied, Purdie had a vacancy; as Irvine later said of himself, he leapt at the opportunity to work under a chemist of his calibre, even at a salary much lower than the one offered by the Nobel explosives factory. Apart from the lure of a university research laboratory, Irvine's gain in moving from the west to the east of Scotland was vastly augmented by the beauty of St Andrews' natural situation: a beauty that became a source of inexhaustible consolation to him. Ardeer was a 'sand desert where the wind always blows, often howls, filling the ears with sand . . . between us and America, there is nothing but water, a sea whose mighty waves are always raging and foaming.'[25] In St Andrews the North Sea is often no less awesome than the Atlantic, but it is tempered by the gentle influence of the little towns and villages of the East Neuk of Fife that run down to meet the sea. Jim Irvine's love of these ancient surroundings became absolute.

In the autumn of 1895, Jim was ready to take up his new job in St Andrews. But despite the importance of all that Purdie had to offer, it was the stimulating, vigorous personality of his Glaswegian professor, G.G. Henderson, that Irvine always acknowledged as his enduring influence. 'When I transferred to St Andrews,' he said, 'I carried with me an example which affected the whole of my professorial life.'[26]

THREE

Civis Universitatis Sancti Andreae

St Andrews. What was this survival of pre-Reformation Scotland where Jim Irvine hoped to find his new life in pure science? St Andrews was, and is, a small town on the north coast of Fife, looking out north and east over the Firth of Tay and the North Sea. From very early times it had been an important ecclesiastical centre, with a castle, a priory, a cathedral and a small harbour. It was the seat of a succession of powerful bishops, and from 1472 it gave its name to Scotland's first archbishopric. There developed in Scotland a need to train young men in divinity in their native land. Before 1410, scholarly youths from Scotland usually sought out European centres of learning, most particularly Paris. There was very little intercourse with Oxford or Cambridge. The Collegium Scoticum in Paris, attached to the Sorbonne, was established in the early fourteenth century, at a time of reaffirmation of the Auld Alliance. The influence of Paris started to creep into St Andrews in the early fifteenth century and a pedagogy, or the nucleus of a university, after the teaching model of the early schoolmen, came into existence in St Andrews, providing scholarly teaching to a resident group of young men.

In February 1411 Bishop Wardlaw granted a charter founding in St Andrews, Scotland's first university. This was ratified between 1413 and 1414 by several papal bulls issued from his native Peñiscola in Aragon by the exiled and schismatic Pope Benedict XIII, who placed St Andrews on a level with the European schools of Paris and Bologna, with power to examine candidates for doctorates and masterships. Before the Reformation, St Andrews University grew into an institution of learning, based initially on the Pedagogy or Faculty House, and finally sustaining three colleges: St Salvator's (1450), St Leonard's (1512) and then finally St Mary's (1538), which was founded primarily for the training of candidates for the priesthood. It is thought that the early St John's College, which pre-dated St Salvator's by some thirty years, was never a 'college' in the full sense, but rather its purpose was as a perpetual chaplainry, supporting the teaching of theology and arts. Its site and buildings were eventually absorbed by the contiguous foundation of St Mary's College. The university in St Andrews kept up a precarious existence, which grew even more fragile after the Reformation. In the eighteenth century, the two colleges of St Salvator and St Leonard were obliged to amalgamate, under the name of the United College of St Salvator and St Leonard.

The nineteenth century, however, saw the introduction of a series of reforms, permitting growth in the number of modern professorships, and a building programme to replace the teaching accommodation of the decrepit medieval colleges with fine new institutional structures. In 1840, an endowed chair of chemistry was finally given life with the appointment of the first professor of chemistry, Arthur Connell. In 1876 the degrees of BSc and DSc were instituted, and in 1897, while Irvine was an undergraduate, a separate Faculty of Science was created. By the end of the nineteenth century, this fledgling cradle of twentieth-century science had in all about a dozen professors and as many lecturers, and as many again in the University College of Dundee when it became affiliated to St Andrews in 1897. The university itself was still small in student numbers: in 1895 when Irvine took up his post with Purdie, the enrolment was 164 in arts, 12 in science, 12 in pre-clinical medicine and 24 in divinity. In Dundee there were even fewer students. Glasgow and Edinburgh had seven or eight times as many.[1]

So how did this strike James Irvine, who had given up the prosperity of Glasgow to seek enlightenment in this struggling institution, as battered by fortune as it was by the waves of the North Sea? To his family, J.C. Irvine was always James, the striving, confident young man expected to get on in life, but on arrival in St Andrews in October 1895 he was cut off from the familiar aspirations of commercial Glasgow. He encountered a different world, one that was devoted entirely to scholarship and the training of the scholars of the next generation. He found himself in the company of new friends: university students with their eyes on the goal of a degree. They were taught by men with an eclectic knowledge of the world. James Irvine adjusted his focus to that of a university. From then on James gradually became 'Jim' to all those with whom he wished to establish a friendship: the name by which he was very soon known to kindly Professor and Mrs Purdie.

Thomas Purdie was singled out for much admiration amongst the university professors in Scotland at that time.[2] He was an organic chemist of much originality and courage, and he introduced to St Andrews the new discipline of physical chemistry and the ideas of the chemistry of stereo-isomerism: that is, the study of the atomic structures of organic chemical compounds. Under Purdie, who was appointed to his chair in 1884, chemistry in St Andrews was changing beyond all recognition.

In the early years of chemistry at St Andrews, when Purdie first arrived there, the subject had consisted of the study of minerals, or inorganic material. There was only one small chemistry laboratory: it was a narrow room formed from an annexe of the chemistry lecture room, which had been provided for the fledgling department in the early Victorian east wing of the college buildings. Conscious of the great divide that had previously existed between the German engine houses of research and St Andrews, Irvine would one day write. 'It is not so long ago that chemistry was taught here in a place that might well have served as an alchemical studio.'[3] The real reason why chemistry remained a rather backward-looking department in St Andrews at that time almost certainly lay in the university's poverty. Furthermore, Purdie's predecessor, Professor Heddle, a distinguished man in his own right, was not the same man of vision as Purdie.

Thomas Purdie, like Henderson in Glasgow, was more than conscious of developments in the wider world beyond Scotland. He too had pursued higher studies under Johannes Wislicenus, who was at that time director of the Chemical Institute in Würzburg.[4] Purdie's mother, the widow of a bank manager from Biggar, was comfortably off. This gave him a degree of independence, enabling him to seek his research experience in Germany, the world leader in exploratory chemistry. Wislicenus was one of the very first to realise that the immediate future for chemistry lay in the analysis and synthesis of the complicated organic compounds, which could now, perhaps, be understood in depth. It was a vast field that would open up possibilities for industries of many types, but particularly the pharmaceutical industry. Purdie's PhD studies with Johannes Wislicenus in Würzburg were shared with W.H. Perkin, the son of William Perkin, who famously oxidised aniline, and produced the mauve dye that Queen Victoria, in her widowhood, made fashionable. It was a brilliant generation that also included Percy Frankland, son of the chemist Sir Edward Frankland.

Purdie was an unusual man, who had come late to chemistry after spending his twenties as a cattle rancher in the Argentine. He chose his path in life in a leisurely fashion, and his pedigree in the field was interesting. The story goes that on his return home from South America he paid a visit to an aunt and uncle in St Andrews. During a walk along the cliffs, he fell into conversation with Professor T.H. Huxley, who advised him to study some branch of science. He took chemistry classes for a year in St Andrews under the mineralogist, Professor Matthew Forster Heddle, a chemist of the old school, but took his BSc in London, where Huxley was in post. It was under Edward Frankland at the Royal School of Mines in South Kensington that he encountered the new studies of organic compounds and their structures. Irvine would later in life describe Frankland thus: 'Always chasing the fairies of organic groups . . . instead of working for his living at something practical as every proper young Englishman is expected to do . . . he emancipated organic chemistry from the empirical study of molecules as a whole.'[5]

Like almost all of these aspirant young chemists, Purdie initially sought a future for his career in London: his first post was as a chemical demonstrator at the Royal College of Science. He was county analyst for Staffordshire when, in 1884, he was persuaded by Principal Tulloch to return to St Andrews as a locum for Professor Heddle, who was on leave of absence conducting a survey in South Africa for the British government. Heddle's health did not permit his return to Scotland, and Purdie's position in St Andrews was confirmed by his election as the third professor of chemistry in the university. Purdie had brought back with him from Europe new opportunities for his discipline, and once good fortune had brought him to the chair at St Andrews he determined on introducing to this remote academic bastion a new outlook for chemistry, with organic chemistry in the ascendancy.

In 1884 chemistry at the struggling university was studied only as one component of an MA degree. Purdie's inaugural lecture as professor was addressed to an audience consisting almost entirely of arts students. He made on this occasion what must have seemed an extraordinary statement: 'I venture to hope that I may soon have some students who will be willing to give the time required for original investigation, and I promise them that, whether the results they may obtain be of scientific value or not, they themselves will be amply rewarded; for among all the methods of scientific training, there is none of such high educational value as research.'[6]

He started as a solitary investigator. His dream was to establish in his department a famous school of advanced chemical research. His senior students might, he argued, be persuaded at first to pursue some original research in the summer months, which at that time did not form part of the academic year. His enthusiasm and his care for the welfare of his students were both repaid, and he attracted a considerable following of bright disciples. He had to overcome the difficulties of working in quarters that were not purpose-built for the practical teaching of chemistry, and that consisted only of the old lecture room, with its ancillary space, that he had known as a student. Here, once the day's teaching was over, the benches were cleared and research work resumed, to be pursued deep into the night.

Professor Purdie increased his staff from the resources of his own pocket. There were personal reasons for this. He suffered from increasing bouts of ill health: he was asthmatic and the haars of the east coast of Scotland did not suit him at all. Time after time he would be bedridden and unable to take his classes. Furthermore, his teaching methods required an assistant. He often taught by means of experiments of great complexity, which had to be set up on the teaching bench in advance of any class. Usually he had not the strength or the inclination to prepare these himself, and it was the job of his young assistant to set them up the night before. He therefore employed young trained chemists to relieve him of aspects of the job that could be delegated, and in return he set several of these assistants on the road to a career in academic chemistry. Purdie's department was, at that time, uniquely attractive to ambitious young chemists in Scotland.

Purdie had other attributes, which made employment under him full of promise. His uncle, another Thomas Purdie, had died leaving a considerable fortune. The elder Thomas Purdie was a fashionable Victorian interior decorator, a new phenomenon of middle-class prosperity in Scotland. He retired to St Andrews from Edinburgh, and built himself a large Scottish baronial villa, Castlecliffe (1869), designed by David Bryce, and overlooking the North Sea. In the early 1890s his widow Jessie funded the first stage of a new, specialist chemistry department, built on garden ground immediately adjacent, on the east side, to the buildings of the United College and its quadrangle.

Jessie Purdie's 1891 benefaction to the chemistry department enabled the realisation of her nephew's dream. By the time Irvine came to join Professor Purdie, young scientists had already gone out from this fledging, now research-led department to make original contributions to chemistry in other laboratories. Important collaborations were evident: the valuable silver nitrate reaction was largely developed by W. Pitkeathly, who was in Purdie's small team during the 1890s. The long series of papers by which his department became instrumental in establishing stereochemistry in Scotland began to appear. Even if a research laboratory was still lacking, the facilities in the big lecture room of the St Andrews chemistry department were first class, so that working there would be exciting compared with James Irvine's other options in scientific employment: the Glasgow and

West of Scotland Technical College, with its poor amenities, or labouring at analysis in a Glasgow chemical factory.

While most of Purdie's students at this time came from modest backgrounds, and lived within easy reach of St Andrews, James Colquhoun Irvine, with his roots in the large, complex web of commercial Glasgow, was something different. Still undecided about his future, Jim came to assist Professor Purdie with laboratory teaching, helping to demonstrate the Professor's elaborate experiments and to explain knotty problems that students might have difficulty grasping. Irvine was eighteen years of age, and this was a job that he leaned towards because of the ambition that was beginning to smoulder within him. He was quite right in recognising that assisting Purdie in his laboratory offered an opportunity that he would not find in Glasgow: as he said himself, he jumped at it. It has to be admitted that the job itself was sometimes tedious, and he was constantly at the professor's beck and call, but Purdie trained and nurtured him. He gave Irvine a vision of a life full of discovery, in which research would reveal new worlds and enable him to do great things with his own team of research workers. The young man and the delicate professor formed an important friendship. Irvine did indeed learn from Purdie what research at the chemical bench really entailed.

To Victorian Glaswegians indulging in the new concept of holiday-making, St Andrews on the sunny, breezy east coast was a polite, rather old-fashioned watering place. This was how Jim had first been introduced to it as a boy, and he was intensely susceptible to the contrast that the medieval town offered with the ugly, ceaseless activity of Glasgow. The imaginative little boy, nurtured on stories of Highland heroes and the romance of Scotland's myths, was stirred by the sense of something that endured in this ancient place, suggesting to him the embodiment of all of Scotland's past. Long afterwards he said: 'I stood amazed beneath St Salvator's Tower and I knew I had come home.' He never renounced those first feelings, and little by little he would come to place himself at centre stage of his new home.

Jim Irvine arrived to take up his new job in October 1895, on a stormy day of driving rain and a biting east wind. The answer to the question of what marked Purdie out must lie in the fact that he was an original worker on the frontiers of modern science. He developed our knowledge of optical activity and chirality. In Purdie's laboratory, Irvine took pride in his own skill with the polarimeter, the instrument that enabled them to observe optical activity. The understanding of chirality, or the asymmetry of substances that have molecular 'mirror' twins, was at the heart of new studies of 'chemistry in space', as Irvine liked to call it, and is still an active part of biochemical research today. In those early days, Purdie strove to move forward his vision of a school of research chemistry, in which the complex factors governing molecular rotation – first observed by Louis Pasteur fifty years before – would be painstakingly elucidated by his team, much after the pattern of the unparalleled research institutes of Germany.

Irvine came to know that strange chemistry lecture room well, 'the lecture table covered with a thick coating of black wax and provided with a huge tank for the manipulation of gases on a large scale'. Otherwise, it carried none of the fittings required for experimental research in organic chemistry and 'the wind, untempered by central heating, drifted continuously into the room, which was warmed only by an enormous open fire, replenished during each lecture hour by the Janitor, who was always greeted with grateful applause'.[7]

Irvine's romance with the beauty of St Andrews was rooted deep in those first days. It was a far more intimate society than can easily be imagined today, and the future of the university was in as great a state of uncertainty as it had ever been: even the affiliation with the Dundee College proposed by the University Commissioners was temporarily annulled in 1895 while a challenge led by the Marquess of Bute attempted to litigate against the union of Dundee with St Andrews. In 1898, the year when Irvine took his degree from St Andrews, the university had only grown to 238 matriculated students, of whom about 25 were in St Mary's College, where young men were educated for the Church of Scotland ministry, just as before the Reformation they had been trained for the priesthood. The academic structure of Scotland's most ancient university was antiquated: professor-led, it was too poorly endowed to permit much in the way of supporting staff. Professors vied with each other for students, because the class fees were the only means of supplementing their meagre stipends and perhaps paying for teaching assistants. It had lost its residential, collegiate quality at the Reformation, but under the impressive rule of Principal Donaldson it had slowly but definitely started to grow. Lord Bute – antiquarian, and a great benefactor of the university – was Rector. Purdie was not, therefore, by any means the only star.

There was an impressive body of professors, among them several with world-class reputations for their scholarship. Butler (Natural Philosophy), Lindsay (Latin), Scott-Lang (Mathematics), M'Intosh (Natural History, and director of the Gatty Marine Laboratory) and Stout (an early father of modern psychology), all brought prestige. The chair of mathematics was a regius chair, and the incumbent later received a political knighthood. Professor Burnet, professor of Greek, was married to a pleasant but mousy woman, but he was noted for the glamour of his academic robes and the number of honorary degrees he had received. 'Professor Burnet,' the gossips said cattily, 'acquires his gowns in Paris; Mrs Burnet does not.' Earlier in the century, Sir David Brewster, the inventor of the kaleidoscope, had been the first scientist to become Principal of the university. In the year of young Irvine's arrival, Principal (later Sir James) Donaldson, familiarly known as Jeames by the students, was in the full flood of his reforms and university development. He was a theologian by discipline, and the appointment of divines to the university's highest office was becoming the norm.

Irvine believed that the master-and-disciple bond he enjoyed with Purdie, another of those father figures whom he found so necessary in his life, was unique to him. That this was not absolutely the case is demonstrated by the fact that, before Irvine, Purdie had nursed in a personal way the careers of other young scientists, in the main all local to the central belt of Scotland. They included J. Wallace Walker and Alexander Mackenzie, among several others, all of whom claimed Purdie's patronage when they were ready to apply for a chair. G.D. Lander, who had come up from London, was the only Sassenach. Observing Purdie in the teaching laboratory, Irvine was struck by his methods. Purdie lectured with an infectious enthusiasm but without the support of notes; and he believed in the efficacy of the numerous and elaborate lecture experiments made possible by his laboratory assistants' hard work. There were temptations to construct grandiose demonstrations that could end dramatically with minor explosions, and even floods of water all over the observers. Purdie was one of those scientists who could fascinate others with his wide-ranging philosophical probings after truths hidden deep in the unknown. He was an exciting influence on these young men, whom he treated like his children.

Jim Irvine repaid the professor's kindness with hard work and loyalty, but it was not always easy. The curse of asthma dogged most of the professor's last ten active years, and Purdie would teach almost sitting on the stove that his new teaching laboratory boasted, with the warm damp air acting as a nebuliser. His chronic illness often made him tetchy, and there would be days when his assistants felt they had been given a hard time. When an attack kept him unexpectedly confined to bed, his young staff would be expected at the last minute to fill the breach in the classroom. It was necessary to pick up Purdie's laboratory technique quickly, and Irvine soon became a favourite with the students, who were of a similar age. He had always liked making himself useful; it was pleasing to be popular, and his new friends encouraged him to consider taking a degree. It is hardly surprising that, by the end of his first year with Purdie, Jim felt ready to matriculate at St Andrews as a student. His contemporary and friend Alexander Imrie recorded that: 'His early training in science at Allan Glen's School and the Royal Technical College, Glasgow, must have been particularly good, for his knowledge of chemistry when he came to St Andrews was nearly up to the standard required for the BSc degree.'[8]

Purdie encouraged him in this idea by assuring Irvine that he could keep his laboratory job while studying towards a degree and thus making it possible for the younger man to attend all the classes that made up the still-embryonic St Andrews degree of BSc. Irvine matriculated in 1896[9] and joined not only the junior chemistry class, but also classes in zoology, botany and physics. He and his student contemporaries were infected with the romance of the old town: 'Being young, imaginative and receptive, we revelled in the beauty of our surroundings, trudged out the West Sands by night or day, scrambled along the cliffs by moonlight to the Rock and Spindle, and at sunrise gazed on the pilgrim's view of St Andrews.'[10]

Imrie, an advanced student with Purdie, invited Irvine to move from his 'bunk' out beyond the Kinnessburn and share rooms with him nearer the department. In the last days of the nineteenth century, the old collegiate life of the university had quite disappeared, and the men students in particular were pushed about from one lodging-house to another. Irvine never forgot this unpleasant experience, which later spurred his mission to develop the residential side of the university. In the meantime, he was grateful to have found congenial rooms with his new friend from the chemistry department. Imrie found that they shared a love of music, and their days were filled in typical fashion for students of the late Victorian period. Irvine was not just a 'grinder', though he may have worked harder than others. He had also developed a certain skill as a raconteur and could make his friends fall about with his mimicry of their professors; he had, too, a ready audience for tales of his limited encounter with industrial chemistry at the Ardeer Nobel factory.

Jim Irvine introduced from Glasgow his passion for sport, for football, for athletics. Encouraged by Jim and his experience as a cross-country runner in the West of Scotland, the University Harriers Club dated from his time as a student leader in the sport. With his friend George Blair, Irvine trained along the sands. 'The antidote to what might have been a surfeit of the academic Muse was provided by the rigours of the football field, by long cross-country runs and by the chastening effect of the Old Course,' he later recalled.[11]

George Blair has left a vivid description of Jim when they first met at the commencement of the 1895–6 session:

> He was a lad of some eighteen or nineteen years of age, of medium build, genial of countenance, with eyes that looked you fearlessly in the face, eyes that betokened a fixity of purpose, yet could twinkle with abundant humour, as he poked fun, or told his stories – a clean-limbed, upstanding youth, who gave the impression of having come from what we Scots call 'a good home' – a vivid personality, with a grace of conversation that at once made him a centre of life and interest in any company into which he came.[12]

In social terms, the student 'diner' had a significance for these students that was gradually lost when the residential system was established. It was here that they had their meals; here, evenings with the Student Song Book, with glees and amateur dramatics, were drawn out and friendships were made. With his gift for mimicry, Jim sparkled at these gatherings. Even then St Andrews was known as the Singing University, and Jim was long after remembered for his customary rendition of an old song, 'By the Sad Sea Waves'. Weekly 'smokers', or concerts, were the order of the day; the young men had good lusty voices and they knew all the old sentimental and comic songs, even if young Imrie had a tendency to sing flat. Male companionship, so foreign to the twenty-first century, was what made 'men's men' of so many of Irvine's generation. Jim adored women, but he knew them as either his little sisters or as mysterious creatures to be cherished and indulged.

The department of chemistry, however, was already notable in attracting good women students. In 1898, the movement to establish a Women's Union took off, in recognition of the fact that the majority of students, both male and female, lived in the town in 'bunks' – St Andrews' slang for lodgings. Students' landladies are known to this day as 'bunk wives'. Irvine, for decades, referred to students as the 'men' of the university, but it cannot have escaped his notice that St Andrews was advanced in admitting women to degrees. Many of them were taking medical degrees, and for the first MBCHB qualification, chemistry was a component part. Henrietta Rusack, daughter of the fashionable St Andrews hotelier Johann Rusack,[13] was one of these. She was one of Irvine's early friends – Hettie to him – and when she married, not long after, Jim felt a small pang of loss.

Purdie was not the only one of his generation to attract benefactors to the university. The great Professor M'Intosh's specialism was marine biology, and a chance meeting with Charles Henry Gatty at the British Museum some thirty years before brought to St Andrews an endowment of £2,500 for building and equipping a new marine laboratory.[14] Gatty was a Sussex gentleman of independent means; he was an enthusiastic member of a learned society, the Ray Society, and his interest in the study of marine life finally drew him up to St Andrews in 1892 to study M'Intosh's work. In October 1896 the Gatty Marine Laboratory was opened in the company of 700 distinguished guests. It was in this month that Jim Irvine returned to matriculate as a student, and he joined Professor M'Intosh's natural history class. He could see for himself how St Andrews was starting to emerge as a university of scientific research institutes. In 1897, as Rector of St Andrews, the 3rd Marquess of Bute, with his fabulous wealth, endowed the construction of the Bute Medical Buildings, south of St Mary's Quad. Irvine was there to witness this development also.

James Irvine was a young man in a hurry. His fellow students noticed his prodigious memory. His capacity for hard work, the ethic of his boyhood, paid off and during the following two years he proved himself every inch the successful student. The fact that he, like all the students who would follow and all who had gone before, wore the St Andrews red gown enabled him, in years to come, as Principal to show how he identified with the undergraduates – sharing, as it were, in their youth and their affection for St Andrews. This sympathy was to prove mutually beneficial. To him the red gown was a symbol of perpetual youth, youth that renews itself generation after generation.

As a matriculated student, Jim Irvine could join in the full life of the university. In his first undergraduate term, the Science Club visited the paper works at nearby Guardbridge. There was nothing extraordinary in this, except that there was a demonstration of the manufacture of high-class writing papers from Spanish esparto grass. This useful piece of extraneous knowledge reverberated in Irvine's life over and over again: it crops up during the lifetime consultancy he held with the far larger Tullis Russell Paper Mills at Markinch; and many, many years later it flooded into his mind when, flying over Trinidad he looked down at the natural resources beneath and pondered the economic problems involved in establishing the University of the West Indies. At another meeting, Mr Lander from Purdie's team gave a talk on the mystical pursuit of alchemy. Jim retained a lifelong fascination with not only the stories of the philosopher's stone but, more importantly, with how the alchemists living close to nature and watching changes they could not understand were driven to attach a supernatural and moral significance to them.

The Science Club was one of the liveliest of the social institutions of the university. Annually it gave a wildly convivial dinner, or gaudeamus. In the dying days of Queen Victoria's reign, students in Scotland were prone to high spirits, and the university constantly fought against their unbridled behaviour. 'We have heard tales of venerated members of Senatus dragging frolicsome "Kates" off the backs of horses, and of becoming in the act somewhat besmirched with mud and gravel.'[15] In Irvine's second undergraduate year, *College Echoes* reported a growing move amongst the student body to have the discredited Kate Kennedy spring celebration of St Andrews' past reinstated – but this would have to wait a generation, for the early years of what came to be known as 'the Irvine era'. The annual procession of students in historical dress had long suffered opposition because of its tendency towards licentiousness and subversion of the university's authority. Its origins may even lie in pagan harbingers of spring, from times when there was no university in St Andrews; but, for centuries, the students' annual festive procession had given rebirth to the figure of a young girl, Kate, the niece of Bishop James Kennedy, who was the fifteenth-century founder of St Salvator's College.[16]

Perhaps Jim Irvine tended to lean towards the more dignified alternative, however. He joined the Conservative Association, and was called upon to sing after the Conservative symposium dinner. In later life, moving with the times, he voted Liberal, but at St Andrews at that time, to be a Conservative was the fashionable political stance.

Irvine in his young manhood was inextricably linked with the several milestones leading towards the gradual emergence of a modernised academic structure at his university. In 1897, the St Andrews BSc degree was awarded in its own right for the first time, independent of any MA degree. In March 1898, after two years of hard work, Irvine graduated BSc from St Andrews.[17] His undergraduate career had shown promise not only in chemistry: in his last year he was a medalist in botany. Professor M'Intosh's magnum opus, *The Life History of British Marine Food-Fishes*, was his prize for coming second in the senior class of natural history. His first prize from the school of natural philosophy in the previous year was Sir Norman Lockyer's lengthy but popular account of solar physics, a similarly handsome book, calf-bound and stamped in gold with the university's seal.[18] Were these personal choices? Did the weighty book on solar physics perhaps provide for him a lingering glance back at the popularisation of science when he was just a boy, and his experience of the transit of Venus? His final examinations placed him top of his year in chemistry (with special distinction) and natural sciences (special distinction), but despite the attainments in other sciences and his bent for botany, he was already committed to a career as an organic chemist.

He was, however, genuinely and easily attracted to botany, and his later development within organic chemistry did, on his own admission, lean distinctly towards biochemistry, which was not then a formalised discipline. He came to realise that he had been somewhat indulgently encouraged to specialise from an early age: he had always been given the freedom to study exactly what appealed to him. It was only later when qualifying for his German PhD that he felt the loss of higher mathematics, and he really had to work at a subject that a twentieth-century scientist could not do without. It formed a constituent part of his PhD, and provided for him a lesson in the ills of too-early specialisation.

To celebrate his graduation, he purchased for himself *Alma Mater's Mirror*, a rather self-consciously precious little anthology that Professor Lewis Campbell had put together for the members of the Students' Union ten years earlier. He studiously inscribed his copy 'Jacobus C. Irvine. Civis Universitatis Sancti Andreae. MDCCCXCVIII.'[19] After graduating he spent a year contemplating his future and continuing to work for Professor Purdie in a research capacity. He was already regarded by Purdie as a brilliant pupil and an able collaborator. Purdie, as he had done with others before, tested him out with the offer of a privately funded assistantship, working jointly with him to further the research of the department in the optical activity of the alkaloidal lactates.

College Echoes, the students' university magazine, reported breathlessly in 1899 that: 'An unusual and extremely startling amount of excitement was observed in the Chemical Department, where through long summer hours five recherche (sic) souls made life miserable for themselves in an unseasonable quest for knowledge.' The university still did not observe the months between Easter and October as being part of their calendar. These were the months in which Irvine found his feet as a chemist and first felt the stirrings of ambition.

He was never a run-of-the mill young man. His family background had already instilled in him this restlessness, and even the belief that his personal destiny would bring honour not only to himself but also to his country. In an age of hero-worship this was not so surprising. 'Honour St

Mungo,' his father said. 'You could be the next William Ramsay.'[20] No son of Glasgow could fail to know of Sir William Ramsay, later to be a Nobel prizewinner and discoverer of the noble gases, and young Irvine's early entry into chemistry by training to be an analyst was the same as Ramsay's. He was a good role model for Irvine who, when he tried to evoke Ramsay's genial personality, imperceptibly sketched out those very qualities that he tried to cultivate in himself:

> Disabuse your minds at once of the idea that the hazard of fortune played any conspicuous part in the achievements of the man.
>
> . . .
>
> All that William Ramsay accomplished sprang from his own enthusiasms, his own indomitable energy, his own indestructible energy, and his capacity to look back and to look forward – back into the records of history, for he appreciated what the past can teach us, forward into the unknown, for scientifically he was a visionary and a prophet.

Irvine also said of Sir William Ramsay: 'It is not always the lot of men to have the verdict of history so uniformly kind and the risk is all the greater the more a man plays as he did the hazardous role of the prophet.'[21]

The year 1899 was remarkable for many aspects of scientific discovery. It was the time of Michael Forster's address to the British Association for the Advancement of Science at Dover, when Dewar succeeded in isolating liquid hydrogen in bulk and attained a temperature within fifteen degrees of the absolute zero. It was also the year when the first Zeppelin floated above Lake Constance, and it was when the first men wintered in the Antarctic. The National Physical Laboratory was founded in 1899 for the centralisation of scientific research for national purposes, a recognition that in the twentieth century a nation should be scientifically self-supporting and should set a standard for research. In St Andrews in 1899 Purdie published an account of the application of his work with Pitkeathly using silver oxide. Irvine was conscious of his times, and conscious of the dramatic developments not only of scientific knowledge but of new ambitions of nationhood that were being played out on the scientific world stage.

Purdie encouraged his young research worker in the idea of spending a year or two in one of the great German chemical research institutes in order to complete his chemical training. In April 1899 the University Court of St Andrews put his name forward to the 1851 Exhibition Commissioners for the award of an 1851 Exhibition Science Research Scholarship to enable him to study in Germany. His candidature was strengthened by several pieces of original work in which he had collaborated with Purdie: 'Active Alkaloid Lactates and the Resolution of Lactic Acid by Means of Alkaloids'; notes on an investigation into Di-methoxysuccinic Acid and Ethereal Salts; 'The Action of Secondary Butyl Iodide on Silver Malate'; and 'The Rotations of Methoxy and Ethoxypropionic Acids'. This last paper was published in collaboration with Purdie, and all were experimental explorations into Purdie's own specialisms at that time.[22] This joint paper with Purdie, in which they published their resolution of lactic acid, represented a milestone in stereochemistry. To arrive at an optical resolution was a novelty at that date, and a considerable achievement.

One of his pieces of work, an experimental examination of optically active dimethoxysuccinic acid, might have been ready to submit to the Chemical Society for publication (and theoretically the award of a St Andrews doctorate), were it not that developments in stereochemistry caused them to halt and accumulate more experimental data. Had the statutory five years after first graduation been passed, Irvine would have qualified for a St Andrews DSc. He felt indignant that this mark of distinction was not yet officially his. As it was, this work was completed during the university vacations when Irvine returned to St Andrews to work with his old professor in the laboratory of the United College through the summer months, according to the pattern first dreamed of by Purdie when he took up his chair.

Irvine was highly-strung by nature. Later he was to write 'I have not forgotten how anxiously I awaited the decision . . . to appoint me [to an 1851 Exhibition Scholarship] nor can I ever forget how much I owe the opportunities the 1851 Exhibition Scholarship brought within my reach.'[23] On 29 June his mind was finally put at rest, and the valuable scholarship of £150 per year, tenable for two years, was his.[24] Another of Purdie's protégés and also the recipient of an 1851 Exhibition Scholarship, Alex Mackenzie, had paved the way and was working in Berlin. Irvine's first ambition had been to join him and take up his scholarship at one of the two chemical institutes in Berlin. He aspired to study with Emil Fischer, the greatest organic chemist of the age, but none of the Berlin laboratories had room for him that year. By the beginning of August, Irvine still had no place at an institute of advanced chemistry.

The 1851 Exhibition Commissioners were beginning to run out of patience, and by August 1899 he was obliged to write to the secretary to the commissioners:

I have been unable so far to fix definitely at which Institution I shall hold the same. My original intention was to proceed to the University of Berlin where special facilities for the study of Technical Chemistry exist. I have received word that the laboratories of Professor Fischer and Landolt are fully occupied, and that Dr Markwald of the 2nd Institute, on account of his impending resignation, is taking no new students. Recent advice informs me that there is still one vacancy in the 1st Chemical Institute for which I have made formal application. At present I am also prosecuting inquiries at the University of Leipzig and elsewhere.[25]

Fischer was the father of carbohydrate chemistry, and the still unexplored state of this important branch of chemistry may have attracted Irvine even then. When the hope of working in Berlin slipped from his grasp, Irvine applied to Leipzig, where Purdie's former professor, Johannes Wislicenus, was director of the Organic Chemical Institute. Purdie wrote to Wislicenus in Leipzig on his student's behalf, and despite Wislicenus' age and failing health, Irvine was accepted by the great man.

Johannes Wislicenus was a man of courage. Not afraid of innovation, a generation earlier he had put Leipzig at the heart of the new stereo-chemistry. Wislicenus wrote to Irvine in the most cordial terms, saying that he expected him at the beginning of the autumn semester of 1899: the German academic year consisted of two terms of classes.[26] A full course of chemical research might take anything up to six or seven years. Irvine had two years at his disposal, and matriculated in Leipzig on 23 October as plain James Irvine, in the same month that the Boer War broke out.[27]

FOUR

A Student in Leipzig, 1899–1901

Jim Irvine spent only two university years in Leipzig, but these two years, in a place so far from home, were to form the most significant period of his life.

He enjoyed a long sea-crossing, and in October 1899 he chose to cross from Leith to Hamburg. In the Leipzig Bahnhofstrasse a line of *droschkas* awaited arrivals from the Hamburg/Berlin train, the fur wraps and sleigh-shaped carriages a reminder that Leipzig lies to the east of Europe, and enjoys extremes of climate more associated with Russia. His student friend from St Andrews, Alexander Imrie, who pretended to more knowledge of Germany than Jim could have, had accompanied him to see him settled in. After a false start in the Brüder Strasse, he chose rooms in Ferdinand Rhode Strasse,[1] a broad tree-lined street of villas and tenement flats in the Scottish manner, all of handsome and recent construction.

He shared these lodgings, in the newly developed sector beyond the Ring Strasse, with the Rose brothers, 'Bud' Rose and 'Cabbage' Rose. Bud was a young musician, and his slightly older brother was a chemist, studying in Leipzig in a more leisurely fashion than Irvine could allow himself. He and Jim quickly established a supportive friendship that lasted many years, stretching over two continents. They were almost inseparable during the Leipzig years. Eventually Cabbage (Robert Eustafieff Rose) joined Purdie's team in St Andrews for a year, between 1904 and 1905,[2] and worked on the development of the Purdie silver oxide reaction. Bud and Cabbage were good-looking, popular students. Their late mother had been Russian, and their father, a genial character known as 'Moss' Rose, was Canadian, though living in Italy. They mixed as much with the musical coterie as with the scientists, neatly representing much that was cosmopolitan in Leipzig at that time. They smoothed the path of their new friend, introducing him into the student society that gave Jim Irvine a social life to add to his experiences in chemistry. Irvine did not find his fellow German students nearly so congenial, however. He increasingly used his matronymic, Colquhoun, as his confidence grew: 'James Colquhoun Irvine' carries an air of gravitas, but his fellow German students took this somewhat outlandish Highland family name to be Cohen, and in Leipzig he encountered an unpleasant anti-Semitism that was new to him: 'What a pity nice Herr Irvine is a Jew,' he overheard.

Irvine was not without some training in German, and he offered himself as a modest interpreter to some fellow British students. His rather technical secondary schooling may have thrown out the classics, but the modern languages of French and German, being important for a business career at that time, were taught to young Glaswegians preparing for careers in industry. At St Andrews, Purdie gave him all the chemical journals to read; many important papers were published by Germans and Irvine grew used to their written style. In his turn, he would be required to write his thesis in German and then translate it for the 1851 Exhibition Commissioners. Although it is unlikely that he had any experience of conversational German when he first arrived in Leipzig, his talent for mimicry and his ability to play by ear on the piano any tune he had heard once were qualities that served him well when he needed to pick up enough German to attend lectures in other branches of science, and to acquire the confidence to converse with fellow students.

On the appointed day in that October, young Jim Irvine nervously attempted to present himself to Wislicenus. Searching for his new professor, he blundered about the various laboratories that stretched along the Liebig Strasse, a fine avenue of new scientific research institutes, eventually recognising, as he said, by the 'fragrant smell of benzaldehyde' (oil of bitter almonds), his organic chemistry destination; this new generation of organic chemists could not avoid the odorants associated with these compounds, and they were beginning to recognise the need to develop a keen sense of smell in order to distinguish the isomers of optically active substances.[3] Irvine's first attempt to use his German and ask the way fell on the uncomprehending ears of a German student, but he was quickly reassured when he encountered Wislicenus, who made him feel more at home. 'You are Mr Irvine from Scotland. Welcome to Leipzig,'[4] he said in excellent English. Not many years later, Irvine was to describe him thus: 'A tall imposing man, with shaggy white hair and venerable beard.'

Yet again a warm relationship between teacher and student grew, developing into something more akin to that of father and son. Wislicenus became Irvine's *meister* in the central European medieval sense. Jim was the great man's last graduate student; but Purdie, it must be remembered, had been his first PhD candidate when Johannes Wislicenus directed the Institute in Würzburg. G.G. Henderson, Irvine's young professor at the Technical Institute in Glasgow, had also sat at his feet in Leipzig. Wislicenus felt strongly bound to this latest young Scotsman.

The triumvirate of Irvine's professors at the First Chemical Institute in Leipzig consisted of men whose memory and achievements still reverberate in chemical circles: Beckmann, whom he found jovial and interesting; Ostwald, aloof and indifferent to students studying organic chemistry; and Wislicenus, whom he loved. Wislicenus was the most stimulating to Jim; he was the type of philosophical chemist whose interests ranged over a vast number of varied and innovative chemical topics and ideas.

Wislicenus' understanding of the then radical concept of stereoisomerism came early in the game; it marched with the discoveries of the celebrated Dutchman, Van t'Hoff. This recognition of stereoisomerism, by a generation before Purdie, enabled chemists to understand the constituency and behaviour of chemical compounds in terms of their three-dimensional structure, particularly when displaying molecular chirality, the characteristic of compounds which have a non-superimposable mirror image. This revelation was one factor that changed the face of the study of chemistry and the chemical industries of modern times. Daringly, Wislicenus struck out to explore these ring compounds and embrace the use of new reactions for this purpose. His classical investigations into the isomerism of the lactic acids dated from the early 1860s, when organic chemistry was only just beginning to free itself from the restrictions of the Type Theory. From his research laboratories, first in Zürich, then in Würzburg and lastly in Leipzig, his students had gone out to all corners of the globe to found schools of chemistry devoted to this newly discovered world. Purdie, whose first specialism was the lactic acids, was one of these. Irvine, with his later school of carbohydrate chemistry in St Andrews, would be another.

Irvine was immediately drawn to Wislicenus' nobility of character, humanity, love of imparting knowledge, and unselfish devotion to the welfare of his students, in whom he inspired a following that amounted almost to idolatry. They in return called their professor Papa. Irvine had joined a select band. Wislicenus was the son of a Lutheran pastor of Polish extraction, a wandering Pole who had known persecution and then endured exile for the modern theology that he preached. The struggles that his family encountered on attempting to reach America, which would become their home in exile, had thrust responsibility on Johannes' shoulders; yet this youthful hardship only strengthened his natural sense of independence. He had, in fact, been forced to abandon his education in Halle as much for his own outspoken political opinions as for his father's. With a degree of self-sacrifice, young Johannes Wislicenus had to become his family's bread-winner, and he obtained an assistantship at Harvard, eventually being able to return from this to his métier in central Europe as a research chemist.[4] There was no insularity in Wislicenus' development.

The chemical problems with which Wislicenus tasked his research pupils displayed his versatility. The topic he gave to Irvine was not connected with Irvine's previous research work. Jim was required to effect a new synthesis of the hydrocarbon, phenanthrene, by starting with salicylaldehyde. Phenanthrene, which is known today to be mildly carcinogenic, occurs naturally in coal tar. Glasgow maintained through the nineteenth century the struggle to develop an adequate chemical industry based on coal tar, and its possibilities would not have been foreign to Irvine.[5] The examiners of the 1851 Exhibition Commission deemed that the subject of the thesis would make a useful contribution to technical chemistry.[6] There were no properly recorded previous studies of phenanthrene that Irvine could turn to, and the 1851 Exhibition Commissioners eventually concluded that the scope of his work in Leipzig was detrimentally restricted. His scholarship's tenure of two years was entirely absorbed by this one thankless task, which proved abortive in one sense: he never synthesised phenanthrene in this way.[7]

The experimental constituent of his German degree proved to be very difficult, and here a distinction must be appreciated between the approach that he adopted to his research in his first year and that which he was able to put into play the next year. The benzoin condensation reaction that he used at first did not and would not produce the goods, no matter how often he repeated his experiments: alas, instead of some of the crystals he so ardently desired, he could only obtain an oily brown mass. The temperatures required for the benzoin condensation were so high that with sealed tube experiments his apparatus often blew up. By June 1901, he could calculate that his thesis had cost him £20 in lost apparatus, for which he had to pay:[8] it was an enormous sum at that date, and the equivalent of about 50 per cent of a labouring man's annual wage. At first Irvine was ignorant of all the difficulties that would face him, and thought he could forge ahead. As he said of himself at this time, he 'was rather a conceited beggar as far as his chemistry'. The experience of his first year's fruitless work eventually left him facing his precious last year in deep despair. In his sense of frustration he accused Wislicenus of deliberately holding him back. His degree required his attendance at courses of lectures on physics and mathematics, as well as botany. In all of these he would be searchingly examined *viva voce* once he had completed his *arbeit*.[9] Classes in these subjects, held in the premises of the university, would draw him away from the attractions of the chemistry research bench, and he found that he really had to struggle to catch up with higher mathematics, something surprising in a young man of high intelligence and with a meticulous approach to his work.

One event during Irvine's first year of studies proved to be of great significance. In March 1900 he attended a series of lectures on the sugars given by Hans Stobbe, who used Emil Fischer's specimens to illustrate his theme. Irvine was very taken with these ideas and in reflection afterwards had an idea that later would make his scientific reputation. For a few years in St Andrews Purdie had been developing and applying a new chemical reaction: the silver oxide methylation technique. Purdie's work was on lactic acids, but Irvine now wondered whether the complex carbohydrate compounds would submit to this reaction as an aid for determining their structure. The sensitive sugars, being polyhydroxy[10] compounds, could be methylated by this gentle method. He was so excited at the thought that he immediately telegrammed Purdie for his views. Purdie famously, but cautiously, replied that he thought it might be productive of much successful work. He suggested to Irvine that he finish his Leipzig degree and then return to work in St Andrews, at his (Purdie's) expense, to develop this idea, a novel approach out of which grew St Andrews' enormously influential and productive school of carbohydrates research, which ran from 1901 to c.1930.

For the next year and more Irvine merely retained in his mind Purdie's suggestion, which only offered the possibility of further work in St Andrews. Leipzig introduced Irvine to a world community of chemists, many of whom worked in research institutes far larger and better-funded than anything Purdie could offer. It is clear that at this time Irvine imagined he would afterwards find a post in London, where he might work in a large team with others of his generation and of his calibre, under the direction of one of the famous chemists at the Royal School of Science or the Royal School of Mines. At this period of his life, Irvine certainly had no thought that he would become Professor Irvine of St Andrews, despite his boyhood romancing.

Irvine's first year in Leipzig was just as remarkable on a social and personal level. Once he had found his feet, he was drawn into the student life that surrounded him and that was to provide him with another vision of his future. In meeting a vivacious young Irish musician, Mabel Williams, he knew that he had met the girl with whom he would share his life. It was an unusually fine autumn in Leipzig that year. As late as November, people went out without their coats, and stood for preference at the front of the trams to feel the cool air rush past their faces. It was popular belief that the comet on 14 November was responsible for this quirk of climate, and that it was going to carry off a slice of the world.[11] Mabel and the other music students with whom she shared lodgings in Schnorr Strasse, in the suburb of Schleussig, took the Schönefeld tram of a morning into town for music lessons, or to attend the Wednesday morning Gewandhaus Probe, for which their teachers would give them passes. The weekly concerts given by the world-famous Gewandhaus orchestra were given their final rehearsal on Wednesday mornings, and the tickets for this were very popular with students of all disciplines.

Initially Jim Irvine did not allow himself the same freedoms. In 1899 Leipzig was not a large city; its medieval heart even today lies just within the Ring Strasse, which in 1899 was lined in the central European manner by grand hotels and by the magnificent new institutional buildings that had grown out of the educational visions of Liebig and of his contemporary Mendelssohn. The chemist Liebig, who was one of the greatest early leaders of chemistry education, and the musician Mendelssohn were in a sense the twin catalysts of Leipzig's late-found fame for higher scientific education and musical studies. Although Liebig never worked in Leipzig, Irvine regarded him as the founding father of laboratory experimental teaching of the sciences of which Leipzig was so notable an exponent, and his name is recorded on the streets and buildings of Leipzig; Felix Mendelssohn was the founder and first director of the famous Leipzig Konservatorium der Musik.

From his digs, Jim could walk to the Liebig Strasse laboratory of the First Chemical Institute. He was at first content to spend his days trying to please Wislicenus and exercising the chemical skills of measurement and accuracy that he had learned in St Andrews. Even nearer to Ferdinand Rhode Strasse were the marble halls and painted ceilings of the university, where all the other elements of the German higher degree were pursued. In addition to following the instruction of his chemical professors Wislicenus, Beckmann and Ostwald, he took classes given by Pfeffer and Wiener.[12] On the inner side of the Ring Strasse, Leipzig's maze of tortuous medieval streets is easily crossed, and in this quarter Jim habitually took his midday meal at the old *weinstübe*, Baarmann's. He eschewed the poker-playing group of students, which in fact included his future brother-in-law, Bert Williams, a student of German philology.

The pursuit of music was everywhere; the residential streets echoed with a polyphony of practising. The music students vied with each other for recognition, and their gossip was all about the respective merits of this teacher or that. Jim, although a scientist, was musical; he could play the piano and sing with considerable charm, and his scholarship gave him the means to attend the opera and, of course, go to concerts. At one of these he met an Australian, a Mrs Usher, who was chaperoning her daughter. She was one of the group of mothers of young musicians brought from all over the world to Leipzig to complete their education. She extended to Jim an open invitation to attend one of her musical soirées, and one early autumn evening he decided to take her up on this. Mabel Williams, a student of both violin and piano, had also joined the throng at the party, made up mostly of musicians. Not all were equally good, and the evening was dull until Jim sat down to play his own accompaniments. Perhaps it was the skill of the scientist, but Jim's prodigious memory served him well, and he had no trouble in singing the ballads of his youth from memory. Both Mabel and Jim afterwards acknowledged that, at this encounter in Mrs Usher's crowded living room, filled with cigarette smoke, they each felt a certain attraction for the other. Mabel's friends teased her for the attention she paid to the curly-headed Scotsman who talked so engagingly. The magnetism between them is perhaps hardly surprising. Jim had been brought up to be good company, and he proved to be just as lively and unaffected as she. They were both good-looking: she was noticeably tall and slim, her dark eyes set into a solemn face, ringed with dark curls. With her four brothers at home in the holidays Mabel was never prissy but, launched on Leipzig, she enjoyed wearing the good wardrobe of elegant clothes with which the local dressmaker in Holywood, County Down, had equipped her.

There were several ways in which the hard-working scientists could regularly meet the musical butterflies. One of these were the highly successful balls and dances which, organised by the English church, would regularly take place in one of the big hotels. In early December, Jim and Mabel met again at one of these. This is how she described the encounter:

I had a great many nice English partners the nicest being a Scotch man!, that Dr Irvine that I met at Mrs Usher's. I danced twice with him & went into supper, & I'm afraid sat one or two extras! Which wasn't at all as it should be – but he was most interesting – talked *splendidly*. He is very very clever – is a Dr, a BSc & now taking out a German degree at the *expense* of the British Government; he has discovered something, a new explosive I think & he is very young for he told me that he has not been *capped* for his BSc yet as he was not old enough – you have to be a certain age. He told me such a lot about explosives, he works a lot with them, & has had some very narrow escapes of being blown up – but it was really tremendously interesting – he wrote his thesis on narcotics and alcoholics.[13]

Mabel was captivated by him, and was happy to flout propriety and spend too many dances sitting out with her 'Dr Irvine'.

The details that she gives her mother about her new acquaintance are rather muddled, but through the muddle it is possible to discern certain of James Colquhoun Irvine's characteristics: that he told a good yarn, and that he wanted to impress. Perhaps his knowledge of explosives was heavily based on the day he spent at Nobel's explosives factory at Ardeer five years earlier. What he may have told Mabel, with some licence, is that he was all but a DSc in principle, having had a research paper already published by the Chemical Society.[14] In fact he had to wait until 1903 to gain his St Andrews doctorate, after the elapse of the requisite five years from first graduation as BSc.[15] However, the fact that Mabel spoke of him as Dr Irvine was quite useful to their romance. All year, her mother back home in Belfast was quite convinced that this gentleman who cropped up so frequently in her daughter's letters must almost be middle-aged, and therefore 'safe'.

From then, Jim's personal life took on a new significance and he allowed more social occasions to compete with the various unpleasantnesses of the laboratory: the furnace heat, the toxic fumes, the professor who was so difficult to satisfy. He now always bought tickets for the Gewandhaus rehearsals on Wednesdays, and he avidly attended all the main concerts, partly in the hope of encountering Mabel. His eyes sought out hers in the gloom of the crowded auditorium, but his seats tended to be in the stalls, and hers would be up in the gallery.[16] Such was the difference in means between a youthful scientist with a valuable scholarship and a young girl dependent on an allowance from her father.

Jim was every inch the romantic lover, tossed about with uncertainty and plunged from sweet happiness into the depths of despond. Mrs Williams of Brook House, Holywood, County Down may have been a stickler for Mabel's observation of the most arcane of social conventions, but Jim's parents, bowed down by the internal struggles of the reformed church in Scotland, were horrified by the development of what they saw as a dangerous, if youthful, obsession that threatened the future of their brilliant son's career.

Far away from home in an alien atmosphere, Jim and his expatriate student friends grew up fast. Absence from home offered them small freedoms from the social straightjacket of middle-class Victorian life, and they learned much from all that was around them in the cosmopolitan city. It was all quite innocent, but they learned to form views of their own and to stand on their own two feet. Students today would recognise much of their voyage of self-discovery. Their views, so forthrightly expressed, were not confined to politics. They were constantly assessing, criticising and chattering about music.

The greatest musicians of the age came to Leipzig to perform, and Mabel's correspondence contains vivid accounts of the interpretative skills of Ysaye, Nikisch, Joachim, Siloti and almost everyone they had ever heard of: all the stuff of fable to subsequent generations. The Russian pianist Siloti was one of the legendary pupils of Liszt. Mabel had wanted, above anything, to be his pupil, but he was so often absent from Leipzig on tour or at the court of the Czar that she only managed to obtain a couple of lessons from her hero. Her violin teacher was a far less elusive character: old Hans Sitt, still known today for his études, was a fixture of Leipzig life, and once or twice a week Mabel climbed the stairs of an old house in the middle of town to learn from him.

One evening, Sarasate, the virtuoso composer of competition pieces of all young aspiring violinists even today, performed at the Krystall-Palast. And who should Mabel bump into but her Dr Irvine, with whom she exchanged heated and lengthy criticisms of the concert. They took a strong dislike to Sarasate's style, 'all rampaging up and down – trills & runs & cords [sic] and harmonics'. He played Bruch's *Fantaisie on Scotch Airs*, which was particularly offensive to them. Mabel would have preferred the Scotch airs on a hurdy-gurdy & 'un-Fantaisied', as she put it indignantly. 'I was speaking to Dr Irvine afterwards & as a Scotch man his spirit rose against the *Fantaisie*! He said it unpardonable to write such stuff & call it Scotch airs! & I think if he could have got hold of either Bruch or Sarasate he would have slain them!'[17]

Mabel enjoyed cultivating her new group of friends, the chemists, but she did not find all of them as interesting as 'Dr' Irvine. There was Charles Crowther, Evelyn Wilbraham and the other young Scotsman, Alexander Findlay, not to speak of Cabbage, and they all distinguished themselves as chemists in later life. Mabel found that Jim's friend Abel, 'a well-meaning but tiresome young man', talked of nothing but himself; as indeed in a sense Jim probably did, but somehow or other Mabel didn't notice it, such was his charm. Jim Irvine's gift of telling a tale, of recounting in dramatic terms some episode of his own experience, eventually met the butt of the Irish girl's teasing. Mabel was used to bringing her brothers down a peg, and warned Jim against expecting everyone to hang on his words – but of course they always did.

Throughout these months of the winter of 1899–1900, the war in South Africa assumed devastating proportions; but what was its impact on these somewhat insular young Brits whose every social need was catered for from within their own community? There was an English church, English sales of work, English balls, and English tennis tournaments in the summer. They also had a Canadian dentist. During the year that Mabel and Jim's romance grew, the war in South Africa progressed, and they could not escape the public hostility of the Germans. Germany did not hold back her sympathy for the Boers. There was quite open and mutual antipathy between the young Germans and the British students. It was even thought that one of their longed-for balls would have to be cancelled. The 'Engländer' were mocked in the street, and rough men on the trams sneered behind their beery moustaches; in retaliation and flaunting their loyalty, the British students wore red, white and blue ribbons in their lapels.

There was a belief in Germany that the Irish, pressing for Home Rule, were lukewarm supporters of the British side – but not so these Irish, who were proud to hear news of the bravery of the Irish regiments. Mabel's response was always spirited: 'All the Germans & French think Ireland disloyal & it does make me mad; . . . some expect a revolution some of these days! Poor little Ireland! & it has done such grand work in the war & they seem to forget all that & remember nothing but those wretched Irish-Americans, & the few wretches of Home Rulers in Parliament.'[18]

Germany's jealousy of England was easily discernable to British students like Bert Williams, who read the German press and had been studying at the university in Leipzig for three years. Bert Williams was Mabel's brother, and his later academic success would be crowned with the Schröder chair of German in Cambridge. He followed with deep unease Germany's suspicion of England's colonial growth. In 1896 his letters home show that he discerned Germany's anxious eye on the Ottoman Empire, concerning which they cast England in the role of robber baron.[19] The increasing diplomatic hostility between England and Germany was fanned by recent discoveries of gold and diamonds in the farming country of the Boer Trekkers. The story of imperial rapaciousness in Africa is of course well-known. The discovery of gold in South Africa in the northern Zuid-Afrikaansche Republiek (ZAR) region coincided in date with the establishment of German East Africa on the very border of Northern Rhodesia. It is not surprising that Germany watched with great interest President Paul Kruger's struggle for political control of these lands.

Letters from home arrived daily with news of the deaths of so many young men they knew. Africa seemed so foreign and far away as a last resting place for childhood friends whom the young students had last seen in the comfortable parlours and drawing rooms of their parents' circle of friends. The German 'reportage' of the war was proclaimed incessantly in Leipzig. On every corner the newspaper vendors shouted the latest news, and extra editions of the German newspapers tried their hand at propaganda, loudly proclaiming: 'Extra Blatt, Extra Blatt. *Ladysmith ist gefallen!*'[20] Ladysmith was not '*gefallen*'; it never fell to the Boers and was relieved on 2 March 1900. Irvine later said that, from the point of view of scientific education, he had found Germany disappointing. 'This may in part be explained', he noted, 'by the fact that my sojourn there coincided with the period of the Boer War and the lot of the Engländer was unenviable.'

James Irvine observed all that was around him and never forgot; fifty years later he found himself lecturing on propaganda to a Workers' Educational Association class of servicemen.[21] His unchanging belief was that Germany had always practised propaganda. When he was a young man, he was witness to the fact that the world was mesmerised by Germany into believing that she was supreme in everything, particularly those things whereby you could control the world: that they would be the Herrenvolk of the scientific age. In later life Irvine liked to contemplate how national characteristics contributed to the development of science. Although he acknowledged that the greatest bulk of scientific work must be attributed to Germany, he believed that France had produced the greatest number of scientific publications, enduring for all time, and that of the new ideas during the nineteenth century that enriched science, by far the largest share belonged to Britain.

It was not only for their politics that Jim and Mabel found the Germans distasteful. The long hair of the musicians, the unkempt dress of the man in the street – these were bad enough. Mabel, fresh from the schoolrooms of her polite Quaker boarding school in Southport, was quick to condemn all that shocked her. 'The women are mostly ugly and badly dressed – the men rude and ugly too – fat, greasy, beery & stare horribly! All wear soft felt hats – & long moustaches curled up Kaiser-wise.' Duelling was prevalent in student circles. The young men wore the slashes of duelling wounds on their faces like a badge of honour. 'Some of the students look so awful with these great cuts and hacks all over their faces. How they can feel proud of it I don't know!'²² The German students were silly and unmanly as companions in the laboratory. With a tendency to be rather plump, they were markedly different in appearance from the clean-limbed young men who had come to Leipzig from the more sophisticated mercantile societies of Glasgow and even Belfast, where custom required a man's dress to be neat and appropriate. The British students thought that the manners of the young Germans were boorish, and that they drank too much beer. Some German students bought tickets for the English balls, and Jim loathed the German manner of obtaining a dance partner. A girl already happily waltzing with one of the young Englishmen would be approached. Clicking his heels, the German would bow and then whisk the lady off to dance with him. The Britishers did, however, make some attempts at fraternising, and tried to teach the rather solemn young Germans the Lancers, but without much success; they just couldn't dance fast enough.

There was also a certain underlying darkness apparent in the artistic life of Berlin and Leipzig at that time. It was out of this darkness that a young painter, Max Beckmann, son of a Leipzig flour merchant and born in 1884, found his medium. Selecting a disturbing side of human life to paint, he espoused the despairing philosophies of Schopenhauer and Nietzsche; a movement in German expressionism developed around Beckmann and his contemporaries. Jim Irvine was aware of this ugliness and carried with him from Leipzig some knowledge of a dark culture that was alien to the cheerful stoicism of his own people.

The Indian summer of November 1899 was succeeded by a harsh winter: glittering hoar frost lay on every branch, and the tram drivers wore furs for protection. As the deep freeze of winter descended, the now firmly established group of friends made plans to hire a frozen pond for private skating parties. At Christmas time, Jim Irvine went to Berlin to visit his St Andrews' chemical friend, Alex Mackenzie: faithful Alex Mackenzie, on whose support Jim depended in later life. Jim may have hoped to encounter the great chemist Emil Fischer in Berlin on this occasion. Later, Fischer and Irvine would correspond and Fischer showed his deep respect for Irvine's work, which he followed closely. There is some evidence that the younger scientist was certainly looking about him for his next move once he had obtained his German degree, and that, at this stage, this would not necessarily be in the direction of St Andrews.

Formal classes ended on 1 March, and many of the students returned to their home countries at Easter. Jim was anxious to maintain his collaborative work with Purdie, and so he spent the greater part of this vacation in St Andrews completing a paper.[23] He then resumed his life in Leipzig in early summer. He toiled away in the laboratory on what he called his '*verflüchte arbeit*' (cursed thesis!). This time of single-minded application to laboratory work allowed Wislicenus to extend his special friendship to his pupil. At midday they would on occasion stroll back, arm in arm, to the *meister*'s house for the noon meal, and there meet good Ernst Beckmann. Stories of old St Andrews would be exchanged for stories of the heroic days of the chemical Institute in Würzburg. Of an afternoon, a game of tennis in the nearby Johannis Park against Wislicenus' nephew might be the order of the day, with the old professor the impartial umpire.[24]

Mabel Williams became increasingly dear to Jim. In May, she pressed on her mother a persuasive argument that a change of digs to rooms in the Robert Schumann Strasse had everything to commend it. There would be a considerable saving in rent; and there would also be economy in travel, as this street of somewhat more superior housing was within walking distance of the Konservatorium. The Fräulein landlady was deemed to be very respectable. What she omitted to mention to her mother was that her new rooms were exactly opposite the corner building in which resided her Dr Irvine, known to her by then as Jim. He had a balcony on which he would step out to smoke cigarettes and – throughout this summer of 1900 – to catch sight of Mabel, who was perhaps practising, or leaning out to say goodnight to him. '*Bist du müde?*' (Are you tired?) they learnt to say, and would repeat for the next fifty years. Thirty years later, a letter to Mabel was still signed 'deine Jim'.

This streak of independence in Mabel brought with it many benefits, and not only sentimental ones. During these last precious months in Leipzig, and eventually living alone in her new digs, she practised and studied her great love, the piano, with increasing intensity. Siloti returned to St Petersburg, where he spent the summer months; a chosen few of his pupils followed him there, but Mabel was not one of them. Perhaps rather late in the day, she commenced piano studies with Robert Teichmüller, an up-and-coming teacher at the Konservatorium. Teichmüller had been a pupil of Brahms, and in his way he became a more important teacher than Siloti, the great interpreter who had far too busy a career on the concert platform to offer in-depth lessons to all the young hopefuls who arrived in Leipzig.

Later in the twentieth century many famous pianists would say they owed everything to Teichmüller, and Mabel owed a great deal. She attacked her practice with renewed faith and pleasure, and the fruits of these last sweet months in Leipzig were not only a courtship, but also a greater maturity and confidence in her playing.

That summer of 1900 in Leipzig enchanted them both. Nightingales sang in the woods beyond their open windows; the days and nights were stiflingly hot, but the parks and fields surrounding the city were scented and bright with flowers, and were cool and inviting. Country inns opened their doors and offered delicious meals and country wines. Boatmen on the River Pleisse got out their skiffs and Jim, keen to display his skill with a boat, took Mabel for expeditions on the pretty network of river and tributary. They were not unchaperoned: Bert and his Agnes were sometimes there, or else it might be Cabbage and Clanis O'Brien, another bewitching Irish girl. Mabel's diary reveals that there were occasions on which she memorably jettisoned her hat. How shocked her mother would have been at this unseemly lapse! In 1900 no nice girl should be seen in public without a hat. Mabel and her brother exchanged conspiratorial glances: 'Lawk a mussy me, this is none o' I!' they whispered. Jim, used to the sensible 'sailor' dresses of his sisters, found Mabel's floating lace-edged muslin afternoon frocks quite unsuitable for a day spent on the river. 'Three-decker dresses,' he called them scornfully. She had hoped she would look like a girl in a painting by Tissot. She was fanciful; he more down to earth. They dreamed and planned their future. Inseparable by now, they took their meals together at Baarman's, at their own accustomed table.[25]

Like all their student friends, they had difficulty in making their allowances last right through the summer and so, as the summer days progressed rather than buy tickets for a concert, they sat in the park, and with a crowd of young Americans heard Sousa conduct his marches.

> Sousa, Sous-a
> He's all right.
> Who's all right?
> Why, Sousa!

chanted the American students. One summer's evening at the Botanic Garden they heard the youngest of the Strauss brothers conduct the famous waltzes, and Jim pronounced: 'If I can't have Bach or Beethoven, give me Strauss.' The pair bade lingering goodnights to each other on the doorstep of Mabel's lodgings.

Queen Victoria's birthday in May was celebrated with another ball. It took place at the Bonorand, a picturesque establishment with a ballroom set in parkland on the edge of Leipzig.[25] On this night, with the characteristic intensity that was evident in all the landmarks of his life, Jim pledged himself to Mabel, as she did to him. Quite improperly but absorbed by the uncertainty of what the future might hold, they sat out all the dances together. Mabel nervously broke her ivory fan into a pile of tiny pieces. Jim swept up the pieces and kept them as a reminder of that portentous evening at the Bonorand ball. Their pledge was a most serious matter for an academic chemist with no immediate prospects of employment. Jim's parents continued to interpret their friendship as an infatuation, but it was the foundation of a life together that would extend to half a century and survive absences in a way that only strong love can do.

Finally, it was time for Mabel to leave Leipzig and return to Belfast. Her year of being 'finished' as a musician was over, and she had lingered so long that none of her friends were left to join her on the journey. She could not travel alone, unchaperoned, and when Jim eagerly offered to accompany her they decided to continue the original deception. Mabel's mother was grateful to think that the man she thought of as a solid, middle-aged scientist, Dr Irvine, was so fortuitously able to bring her home. They crossed from Flushing to Queenborough, on the Thames estuary, in the worst storm for fifty years. The foremast and bulwarks of their packet were carried away and, nine hours late, they limped into harbour, where Mabel's father was anxiously waiting.[26] To his surprise he found that his daughter's companion was a cheerful, very young-looking Scottish student: plain Mr Irvine who, unlike Mabel, seemed none the worse for the stiff crossing.

During the summer of 1900 Jim paid the first of many holiday visits to Brook House, the comfortable home in Holywood where Mabel lived with her boisterous family. 'It's a poor home that can't afford one spoilt child,' was one of her mother's favourite sayings. Jim's family might have every reason to suspect that Mabel was spoilt, though in truth this was never seriously so. No engagement between the two sweethearts could take place for many years, and propriety meant that Jim could only be invited to Brook House as the friend of Mabel's brother, Bert. Propriety was the cause of many hardships and difficulties they would bear during the next five years, but the warmth and lightheartedness of the Williams family, with Mabel in their midst, was a very great pull to Jim, who from then on had a tendency to neglect his own more serious family in Glasgow. Mabel herself described her family as 'inconsequent'. Her mother was indulgent and old-fashioned.

Even if she knew it was really only Mabel's company that Jim yearned for, outwardly Jessie Williams had to treat him as another of her four sons and not a future son-in-law.

Mabel's father's business life had grown from modest beginnings as warehouseman to the position of partner in the cotton and embroidered muslin business of Williams and McBride. He was able to keep his large family in some style. John Williams's and John Irvine's experiences of business were not too dissimilar, although Jim's father in Glasgow was never made a partner of Walter MacFarlane. John Irvine had acquired impressive qualifications and the skill of draughtsmanship, while John Williams, who became the richer man in old-fashioned Belfast where the pace was slower, was purely a businessman. Both were devout Presbyterians.

Sadly, Jim's second year in Leipzig, without Mabel, was as unhappy and arduous as the first was carefree and happy. With the prospect of enduring that Victorian convention of a long 'understanding', and not an engagement to marry, Jim faced the great difficulty of winning a foothold in a career that at that time offered very few opportunities. Mabel's return to Ireland created a separation that made him introverted and melancholy. His experimental work was producing very few results; and even those few were dependent on what he called his 'sheer Scotch stubbornness'.

It was not until later that winter of 1900–01 that he decided to apply Purdie's silver oxide methylation reaction to the salicylaldehyde. The process had the merit of being a rapid one, as all the operations could be conducted in one day. The methyl ether of salicylaldehyde had first been prepared by W.H. Perkin more than thirty years before,[27] but Irvine's method was capable of producing 90 per cent of the pure substance very quickly.[28]

Jim relished the fact that in Leipzig he felt on the cusp of new knowledge. It was still with the old pride in himself that he wrote to Mabel Williams: 'Can you realise the enthusiasm of a cracked scientist, Mab, when he takes a synthesis another stage further than anyone else has managed? It has given me back some of the keenness and vim that I used to have for the investigation of the vast problems of the unknown.'

Jim's letters to Mabel reveal the return of something of his old spirit, despite his having to work against the clock and encountering continual disappointments.

> I have had such a terribly trying week – I never knew such a series of misfortunes to overtake my work – two explosions with consequent

wreckage of apparatus and you may well imagine my consequent despair.

. . .

This cursed analysis takes a whole day – from 8 am until 8 pm and during that time I am working over an apparatus at furnace heat – with my nerves on stretch – on some occasions this week too busy to go to dinner. No wonder then I came home a perfect mental and physical wreck and only by the most obstinate Scotch endurance could I set to work again – write up all my day's work and read up for the morrow . . . I cannot explain my difficulties to you but I can hardly imagine a chemist confronted with such a stupendous irritating task as I am at present tackling.

A fortnight ago everything looked rosy. I had at last got one stage further and secured a beautiful new compound. Yet curiously enough this substance apparently defies analysis and I have had to resort to a most elaborate and expensive method. By dint as I have said of successive days' torture (without dinner) I have sweated at it in the furnace room. – I have analysed it eight times. On three occasions my apparatus has exploded and the other five were unsuccessful. The Prof says it is the most stubborn case in his experience and I can believe him. This one stage has cost me more worry, more work and more money than all the rest of my arbeit put together. Small wonder I have been half crazy over it. – I am maddened at the thought that this unfortunate series of mishaps should come at this time and indefinitely postpone the end of my degree – and not only that my return home.[29]

Slowly the results began to tumble out; the reaction was still in its infancy and required great pains and tenacity to effect. Hydrogen cyanide, or prussic acid, present in his process, made him ill when the reaction was carried out in an open vessel.

That year he spent Christmas in Leipzig. He could not leave the laboratory bench. To let off steam early on New Year's morning he and Cabbage engaged in a snowball fight with the young English chemistry student, Charles Crowther, who was in Leipzig like the rest in order to acquire a German post-graduate degree; he and Crowther would not meet again until the period of the First World War. As he stood on his balcony listening to the church bells ring in the New Year of 1901, he thought of Mabel.

The death of Queen Victoria on 21 January curtailed the few midwinter social events that Jim and his colleagues looked forward to. Spring came, but it had lost the allure of the previous year and his entanglement with Miss Williams. Every woodland walk, every inviting seat was now imprinted with a memory. He was overwhelmed by a sense of loss. There was to be very little fun in this year. He tried desperately to obtain some paid employment for his eventual return to Britain, but an application for a lectureship with the Govan Education Board amounted to nothing, to his immense relief.[30] The Govan Board was the third most important in Scotland, but training prospective school teachers was not an appealing thought to a chemist who dreamed of the new discoveries waiting to be unlocked.

He had to acknowledge that his work in Leipzig was inconclusive, and on 4 June 1901 he applied for a third year's scholarship from the 1851 Exhibition Commissioners, hoping that he could pursue these threads further under a London chemist. Unfortunately, his case was not strong enough.[31] He had to keep his mind, however, on the immediate problem of completing his Leipzig degree. He never conquered his tendency to overwork, and headaches confined him frequently to bed. He endured lack of sleep, and he learnt to rely on the stimulus of cigarettes. Although he and Mabel knew that nicotine would one day damage his health, he chain-smoked his way through these last months.

With a characteristic sense of being misjudged, he felt that he already had enough material to satisfy the requirements of his degree, but still Wislicenus pushed him on, recognising in his pupil latent stirrings of high ambition. He advised him not to leave his results unresolved and open for others to take the glory. Irvine started to measure himself against what he called the chemical toffs: the great Professor Goldschmidt of Marburg had already published findings that corresponded with some of Irvine's results,[32] but it was Goldschmidt who had shown no analytical data. This gave life to Jim's competitive spirit, and finally – still without the synthesis of phenanthrene – his investigation, with analyses, of the derivatives produced from the methyl ether of salicylaldehyde was sufficiently new to merit the degree of PhD *summa cum laude*[33] – the highest ranking given by Leipzig, and never previously, he believed, awarded in Leipzig to a non-German.

It was won on the strength of his thesis and at a cost to his health. The headaches multiplied, and he became a liability to his friends because of his tendency to fall into prolonged dead faints. Owing to his rundown state of health, he succumbed to flu during the last weeks. He had to admit afterwards that he had overworked and that his viva examinations had suffered as a consequence – although his gentle mother had insisted he return to Glasgow for a short recuperation at Easter, with strict instructions not to cross over to Belfast to see Mabel. The viva examinations were, in themselves something of a throwback to the medieval student's test of learning. In German, and for an hour, a PhD candidate was required to debate with each of his professors in turn, and to defend his point of view.

The formal reading of his results took place immediately after the viva:

'*Herr cand Chemie Irvine! Es feut mich sehr ihnen zu mittheilen das sie haben die mundliche Prufung mit "Magna cum Laude"* (seconds) *gemacht und ferner das die wissenschaftliche Facultat ihre Doctor Dissertation* (the thesis) *mit die Marke "summa"* (firsts) *bezeichnet hat.*' 'I have therefore seconds for the exam & firsts for the thesis and had I only known German perfectly I know my answers were worth firsts in the Prufung easily,' he wrote to Mabel Williams.

His departure from Wislicenus, his *doktorvater*, moved them both greatly: You have been very dear to me, the old man said.[34] They never met again.

Despite the success of his examinations, the melancholy of his struggle to survive the final endurance test still hung over him. As he left Leipzig, he was still weakened by the nervous illnesses of that summer, and a pall of depression refused to lift. He knew not what the future held for him, and he had failed in all his attempts to gain some remunerative employment that might enable him to continue his courtship of Mabel Williams. He felt unloved and unresolved. It was, however, in his return to St Andrews that he would in time find what he had been seeking. Like Virgil's Aeneas pursuing his goal of Rome, through hardship and tragedy, so Irvine unknowingly carried the idea of St Andrews before him: it would form his life's course.

FIVE

Return to St Andrews

Jim Irvine's two years in Leipzig had turned a rather undeveloped and spoilt young Scotsman into a man who was able to look his future in the face. But this future carried with it none of the inevitability that has been suggested by earlier commentators. With many backward glances at the opportunities offered in the powerful research institutes of London, and rather sorrowfully, Jim returned home to Scotland during the summer of 1901.

His friend Alex Mackenzie, whom Professor Purdie also favoured, had had more luck. Not only had the 1851 Exhibition Commissioners been prepared to support his studies in Germany for the coveted extra year, but his doctoral work had been conducted in Berlin, first in Ladolt's laboratory and then under Marckwald. His was a Berlin PhD, also of 1901 in date. On his return from Germany, Mackenzie took up a research studentship at the Jenner Institute in London, with the all-important funding provided by the Grocers' Company. Was Jim Irvine jealous? Probably not; but he did, at this stage, measure himself against the slightly older chemist, son of a Dundee schoolteacher.

Of course, he still had in mind the possibility that with Purdie's support and collaboration he could strike out in the St Andrews laboratory into developing knowledge of the sugars. However, Irvine returned to St Andrews in 1901 initially under the same terms as previously: collaboration with Purdie in his work on succinic acid,[1] an extension of Purdie's own optical activity research. Patience was another virtue that this impatient young man had to learn. The sugars programme would be lonely work at the outset. There would be no large team of other eager young chemists on whom to rely. Purdie's involvement at first was lukewarm. The acknowledged authority was Emil Fischer, and most of his carbohydrate work dated from before this time. Fischer made no pretence of his belief that current chemical knowledge did not permit any further exploration. It is undoubtedly true that the very inconclusiveness of Fischer's work rendered it alluring to Irvine. It wasn't until 1910 that he purchased for his own library the recently published checklist of all Emil Fischer's published sugars work, most of which had been done before the turn of the century, something that would reassure Irvine.

Years later, in the States, Irvine was honoured with the Willard Gibbs medal of the American Chemical Society. In giving the required attached lecture he attempted to make an explanation as to why, as a young and inexperienced chemist, he had gravitated towards a scientific life devoted to the carbohydrates: 'First importance must be attached to the fact that carbohydrates are essentially the products of natural, as opposed to artifi- cial, synthesis . . . To study the sugars is . . . to study the great molecular channel through which solar energy flows to us.'[2] He liked the variety demanded of the sugars chemist, who must be something of a biologist and something of a physiologist but, 'above all, he must be a physicist'. This diversity of scientific interest found in Irvine would account for the success of the several ways in which, as a chemist, he would be called upon to serve his country in the Great War.

Purdie had the financial means to encourage this new departure, and his hope of founding a new school of stereochemistry in his department still waited to be fulfilled. The return to the fold of his brilliant pupil was all that he could have hoped for. Irvine was hard-working, painstaking in the laboratory and personally ambitious; together the two men set out to conquer new worlds.

Before 1905, the Professor's retiring room, adjacent to the splendid new teaching laboratory, still had to serve as research laboratory. The gift of Mrs Purdie – Professor Purdie's uncle's widow – had not yet provided for research. In his characteristically playful style, Jim described this inner sanctum in a letter to Mabel:

Scene 1. The private room in the chemical laboratory of the most ancient university in Scotland . . . I have a big fire going and every gas-jet in the place lit and all around me sparkle the fancy apparatus which play a part in the great sugar research. Outside it is a wild night – a perfect gale is blowing & I can hear the moan of the sea as it beats on the cliffs not fifty yards from my windows.[3]

In giving a paper on the chair of chemistry in 1940, Irvine came to recol- lect that: 'In that same room a certain young lecturer, greatly daring, took the bold step of launching out on researches remote from the St Andrews programme of optical activity, despite his professor's warning that if Emil Fischer was forsaking the field of carbohydrate chemistry there would be few gleanings left for others.'[4] Jim Irvine's first steps into his new approach to the world of the sugars are written up by him in half calf-bound notebooks, and that of 1901 outlines the first experimental work. Starting at the beginning, he examined the action of silver oxide (Ag_2O) on, first, methanol (CH_3OH) alone. He then examined the effect of silver oxide on a solution of glucose in methanol. His notes included observations on the appearance and the smell in this second experiment.[5]

Soon after his return to St Andrews, Irvine was appointed to a university assistantship, a post that carried rather more hope of security and advancement than the job of private assistant to Purdie, although it was without a great deal of remuneration. A system of extension lectures existed in Scotland at this time during the winter months, and in October 1901, before he commenced in St Andrews, Jim was dispatched by Purdie to Aberdeen for the experience of giving a week of hastily put-together lectures.[6] The Carnegie Trust for Scotland, the main source of funding for university teaching in Scotland at that time, paid the lecturer's fees. These lectures were given to the department of Professor Japp, who had once been moulded by Purdie and whose ideas regarding the chemistry of life continued to interest Irvine for many years to come.

Jim Irvine returned to his old digs in St Andrews, to the house on the Scores owned by the family of his friend, Alexander Imrie. This was Scores Villa West, which in the days before the Catholic church and its presbytery were built, had a direct view of St Andrews Bay and the stretch of the West Sands. It was but a step away from the chemistry laboratory.

From this house he resumed his correspondence with Mabel Williams, who had returned to her musical studies in Belfast. Dr Walker, with whom she studied the piano, thought it might be a good thing for her to take the Licenciate of the Royal Academy of Music (LRAM) examinations sometime in late December 1901. Although she recognised the virtue of being made to practise, she was very quick to dismiss an idea that threatened to clash with a visit from Jim at Christmastime. Her arguments stand in marked contrast to the values of the Irvines, who would have been proud to pursue such a qualification and at this time were encouraging their younger daughter, Annie, along the path towards taking a degree and entering the teaching profession. 'As to the exam darling,' Mabel wrote, 'I don't know what to say. I don't believe it would be possible to go in for it – if by doing so I prevented you coming over here. I should be miserable . . . Afterwards it would do me little good, except the results of additional practising, for I don't suppose I shall ever want to teach or play in public & that is what the certificate is for.'[7]

Mabel was clearly to be a lady of leisure, kept pleasantly at home as the companion of her mother, and waiting for marriage. Even the idea of this talented girl becoming a serious recitalist and professional musician was anathema to her mother's complacent view of life. All this produced serious unease in Mr and Mrs Irvine, who refused to meet Mabel and worried that she had not been brought up to be a good housekeeper, fit to marry their son. Their opposition was enough to make Mabel feel she should release Jim from his promise: 'I hope I shall hear of you some day in the scientific world,' she wrote sadly on New Year's Day 1902.[8] Poor Mabel was made to feel less than adequate by the two opposing forces. 'I would have been a musician if I could,' she wrote. 'I commend a life's devotion to it. I don't think music is only a play on the emotions & it is quite as intellectual as any other art or science if we choose to make it so. Music is a moral law.'[9]

Young Irvine was in petulant mood, and he was brittle enough in his mid-twenties to accuse Mabel's musical life of coming between them, of absorbing the better half of her nature. He agonised that Mabel's parents expected her to make a 'good' marriage, and not to an academic chemist who as yet had no lectureship and no real hope of immediate advancement. He angrily imagined that his lack of money had turned Mr and Mrs Williams against him. The letters exchanged throughout such a long absence inevitably brought many misunderstandings between them. 'It was so very like your dear hot-tempered headstrong self that I had actually to smile in the middle of my misery!' was Mabel's retort, in defence of her mother. She had a number of suitors from within her parents' prosperous circle, and to all of them she turned up her nose. Jim, her 'dear old fossil', was everything she wanted, and he worked with a passionate persistence in an effort to get a university post sufficiently well paid to allow them to marry.

A long period of time spent mostly apart, when they had plenty of opportunity to have second thoughts about their commitment to each other, was not conducive to their happiness. Jim's parents thought that it would have been madness for Jim to propose marriage in any formal sense until he got a lectureship. Mabel's mother began to think that they were incompatible: two such strong characters, who seemed to do nothing except make each other miserable. On several rather fraught occasions the couple tried to break the pact they had made to each other in May 1900 at the Bonorand Ball in Leipzig. Could they turn their backs on each other?

Deeply conscious of the pathos of their situation, Jim wondered if he should go abroad, far away from any old association, across the Atlantic: he'd heard that 'there is a good post going in the Govt. Lab in Jamaica and I would stand a good chance of that with my experience of sugar analysis';[10] on the other hand, perhaps he should see if he was not too late to offer himself for a post that had been advertised in Montreal. How bitterly ironic it seemed to him that he and Purdie had been invited to give a paper at the Belfast meeting of the British Association for the Advancement of Science in 1902. This accolade should have commended him to Mabel's parents, and yet the rupture forced on the two sweethearts forbade their meeting. To be in the same city as Mabel, and not be with her, was more than Jim could bear. They resolved to put their misunderstandings and tensions behind them, and were more prepared than ever to endure this most testing period of their lives. The meeting of the British Association in Belfast became for Jim a new beginning in more than one sense, because here Purdie and Irvine made public the first fruits of their new sugars collaboration.[11] The collaboration was mutually valuable to Jim and to his professor: the name of Purdie gave status to Jim's novel work, and Purdie increasingly encouraged this new turning that his laboratory had taken.

One year later, Irvine reported to the assistant secretary to the 1851 Exhibition Commissioners:

On terminating my 1851 Exhibition Scholarship in 1901, I was appointed University Assistant in Chemistry at the above institution, an appointment which I still hold. In this capacity I undertake all the lecturing on Organic Chemistry and superintend the work of the advanced students in the laboratory.

The research students also work under my direction, although the subjects of their investigation are chosen for them by Professor Purdie. Conjointly with the latter I have undertaken an investigation on the 'Alkylation of Sugars' an account of which I delivered recently before the chemical section of the British Association.

I have been engaged to carry out the same academic work during the present session.[12]

St Andrews University was preparing itself for growth and was well aware of the needs of the burgeoning pure science departments. In the first session of Irvine's return to St Andrews, Professor Herkless, an ambitious man who would become Principal after Donaldson, prepared a statement for the trustees of the Carnegie Trust for the Universities of Scotland in which he outlined the great difficulty under which the underfunded university was labouring to meet the demands of modern education.[13] In 1901 the Carnegie Trust, swollen with J.P. Morgan's multi-million pound payment for his share of Carnegie and Co., was ready to intensify Carnegie's educational philanthropy. This was fortuitous for Jim Irvine's career.

Student numbers in St Andrews began to grow, but the poor provision for teaching and for research still did not encourage growth, and Herkless reported to the Carnegie trustees that there was already overcrowding in the modern chemical laboratory given to the university in 1891 by Mrs Purdie of Castlecliffe. In 1901 the chemistry department was so full that two students had to be turned away. The laboratory provision for Purdie and Irvine's groundbreaking sugars research was pitiful, and Jim was still inadequately paid.

The report to the Carnegie trustees claimed that by its size and situation St Andrews was the most suitable centre in Scotland for post-graduate work in pure science. It went on to state that certain departments, of which chemistry is first cited, would be very beneficially served if there were scholarships available to encourage able students to do research. The department desperately needed an annual grant for apparatus and materials but, more than this, they needed a salary to secure the services of a young chemist of some standing and experience. Irvine was initially paid out of Purdie's own purse, but the weight of his duties – teaching an advanced course of lectures, in addition to taking a general course in the teaching laboratory – demanded a salary. If the university could find their way to providing for the chemistry department a salary for a lecture assistant and a laboratory attendant, might it be hoped that the Carnegie trustees would finance the further services of a 'young chemist of some standing'?

The trustees, impressed by the quality of research already undertaken in Purdie's department, came up with a solution: Irvine would be that 'young chemist of some standing', and in 1903 he was appointed to an inaugural Carnegie Research Fellowship. His fellowship was worth £100 per annum, to which was added £50 contributed personally by Purdie. The sum of £5,000 would be given to match Professor Purdie's further endowment of a new research laboratory. This all represented a new departure for the Carnegie Trust, which had until then confined itself to supporting the essential work of undergraduate teaching in Scotland's universities, and no more.[14]

Finally, a statement concerning the endowment grants assigned by the Carnegie Trust to the University of St Andrews contained the following

interesting information about the better funding of the chemistry department.

> In regard to Grant 1 (see page 41 of the Court Minutes) of the capital
> sum of £5,000 given for Chemistry, no difficulty exists. Professor
> Purdie has given £5,000 for building a Chemical Research Labora-
> tory, and the other £5,000 [from the Carnegie Trust] is to be spent on
> the same laboratory, part of it being a contribution to the building of
> it and the rest to its upkeep.[15]

This was the foundation of the exceptional way that appliances and materials
for this department were funded throughout the 100 years that followed.

The award of one of the very first Carnegie research fellowships came to
Jim when his ripening powers most needed this recognition and support.
Purdie's presence in the department was beginning to be cut short by his
deteriorating health. Jim worked sixteen-hour days in order to compensate: that was the deal with his professor. He actually enjoyed being left in
command of the department during Purdie's illnesses; he was developing
a taste for being more capable than others. His fury at having to undo the
work of an incompetent assistant is tinged with the satisfaction of being the
one who could get things done.

Purdie's testimonial for Irvine's 1903 application to the Carnegie Trust
commented that 'Dr Irvine has the faculty of inspiring others with his own
eagerness for research, and several students have been engaged here in
this work under his supervision during this past session'.[16] Purdie noticed
his 'suggestiveness with respect to both ideas and methods of work'. Many
of these same students in succeeding years were awarded Carnegie Trust
fellowships. Irvine's fellowship was renewed in 1904 and 1905, by which
time he had a lectureship. The Carnegie scheme played a major part in
the advancement of the sugars programme in the St Andrews chemistry
department.

Purdie and Irvine began to plan the development of a new research
laboratory capable of accommodating initially ten research students, with
small subsidiary rooms, about eight in number, for special operations. Thus
it came about that in the declining years of Thomas Purdie's life, Irvine with
his energy and searching mind was able to partner his old professor and
create a name for his laboratory. When Purdie and Irvine first applied to
their new study the silver oxide reaction that now bears their name, little
was known with certainty of the detailed structure of even the simple sugars,

and still less about the disaccharides and complex polysaccharides, where Emil Fischer's work had come to an abrupt end. Suitable methods of investigation had not been available to Fischer, and many fundamental problems remained unsolved. Irvine soon found confirmation of his Leipzig idea that Purdie's methylation technique, when applied to the reactive hydroxil groups present in the sugars, would provide a method by which the next stage in the development of carbohydrate chemistry could be initiated. Within a year he had isolated trimethyl- and tetramethyl-glucose, the first methylated sugars.

Far from challenging Fischer's work, Irvine came to provide the strongest experimental evidence of Fischer's formulation of the methyl glucosides.[17] Irvine's notebooks continue to record the nascent sugars school in its infancy. His notes of 1903 demonstrate that he never ceased to use Fischer as a standard, but that he used different reagents to him. Irvine kept his sights on the polysaccharides; the success of his activities in the chemistry laboratory over the next fifteen to twenty years owed much to his characteristic originality of thought and clearness of vision. His slow, painstaking work at the laboratory bench would become singularly fruitful. There would even be real adventures in the chemical community, such as would appeal greatly to the boyishness in Irvine. But in the meantime, Irvine and Purdie together built up their knowledge by applying their methylation technique to the methyl glycosides of the sugars. At the British Association meeting in 1903, they reported on this development from their historic paper of the previous year.[18]

All this while, Jim tried desperately to resolve the gnawing problem of his love affair with Mabel. It was becoming clear to him that matters of the heart and domestic peace would be as important to him as his ambitions as a chemist, even if Mabel felt that she had to learn to 'be your very loving runner-up'. He could never give her up, and he met this with constant worrying. Mabel's attempt to reassure him was typically Irish: 'Don't worry about things, even if it is a Scotch characteristic – it is not an Irish one certainly. We always "up & look for better luck about the morrow's morn".' Mabel and Jim learnt to lean on these two extremes. He was young and inexperienced in such things, but his instincts were to be constrained. He still knew that he could not propose marriage until he had secured a rare thing at that date: an established lectureship in a university; and in a university, moreover, to his liking.

Edwardian social mores, as practiced in aspirant middle-class Belfast society, were of a subtlety that seems ridiculous a century later. Mabel had been put in an ambiguous position by this prolonged commitment to something that was not an engagement of marriage. The winter season of dances and concerts was particularly hard to bear, and of course she would have loved to have been engaged to her fascinating, good-looking and ardent Jim: to have been able to love him openly, to show him off in public, to dance every dance with him without causing talk and scandal. To be free to dream of a bottom drawer full of fine linen, and of cupboards full of pretty dresses, was what she and all the girls at Brighthelmstone School, Southport had always wanted.

Mabel's mother felt that it was not honourable for a girl to be privately engaged when other men she met did not know about it. 'If you come here so often,' wrote Mabel to poor Jim, '& people talk so much, they must be told. Also – a reason I hate to give – if I go out so much as I have been doing lately to dances & things I should go as an engaged girl, since my "affections are already engaged"! I might perhaps wear a little placard on my back – "this heart already taken – no-one need apply here" . . . if not I must not dance every dance, & never sit on the stairs, in fact I must steer clear of men altogether!'

Finally, it was made quite plain to Jim, who had only been able to visit the comfortable Williams family circle 'as a friend of Mabel's brother', that his visits must be suspended. What a difference there was between Jim's life as a chemistry assistant in the old-fashioned university and the life of his unattached sweetheart in Ireland! Jim bitterly resented the fact that, while he laboured, Mabel spent her time in the relative idleness of long visits to her girlhood friends and in accompanying her mother in paying calls. To feed her daydreams, Mabel immersed herself in Andrew Lang's book *St Andrews*, Jim's Christmas present to her.

These five years of testing gave both Jim and Mabel time to grow up. Jim learnt not to be quite so self-righteous, and much more sympathetic to Mabel's difficulties. The promise of her wit, her native intelligence, her beauty and her understanding of the human spirit was his constant consolation. It was she who finally devised a new way by which they might meet. The family of her future sister-in-law, Agnes Reid, lived at Broughty Ferry, a well-to-do suburb of Dundee, located across the Tay from St Andrews. Mabel wrote on 7 December 1902, disclosing her plan to visit Agnes Reid: 'After all it doesn't matter how people talk over there – & that is their only reason for not allowing me to see you.'

Before she could embark on her trip, Mabel had to buy a new wardrobe of clothes, and then the lengthy visit early in 1903 could take place.

Throughout these six weeks Mabel and Jim met only once, and that at The Wylde, the house of Agnes' stepfather;[19] Mabel had still not seen St Andrews for herself. The two girls, who had lived in the same household in Leipzig, busied themselves with going to concerts in Dundee and socialising among the families of the jute barons of Broughty Ferry. Mabel gazed across the bay to where Professor Purdie was too ill and Jim too overworked to see her.

Wistfully, and still in Dundee, she wrote: 'Your St Andrews has been a city of dreams to me – a cloud city & that I shall see it & walk its mystic streets with you must be a dream too.' Addressed to: 'JC Irvine, Esq. PhD, DSc!! Hurrah! Wave your hat!'

Jim was now in possession of the St Andrews doctorate. Following the publication of 'The Alkylation of Sugars' in the *Journal of the Chemical Society*,[20] in March 1903 Jim was finally awarded the higher degree that in Leipzig he had at first allowed Mabel Williams to believe was already his. His external examiner was Norman Collie, a London chemist who in 1903 was a chemical colleague of Sir William Ramsay at University College London. Norman Collie was primarily an inorganic chemist, but he was one of that select company of scientists: he had been a graduate student of Wislicenus. At the time that he examined Irvine he held the chair of organic chemistry at UCL. He unhesitatingly recommended the St Andrews University Faculty of Science 'to grant his request'. Pointing out that the subject of Irvine's DSc thesis was not an easy one, he commended the fact that Irvine had successfully worked out his subject in a careful and orderly manner.[21] The alkylation of sugars was to furnish the whole of Jim's rich chemical life. On formal academic occasions Jim could now proudly wear the gown of amaranth silk that was the St Andrews DSc gown. A hierarchy in post-graduate degrees was starting to emerge, and with it an awareness that the British DSc was more difficult to attain than the German PhD.

The DSc and the Carnegie fellowship gave a boost to Jim's career; little by little he and Mabel planned for marriage. But would the city of their dreams become their home? In October 1904 Jim was offered the senior lecture-ship in chemistry at the University of Sheffield. Wise Mrs Purdie advised him to do nothing until he had talked to Mabel. Early one morning Mabel was woken by the whistle with which from the street below Jim would call for her in Leipzig. He had crossed on the night boat to Belfast. Was the grimy industrial town of Sheffield worth £200 per annum to them? Its only advantage seemed to be in letting them get married. No, Mabel would not have Jim move from his by-now distinguished work in the place he loved so much. They would do what others might not have done: they turned the job down. A pattern emerged over the following thirty to forty years: time after time Jim would be offered a position in academic life that a more worldly man would be tempted to regard as a distinct prize. All were ultimately refused.

These increasing signs of professional recognition had strengthened Jim's position with his future parents-in-law. Mabel's brother Bert became engaged and then married to Agnes Reid of Broughty Ferry. It was hard for Jim and Mabel to watch their Leipzig companions marry when they could not. As 1904 drew to a close, they planned to be married the next year, even if their household budget would have to depend on Mabel's dress allowance from her father. As it chanced, their patience was rewarded soon afterwards, with the longed-for lectureship in chemistry in St Andrews. Purdie admitted to the Principal of the university that his weakened state of health demanded that there should be someone in post in his department who could legitimately act as his deputy. Irvine liked to describe his job as that of the understudy. On 19 November 1904, the University Court agreed that a lectureship in chemistry should be instituted, and that James C. Irvine should be appointed to it.[22] The lectureship in organic chemistry had not previously existed, and the salary of £200 was made up from several funds and guaranteed by the Professor, who could not continue without Irvine.

The offer of the post in Sheffield must have awoken Dr and Mrs Purdie, as well as Jim and Mabel, to the fresh realisation that Jim belonged in St Andrews. Jim's mother thanked divine providence, both sides of the family were united and Mabel was welcomed with open arms into the Irvines' life in Scotland. The house on Balgrayhill Road overlooking the Campsie Fells, shopping with Jim's two sisters in the smart streets of Glasgow, visits to the wealthy aunt at Dalmeny House, and a holiday on Arran: all were hers. Jim had quietly brought her to visit the rich widowed aunt, Agnes Colquhoun, just over a year previously, as he escorted Mabel to the boat train after the Broughty Ferry visit.

In the autumn of 1904 Mabel's family moved from the comfortable suburban home in Holywood. The purchase of a country house with a small estate at Dunmurry represented the Williams family's social apogee. In addition to extensive gardens with large glasshouses, there was a farm with a farm manager and a lodge with a keeper at the gate. There was room for a cricket pitch for the younger brothers. Jack and Jessie Williams were adamantly old-fashioned, and so there were two carriages in the coach house, but by choice no motor car. The move, however, was the cause of a severe breakdown in Jessie Williams's health, and therefore also the postponement of the wedding until June 1905. Jim, who was given to angry outbursts, could not hide his disappointment.

The next handicap that lay in their way was the difficulty of finding somewhere to live in St Andrews. Mabel visited St Andrews for the very first time early in the year of 1905; she stayed with the Purdies in South Street, which is considered the finest sixteenth-century street in Scotland. She found that Mrs Purdie gave very sensible advice. Even a flat above a shop in St Andrews was quite acceptable for the households of university people, advised Mrs Purdie. Yet they found nothing. Mrs Purdie explained the reason: once settled in St Andrews, no-one ever moved. Of course, neither Jim nor Mabel would have guessed that this would be their own experience. Very few houses were 'to let', and at the turn of the century it was not the general thing to buy property. Jim would not agree to anything that was not fully modernised. On the eve of signing the lease on a house in smart Queen's Gardens, Jim tore up the legal papers because the only bath lay beneath the floorboards of the kitchen, and the drainage could not be guaranteed. They decided that, to start off with, on their return for the Michaelmas term they would live in 'rooms'.

Jim and Mabel were married on 28 June 1905 in Dunmurry Presbyterian church, County Antrim. In the morning Mrs Williams had gone out into her garden to pick sheaves of the special 'wedding-day' gladioli that she had grown for the occasion. The garden was her great joy and through this she formed a strong bond with Jim, who could always supply the botanical name of a favourite flower. The wedding day became the occasion for a large house-party, which included Jim's two sisters, Mary and Annie, who stayed on afterwards, and Jim's parents. Mrs Irvine was known for her soft and kindly heart, and she took greatly to Mabel's younger brothers.

There were absentees: notably Mabel's brother Bert and his wife Aggie. A *froideur* between Jim and Mabel and Bert and Aggie, which had grown up a year before, came to a head in the year of the wedding. Aggie's step-father, a Mr Paton, was in the Dundee jute business, and during Mabel's visit to them at Broughty Ferry in 1903, Jim had come over for a weekend. Mr Paton had consulted him about an idea he had for manufacturing a new textile from the ramie fibre.[23] The association between ramie and jute was that the jute machines could be adapted for the production of the ramie textile. Jim had been led to understand that he might become associated with a very lucrative enterprise, and so he had addressed the chemical problems that lay in the path of preparing the fibre for spinning.

Ramie had been known to the ancient world. It grows perennially in Asia, particularly in northern India, which was also an important source of the raw material of jute. Ramie, however, was something quite new in Dundee, and it did demand challenging work from an organic chemist. Having given the proposal a good deal of thought and written up his findings for Mr Paton, he was shocked to find out later that Mr Paton had quietly gone ahead and used Jim's scientific contribution without any acknowledgment, and without drawing him into the enterprise. Jim took advice from his colleagues and was forced to admit that since Mr Paton was not ultimately in a hurry to take their joint discovery into full production, he must abandon his hopes. Jim had acted entirely in keeping with his commercial upbringing, and it was a natural instinct for him to assume that his chemical knowledge might have an industrial application that would work to his advantage. He took it badly that his old friend and future brother-in-law did nothing to help him in his vexatious position with the unpleasant Mr Paton.

Jim and Mabel had to do everything they could to avoid meeting Bert and Aggie during the summer of their marriage. It was questionable whether or not Jim's brother, Alec, would feel able to come to the wedding as best man, so keenly did he feel that the Williamses had let his brother down. Jim himself continued to harbour his grudge against Bert Williams in the strange case of his first close experience of cut-throat lack of principle in matters of industrial business. Bert was Mabel's special brother, who had shared all her Leipzig life and had been her conspirator in her romance with Jim; but Jim was bad at forgetting old scores and could not forgive him.

Their honeymoon – a whole summer spent in Ireland – was all that their Leipzig romance had led them to expect. With the ballads of Tom Moore on their lips, they explored the wild and romantic countryside of County Wicklow. They found the Meeting of the Waters and the Sally Garden, and Jim learnt through Mabel what there is of humour and sadness in the Irish spirit. Jim delighted in talking to the country people they met on their way, and his kind heart was smitten by what he took to be an old woman's tragedy: 'Does your fine son live with you?' he had asked. 'Och, shure it's away he is, away in the far country.' 'Does she mean her son is dead?' whispered poor Jim, who was used to polite Presbyterian euphemisms. Mabel laughingly told him that all it meant was that the son was in America. Jim, who thought that it could have meant heaven or Chicago, was touched by the beauty of the Irish turn of speech, so far from and yet so near to the people of the West of Scotland that he knew. Mabel, however, reminded him that Ireland, for all her poetry and beauty, was not a happy country. She was glad that she was now legally Scottish and going to live in Scotland.[24]

In Dublin Mabel unpacked her new frocks, and they attended the fashionable garden parties and dinner parties of the viceregal capital under the kindly eye of Jessie Williams' old school friend, Mrs McComas, whose family owned the Shelbourne Hotel. Jim, resplendent in morning tails with a topper in his hand, would slip away from the shaven lawns to have a quiet smoke. Mabel was happy and secure as never before; boisterously, they played tennis, billiards and golf by day, and then danced and dined in all their finery by night.

By the end of the summer Jim was tired of the vacuous round of Irish country house-parties and anxious to get back to his work. They returned to the small house on the Scores that had been Jim's home for many years. The innumerable cases of their wedding presents had to be stored in the cellars of the laboratory, and Mabel's trousseau, which must have surprised the university folk of St Andrews, was far beyond the needs of the wife of a humble lecturer. Yet Mabel found a good deal of style amongst these distinguished dons and their families. On one occasion she found herself sitting next to Andrew Lang at dinner. The great man uttered not a word to her all evening; later she got her own back on her discomforture in a witty essay she wrote for the *Glasgow Herald*: 'Genius at Dinner'.[25] The town's old-fashioned etiquette expected her, as a new bride, to wear her wedding dress to dinner parties, where she would be the guest of honour, but Jim quietly grumbled that the wedding dress of taffeta and Limerick lace had cost him a fortune in cabs. In future they would walk or bicycle to evening engagements.

Mabel's letters to her mother provide a most vivid picture of St Andrews when she first arrived as a young bride. In 1904, Andrew Carnegie, the Pittsburgh Ironmaster, was for the second time elected their Rector by the students of the university. His installation in October 1905 was Mabel Irvine's first experience of this colourful student ritual, at the heart of which was a torchlight procession, with the students dressed up in comical dress. Her description of the bonfire in the middle of the quadrangle serves to illustrate the wild, ungoverned antics of this survival of student life from before the twentieth century.

> They all assembled in the Quad & Jim and I went up to watch them gather & form into procession. They had a fire lit in the middle of the

Quad, the effect was splendid. The flickering lurid light on those old rugged grey colleges & to think that this same ceremony has gone on for more than 300 years! The glare on these weird figures & in such romantic surroundings was a sight not easily forgotten. There were soldiers & sailors, & clowns & fishwives & Mephistopheles & executioners, & ladies & babies & nurses & maidservants & old English figures & Frenchmen & Japs & Chinese. – every conceivable imaginable creature! They all lit their torches at the fire & marched round the Quad – headed by two highlanders playing the pipes & a soldier with a tiny pony & four men on horseback. The long line of flaring torches looked splendid against the dark buildings – then out under the old archway into North Street – blowing trumpets, ringing bells & banging drums! They march through all the streets, calling at the Professors' houses where they cheer & sing 'For he's a jolly good fellow'. Their longest stay was at the Principal's house & there Carnegie came out & spoke to them. Jim and I went up on to the roof of the Lab & watched from there for his house is right opposite. It looked wild from up there.[26]

Mabel was never afraid of forming her own opinions, and interestingly she felt strongly critical of the American bias to Carnegie's speech at the next day's installation. 'The man has no learning or culture, he is not a great man, tho' he may be good.' Despite the fact that their tenure in St Andrews was so heavily dependent on Carnegie's largesse, she felt able to say: 'I don't think the almighty dollar is sufficient claim to the Lord Rectorship of St Andrews.' The evening reception was certainly after her own heart. 'But last night's function was most interesting of all. It was very crowded but I was glad I wore my wedding dress. It came through the fray nobly. I love an academic gathering. The men look so fine in gown & hood & everybody interesting.'[27]

Jim and Mabel set about anxiously looking for a house. Jim would dash back at lunchtime from the laboratory, and they tried to be calm as they considered several possibilities: an old house, 62 North Street, was offered at £45 per annum, but Jim thought it would not do. He had once lodged in one nearby, and found it ramshackle and inconvenient. He was shocked by the high rents commanded in St Andrews. Not surprisingly in someone raised in the new Glasgow of North Kelvinside and Possilpark, he leaned far more towards living in a modern villa, such as were springing up in the new western suburb of Rathelpie out on the Strathkinness Road. They settled on a house with lovely views but also with a fifteen-minute walk into college. Even if it was a step in to town, it was also close to the links and to the men's bathing pool where Jim bathed almost every day. The rent was £42 per annum.

The house, which they named Little Dunmurry after Mabel's home, was owned by the developer–architects, Gillespie Scott, who had recently built the row of semi-detached villas overlooking the university's playing fields. It was fitted up in a modern way, with electric bells throughout the house, and Mabel and Jim were its first occupants. The rooms were not overlarge, and in fact it was not as convenient as they imagined. They were, however, supremely happy. At weekends they explored the country hinterland on their bicycles and amused themselves with furnishing their home. The intimacy of the early years of their marriage can be illustrated by a game they devised for themselves. By the evening fireside, Mabel, ready with paper and pencil, and a complete ignoramus in matters chemical, would try to read Jim's mind, while he attempted silently to project into her mind sets of chemical formulae for her to write down. Like other happy couples, they were remarkably successful at this innocent mind reading. Perhaps it was an extension of the amusement that the then-fashionable game of planchette had given them when they were students in Leipzig. But when their friend, Alfred Hoernle, the empirical philosopher, asked if they would take part in measured, scientific experiments at Oxford University they refused, feeling that this would be taking what was essentially a game into dangerous territory.

True to Jim's Free Church upbringing, they attended the fashionable Free Church of Scotland Hope Park church, which was presided over by Dr Sloan, a notable character in Edwardian St Andrews, and who served as Provost of the town. Married life also gave Jim the opportunity to reveal his canniness with money. Mabel was surprised to learn that, throughout the previous four years, he had managed to build savings out of the small salary he had received as a lecture assistant to Purdie. This sum Jim had kept against the certain day when he and Mabel would sally forth to Justice's of Dundee and furnish their house. Mabel's father and mother pressed all manner of gifts on them for their home, but Jim, proud to be in charge of his own household, thought they should not be greedy. To spend his savings now in his own way was part of the pleasure he had so longed for. They allowed Mabel's parents to give them their carpets and curtains, and Jim's family gave them their dining room furniture.

For Jim, keeping house with Mabel was a most delightful game, and nothing was too much trouble. No longer was he the character who felt hard done-by, with a whole list of complaints against Mabel's family, his professor and his colleagues. If the Irish maid that Mabel had brought with her let the range go out, Jim now hurried back from the lab, rolled up his shirt sleeves and examined its works. Their neighbours at Rathelpie were mostly of the wealthy class of Dundee businessman, with a few independent 'county' people and one or two of Jim's colleagues thrown in for good measure. Several of these, such as the Boases, formed long friendships with the Irvines because of shared enthusiasms for golf and tennis. Mabel was selective in forming her social circle, in case the business of returning calls got out of hand. She took pleasure in seeking out those who were artistic, interesting or merely unusual, and at that time the Scottish RA, Peter Graham, and his family lived nearby: they were both interesting and 'county'. Jim for a while encouraged her in a whim that she might even take up hunting, and she sent back home for her riding habit.

The university made efforts to widen an intellectual and cultural base that could be shared between town and gown. The Bell-Pettigrew Museum dates from 1907, and in accepting the generous gift of a natural history museum from Professor Pettigrew's widow, the Court minutes acknowledged that the whole town community, their interest already aroused by the popularisation of science, would gain from this addition to St Andrews. Nor was music neglected. Encouraged by the university, Mr Curran of Abbotsford Crescent, an Irishman of independent means with a fine voice, gave a series of illustrated lectures on song, and Mabel played his accompaniments. She was amused by his habit of nipping behind a screen, shortly before he sang, to swallow a raw egg, which he believed lubricated the vocal cords.

Mabel had much to learn about household management, but St Andrews soon learnt to admire her good taste and cleverness in making their home pretty. Her indulgent mother would send wonderful things from the farm and garden at Dunmurry in order to help Mabel eke out her budget. Hampers of peaches, grapes, vegetables, tomatoes, jam, bread, chickens, fresh butter, eggs, bacon, pork pies, tea and so on were sent to St Andrews during the next seven years, and lying on top would be a big bunch of violets or some roses.

Einstein's *annus mirabilis*, 1905, was a landmark year for the department of chemistry in St Andrews. The new research laboratory neared completion and Purdie's team was expanding as news reached beyond Scotland of the new school of sugars research that Jim Irvine was developing. Early in the year, Jim and Mabel's old friend 'Cabbage' Rose, complete with his Leipzig PhD, joined the team. Robert Rose was a welcome ally, and by 1906 he had ready a paper, which he published jointly with Jim on the constitution of salicin.

Prizes and scholarships were taken seriously in the days when the student could look for very little financial support from government sources. Under Ordinance 57 passed in 1889 by the commissioners to the Scottish Universities Act, graduate holders of a scholarship were obliged to engage in some teaching. Strictly speaking, their scholarships would not stretch easily to their remaining at the university for the third term, and at this time there was strong opposition in Scotland to classes during the summer session. It was, however, during the summers that Purdie had from the first attracted his best students to work at research. More money had to be found to support this: chemistry was put forward as a special need, and a claim for £250 per annum was made to the Court.

But first, Irvine, on behalf of his professor, had to supervise the finishing touches of the new research department, made possible by the Purdie family and aided by the Carnegie Trust. The 1891 teaching laboratory had been a single-storey building; the new research laboratories were built on top of the earlier building, and included a fine room overlooking the North Sea for the director of the Chemical Research Institute. On 16 November 1904, Purdie wrote to Principal Donaldson, reporting on the expenditure of fitting out his new building. The budget of £7,000 made up by himself and the Carnegie Trust was not sufficient to pay the architect's fee or even to finish the building work in the correct manner. He gave a further £2,000. Items that were added to the brief at this stage included provision for better ventilation and for ventilation cowls. In the early years of chemical research on this site, it was not uncommon for young research chemists to fall into dead faints from the toxic fumes. They would be laid out, like dummies, to recover on the lawn outside, where the eighteenth- and nineteenth-century professors had played bowls and where the staff at that time played tennis.

From these premises, between 1904 when Irvine took up his lectureship and 1907, St Andrews produced seventeen published pieces of original work, making Purdie's department rank third in the kingdom after the far larger institutes of London and Manchester. Of these papers, Irvine was responsible for thirteen, either solely or jointly with others. Irvine's remit as lecturer in organic chemistry, in addition to giving the qualifying courses of lectures to first-degree students, included the day-to-day running of the research department, the training of research workers in the special manip-

ulative processes for which Irvine had acquired considerable expertise, and
even the allocation of research topics to suit his own research programme.[28]

Purdie's syllabus for the first degree in chemistry at St Andrews reveals
a magisterial mind. Week by week, his students – many of them new to
chemistry – were given a complete induction into his subject. This was
not textbook stuff: much was being still revealed and discovered. We find
Sir William Ramsay's nitrogen there, along with the whole of the periodic
table, insofar as it was understood. As soon as Irvine returned from Leipzig,
however, change crept in to the department. During the winter of 1902–3,
Purdie was too ill to take his course. Dr Irvine picked up the syllabus where
his professor had left off, and made it his own. At first Purdie was critical;
nervous that Jim might be leaving sections out, he guided and warned his
young protégé that he had a tendency to omit giving the formulae in full.
But Irvine's lecture notes reveal an energy and liveliness that is different
from the style of his professor. He engaged his audience with much reference to the manner in which the elements and their compounds are found
in nature. He enjoyed illustrating their industrial uses, and their occur-
rence in everyday life. He defended his approach, and he devised many of
the final examinations.[29] It is quite clear that, although young and inexperienced, he was enjoying himself. During the last years of Purdie's tenure
of the chair, Jim frequently and readily slipped into the professor's shoes.

Preparing for a time when the 'prof' would no longer be there to lead the
department, Purdie and Irvine put considerable pressure on the university
to increase by £100 the salary of the lecturer, and to make the post more
secure. This was but the first stone in the building of a modern department.
Otherwise, Purdie depended on a yearly succession of lecture assistants
who, being recent graduates, were happy to receive £50 a year and continue
some research. The 1907 departmental return to the University Court drawn
up by Irvine reveals far and away the greatest vision of all the departments,
and makes a good case for formidable investment in chemistry. Personnel
were to be the key to the establishment of a modern scientific institute, and
Purdie began to make arrangements to finance chemistry in St Andrews in
case of his death.

In the spring of 1907 it became clear that Mabel Irvine was acutely
anaemic. She decided to go home to Ireland and consult a physician known
to her parents. In the comfort of Dunmurry House, Mabel recovered from
gynaecological surgery while Jim tried to offer her assurances from his
knowledge of physiology gleaned from his BSc degree. Whether or not he
really wrote with any medical authority is doubtful, but it helped him to

try and reassure his poor wife in this way. Alone in St Andrews, he worried about her sufferings. He spent increasingly long hours in the department, mostly with sole responsibility for its smooth running. He became petulantly angry at how his work expanded while his salary did not. It was once again an unhappy time for him, not made any easier by a tendency to overestimate his own importance.

In fact, Jim had grown to value the months of summer, which were still outside the university calendar. This was when he could nurture his research students and pursue his own research more single-mindedly. It was also the time of golf championships in the town, and Jim couldn't resist laughing at his good neighbours, who sallied forth, braving the foul weather and wearing the strangest of protective clothing. One man donned both fishing kilts and plus-fours, the crowning act of his rig-out being a bowler hat. Another, whose mackintosh had got soaked in the morning, strode about the links in a dressing gown. Others in the university spent their summers differently, many in fashionable spas in Europe. Principal Donaldson took his wife for two months to Baden-Baden in May and June 1907, and wrote back to St Andrews to say that their return would be entirely dependent on the state of the sea at Calais.

Jim's marriage quite naturally marked yet another momentous turning point in the development of his character. His life in Glasgow was 'in the past', as he looked forward at a career that was already being conducted on a European stage. He continued to climb the uncertain ladder of academic advancement. He relished throwing himself into this new circle of scientific scholars, to whom research was a siren that beckoned unrelentingly. Mercantile Glasgow grew further and further from his mind. He continued to visit Heathfield dutifully, but the stern papa – the 'governor' – and the gentle mother were left more and more to live their own lives. Only sentimentally would he revisit the memory of sailing in the Firth of Clyde, and of the holiday hustle and bustle of the steamers at the Broomielaw Quay.

SIX

The Professor

There was a stirring of excitement among British academic chemists in July 1908: Professor Walker, who had been appointed to a chair in Edinburgh, tendered his resignation of the chair of chemistry in University College, Dundee, which was an integral part of the Faculty of Science at St Andrews.[1] All applications for the vacant post had to be in by September. The phenomenal number of good candidates was perhaps an indication of the current frustration felt by chemists anxiously looking for career advancement in British universities. The candidature of twenty-two was the largest there had ever been for any chair at St Andrews. Three of the short-listed candidates had been students of Purdie, and looked to him for support: these were Alex Mackenzie, Wallace Walker and Irvine. Irvine was by far the youngest, and although he was bursting with promise, he had perhaps less career experience than any of the others.

An Edinburgh chemist, Hugh Marshall, was eventually appointed. Hugh Marshall, FRS, had taught for a period of twenty-four years in Edinburgh, and testimonials from the Royal Society and Sir William Ramsay attested to his long-established European reputation. Irvine did not stand a chance, despite his twenty-three published scientific papers. But even the heavily political appointment board, dominated by nominees from the city of Dundee, found themselves at first unable to make a decision. Finally, ten days later, out of two selected candidates, Alex Mackenzie and Hugh Marshall, the older man, Marshall, won on a show of hands. As an inorganic chemist, Marshall's work might have been considered a useful counter-balance to the rapidly expanding carbohydrate specialism in St Andrews. As far as the university was concerned, it was thought to have been a most undignified election, which seemed to slight the three stars in the St Andrews firmament.[2] The university soon became disenchanted with Marshall, who had no social graces.

It might quite legitimately be asked why Irvine aspired to a chair so soon after having obtained the lectureship for which he had struggled over a period of three years to secure. His ambitions extended to more than his own career. He aspired to being able to afford to run a fine house, to be at the top of the university social ladder and, increasingly, to be of real influence in the university's growth. He remained sensitive to the fact that he had brought his distinguished bride to live modestly as the wife of a mere lecturer: he imagined that his mother-in-law expected her daughter to be at least the wife of a professor. He once reflected: 'I remember a girl who lived in and loved a beautiful home, yet she left it to go with a young lecturer to a little suburban house. I remember other things she gave up and many things she has done for that turbulent youth.'[3] His salary of £200 per annum was a poor thing compared to the £600 per annum that went with the professorial chair.

Even more, Jim was beginning to resent being at Purdie's beck and call. This had been noticed by others, and Professor Walker, the outgoing professor of chemistry in Dundee, actually said to him: 'I've often thought your work with him wasn't all a bed of roses . . . I don't wonder you want to get away.'[4] The appointments board were confused by the fact that Purdie seemed to recommend each of his candidates, and would not give Irvine his sole support. Irvine felt this most bitterly, but he ignored the touching terms in which Purdie actually wrote about him in his testimonial:

> I owe more to Dr Irvine than I can well express. In recent years, owing to my indisposition, it has frequently fallen to him to undertake my lectures and much of my duty. At such times I have always known that my work was in safe hands.
>
> Dr Irvine is a particularly good lecturer. He prepares carefully and speaks fluently. Avoiding needless detail, he seizes his main points, and sets out his subject in clear and lively style. The influence of his Master, Wislicenus, is evident in the faculty – which he shows in a remarkable degree – of rousing the interest and enthusiasm of his students.[5]

Purdie could but recommend Irvine cordially for the vacant chair in Dundee. Irvine had hastily misjudged his old friend's honesty.

It was the accepted custom early in the twentieth century for candidates for a senior post to lobby all the most influential people concerned in the appointment. Jim went to see the Lord Provost of Dundee and thought he was the stupidest man he had ever met; he went to see the Principal of

University College Dundee, Mackay, for whom he formed a high regard, as well as the 'big, jovial, kindly' Principal Donaldson in St Andrews. He had a long session with Professor Walker, who took his young colleague under his patronage. In fact, it would appear that Irvine was universally recommended for the post by all those most qualified to speak for him. Jim found that these exacting, long interviews placed enormous nervous strain on him, and he disliked having 'to talk about himself and exert every nerve in order to gain points'.[6]

Jim Irvine's curriculum vitae also covered his interest in student societies and other university institutions, as president of the Science Club, president of the Tennis Club and vice-president of the recently instituted University Chemical Society; he was also on the Athletic Union and the Library Committees. The student vote in St Andrews naturally enough had little effect on the minds of the Dundee jute makers. The library committee had just overseen Sir Robert Lorimer's large-scale and costly addition to the university library: a reordering that was desperately needed because of the loss of library quarters to the Senate room, which had recently been remodelled by Robert Anderson. This loss, coupled with the introduction of new subjects and the rapid accumulation of accessions, had brought the library to breaking point.[7]

By early October and the opening of the new academic year, Jim had gone back to his old labours, continuing to double up his job with that of his poor professor, whose asthmatic problems returned to him annually along with the mists of autumn. His students were evidently pleased that they had not lost Dr Irvine, and gave him a roaring reception. Fifty-four of his former and current students had signed a testimonial supporting him for the Dundee post, at the same time remarking how keenly they would feel his absence. Jim's haste to get a chair had blinded him to the fact that the upheaval that the Dundee chair had brought to the summer months was but a dress rehearsal for a vacancy in St Andrews. Purdie was only too well aware of it, and by the following January the gossip was that Purdie was preparing to relinquish his chair: something bound to cause shock at that time, when these appointments were for life.

Both Jim and Mabel became the talking points of the St Andrews drawing rooms. The town's social attitudes around 1909 were shaped by the old-fashioned introverted intimacy of the university, as well as by the survival of Victorian class interdependency. It was distinctly to Jim Irvine's advantage that his wife gave the air of having a small income of her own and knew how to behave in society. It was also hoped that this time the university would choose 'one of her own'; it was felt that in choosing Marshall, Dundee had made the mistake of buying a pig in a poke. Of the three St Andrews candidates, poor Wallace Walker was condemned for having married the daughter of a small farmer from outlying Strathkinness; but, luckily for Jim, Mabel was a great favourite among the gentlemanly but elderly professors and their wives. She set about demonstrating quite how she might play her part.

Early in the year, she gave two ladies' luncheons, for which she hired a 'waitress' to augment the services of Mary, her Irish 'cook-general': 'It may do a lot of good, one never knows. At any rate it will show that this wife would not be a disgrace to the University,' she wrote.[8] Poor Mary had earned a rare day off, and she took herself to Dundee to spend the day with a friend. She bought a hat for 13s, and she and Gladys bought tickets for the theatre. It turned out to be Wagner's *Tannhäuser*. Her account of a day out in Dundee offers an unusual and comical record of 'downstairs' St Andrews servant life: 'Och there was a woman singing all the time, & she was a princess I think, but if their throats don't be sore this night after all that *screechin*! I couldn't hear what it was all about for the noise they were makin'. I never was as tired in my life, & my head was *cleevin'*.[9] Mabel and Jim, who had learned to adore Wagner's operas during their Leipzig days, could not permit themselves an escape for the day to Dundee, even to hear Wagner.

Mabel joined a committee of wives formed by Mrs Herkless and Mrs Stout to oversee the licensing of lodgings for women students:

> I am to inspect two houses in Argyll Street . . . and one in Kinness Place. I want to do it very well & in business-like fashion, also with a view to Jim's chair!! . . . I have always felt very keenly the way the poorer women students live who can't go to the Hall. Most of the Carnegie students, teachers in training, who ought to be housemaids and cooks. They live in twos.[10]

Perhaps we can attribute her little snobberies to her desire for a leading social position in St Andrews to help her husband's advancement in his career. She planned to give a concert to raise money for the extension of the women's residence, University Hall.

Andrew Lang's 'haunted town by the northern sea' was not entirely immune from the influences of the outside world. The university, which was already pioneering the higher education of women, acquired some notoriety in the matter of their enfranchisement. Christal MacMillan, a young lawyer and graduate of the Lady Literate in Arts (LLA) course at St Andrews, was the first woman ever to petition the House of Lords: her plea was for votes for women graduates. Suffragist meetings were all the rage among the professors' wives and daughters. Keeping an open mind, Mabel busied herself with attending these public meetings, to one of which, in the March of that year, Christal MacMillan came to speak, as Mabel recorded: 'On to a suffragist meeting with Lucy [Menzies]. I had to promise her to, as she came with me to my anti-suffrage meeting . . . Miss Chrystal MacMillan, the heroine of the House of Lords episode, is to speak.'[11]

Despite the fact that Lucy Menzies was pronouncedly pro-votes for women and she, Mabel, declared herself opposed, Jim Irvine's wife went with Lucy to them all, indiscriminately. It is hardly surprising that Lucy Menzies was a suffragette: she was a scholar in her own right, and she grew up in an intellectually liberal household. When her father, Allan Menzies, a theologian of 'advanced views', who had a cleft palate and was slightly deaf, was appointed in 1889 to the chair of Biblical Criticism in St Andrews, Andrew Lang was overheard in the Athenaeum saying, 'I hear they've appointed a deaf and dumb atheist to the Chair of Biblical Criticism in St Andrews'. Andrew Lang's waspish gossip was no measure of this endearing family. Lucy, who today is commemorated by the Episcopal Church for her life of saintliness, was a mystic and became a close colleague of Evelyn Underhill. She, like Mabel, had been sent to Germany by her parents to be 'finished', and she studied the piano in Heidelberg. Jim and Mabel's constant and intimate friendship with Lucy was a strength to them throughout their lives.

Mabel delayed her usual departure to spend the Easter vacation in Ireland so that she could attend the graduation ceremony on 31 March and keep in the public eye. Jim would take no spring holiday this year, because he knew that just as soon as the chair was declared formally vacant and was advertised, he could begin lobbying and he would be able to talk to the members of the University Court. He was already preparing the ground behind the scenes with the members of the Senate, all friends. People were beginning to fear that, if Irvine were not chosen for the St Andrews chair, Jim and Mabel would not stay long in St Andrews. Some other university or research institute would lay claim to him.

Jim found sound support in the Professor of Anatomy. James Musgrove, an Edinburgh man, was quite a smooth operator and well used to these difficult machinations. Jim had been working on a new book on research methods and he thought that a published book would be a feather in his cap, but Professor Musgrove advised him strongly not to publish it before the outcome of the chair was resolved. He wisely commented that, no matter how good a book of that kind was, it was certain to attract some adverse criticism. Irvine might even tread on somebody's toes, and this could run against him. It would be far better to circulate the manuscript of the book in private to one or two key people, including Purdie; who, surprisingly, seemed not to have been aware of Irvine's publishing aspirations. Jim boasted that a draft of this manual was already making a most favourable impact on the work of two or three research students in the laboratory. 'He gave the MSS to a couple of his students, Hind and Garrett, before their degree exams came off – that they might study his new method – & they both came out with almost full marks', wrote Mabel proudly to her mother. It would appear, however, that the book never got beyond the manuscript stage.

Mabel and Jim were convinced at this time of Purdie's perfidy towards Jim: that he was ungenerous in every way, that he would lose his temper on the few occasions when he felt well enough to be in the laboratory and that he seemed still to withhold his exclusive patronage to Irvine. Little did they know in what ample terms Dr Purdie spoke of his protégé, as evidenced in his report to the Carnegie trustees during the spring of 1909 in which he refers to James Irvine's already distinguished career and describes the St Andrews school of 'sugars' research as the creation of Irvine alone. Purdie was saying privately that if the Senate wanted the chemistry department to 'hum', they would choose Irvine without any hesitation. It is clear that in Purdie's mind Irvine was his heir apparent.

Once Mabel and Jim had shaken off the tensions and anxiety that the issue of the chair of chemistry had laid on them, their resentment of Purdie evaporated. Jim later recorded that '[Purdie's] election to the chair in 1884 was the turning-point in the history of chemistry in St Andrews, and it is not too much to claim that it was also a turning-point in the history of the University'.[12] Jim drafted the university's encomium for his old professor, in which he recorded 'the affection and esteem which [the whole university] entertained for him, and [the hope of all his colleagues] that he might be long spared to be in the midst of them and to see the educational and scientific work in which he has laboured so strenuously and generously during his professorate continued and carried forward with energy and insight'.[13] Surely Irvine had long seen himself as the one who would carry Purdie's work forward in this way?

Jim took enormous pleasure in the numerous testimonials he received from continental chemists in the research institutes of Germany, Holland, Switzerland and France. These distinguished men, who included Professor Bertrand of the Pasteur Institute, had no hesitation in commending their young scientific friend – '*cher et très honoré collègue*' – to the St Andrews Senatus. Hans Stobbe, whose lectures on the sugars had triggered the young Irvine's interest, added his name. The great Emil Fischer 'stated most willingly' his admiration of the 'considerable advance in the experimental treatment of the sugars' that Irvine had achieved, and he added that Irvine had 'thrown a new and interesting light on many important theoretical questions connected with the sugar group'. In eight years a transformation had taken place, and, no longer the pupil, Herr Doktor Irvine had become the '*Sehr geehrter Herr College*' of his Leipzig professors, Beckmann, Pfeffer and Stobbe, who stepped out of the shadows of the past to honour their pupil.[14] The author of *Chemie der Zuckerarten* (1904), Professor Edmund von Lippmann affirmed his close and valued collaboration with Irvine, whose treatment of the fundamental problems with the sugars he felt was based unusually on original and illuminating thought.

To turn to the St Andrews University Court, it would be swayed by an interesting role that Irvine had as recently as the previous year been able to play in the development of the university which, under the able direction of Principal Donaldson, was experiencing a revolution. The old order whereby subjects would be studied by a haphazard collection of students, under the exclusive care of their professor, was completely played out. The four Scottish universities banded together, with the Carnegie Trust backing them, in a bid to obtain a forward-looking structure and financial provision for fine new faculties of Science, Medicine and the Arts. Lectureships in all the departments would be provided for out of central funds – lectureships with salaries, permanence and job descriptions. During the year 1907–8, a new ordinance for restructuring all the departments in St Andrews was drawn up, and Irvine on his professor's behalf wrote the submission for the department of chemistry. Emphasising the value to the university in encouraging the growth of chemistry, he staked his claim far more boldly than did any of the other professors for their departments. Irvine had a determined streak when it came to obtaining money for the institutions that fell to his care, and this streak was beginning to emerge.

Using the excuse of a perfectly innocent departmental report as his vehicle, Irvine was able to demonstrate two things: how the research department had flourished since the inception of all the new facilities and buildings given by Purdie in 1905; and how much the reputation of the department had grown since he had taken up the post of lecturer. Irvine took pleasure in the neat tables he produced to demonstrate St Andrews' position, which had the most productive chemical research institute in the kingdom, after the enormous laboratories of Manchester and London. This was a competitive little trick that Irvine used to great effect many times during his life. One could almost call it public relations. Purdie disliked these quantitative ways of assessing the value of a department, but Irvine knew that it was the way to attract money.

In a letter written privately to Principal Donaldson, who was preparing a case for St Andrews' science research claims against the Carnegie Trust's second quinquennial, Irvine went so far as to say that:

> Possibly the qualitative statement that, between St Andrews and Dundee the output of papers in pure chemistry equals the combined product of Oxford and Cambridge is a striking enough fact to empha sise the effort which is being made to stamp the University as one of the most prominent seats of chemical research in the country. I trust that . . . the statement may be of use to you.[15]

The result was that Principal Donaldson reported to the university commissioners and to the Carnegie Trust that chemistry in particular cried out for singular treatment: '[The new chemistry department] cannot have its full effect unless it is supplied with more educational power than it has at present. There is need of more assistants and possibly of one or two additional lecturers.'

Mabel wrote to her mother: 'I do think all this Ordinance business has come in the nick of time. Jim's new degree has made quite a sensation and everyone is greatly struck with it. The time has not yet come for him to speak on the subject, he spoke at the meeting yesterday but not on his new plan. Burnet[16] mentioned it yesterday in his speech and called it very ingenious.'[17] The 'new degree' was the St Andrews PhD, which Irvine devised, after the German model, to enlarge the experience of research in both the Arts and Science faculties. It would allow higher rank to be given to the DSc, but it would encourage research opportunities in the Faculty of Arts.[18] Its introduction was delayed, however, by the 1914–18 war.

In 1909, as with the Dundee chair, there was a formidable list for the St Andrews chair of chemistry: thirteen strong candidates. The new research laboratory, backed with further funding, was a major attraction. On 19 June the list was submitted to the University Court, which considered all the applications and testimonials there and then. St Andrews determined on a different and more forthright approach from that of Dundee: no short-leet was to be drawn up, and all the candidates apart from Irvine were told straightaway that they would not be expected to call upon members of the Court. On 26 June, Irvine's unopposed election as St Andrews' fourth professor of chemistry was made public; his letter of acceptance is dated 28 July. He and Mabel had got what was, for the time being, their hearts' desire. Mabel wrote that they experienced with relief a new feeling of permanence in St Andrews. Whether or not such a thrusting and capable man would remain content, only time would show. Distinguished Professor Perkin hoped that young Irvine's ambitions would now be satisfied, and so for some time they were. He was thirty-two years of age, a fact perhaps unremarkable in later times but extremely rare in the strange world of early twentieth-century British universities. The appointment aroused criticism in his older colleagues: this was Jim's first experience of back-biters. The enormous importance to Irvine of this step in his career cannot be under-estimated. With Percy Herring, who had got the Chandos Chair of Physi-ology the year before, he led a new generation of young professors.

Purdie had found the department of chemistry very poorly equipped, and he left it in the highest state of efficiency. The world looked admir-ingly at his growing school of chemistry: Purdie's final accolades were his just reward for the remarkable way he had kept the faith and brought his department from nothing into the international company of the great research institutes of chemistry. As far as Irvine was concerned: 'I was batting on a good wicket, . . . we were opening out a fruitful field of carbo-hydrate chemistry and were allowed to cull the fruits of peace.'[19] He could not have imagined how short a lease he had, and how the Great War and the chemical needs of the War Department would fracture the work of the school he was developing.

'It was a striking act of generosity to hand over in this way an inheritance which had come to him unexpectedly, and equally an act of faith, for it was the first laboratory of the kind in this country, and the smallest univer-sity in Scotland was a strange locus for such an adventure,'[20] was Irvine's comment on the Purdie bequest. Purdie had worked all his professional life to establish an important school of chemical research only to hand it over to this young man at the very point when it was beginning to show the first signs of its promise. This too was an act of great generosity.

Irvine picked up the ball and ran with it.

Irvine's inaugural address strayed from the usual path whereby the eager newly appointed professor would traditionally lay out his stall. Not for him the desire to use this opportunity to describe all that he hoped to achieve with this, his great chance. He did not puff himself up with ambition for the school of chemistry. After graciously paying great tribute to Professor Purdie's legacy, he played a trick of oratory such as he would, in his future life as Principal, often use. His romantic resumé of the history of chemistry in St Andrews manages to embrace an alchemical capriccio; it plays on the then landmarks in the development of our knowledge of chemistry, and somehow connects them all with St Andrews: Dalton, Davy, Joseph Black, Rumford and even Lavoisier are all there, and he conjoins them into a glorious exhortation to his young listeners to thank their great blessings that they found themselves in the calm and beauty of St Andrews. He contrasts the lives of the young people in front of him with those chemists working in what he called 'slumland': 'The remote and hideous parts of London which suggest to most of us ... the philanthropic efforts of Dr Barnardo.' They nevertheless eagerly turn every day to their laboratories, because their subject 'exercises on them a fascination as subtle and magnetic as that which draws the common-place Englishman to the golf-links, the cricket field or the race course'. What began as a pleasant canter through the fields of pioneering chemistry has become a stern plea to all to do their best (never an easy goal in Irvine's scheme of things), to maintain a robust sense of duty even when faced with the routine of the daily work, and never to lose enthusiasm for the subject. In return Irvine offers them not so much his service as professor, but rather his friendship. He considers it a privilege to further his great work by means of this mutual confidence and singleness of purpose.[71]

Knowing Irvine as we do today – a towering figure who breathed new life into the higher education of the twentieth century – it would be easy to lose sight of the committed and inspirational young chemist of 1909. Research was a constantly burning flame within him; his notebooks and even small scraps of paper covered in formulae and ideas show that, as a young professor, he felt chemical ideas were inexhaustible. At this period of his life all of his colleagues and students were eager to attest to his remarkable powers as a teacher: a man who could present even the most unpromising facts in an interesting manner, and impart a genuine and abiding love for the subject he had made his own.

Irvine's infectious enjoyment of his lectures to the General Class made its mark on the university as a whole. He was an instinctive teacher who approached this side of his duties wholeheartedly. News quickly spread about the chemistry professor who was a wizard at the lecture experiments, and who courted his audience with a command over his whole subject. He revered the scientific thinkers of the enlightenment who had made it all possible, and he persuaded his audience that there was far more yet to discover. It was still possible for an Arts student, with no previous experience of chemistry but attracted to this electric and youthful department, to choose first-year chemistry as a component part of an Arts degree. There were several notable examples of former Arts students who went on to make a career in chemistry, armed with that peculiar feeling of pride in their profession that Irvine loved to instill. Edmund Hirst, who would hold chairs in chemistry at Bristol, Manchester and then Edinburgh, was just such a student. He came to St Andrews in 1914 from the local school, Madras College, to study towards a classics degree. He fell under the spell of the chemistry department, and once drawn into Irvine's team he was transformed into a chemist.

The staffing of the department was depleted by Jim's promotion from lecturer. There was no permanent provision for a lecturer in chemistry in the university, as Irvine's salary had been made up for him by sums from Professor Purdie's own purse and by his Carnegie fellowship. His had been a precarious position. The next generation of Carnegie research fellows provided the department with assistants, who would straddle the two responsibilities of helping in the teaching laboratory and pursuing fields of research under Irvine's guidance. These young people comprised both Irvine's first team of research workers and effectively his staff.[22]

The old wood, Purdie's former chemical assistants, did not survive the change of professor. Irvine appointed his own nominee, William Denham, in their place as his first personal assistant. Denham, a Fellow of the Institute of Chemistry, with a London BSc degree, had been teaching at the Glasgow and West of Scotland Technical College, and like Irvine before him he yearned for a foothold in a university chemistry department. He had the presence of mind to write to Irvine only that summer, congratulating the young professor on his preferment. Irvine warmed to the fact that a stranger so much admired what was happening in his department, to the extent that he would give up what was undoubtedly a better-paid job, in order to work in the St Andrews chemical research institute.[23] He must have reminded Irvine of his younger self. It was not until 1912, however, that Denham could be appointed lecturer and assistant to the professor. Irvine looked for staff with experience of the large chemistry departments south of the border. Six months later W.N. Haworth,[24] who would in 1937 be awarded the Nobel Prize for his carbohydrate research programme, took up the appointment to a further lectureship, and with him Irvine embarked on an important period in his life. Thus began a new chapter for chemistry in St Andrews, when it would acquire international acclaim. Emil Fischer, the greatest organic chemist alive, offered an exchange of research programmes: 'I wish to avoid any possibility of collision or competition.'[25]

Irvine approached his new responsibilities as a man of the twentieth century: in the weeks leading up to the opening of the university year in September 1909, he applied for a central lighting system in the department, for a telephone and also for an 'ambulance set'.

Edwardian St Andrews had its fair share of 'characters', and of these Coutts, the university janitor, was one of the largest. He finally came in for a good deal of criticism for the licence he took with the professors and the students, whom he called the 'menagerie'.[26] In his eagerness to modernise the university, Principal Donaldson entrusted Coutts with the wiring of the chapel and the lecture rooms for electric light, and Coutts had provided his dangerous best. Irvine used all his influence to have Coutts' wiring systems ripped out and professionally replaced.

A chemistry department of the early twentieth century was by no means free from danger.[27] An explosion that took place in the laboratory in 1911 shook the houses on the the Scores   the street that divides the college buildings from the sea – and his own house felt the blast.

Irvine became a master at manipulating the class grant system in favour of chemistry, and in 1911 he demanded the princely sum of £330, from a variety of sources, with which to finance the day-to-day running of his new empire. Jim's attitude towards his young colleagues in the laboratory and his colleagues in the Senatus mellowed. He explained this inner peace in this way: 'From the nature of my work I had to spend many hours in darkness, observing a beam of polarised light in its transit through sugar solutions, and it was in these times of solitude that this spirit of gratitude was born.'[28]

Jim and Mabel's own vastly improved finances gave them a sense of new freedoms. Mabel felt she had earned the occasional trip to London, which would allow her to keep up with the musical world. They both had begun to think that their little house situated so far outside the town and so far from the department was not such a good idea after all. Jim was determined that his wife would live in as fine a house as St Andrews could offer. The house they found was Edgecliffe East, and in November 1909 they were ready to take on the lease, which at £100 per annum was double what they were paying for the little house out in the westerly suburb of Rathelpie.[29] Edgecliffe East is a distinguished semi-villa, built (1864–6) to the designs of the St Andrews architect, George Rae. It is sited on surely one of the best sites in St Andrews, immediately overlooking St Andrews Bay on the north side of the Scores. Externally it conveys an exaggerated baronial style: Mabel admitted that she could never describe it as beautiful, but it was large and elegant on the inside. It was immediately opposite the chemistry laboratory, and its gardens ran down to the cliff. Many of the wide windows in the public rooms overlooked the bay, and presented the ever-changing panorama of the seascape that would never cease to delight them, whether in the frosty sharp air of their first winter or the balmy nights of June.

During their first spring in the new house, King Edward VII died. Mabel, now the professor's wife, declared that she owed it to her husband's position to go into complete mourning. Early on the morning of 7 May she rushed out to buy herself a new coat and skirt of fine cloth, a black lace blouse and a dashing three-cornered hat of fine straw at 22s. The St Andrews dress shops were fast selling out of black. That night Jim and Mabel sat in the drawing-room window watching battleships in the bay, their flags at half-mast, playing their search lights. General opinion amongst the St Andrews wives was that the old King had been greatly beloved, and that his son was not fit to follow in his footsteps.[30]

Little happened, however, to diminish their pleasure in Edgecliffe. Gardening became their latest hobby and, as with most things he took up, and with his usual thoroughness, Jim threw himself into acquiring a new expertise. He bought a lawn mower and an assortment of garden tools, and he became their gardener. They worked hard together, like a couple of children, weeding and clearing back the shrubs. Soon the garden, which had been allowed to become overgrown, was presentable, and Jim enjoyed this return to his youthful interest in plants, an interest that would increasingly feed his chemical research.

Edgecliffe East had the added attraction of nurseries at the top of the house. By the winter of 1910 they eagerly looked forward to the birth of their first child. Jessie Veronica was born in Edgecliffe on 26 April 1911, and with her a succession of nurses and nannies joined the household. So began Mabel's lifelong struggles in the search for good domestic staff. In 1911, there was Sara in the nursery, Janet in the kitchen and Kate the house-maid. On the nurse's day off, Mabel would take the baby down to the cathedral grounds, where they could spend a sunny afternoon in a sheltered spot, amongst the memorials of the great and the good of the little town. St Andrews was still, for the most part, a community of grey-beards, and one and all were amused and delighted by the arrival of a child in their midst. The baby's baptism, at which Dr Herkless, Professor of Ecclesiastical History, stood sponsor and minister, was the first that had taken place in College Chapel for fifty years. Veronica was the toast of many a dinner party and, as a talking point, she almost eclipsed the preparations for the university's quincentenary celebrations.

During the summer of preparation for the quincentenary, the Irvines' domestic peace was ruffled by a most disturbing piece of news that would become an unexpected turn of good fortune. Their landlord, David Foggo LLD, who lived next door, was obliged to make his financial difficulties public: his chief creditor wanted to call in his loan, and the investments that had stood surety for this loan.[31] Jim and Mabel had no experience in business matters, although their backgrounds were in commerce. They were at first deeply anxious. A sheriff's writ was served on Jim on 20 July. Might they be turned out of their house, with a new baby to care for; and how then could they measure up to the social demands of the quincentenary?

Initially they felt they were in deep water, but they remained as tenants to the 'trustees to the heritable creditors'. Dr Foggo was finally declared bankrupt in 1913, and after those two years of uncertainty Jim had the presence of mind to approach the St Andrews lawyers, Hotchkiss, with an offer for the freehold. This was his first opportunity to exercise something of the same business acumen that the University Court recognised would be so desirable to them when he applied for the vacant principalship in 1920. It was extremely unusual for a young don to own such a fine house at that date; it was not the custom of the professional class, who tended to rent. With the sole exception of the newly married Professor and Mrs Musgrove, who lived opposite, at The Swallowgate, Jim and Mabel's property-owning neighbours on the Scores were not university colleagues. Mrs Musgrove was rich and remarkable for having been married four times. Edgecliffe would become Mabel's pension.

In three years' time, the Great War would turn everyone's world upside down, but in 1911 St Andrews was the very essence of the golden Edwardian idyll. Within the peace and security of the years after Queen Victoria's death, the world apparently ignored the imminent cataclysm. In June 1911 – the year of the university's quincentenary – Jim was elected dean of the Faculty of Science.[32] He now had charge of all the scientific departments both in St Andrews and in Dundee, including medicine. As faculty dean at this early point in the development of his career, he was thrust into a position of authority during the quincentenary: something he very much enjoyed.

Many later thought of the 1914–18 war as a chemists' war in the sense that the Second World War was a physicists' war. It would be for its chemical war work that St Andrews would achieve high eminence in the academic world, but in the year of the quincentenary, the world turned to St Andrews in a spirit of celebration for its past 500 years of romance and even scientific distinction. There was not even the suspicion of a lull before the storm as the university proudly prepared itself as host to an event of magnificent and glamorous proportions. The germ of St Andrews' fifteenth-century foundation lay in Bologna and Paris, and its fellow medieval universities in Europe were all represented at the celebrations; so also were places of learning as far-flung as Tasmania and Dalhousie, Helsingfors and Lahore. Lord Rosebery's unusual arrival by sea in his yacht was met by a long procession of red-gowned students walking along the pier, and this event is perpetuated even now every Sunday in term-time by the tradition of the pier walk. The rolling cadences of his speech as Rector contributed an example of the old-fashioned oratory that would so soon be associated with a bygone age.

To the ordinary observer, it might have seemed bizarre that this tiny and still struggling institution, with a student headcount in 1911 of only 353, should be so confident in a historic heritage that had survived 500 years of ecclesiastical foundation, reformation and then decay, that it did not quail at inviting delegates from every conceivable learned body in the world. It ordered 86 honorary LLD hoods and 14 honorary DD hoods from the two St Andrews purveyors of academic dress. Enormous numbers were involved in the four days of functions, from 12–15 September.[33] A 'temporary' hall to seat 3,500 people, 217 × 96 feet in scale, was erected on the tennis lawns beneath Lower College Hall, behind the north range of the college quadrangle. Green and white was the theme, and in what was described as a temporary drawing room, the chancellor, Lord Balfour of Burleigh, and his wife received the guests at the large evening reception on the first night, assisted by the joint convenors of the receptions, Professor Herkless and Professor Irvine, with their wives.

The orchestra of the Scots Guards provided a programme of suitable symphonic music, in which predictably Brahms' *Academic Festival Overture* was played. A certain diplomatic skill had to be deployed in the case of inviting delegates from Hungary and Finland; both of these countries demanded nation status, independent of Austria on the one hand and Russia on the other, and so Dvorak's *Humoreske* and Sibelius' symphonic anthem to his country, *Finlandia*, could be heard by the first evening's vast throng.

By far the most memorable event in all this panoply of just pride was the academic and civic procession that filled the St Andrews streets with the rich rainbow colours of academic dress that well evoked the medieval schoolmen of their mutual past. Holy Trinity, the town kirk, received them all for their thanksgiving. The University Chapel of St Salvator's College was at that date still in urgent need of repair, but the pre-Reformation church of the Holy Trinity, as old as the university, had recently been restored and rebuilt. Under a clear blue sky, the nations of the world met in peace. The Rector of the University of Berlin strolled down South Street, in his gown of red velvet, his tall cap embroidered in gold, beside the representatives of Belgium, France, Italy and Britain, all members of the freemasonry of the mind. No-one on that happy day thought that, in three years' time, Britain and her allies would be at war with Germany. An evening of historic tableaux presented to a spellbound audience of guests the history of St Andrews, from Laurence of Lindores to the murder of Archbishop Sharp. Were there perhaps echoes of this successful event in Irvine's mind when, in 1926, he felt inclined to encourage the revival of Kate Kennedy's Day and the procession of students in historic costume?

The quincentenary was the ideal occasion on which to inaugurate the spacious Bell-Pettigrew Museum, endowed by Mrs Musgrove in the name of her late husband, Professor Bell-Pettigrew, and here was planned an elaborate dinner for between 500 and 600 guests, at which white tie, evening tails and orders were to be worn. The catering was no less lavish at the students' ball. A further day of functions and outings on Tayside and in Dundee gave the university ample opportunity to show off the full range of its buildings and departments, and offered the visitors the chance to view one or two local beauty spots.

The honoured guests were, for the most part, offered hospitality for the four or five days of graduation, speeches, banquets, balls and the presentation of addresses; they stayed in professors' homes and in the country houses of the landed and aristocratic Fife neighbours of the university. Great care was taken to match guests with hosts. An expansive spirit of goodwill and eagerness to help made this incredible operation possible, and local industrialists, including David Russell of the Markinch paper mill, contributed their organisational skills. The guests nearly all wished to bring their wives; many brought their daughters, and even their sisters, as was perfectly proper in Edwardian society. A section of the chemistry laboratory was handed over to the fashionable photographer Lafayette, to act as a studio for portrait photography.

St Andrews was distinctly proud of the current development of scientific research within its walls. The festivities were reported at length in the scientific journal *Nature*. The emphasis of the quincentenary was on the celebration of science, and the presentation *Memorial Volume of Scientific Papers*,[34] edited by Professors M'Intosh, Irvine and Steggall, the Dundee mathematician, is testimony enough that St Andrews was ready to look confidently at its future. The Purdies and the Irvines were to have the chief chemists to stay in their houses. Jim and Purdie were firm friends again by this time, and the two couples arranged a most complex programme of luncheons and dinner parties, by means of which Jim could meet round his own dining table most of the important chemists of the day. T.P., as Jim and Mabel would refer to Thomas Purdie, made no bones about what he was trying to achieve: an FRS for Jim. 'Oh, you needn't ask them, they'd be no use to you,' the wise old professor would say.[35]

During this charmed year of 1911 Jim Irvine felt that he was in the ascendancy, although it was not until 1918, and after Purdie's death, that he was elected FRS. By that time, the chemistry of war had drawn Irvine into hitherto undreamed-of chemical circles. The Irvines' house guests in September 1911 were the Cambridge crystallographer Professor Pope and his wife, and Professor and Mrs Perkin from Manchester, as well as Jim's former colleague, Dr Lander and his wife. Professors Perkin and Pope were to be given honorary degrees, and when the time came (1918) they were both proposers of Irvine for his election as FRS. Professor W.H. Perkin was the eldest son of Sir William Perkin, who at the age of eighteen patented his discovery of an aniline dye of an intense purple shade, favoured by Queen Victoria. Over tea, the Popes made Mabel laugh by warning her that Mrs Perkin was in the habit of wearing an evening dress died mauve by the application of her late father-in-law's famous dye. Jim went down to the station to meet the Perkins, and as he approached them, he could hear Mrs Perkin say to her husband: 'Oh, kind Professor Irvine has sent his son down to meet us!' 'That's not his son,' Professor Perkin laughingly replied. 'That's Professor Irvine.' Jim loved this story that so well illustrated his air of eternal youth.[36]

It was undoubtedly true that the trouble Jim took to show off his beloved St Andrews to the chemical grandees did more for his success than the rare port he had laid in for his dinner table. These were days of informal conversation, of walks through the old town in the September sunlight.

That year, the summer's drought extended into the autumn. Jim's gift of storytelling, coupled with his deep love of the place, served to illuminate its essential and breathtaking beauty. This was a formula that never failed to impress, and in the forty years of his service to St Andrews that lay ahead it brought wealth, prestige and the attachment of great men and women to the university's cause. The days of the quincentenary comprised a week that all who participated in it remembered for the rest of their lives. In the train bearing the last of the guests away, a golfer turned to his companion as they looked back at the links and the outline of the old grey town: 'Go-ahead little place, St Andrews, I hear they've got a university there now,' he was heard to remark.[37]

The quincentenary changed Jim Irvine. When it all was over, his wife could see reflected in his face a look of determination and inflexible purpose. Here, already in their midst, waiting in the wings, was the leader of St Andrew's twentieth-century renaissance. Did Jim Irvine recognise that from that time he would devote himself to planning how he could help bring it to a glorious future? All that the quincentenary had represented: the past and the future, he would restore to the university in full: the collegiate life, the beauty of her material estate, and her growth into a larger, modern institute of higher education of the new age. It would become a seat of universal discovery, which surely must be the definition of a university.

SEVEN

The Great War

In the summer of 1914, Jim was invited by Professor and Mrs Purdie to join them for a week's fishing on South Harris. The Purdies regularly took holidays at the Hebridean Sporting Association's exclusive fishing establishment based at Finsbay Lodge in this far outpost of Scotland. In the clear air of the Western Isles, Thomas Purdie's asthma cleared up and something of his old athletic self returned as he fished the fine sea lochs maintained by the Association.

This was not Jim's first taste of Highland fishing: the previous year's summer holiday had been spent delightfully *en famille* at Marchmont in Glenurquhart. Much of the success of this first Highland holiday came from Jim's discovery that fishing these remote waters provided the best possible escape valve for the pressure he lived under during the years of his professorship, and during the whole of the war to come.

The invitation to a gentlemen's private fishing club was, he felt, something special and merited a new wardrobe. His first professor, George Henderson, would be there, together with a full complement of Glasgow businessmen, shareholders in the venture, who all had half an eye on the telegraph exchange for news of the imminent war. Alas, Jim's new fishing clothes were far too elaborate and his expensive silk-lined waterproof marked him out as a new boy. However, he loved the clubbish atmosphere and the gentle competitiveness of each man's 'bag' at the end of a day, every man with his personal ghillie. He savoured every moment of this new world, characterised by the smoking-room stories of fish once caught and of the fish that were undoubtedly waiting for them in the desolate waters of the chain of little lochs. A wild and stormy night was to be relished for the spate that would surely follow.

The week's holiday on Harris would have been no more than that, had it not taken place at the beginning of August 1914. Jim felt that his experience of Germany when he was a student in Leipzig gave him an insight into

European politics denied to most of his fellow countrymen; he believed that Britain had become far too obsessed with home issues, such as the vote for women and Home Rule for Ireland, both of which he dismissed as small-minded. The war, he felt, would teach his country something about the graver issues of the balance of power in international affairs.[1] Closer to home, his kind heart was deeply moved by all that he witnessed of the crofters' response to an event miles away from the outer isles. He wrote vividly to Mabs, who was expecting the birth of their second child in September, and his letter of 4 August provides as telling a record of the stirrings around the outbreak of war as any news-stand on a Westminster street corner.

> Imagine a little lonely loch, dreary and grey, with the rugged hills all around and the mists swirling over the rocky precipices – I am quietly fishing in company with my ghillie, John, who as a sergeant in the Reserves lives in the hourly expectation of being called out. For the moment we have given up talking of war and casting for a big sea trout who is coming again and again at the line, when out of the mist, leaping from rock to rock, comes an old white-headed man who shouts to us in Gaelic. 'My telegram', cries John, and he bends to the oars and we dash across the loch. A quick question and answer in the unknown tongue.
>
> 'Have you any news?', I ask the messenger – a shake of the head and 'I hav no Engleesh' is his reply. He has telegrams for the ghillies, who are in the Naval reserve and he dashes off from one loch to another so as to find them. Half an hour later three men in oil-skins with sacks over their shoulders march down the rocky path. They have in a moment's notice left homes, wives, children and their scanty livelihood to obey the call. A shouted farewell in Gaelic and they disappear – we got on casting with the feeling that it is unworthy for men to play themselves at such a time, – meanwhile three brave men trudge through the rain to Stornoway.

Back in St Andrews, the *St Andrews Citizen* reported that in the forenoon of 3 August several of the merchants in the town had to close their premises in order to cope with the orders they had received, and prices rose steadily. Sugar fluctuated between 4d and 9d per pound; oatmeal, flour, butter, eggs, jams, rice and sago all went up in price. The banks closed, and citizens temporarily ran out of cash.

Apart from a degree of inevitable domestic panic that involved laying in larger stocks of those staples of an Edwardian Scottish household – flour, oatmeal and coal – the young Irvines initially experienced the war by proxy. As head of department and now a leading member of the Senatus, the university's governing academic body, Jim would not be called up, but he joined the Officer Training Corps (OTC) and did his patrol duty in a khaki greatcoat, shared amongst his colleagues. A minor battle throughout this period would consist of his struggles to persuade the War Office that many of his colleagues should be allowed to stay at their teaching posts in St Andrews.[2] Mabel's youngest brother, Ron, was called up, but all the other men close to her were in reserved occupations. One brother was now the senior partner of the family business; another, the German philologist Bert, had a chair at Trinity College Dublin.

St Andrews was still strikingly small, even compared with the other Scottish universities. Immediately before the outbreak of war, there were 508 matriculated students, of which 308 were men, the numbers being distributed between St Andrews and Dundee. As the war progressed, the student body diminished dramatically. When the university opened for the first term that fell during wartime, about 100 students put their names forward for the commissions offered to those who had trained in a territorial unit in peacetime. One by one, many of the best chemistry students were called up.

In London, The Royal Society, at the request of its war committee and in support of the government, drew up a list of British pure chemical research institutes, among which was Irvine's research department at St Andrews.[3] In this way St Andrews commenced its co-operation with the War Office Department of Supplies.[4] Without hesitation Irvine offered all the facilities of his modern chemical research laboratory to the war effort. This meant suspending the programme of his school of sugars research, his life's ambition, and substituting in its place the demands of the War Office. His was an outstandingly well-equipped laboratory: Purdie's endowment and Irvine's persuasiveness with the Carnegie trustees had seen to that. It was staffed by eager young scientists, all keen to obtain the training and experience that Irvine offered. All were offered up to serve the needs of the war with Germany. Ironically, only a couple of years previously over £200-worth of new apparatus had been bought for the St Andrews Chemical Research Institute, and much of it was ordered from the catalogue of a German supplier.[5]

During those halcyon five years of Irvine's professorship before the outbreak of war, St Andrews continued to consolidate its growing reputation as a science university. In 1912 the British Association for the Advancement of Science met in Dundee and St Andrews, and the delegates were taken to visit Glamis. At thirty-five years of age, Jim Irvine still looked no more than a boy. 'You don't want to go round with all those old fogies! do you? I'll show you round,' offered a young girl with a merry face. Jim Irvine began a friendship with Lady Elizabeth Bowes-Lyon, who would one day be King George VI's consort: a friendship to last all his life.[6]

Throughout this time, Irvine struggled to staff his popular department. Although there was no financial provision for additional departmental staffing in pre-war St Andrews, he attempted to solve the problem by giving teaching responsibilities to his most promising research students, all young men and women whom he could regard with pride as highly trained chemists. He sought out scholarships and bursaries with which to pay them. He was noticeably successful in laying claim to more than his fair share of Carnegie teaching fellowships and Berry Awards for his protégés; the number held by women noticeably increased as the war progressed. This trained and very adaptable team proved a great advantage when it came to war operations in the chemistry research department.

Professor Irvine returned to his department to commence the Martinmas term of 1914 with the obligation to maintain undergraduate course teaching. If the somewhat breathless tone of the student magazine *College Echoes* is to be believed, he continued his undergraduate teaching throughout the period of the war with his accustomed verve. 'Even his tutorial classes in the summer term, which he jocularly referred to as a "refuge for the destitute"', came to be described as 'thoroughly enjoyable'. Above all, he had to keep his research team in readiness for government instruction.

The government instruction that soon came was surprisingly apposite. During the first weeks of the summer vacation of 1914, Jim had become fascinated by a compound which was registered pharmaceutically in Germany as dulcitol; it fell into a rare group of sugars, and this may have been what initially attracted him, as Irvine's own speciality lay with the more complex sugars. For some reason, perhaps even lying within his subconscious, he was fascinated by the fact that British research in the sugars required for pharmaceutical medicine fell woefully behind German knowledge. Jim even cut short a holiday with his family at the beginning of the summer vacation of 1914 to rush back to St Andrews and pursue this engrossing private research during the fateful summer in which war broke out between Britain and Germany.[7]

The first requirement that the British government, through the agency of the Royal Society, sent to St Andrews was for this same product, dulcitol, to serve the Navy and Army Medical Service in the field hospitals. Dulcitol is actually a sugar needed in diagnostic bacteriology to identify strepto-coccus typhii, the bacterium that causes typhoid. Germany, always a leader in pharmaceutical manufacturing, was the chief producer of this drug. Suddenly dulcitol, which had been manufactured from the now-unobtain-able raw material of Madagascan manna, sprang into a position of first importance, and the search was under way for British research laboratories that could commence making its synthetic form.

Initially and irresponsibly, the government made light of the shortages. Dulcitol was brought to the attention of the War Office Department of Supplies more by force of economics than by any real appreciation of the effect of the pitiful absence of bacteriological medicine at the front. By the beginning of 1915, a statement was made that 'the War Office is at its wits' end for further supplies'.[8] Shortly after the outbreak of war, dulcitol became exceedingly scarce and, at the close of 1914, it was practically unobtain-able and the price consequently soared: from 65 shillings per ounce in July 1914 to 300 shillings in January 1915. Within a few weeks dulcitol was being sought all over the world. Even a few grammes of the compound were in great demand, and the cost of one ounce rose to £920 sterling. Allied forces were calling for supplies of dulcitol at the rate of 5 lb in weight per week.[9]

The synthetic approach to making dulcitol required taking the prepara-tion back to lactose (milk sugar). It was Irvine's hero, Emil Fischer, who had first synthesised it in Germany, but he had only obtained less than one-fiftieth of an ounce. The collaboration between Irvine and Fischer's laboratory, which had been Fischer's suggestion, was now not possible. Because the chemistry of sugars was already a special feature of the research carried out in the St Andrews laboratories, trained workers were available who were thoroughly familiar with the techniques necessary for experi-mental work of this nature. The ordinary fittings of the research labora-tory were dismantled and large-scale apparatus installed in order to cope with the work. A number of unskilled workers were admitted and, under the supervision of research graduates, they mastered the more mechanical stages of the process. In the course of the first ten weeks, over 1 cwt of milk sugar was converted into dulcitol. This satisfied the requirements of the government for the time being.[10] A leader in the *Daily News* (26 December 1914) reflected that the remarkable response of the universities to the drugs crisis may 'increase materially the respect of the practical business man for the theorist cloistered among his retorts and test tubes'.

After an interval of five weeks, during which the laboratory was engaged on other government work, Irvine was required to recommence production, and the preparation of large quantities of pure dulcitol was resumed in October 1915. This time the scale of working was increased, and about one-fifth of a ton of milk sugar was converted into dulcitol in the course of five weeks. 'What a peculiar sight the lab must be from what I hear. Men, women and children (or is that an exaggeration?) working on compounds,' wrote a former student from an unstated address in northern France.[11] Students of all disciplines who were not called up and who were left behind at their undergraduate studies were begged to give up their vacations and leisure time. There were no vacations taken in the laboratory; work continued on Sundays. The untrained workers, for the most part, were drawn from the homes, offices and shops of the tiny provincial town. Many were women of the type of 'golfing-girl' that before the war Irvine had despised, and they stood at the benches for eight to ten hours daily in an atmosphere reeking of boiling acetic acid. Many of these 'laboratory assistants' contracted skin disorders, but with enthusiasm they kept pace with the growing demand and the need for speed. Uncomplainingly, they put up with the physical dangers of their work.

In addition to supplying the War Office, it was found possible to deliver all the material required by the Lister Institute and several public health authorities. Irvine's band of chemists was successful in providing not only a substitute for dulcitol, but actually 'the same compound, identical in every respect' (according to Irvine) to the natural drug. The final cost of the synthetic product, of which nearly half a ton was prepared in St Andrews, was considerably less than the pre-war rate for German dulcitol. Irvine's account of his research team's remarkable achievement in responding to the British government's first SOS demonstrates most vividly how he had long learned to suspect the German mind, and how pleased he was to beat them at their own game. 'I don't wish to romance,' he later said, 'I know there were many factors which dictated the date of the great war, but I shall never have the conviction removed from my mind that one of the factors was that Germany believed that the British Empire would be unable to provide this bacteriological sugar on which the troops would so largely depend.'[12]

Irvine, let us remember, had been a student in Leipzig during the years of the Boer War. He had absorbed far more than the experience offered by the narrow pursuit of his thesis while he was a student in a German research laboratory. He felt strongly that the hardest lesson that the British government should have learned from the tragic loss of life in the South African campaigns was that more men died from typhoid and other fevers than from shells or bullets. It appeared, in November 1914, that the British government had not learned from that bitter experience.

Irvine, no more than all his colleagues in the research chemical institutes of Great Britain, was caught up in the increasing need for other sugars. What differentiated him from some others, perhaps, were his energy and creative imagination. As the fighting spread to the Near East, so the British forces were exposed to the new dangers of the treacherous climate and infected swamps of Mesopotamia. Many complex bacteriological sugars were needed to combat these serious threats to health. In response to the request of the National Health Commission, Irvine was asked to take up the preparation of fructose and inulin in the autumn of 1915. At this same date, it was resolved by the Royal Society that, as Irvine's reports were so arresting, they should all be printed and circulated.[13]

Fructose, a particularly fickle substance, may be prepared from cane sugar, but not in a sufficiently pure condition for medical use. There was only one source for pure medicinal fructose, and that was inulin. Irvine suspected that a natural source of inulin was to be found in the fibres of the dahlia. He finally set about manufacturing the precious substance in large quantities from dahlia tubers, sent to him by parcel post from all over the British Isles in response to an advertisement in the national press. The boy scouts were commandeered to collect the old dahlias being dug up from their summer displays. Municipal parks and botanical gardens all made their contributions. A deluge came from all the private gardeners who in time of peace had so proudly cultivated these gorgeous blooms.[14]

A source of amusement at the Irvines' breakfast table was found in Jim's daily post: letters from ladies and head gardeners whose dahlias had won prizes that summer, asking if these precious strains might not be of more value to the war work than common or garden dahlias that had not won prizes. And would double dahlias be more efficacious than single? How could these good people be adequately thanked for their sacrifice, when all were sent indiscriminately into the mincing pot? These were but the first steps towards the almost industrial proportions of bacteriological and biological substances that Irvine's St Andrews laboratory contributed to the nation's need. He encapsulated the value of his work when, looking back, he wrote: 'In the summer of 1916 there were fewer dahlias in the gardens of England and other parts of Great Britain, but at the same time there were

PLATE 1. *Above*. The Irvine family's weaver's cottage at Ladycross, near Maybole, Ayrshire. The Irvines were yeomen farmers as well as weavers of fine cotton. James Irvine's father was born in this cottage in 1846.

PLATE 2. *Left*. Mary Paton Colquhoun Irvine (1851–1923), James Colquhoun Irvine's mother. This portrait was taken at the time of her marriage in 1874.

PLATE 3. *Above left.* James Colquhoun Irvine, aged three years.

PLATE 4. *Above right.* James Irvine at the Free Church Normal School, aged seven years. His father was a prominent member of the Free Church of Scotland and sent both his sons to this pioneering school in the Cowcaddens district of Glasgow.

PLATE 5. *Right.* James's father, John Irvine, in the garden of Heathfield, with James's brother Alec on the left. John Irvine (1846–1926), engineering draughtsman and ironfounder's clerk, was an amateur horticulturalist.

PLATE 6. *Left.* Springburn Harriers in the early 1890s. James seated right, with Alec Irvine standing right. Alec, who was two and a half years older than James, persuaded his brother to take up cross-country running.

PLATE 7. *Below left.* James at the time of his departure from Glasgow in October 1899 to study in Leipzig under the chemist Wislicenus, as an 1851 Exhibition scholar.

PLATE 8. *Below right.* The microscope used in the St Andrews Chemical Research Institute by James Colquhoun Irvine.

PLATE 9. Mabel Violet Williams, before her departure (1899) from Belfast to study violin and piano in Leipzig. Her violin was a Vinaccia, bought from Hills and made in the late eighteenth century in the Neapolitan workshop of the Vinaccias.

PLATE 10. Mabel Violet Williams c.1900, as she was when 'Jim' first fell in love with her.

PLATE 11. Irvine (left) in the Erste Institut für Chemie in Leipzig. It was in this laboratory that the experimental side of his German PhD was conducted.

PLATE 12. James Colquhoun Irvine, DSc St Andrews, March 1903. The St Andrews DSc was senior to the German PhD. Mabel described his DSc gown as being of 'amaranth' silk.

PLATE 13. James Irvine (1904), when appointed to a lectureship in Chemistry in St Andrews.

PLATE 14. Irvine (left) with Professor Purdie in the new Chemistry Research Laboratory, St Andrews, c. 1905. The Purdie bequest from Professor Purdie's aunt and uncle made possible the development of the outstanding chemistry buildings that served the university for over fifty years.

PLATE 15. Irvine, 1909, at the time of his induction to the Chair of Chemistry in St Andrews.

PLATE 16. Jim and Mabel's wedding day, 28 June 1905. The wedding party is seated outside Dunmurry House, County Antrim. In the back row can be seen James's father, talking to the Minister. On Mabel's right is her father, and her mother is on Jim's left.

PLATE 17. Edgecliffe (right) viewed from the roof of the chemistry laboratory, St Andrews. It was from this roof that Mabel, a young bride, watched the Carnegie rectorial festivities in October 1905. Jim and Mabel bought Edgecliffe in 1913.

PLATE 18. St Andrews chemical workers during the First World War, including many of the previously untrained workers: women of St Andrews who volunteered to work in the laboratory. Professor Irvine is bottom centre.

PLATE 19. Playing with Veronica and Nigel, Jim and Mabel's elder children, in the garden at Edgecliffe.

PLATE 20. *Above.* Alison Russell (left), wife of David Russell of Tullis Russell of Markinch, with Mabel and Jim on holiday in Glen Urquhart 1918. David Russell, and his son after him, was a generous benefactor to St Andrews University.

PLATE 21. *Left.* Jim and Mabel – tennis doubles partners c.1922. Jim was President of the University Tennis Club for many years, and both he and Mabel were keen players; they represented the university in doubles championship matches.

PLATE 22. Veronica, Nigel, their parents and J.M. Barrie in May 1922. The other man in the picture is Dr William Low, the Rector's Assessor when Barrie was Rector.

PLATE 23. Mabel Irvine, J.M. Barrie and Felicity – the 'Hip, hip hooay Baby'. On receiving the Freedom of St Andrews, Barrie described Felicity as 'the most remarkable woman in St Andrews' for having been coached to say 'Hip, hip hooay', and the London newspapers picked this up.

PLATE 24. Principal Irvine with J.M. Barrie and Haig. Barrie was installed as Rector of St Andrews on 3 May 1922 and Field-Marshal Earl Haig was installed as Chancellor on the same day.

PLATE 25. Ellen Terry and Squire Bancroft in the garden of University House, 1922. Ellen Terry, the actress, and Squire Bancroft, the actor-manager, received honorary degrees from St Andrews University at J.M. Barrie's rectorial installation.

PLATE 26. *Above*. The Prince of Wales receives the Honorary LLD of St Andrews, September 1922. The Prince was in St Andrews to play himself in as Captain of the Royal and Ancient Golf Club, and the university took advantage of the occasion to give him a degree.

PLATE 27. *Right*. The two cousins, Baldwin and Kipling, with Irvine, October 1923. Stanley Baldwin and Rudyard Kipling's mothers were sisters, and when Kipling was installed as Rector of St Andrews, Stanley Baldwin, recently made Prime Minister, received an honorary degree.

fewer victims of meningitis and other deadly troubles.' Meningitis was the scourge of the campaigns in Asia Minor, and could have killed more men than were killed under enemy fire.[15]

In June 1915, before the St Andrews team was asked to intensify their production of dulcitol, a new demand came their way. Movingly, this urgent need was for 'novocain', a well-known local anaesthetic in general use today.[16] The synthesis of novocain is a complex operation: seven different compounds had to be prepared on a large scale, and for this over sixty workers were engaged for a period of three months – from the middle of June to the end of September 1915. Many of those employed this time were old students and graduates of the university, now engaged in teaching, who gave up their summer vacation for this purpose. In addition, about two dozen untrained workers, not directly connected with the university, once again volunteered their services. The professor fought to obtain some financial compensation for them; he claimed class grants two and three times the size of any other department. He ensured that call-up papers for his students were delayed until they had taken their final examinations.[17]

Jim's modern research department, with its well-equipped bench room for eighteen advanced students, must have been distinctly crowded. It was an almost 'Boys' Own' operation using 7 lb jam jars, and for which he invented a number of ingenious additions to the facilities of the chemistry department, notably the 'shaking shed' for the large-scale coagulation of his material. One of Jim's advanced research chemists was a young woman, Ettie Steele, whose career in St Andrews had commenced in the botany department; her work was largely instrumental in obtaining the synthesis of novocain.[18] In later years, she became Irvine's devoted personal secretary throughout his principalship of the university. The success of the whole operation, however, owed everything to Irvine's great organisational ability, sustained concentration, and a remarkable ingenuity of thought and technique, all qualities recognised by Purdie when he put Jim forward for a Carnegie fellowship in 1903.

Behind the sombre facades of St Andrews' streets, most of the townspeople must have known something of what was going on, and yet the utmost secrecy was maintained and the old grey town closed ranks against the outside world: this was war-time. Occasionally, a student rag could not resist an oblique comment, and in December 1915 the *College Echoes* Christmas editorial contains this snippet:

This is not the place for details, but we think it only fair that the splendid services rendered, and being rendered, by [the chemistry laboratory] to the government should be brought before the notice of all cives.[19] During the past summer, and ever since, the war work has gone on unceasingly, and the output of the material required has been so great and continuous that St Andrews laboratory has created in this line a record created by no other scientific institution in the country. This is something we can all feel justly proud of, and if any student finds he can spare several hours per diem, he ought to offer at least his services to the science department.

In return, Professor Irvine offered to his workers something of the atmosphere of an elite club. Some light relief from war was found for those suffering the heat and dangers of the chemistry laboratory. Encouraged by the fine autumn weather of 1915, Jim Irvine's wartime frivolities stretched to picnic parties for the chemical staff out on the cliffs,[20] and tennis matches on the courts just beside the laboratory. These were particularly good courts, maintained by the University Tennis Club, whose President was Professor Irvine; and the professor, rather a good player himself, saw to it that there was money from the university to have the tennis lawns kept free of weeds. The exhausted workers of the laboratory, in need of some fun, could claim preferential order in booking the courts. The professor brought a gramophone into the laboratory, and soon strains of the latest hits, including 'If You Were the Only Girl (in the World)', written in 1916, could be heard drifting over the college.

Rather daringly, in March 1917 the St Andrews University Missionary Association brought the chemistry department into the public eye under the guise of a dramatic entertainment featuring a newly written play, *In the Shadow of the Tower*. The play took as its subject the chemistry research laboratory's current wartime activities, presented in a sentimental way as seen through the eyes of a modern female blue-stocking and her old-fashioned aunt. Cameo parts were played by Mabel Irvine and Dr Haworth, Jim's colleague in the department.

Mabel found life as a university wife in the little town quite stifling, and towards the end of the war a holiday with Jim's friends, the Kerfoots, chemical industrialists in Cheshire, provided her with a break from St Andrews and a glimpse of the wider world. With Margaret Kerfoot, she took up her musical studies again, finding in this considerable personal development as a musician and composer of lyrical works. The war effort gave her opportunities to use her talents, and one of these was musical composition. In 1917 her *Fairy Opera* for children was performed to raise funds to provide comforts for the troops. Veronica, Mabel and Jim's eldest child, now aged six, played a leading role. The musical play itself was well reviewed, with thought of a London publisher, and it certainly gave a taste for the stage to Veronica who, when she was grown up, entered RADA.

Jim's students had often enjoyed the welcome that Mrs Irvine extended at the comfortable family home just across the road from the laboratory. Seated at her piano, playing to all who cared to listen, she was often 'at home' to Jim's devoted department. Four-year-old Nigel could be relied on to make people laugh. He play-acted the scenes around him: 'Here's a soldier home on leave from the Front with all his paraffin-oilia.'[21] To play with the two bonny Irvine children was a delight to the hard-working students, removed for a space of time from their own families. In fact, they soon discovered that Professor Irvine liked nothing better than to be 'one of the boys'. Their 'prof' was bound to these young people through loyalty and empathy. The special relationship that James Irvine had so much enjoyed with his professors was reversed: although now the revered *meister*, he was young, and he drew each and every one of them, with a pretence at equality, into a great chemical collaboration. It was soon apparent that Professor Irvine put his students centre stage, a practice that would inform the guiding policies of his subsequent career as Principal of the university.

One by one, posted to the Argylls, the Gordon Highlanders, the Black Watch or the Cameronians, his boys left him for the war. The Highland Brigade was in the thick of it during the Battle of the Somme. With nonchalance his old pupil, Charles Soutar, described for him the taking of Eaucourt l'Abbaye: 'The field was absolutely covered with Bosche [sic] souvenirs such as helmets, caps, machine guns, prismatic compasses, automatic pistols and thousands of unexploded shells . . . there were thousands of dead lying in the open.'

An example of how intimately the fate of those who did not come home was felt in the Irvine household is to be found in James Mackay, who came from Mabel Irvine's home city, and had been quite adopted by the family. His professor had fortunately urged him to take his BSc the summer before the outbreak of war. He fell at the Battle of Ypres, and the tragedy of his death was made known to the professor by telegram, as if Jim Irvine really were an elder brother.

The chemistry professor conducted a remarkable correspondence with them all. They never ceased to be chemists in his eyes; if they needed to brush up a bit before the day came when they could return to St Andrews, he sent chemistry textbooks to the front. One kept a photograph of his professor with him in the trenches, and mused that if he needed cheering up, he imagined he was back once more in the dear old chemistry laboratory overlooking the North Sea, exploring some new adventure with the prof.

Halfway through these years, Jim Irvine and the whole university community suffered the death of Thomas Purdie. His funeral took place in College Chapel on 16 December 1916, and much tribute was paid to the genius of his life's work and the generosity of his endowments to the university. With the death of his mentor, Jim felt alone and exposed, but proud to succeed him as leader. To his close friend David Russell, the paper magnate of Tullis Russell mills, Jim wrote of his deep sorrow at the loss of 'my esteemed friend Professor Purdie who was my scientific father and inspiration of all that I have done'.[22] His professor left, as a bequest to him, his signature as chief sponsor of Irvine's eventual election to the Royal Society.

By September 1917 an official report on St Andrews' chemical contribution to the war had been sent to London. It bears no signature: all St Andrews' war work was to be anonymous, but internal evidence coupled with some small hand-corrections tells us that it was written by Irvine, and Irvine left a copy with the secretary of the university:

> The work was divided into ten departments, which were under the supervision of trained research chemists. Each worker was drilled in the special operations required in his department and, as the different stages of preparation had to be dovetailed into one another, the time-table of each person in the laboratory had to be adjusted with the utmost care. The results justified the experiment of entrusting some of the preparations to untrained workers as they quickly mastered the technique of the processes, but, in order to keep to the required programme, it was necessary in two instances to triplicate the work of departments by running three eight-hour shifts in the day.[23]

What he does not say is that this production line was at all hours and at all times dependent on his own administrative skills and sense of responsibility, and on his very able lecturer, W.N. Haworth, promoted to the position of reader in chemistry in November 1915. The professor himself carried out the final stage in the making of any one product. It was groundbreaking work, for all these substances had to be produced *ab initio*.

A detail that illustrates the extent to which Irvine was emerging as a first-rate business administrator is to be found in the persistent way that he wrote to the Royal Society to ask if any of the authorities had thought of the need for employers' liability insurance to protect the workers in all of these university laboratories. Irvine was the only one who had picked up on this need, perhaps because in St Andrews the question was particularly alarming due to the number of unskilled workers that he used. At first Irvine's point was met with resistance by the government, which was not eager to commit money to this, but eventually his demands were too compelling to resist. In May 1917 he asked, via the Royal Society, for permission to take out provisional protection for processes connected with the production of dimethyl and diethyl sulphates. Late in the day, the National Health Insurance Commission set up policies for the employment of chemical war workers.[24]

Soon, news of the relief brought by novocain came back to St Andrews from France. A St Andrews chemistry student wrote:

My brother, who joined the Chemical section of the RE, has been moved to a V.A.D. Hospital. I called to see him in hospital and he informed me that the stuff they used to kill the pain during an injection was some kind of chemical they had prepared at St Andrews.[25]

Professor Irvine's report to the War Office describes some of the innovative processes developed at St Andrews. War, the mother of invention, had certainly provided a challenge to St Andrews, and Irvine was proud to pick up the gauntlet.

At the end of the summer over 20 kilogrammes of the compound known as Diethylaminoethanol, all the materials for which had been prepared in the laboratory, were handed over to the Government at cost price. In the course of the work a new process was devised for preparing one of the constituents of Novocain. As this method is not only much quicker but is also more economical than those hitherto available, it has been adopted as the standard method to be employed in the preparation of Novocain for Government use, and the St Andrews University has been entrusted with the supply of the whole of this constituent. This preparation was accordingly resumed in October 1915 and regular consignments of 12 kilos monthly are sent off.

The general principle adopted in the laboratory has been to use the research chemists to work out the details of each process and thereafter to instruct the others in the manipulations. As during the current session the services of eleven research scholars and fellows were at our disposal it has been possible to keep about 25 untrained workers fully occupied and at the same time to undertake the investigation of new problems. Of these may be mentioned the various steps necessary for the synthesis of the drug known as 'orthoform new', the preparation of pure lactic acid, and of the bacteriological sugars, glucose, galactose, and sorbitol.[26]

The government found in St Andrews a specialist resource of enormous competence to which they turned increasingly. This was far-reaching work that informed commercial pharmaceutical science in the United Kingdom in the years after the war, and ensured that Great Britain could be, even in peacetime, self-supporting to a far greater extent than ever before.

Throughout 1916 and 1917 the little 'chemical factory' on the Scores in St Andrews, co-operating with the National Health Commission, produced supplies of numerous substances in addition to dulcitol and novocain, as well as providing methylating and ethylating agents for other laboratories: for this latter service, Irvine and Haworth were marked out for special commendation by the authorities in London. They made mannitol (a diuretic drug in frequent use in hospitals). The Royal Society recorded the fact that Irvine's laboratory was the exclusive supplier of not only dulcitol and inulin, but also fructose – known as levulose (8½ lbs) in the official minutes – and the disaccharide maltose (which had to be made from potato starch). Other sugars could be extracted from bladderwrack, the seaweed native to those shores, and there were expeditions out to the sands and the rocks to collect this now precious resource. The Food Controller, who seemed to care more about civilian food stocks than the lack of medical supplies for the soldier, only grudgingly released the potatoes required by the ingenious professor of chemistry.[27]

Having already built up some familiarity with the industrial chemists, who were all eager to get in on the processes devised in St Andrews, by the end of 1915 Irvine was ready to move on to the second stage of his undertaking: instructing pharmaceutical manufacturers in the processes developed in St Andrews. Information was sent to Boots, the Abbey Chemical Company, Messrs Burroughs, and the Wellcome Company. The north-west family firm of Kerfoot took over the manufacture of novocain under the trade name Kerocain.[28] This work extended throughout the whole period of hostilities, and Jim was able to introduce several improvements into the processes undertaken in the Kerfoot factory. Ernest Kerfoot and his family developed an enduring friendship with the Irvines, and Messrs Kerfoot continued to play a useful part in the relationship between university and industry long after the war ended. For the duration of the war, Jim Irvine lived in the parallel worlds of the academic chemist and the industrial chemist, and amongst these last he was delighted to find once more several of his old Leipzig chums, notably E.C.B. Wilbraham, whom he had last seen at Wislicenus' research bench in another life.

The connection with industry corresponded with the Royal Society's plea in May 1915 to the boards of Trade and Education to offer government support for the establishment of closer relations between the triumvirate of manufacturers, scientific workers and scientific teachers. The Royal Society was playing its part in a movement that led to the establishment of the Department of Scientific and Industrial Research in 1916.[29] It quickly became apparent that there was an abysmal lack of communication between the government scientific agencies on the one hand, and the research laboratories of both the universities and industry, where advanced work on chemical products was being pushed forward to serve the war effort. Irvine, with his instinct for business practice and his training in a German research institute, found himself caught up in a movement to unify Britain's scientific capability. In Germany the technical institutes, such as that at Charlottenburg in Berlin, had long provided a concentration of industrial research for many important products, thus placing Germany in the lead. In wartime Britain, the pressure to modernise was on, with demands from organisations such as the Paper Makers Association, for the government to make a forward move into establishing what became the Department for Scientific and Industrial Research. It was significant to Irvine's future career that between 1914 and 1918 he acquired a reputation in London for scientific administration and vision. These were not lost years for him.

In the shadowy, secretive world of wartime Whitehall, Irvine became used to receiving summonses to serve a large spectrum of needs, the most curious of which was to interview a brilliant American chemist, Captain Matthews, who had been detained on suspicion of being a spy. Irvine was able to reassure the authorities of Matthews' bona fides as a scientist pursuing wartime work in the US Quartermaster department, and thus he secured his release.

Work not directly related to carbohydrates, beginning with investigations concerning acetone, came to Irvine as his reputation for speed
and ingenuity grew. His association with munitions work came into his
life during the time that his laboratory was making its investigation into
novocain. In his capacity as adviser to the Department of Propellant
Supplies, he was responsible for a series of researches on the manufacture
of acetone used in making cordite. During these visits to London, Lord
Moulton, the director-general of the Explosives Department, slowly drew
Irvine in to working for the proactive aspect of the British war effort: the
manufacture of explosives materials, and then the very gases that the shells
dispersed. Penetrating the bombed oases of the east of London and the
blacked-out Hertfordshire hinterland, he visited factories in search of those
who would make chlorhydrin for him.

In August 1915, Charles Yule, one of Irvine's soldier students, received a
long list of asphyxiating gases from his prof, whose instruction on gases was
found to be far more informative than the rather footling trench instruction in gas warfare that the army gave to Yule and his companions. More
than this, the professor devised a little private line of research for each of
his former students: he asked them, for example, to obtain observations
on the Germans' use of gas. It was in April 1915 that the Royal Society first
brought to the discussion table the Germans' use of poisonous gas. The use
of poisonous gas explosives contravened the Hague Convention of 1907,
which both Germany and Great Britain had signed, Britain reserving the
right to inflict reprisals on any signatory that broke the convention. Irvine,
keeping ahead of the game and already advising the Royal Society on the
progress of his drugs production, thought he could play a part in defeating
the new and deadly hazard of chemical warfare. The information that
reached St Andrews from the front had an immediacy and an air of reality
that no government report would convey.

James Mitchell, who did his best to send snippets of chemical interest
back to St Andrews, described a 'gas course' in the field:

> We have had no experience of 'hostile' gases yet but I, personally
> have encountered gas. I, along with four other officers, attended a
> demonstration. A trench was filled with a mixture of Chlorine and
> Sulphur Dioxide. We fixed on our smoke helmets and walked along
> the trench. The helmets were very efficient. By putting my mouth
> close to the nozzle of the cylinder I felt a slight taste of chlorine in my
> mouth. As far as I can make out the respirators and smoke helmets

are moistened in 'Glycerine' and a solution of 'hypo'.

There are several helmets and appliances in use which are all very good. We saw a Bosche smoke helmet. It is made of rubber with goggles and mouthpiece. Chemicals are held in a pepperbox nozzle through which the Bosche breathes in and out.

The German goggles have eyepieces made of a singularily [sic] hard sort of mica. It is very difficult to break and does not get moist when breathed upon.[30]

Irvine had an interest in the respirators, the design of which had constantly to be improved. By 1917, Colonel Harrison, a consultant chemist in peacetime, had developed a gas mask so successful that it was hoped it could turn the war. The St Andrews physiologist Percy Herring, and the chemist James Irvine, gave significant assistance towards the design of the Harrison respirator, and Irvine's rather unorthodox sourcing of information from his students was useful, and never frivolous.

James Macdonald, son of a St Andrews doctor, who graduated BSc in 1911, was held in particular affection by Mabel and Jim, and he wrote back in the style of an old friend.

There is just one little incident that will interest you. One night some little time ago I had just made my report about midnight to my Brigadier in a dug out in a village that has been mentioned plenty during the past month when Mr Bosche opened what one might call a 'silent bombardment' – at least it was silent by comparison with the normal. Suddenly not 100s but 1000s of small shells whizzed over the village – whence they came & whence they were going it was difficult to say. My way lay through the remains of the village and a mile or so down a valley. When I reached the outskirts of the village the mystery of the shells was solved: they formed a barrage down the valley – and were apparently all 'duds' – at once I concluded 'gas' – and as no lachrymatory effect was apparent I concluded them to be asphyxiants – which proved to be the case. Anyhow they were coming so thick that I thought it as well to wait until they stopped, so I sat down against a steep bank about 10 ft high and waited about forty minutes when HE coming along made the place rather too hot so there was nothing to do but risk the barrage which we – myself & another officer did. There was a moon by this time and the whole valley seemed to be and in fact was 'alive' with falling shells.[31]

Both Charles Soutar and James Macdonald survived the war, and were collaborators of Irvine's in several published chemical papers.

The professor looked out for postings within the British Expeditionary Force (BEF) that would allow his students to use their chemistry, and he searched for possible forms of employment for them once the war was over. James Mitchell heard 'that you had forwarded my name for work with dyes. I could hardly believe it, as I have thought of that work for a long time now'.[32] The wounded kept up their letter writing from the hospitals for officers in Mayfair, which were run by society ladies. All longed for the day when they could return to St Andrews.

For the professor of chemistry, St Andrews was not by any means the safe, otherworldly place that his soldier students liked fondly to imagine. Irvine, not yet himself an FRS, was starting to command considerable respect among the chemical grandees on the Royal Society's war committee. Drugs were not the only chemical substance that the War Office came to require from Irvine. The gases of varying degrees of toxicity that characterised the war were creating vexatious demands of the chemists working in the research institutes. As early as the summer of 1916, Irvine had thrown himself into further technical chemistry at Kerfoot's laboratory, and oversaw the industrial production of ethylene, a key component in some chemical warfare. That most mild-mannered of chemists, Thomas Purdie, in his last letter to his disciple, expressed deep admiration for Irvine's ability. 'To me who have never made C_2H_4 except for the lecture table, it seems indeed miraculous to turn out 200 gallons per hour, and 1½ cwt of chlorhydrin sounds like Lloyd George's accounts of the national output of munitions.'[33]

Just when it was thought that the fortunes of the British Expeditionary Force had taken a turn for the better, on the night of 12–13 July 1917, a new shell was released on the Fifth Army front at Ypres. It was not strictly speaking a gas shell: it contained a yellow oily substance that wormed its way into the soldiers' clothing and onto their skin; it attached itself to their heads, faces and eyes. Two unexploded shells of this new danger were secured on 14 July from the battlefield. One was sent to St Andrews for its unidentified contents to be analysed by Irvine. Irvine's approach to his chemistry was not narrow: it had always had something inclusive, even philosophical, about it. This shell was supposed to be extremely dangerous, and possibly lethal. Perhaps it was not mere curiosity, then, that had prompted him to ask his students to observe the nature and effect of the German use of gas. The term 'gas' in chemical warfare is a misnomer: chemical warfare is only gas warfare in the sense that the toxic or irritant chemicals within a shell are carried by the atmosphere once the shell has been caused to explode.

The shells released at Ypres in July 1917 became an infamous aspect of the war; they contained what was known as 'mustard gas'. It formed horrendous blisters, and caused blindness. It inflicted great pain, and was the cause of a new wave of severe casualties: more casualties than from any other cause, although the number of fatalities it inflicted was comparatively low. Both sides at this point in the war resorted to the use of strategic devices, such as smoke screens, and inflicting casualties by any means available. In releasing mustard gas, the German strategists played a clever game. The imposition of such a large scale of casualties at this point in the war was more damaging to the capability of the British fighting force than the fatalities, because with mustard gas every casualty required evacuation. At Armentières, which was deluged with mustard gas by the Germans, the BEF had to withdraw immediately.

On a Sunday morning two days after the event at Ypres, when the rest of St Andrews was safely in church, Irvine opened the specimen shell, using gauntlets and goggles. Only a doctor and Irvine's wife waited anxiously, and at a distance, in the street outside. He identified the contents, worked out how the Germans had made it, and then devised a process for its manufacture, all within a matter of months. He wrote in his notes: 'We pulled ourselves around this time. Mustard gas – and better. A great triumph for Allies to do this so quickly. Germany beaten at her own game.'[34] The other unexploded shell of mustard gas was sent to Professor Morgan at Finsbury Technical College for analysis.[35] The commander-in-chief of the British Expeditionary Force, Douglas Haig, who was a keen golfer and had been elected Rector of St Andrews in 1916, was surprised to hear that the latest toxic shells sent out to him came from anywhere so innocent as the home of golf, but he lost no time in writing directly to Irvine: 'I wish to obtain a shell filling equal to and if possible superior to that used by the enemy.'[36]

Mustard gas had, of course, been known for a period of at least twenty years, but so far the allies knew of no large-scale production method suitable for use outside the university laboratory. Irvine's private memorandum on his mustard gas was characteristically optimistic, and at first he followed the method of French physiologist Victor Meyer, but this only produced low yields. In September 1917 Irvine's report to Captain Basil Williams at the War Ministry contains the following oblique reference to this top-secret work: 'In addition, a series of investigations are now in progress which are being carried out on behalf of the Ministry of Munitions but the nature of these inquiries cannot be specified at present.'[37]

An industrial process was required for the production of this obscure compound known to the organic chemist as dichloroethyl sulphide and, if adopted, mustard gas could be made in the factories that before the war had manufactured chlorine for the dye industry. The existing plant in these factories would require little alteration to begin their work in support of this new phase of the war. Irvine turned to F. Guthrie's approach and resorted to variants of Meyer's work. He issued seventy reports to the Chemical Advisory Committee between August and December 1917, but even the impressive three-pronged activities of Pope in Cambridge, Baker in London and Irvine in St Andrews were slow to get results. The chemists at Imperial College recommended the thiodiglycol method of manufacture, but this took too long, and there were grave problems with obtaining manufacturing plant suitable for making it in very great quantities. General Thuillier's letter to Irvine early in 1918 gives some idea of the world of the vast chemical industries that Irvine had entered. The Castner-Kellner Company at Runcorn were peacetime producers of alkali chemicals, and had already been harnessed to produce chlorine for British gas shells. Now, it was to be chlorhydrin, and then mustard gas:

> I was at Castners on Thursday, and they have constructed quite a fair sized plant, with two brick tanks about 100 cubic feet capacity, and their Dr Howarth [as distinct from Dr W.N. Haworth, lecturer in St Andrews] is quite sure the plant will produce chlorhydrin. This, of course, is in accordance with the arrangements made at our general meeting at Castners in November, when each contractor was to do what he thought best, and get ahead but the shakers were to go in in any case, until we had found another method.[38]

There was a race on amongst the chemical giants to see who could produce the 'Hun Stuff' the most quickly and at the lowest cost. Like the boy athlete he had once been, Irvine showed that even at this game he was a sprinter; even Professor Pope and Professor Baker of Imperial College had to admit that the Irvine approach to obtaining the mustard gas was the best. From the Ministry of Munitions came this news: 'I dare say you have now heard of the apparently simultaneous discovery of Pope, Baker, two men at Manchester and one at Liverpool – of the possibility of making H. by SCL_2 using a charcoal catalyst. Naturally, there is much stir in the Professional dovecot! They wanted to stop all work on present plants and turn right over. We naturally gave a point blank refusal.'[39]

In her memoir of her husband, Mabel Irvine underlined the fact that this service to his country was morally repugnant to Irvine.[40] Lecturing on the subject in 1921 to the St Andrews Women's Citizen's Association, he stated that this was not happy work for a chemist, but he felt he had to embrace with his skills two essentials of warfare: protection of the troops and retaliation. He was of the opinion that not to retaliate would lead to surrender. At least he was reassured that the government now trusted him to play a very large part indeed in conquering the enemy and in protecting our troops.

It might be said that his chemical counterpart in Germany was a distinguished chemist of Swiss extraction, Fritz Haber, who had been working on the development of poisonous gas for over three years; he has been described as the father of chemical warfare. Haber, who was responsible for the first successful use of chlorine gas and then mustard gas at the second Battle of Ypres, did not share Irvine's scruples, but his wife, Frau Doktor Haber, was so appalled at this new distortion of science that she went out and shot herself in their garden with her husband's service weapon. Haber, on the other hand, exulted in what he could do, and personally oversaw the deployment of his gases at the front.

The British cabinet stuck to a moral high ground that the scientists felt lacked definition and was quite unworkable. 'Only gases were to be used which were as harmful, but not much more so, than those used by the enemy.' Haig, frustrated by the government's opposition to retaliation, called for more and yet more of Irvine's mustard gas shells. Irvine wrestled with his conscience. He saw Britain's great need, and also that he could supply something that might save the lives of thousands of troops – something that would shorten the war. He became tense and irritable, unhappy that the science he loved had to be turned to a use that went against any human ethical standard and was, in his mind, contrary to God's law. He retained in his pocket book a quotation from Charles Lamb: 'Alas! Can we ring the bells backwards? Can we unlearn the arts that pretend to civilise, and then burn the world? There is a march of science, but who will beat the drums for its retreat?'[41] Irvine, trying to preserve some secrecy in his correspondence with his friend, David Russell, refers to his latest gas as 'HS', or Hun Stuff. 'I am not surprised that Haig had never heard that HS comes from his own University. The quest for ribbons and KBEs is too keen for the London Ring to depart from their "official secrecy"', wrote Irvine defensively to Russell.[42]

Irvine could be excused for thinking that the award of gongs for the scientists was confined to the south of England. Professor Edward Thorpe's knighthood in 1917 caused the poor man enough embarrassment for him to write to Irvine: 'Everyone knows that without the wonderful work which you have initiated and carried through at St Andrews the general scheme would have been a failure.'[43] Thorpe was an inorganic chemist of the previous generation, and he held a government scientific post that had already enabled him to make a contribution to public health. Nevertheless, he had the imagination to acknowledge that scientists like Irvine, working with specialist knowledge and ingenuity at the laboratory bench, were the ones who were really doing the government's work.

While it has been said that the central organisation of wartime scientific research was conducted in France on rational lines and in Germany along strong, simple lines, the British Ministry of Munitions was notorious for quarrels and intrigues. Professor Pope complained that British chemical research 'is being run in the spirit of the little village publican doing his two barrels a week.'[44] Until July 1917, increasing chaos prevailed among many of the scientific advisory groups and the ministry that they were advising. No official liaison between the scientific advisory groups and the Special Brigade of the British Expeditionary Force was encouraged, despite the brigade's responsibility for the deployment and commissioning of gas shells. On July 16 1917 Lloyd George invited Winston Churchill to become minister of munitions, and a complete reconstruction of this department was put in hand. The events at Ypres shook the several British authorities deeply, and in September 1917 an advisory panel of twelve scientists was appointed by Winston Churchill's ministry to advise Porton Down and Imperial College, the two chief centres of the government's attempt to co-ordinate chemical warfare. Irvine was one of these scientists. They first met on 27 October, with General Thuillier at their head, a man whom Irvine learned to admire and confide in. Out of this motley group of civil servants and scientists, four men emerged to take the lead. They were all able administrators, bucking the trend of so many of the scientists of that time: the well-known Professor Pope from Cambridge, who had become incensed at the uselessness of the earlier Scientific Advisory Group; Harrison, the brilliant deviser of the respirator that had begun to turn the war around; A.W. Crossley, who since 1916 had been head of Porton; and James Colquhoun Irvine, the maverick young professor from that tiny university on the east coast of Scotland. This is the first recorded occasion on which Irvine learned to make his voice felt amongst those same entrenched but powerful committees that, as a university vice-chancellor, he would later seek to command.

When so many young men close to him – his brother-in-law, his students – were fighting in France, Irvine's munitions work gave him the pride of knowing that he too could engage with the enemy. Although secret to the outside world, this work brought him into the limelight in official circles and attracted the admiration of his senior colleagues in the Royal Society.

By Christmas, Professor Irvine, exhausted by overwork, had succumbed to the 1917 outbreak of influenza and was seriously ill. He was frequently absent from St Andrews throughout 1917 and 1918, briefing Brigadier General Thuillier, Controller of Chemical Warfare at the Ministry of Trench Warfare. What a little space of time had passed, Irvine felt, between the day when he made his first gramme of dulcitol and that day when he stood in a factory in the north-west of England listening to the thunder of 16,000 gallons of liquid glycol chlorhydrin being manipulated. He forged an important relationship with the Wilton Research Laboratories in Manchester, manufacturers in peacetime of synthetic dyes and other organic chemical products. Irvine's trump card was the speed with which he discovered methods of production that would cheaply and quickly respond to what was a desperate situation. Ironically, Fritz Haber received the Nobel Prize in 1918 for his work in devising the Haber process of producing nitrogen products such as fertiliser and explosives from hydrogen and atmospheric nitrogen. Haber's fortunes sank after the war. As a Jewish scientist, he was banished from Germany; many of his family were exterminated in the death camps. Hitler, who had been temporarily blinded by mustard gas at the front, wanted nothing more to do with the father of chemical warfare.

Irvine, on the other hand, prospered. In May 1918 he was elected FRS for his advancement of our knowledge of the carbohydrates, and for the pharmaceutical chemicals that he developed during the war. He was proposed by not only the late Professor Purdie, but by Pope, Frankland and Walker – all guests at the St Andrews quincentenary in 1911 – and, importantly for Irvine, by Professor Crossley, the chairman of the Chemical Sub-Committee of the Royal Society's war committee. On his citation, the Royal Society does not neglect his peacetime distinction as an organic chemist, but it is worth observing the names of some of his new wartime chemical colleagues amongst his proposers. A.W. Crossley knew better than most what Irvine had achieved, and there is the reference to chemical warfare: 'He has devised and practised successfully a new process for the manufacture of Glycol Chlorhydrin.'[45] In May 1918, the war was not yet over, and Irvine's wartime achievements were fresh in the minds of the more senior fellows of the Royal Society. A few months later, James Colquhoun Irvine was elected a fellow of the Royal Society of Edinburgh.

Those beyond St Andrews could only guess at the importance of the work, which was, as with all the chemical research at this time, conducted under the rules of war-work secrecy. The *Glasgow Herald* ran a paragraph in its 'War and Political Gossip' column, from London: 'Many weeks ago a munitions expert described to me various forms of concentrated horrors which were being prepared for the entertainment of Fritz when the spring push came. Among them were the new gas shells, which are now said to have been chiefly responsible for the German retreat on the Ancre ... Meanwhile, it is sufficient to say that the credit for the discovery belongs to a provincial university, and chiefly to a clever professor there.' Jim's father longed for some details with which he could enjoy some 'swank' at the smart new Springburn golf club with his circle of business friends. Knowledge of Irvine's war work remained something of a secret for many years; although in point of fact, over the next twenty years, Irvine judiciously chose several different audiences to whom, with a proper sense of achievement, he carefully outlined the edifice of wartime production that his research laboratory became. He and his like felt that their remarkable achievement in the interests of the health of our fighting forces, and of bringing an end to the war, had been inadequately acknowledged.

In January 1919 Sir William Graham Greene, the uncle of the novelist, wrote on behalf of the minister of munitions to both Professor Herring (physiology) and Professor Irvine (chemistry) at St Andrews:

> The Minister fully apprehends the extent to which the science of this country has contributed to the successful result of the war. The solution of many problems of vital importance to the Armies in the Field has been rendered possible only by the patriotic and self-sacrificing manner in which scientific men have placed their services at the disposal of the Ministry. In many cases the investigation of the problems has involved considerable risk and danger to those who have devoted their scientific experience to the task of finding practical solutions. In particular, the success of both the offensive and defensive gas measures had been due in no small degree to the researches carried out by the Members and Associate Members of the Chemical Warfare Committee.[46]

Finally, on 20 May 1919, Field-Marshall Sir Douglas Haig visited the St Andrews laboratories that were the fount of so much of the chemical support he had cried out for in the theatre of war.

In recognition of his services during the war, Irvine was awarded the CBE in the New Year Honours of 1920: the 'Nation's Scientist', as one of his peers described him. A fellow chemist was able to reassure him that, since the armistice, the accuracy of Irvine's speedy conclusions in 1917 had been verified, and the chlorhydrin process proposed by Irvine from his investigations in St Andrews was the same approach as the one that produced all the German mustard gas.

During these four years, the War Office had dictated the programme of chemical research to St Andrews in a somewhat haphazard way. Before war broke out Irvine had planned to work his way systematically through the fundamental work of the whole spectrum of the carbohydrates. The fact that he had to suspend his longed-for role as director of his own research institute was a sacrifice to him: something far removed from the picture of his future career that he had formed in 1909 when he succeeded to his chair.

A printed paper sent from a body in the Netherlands to the Fellows of the Royal Society and to other similar institutions, urging scientists not to recognise the divisions which the war had created, is suitable to describe Irvine's thought as a scientist, but also as a humanist, as the succeeding chapters of his life unfolded.

Next to pure science let the great practical needs of humanity take a place in your considerations. The task of science is not only to enlighten the world but also to find the means which may render life in this world more bearable . . . Recover the high scientific point of view which on his deathbed, made Ampère say to a fellow worker: '*Il ne doit être question entre nous que de se qui est éternelle.*'

EIGHT

The Principalship of St Andrews University

In the aftermath of the war, James Irvine suffered a serious crisis of confidence in his career. The hopes of national reconstruction seemed to him to be doomed to bitter disappointment. He became deeply introspective and dissatisfied with himself. He was angry and impatient with his colleagues. He felt undervalued and trapped in a poorly funded, provincial university, which he feared might offer him nothing but despair.[1] Momentarily, the old imperative of leading his own school of research disappeared, and in its place came the conviction that he would like to taste of the power and influence that a senior government post would give him. Or perhaps he should submit to the overtures of the large-scale commercial interests that were waking up to the need for specialist research stations. His ability as an administrator had been a factor in his wartime success and made him attractive now to spheres beyond university life. Jim was becoming increasingly aware that he had certain great abilities that had lain dormant: talents for business; talents for administration; talents for the cultivation of powerful personal friends; talents for oratory and the power of persuasion. These would all in time come to be harnessed to the greater service of St Andrews University, but in 1919 he felt he could hardly face a life where he had to fight in some pathetic way to introduce breadth of vision to his alma mater. The noble future with which he had determined to associate himself after the success of the quincentenary celebrations in 1911 was now clouded by the university's post-war exhausted state. In 1911, St Andrews had been celebrated as a scientific university of the new age. M'Intosh, Irvine and Steggall's *Memorial Volume of Scientific Papers* (1911) was intended to have consolidated St Andrews' mark on the scientific world. The economic collapse of Western Europe after the war seemed to drain away any immediate hope of realising such ambitions.

Although he was still young, the war had thrust him into the limelight of Whitehall and the chaotic web of government research agencies. He had learned how to make his voice heard above the others, how to be invaluable to great men. His lively, energetic and forthright approach to solving the chemical problems that the war threw up made him a marked man. True to his motto, *Ecce ego, mitte me,* he loved the thrill of being of service to the greater good. It was as a government servant rather than as a humble academic that during the war years he was so frequently to be seen standing on the platform at Leuchars Junction, armed with his official pass to travel first class[2] and waiting for the London train to steam in.

It was still the fact that, although the life of a senior academic scientist was in many ways an attractive one, the professor had very little standing, socially or politically, outside his university. His salary allowed him very few social appurtenances, such as a motor car. In his post-war depressive state, the glamour of running his own department had worn thin. His confidence in the staffing of his department was shaken by the war. William Denham, the lecturer he had appointed to be his personal assistant, was drafted off in May 1916 to work in the Chiswick Laboratory, a branch of the Department of Explosives Supplies. Denham resigned his position in St Andrews, never to return.[3] The disintegration of the fragile structure of Professor Irvine's department had begun. His other lecturer, W.N. Haworth, who departed for a chair at Armstrong College, Newcastle, at the end of the academic year of 1920, had long irritated him beyond words.[4] Haworth was never an easy man, and the war work revealed him as a pedant, and one intent on self-glorification. Another chemist, one of Irvine's London friends, described him as 'a kind of Methodist Pope'.[5]

Deeper exploration into solving the question of why Irvine was so ready to give up his department reveals even a smouldering personal dissatisfaction with the direction that his school of sugars research was taking; and this despite the fact that his chemistry war work had pushed forward his specialism, and had assisted him in notching up knowledge of a final tally of over 700 sugars and sugar derivatives. We must wait until 1931 for an explanation of his post-war malaise. Only then was he sufficiently at ease with himself to confess in *Nature* that:

> It must be admitted that the advances in chemistry made by [Irvine] on the structural chemistry of carbohydrates do not lead very far towards the interpretation of fundamental problems.
>
> . . .
>
> So many questions remain unanswered: Is glucose the first product of photosynthesis? Why are sugars optically active, and why is the

glucose configuration favoured above all others? By what processes are the hexoses converted one into the other? What is sucrose and how is it formed? . . . If I had my scientific life to live over again, I would study these additional problems, but would do so under conditions approximating to those which prevail in plant and animal life . . . a sugar is unlikely to reveal its true characteristics when exposed to the fierce reagents of the organic chemist.[6]

Irvine loved the story of how the youthful Lyon Playfair, a St Andrews FRS of a much earlier generation and one of the founders of the Chemical Society of London, was inspired to experiment from nature by the lectures in chemistry given by Dr Briggs in St Andrews: 'One day he [Lyon Playfair] was discovered in the kitchen at his home struggling with pot and pan to extract sugar from beet-root.'[7]

The quirky enthusiasm with which Irvine, throughout his chemical career, sought always to conjoin chemical studies with plant studies indicates that he was probably more naturally inclined to be a biochemist. In 1909 when he took up his chair, his inaugural address noted with admiration how earlier chemists had examined organic substances such as the essential oils and the sugars by isolating them from plant sources, thereby side-stepping the then shunned production of substances *de novo* by synthetical methods.[8] Vitalism, good or bad, certainly haunted his thoughts. He had had several papers published in the new *Biochemical Journal*,[9] and for some time he had attracted the admiration of German biochemists. In 1909, when Irvine applied for the chair of chemistry in St Andrews, Carl Neuberg, who is credited with formalising the coinage of biochemistry, wrote one of his testimonials.[10] Here Neuberg acknowledged that the young Irvine's work had already enriched the knowledge of not only the chemist but also the biologist. Carl Neuberg suggested to Irvine that he should be a regular contributor to the *Biochemische Zeitschrift*, of which he was editor, and asked for permission to publish Irvine's paper 'A Contribution to the Chemistry of the Humic Acids'. Had biochemistry been a formalised discipline in 1899, offering genuine challenges and a secure career to the brilliant young man, he might have remained at the forefront of scientific discovery and never left the research laboratory. In 1909 he could see that the leaders of research in the carbohydrates and then in the chemistry of the proteins, such as Emil Fischer, would 'bring Chemistry to the beginning of an extraordinary development in the biological direction'.[11]

It would appear that, by 1919–20, some unhappiness with the very pursuit of pure chemistry had taken root within him. He disliked what he saw as the tendency for research students to be mere links in a chain of research development. Would there still be room for the lone investigator? In the reflective mood of his late fifties he spoke critically of early extreme special-isation and of 'the almost mechanical quality of much of the work termed research. The ladder of research was once difficult of access and steep to climb; – only the strongest survived. It may have been a cruel process but natural selection is never kind.'[12]

To his troubled mind, even his domestic happiness had been fractured by the war years. Irvine was sensitive to the fact that his wife had become unhappy and frustrated in St Andrews. Their limited means acted as a brake on her desire for some fulfilment of her talents. Mabel had gone back to developing her musicianship, and the classes at the University of Edinburgh in advanced counterpoint and composition that she took from the distinguished musicologist Donald Tovey only served to expand her sights.[13]

How quickly had evaporated those happy, carefree days of Jim and Mabel's early married life. After that last summer of 1914, Jim's life had become entirely absorbed by the war and his new importance. On top of this, the needs of his department left very little time for Mabel. Her wartime pregnancy ended in a stillborn child. Jim even wrote of a shadow that had come between them, and he resolved to make a better life for his family by turning away from the university.

During the war, Jim built up powerful relationships with the industri-alists of the north-west of England whose factories he had all but taken over. He became a familiar figure in the Manchester Chemical Club. In the summer of 1919, he was approached by the Council of the British Cotton Industry Research Association, a consortium of Manchester cotton producers which, under the watchful the eyes of the new Department of Scientific and Industrial Research (DSIR), was putting together the type of specialist research station that Irvine had so much admired in Germany and which the DSIR was doing so much to promote. They were looking for a chemist to be the first director of their research institute at Didsbury. Throughout August 1919, Jim was called for interview after interview, once again leaving Mabel at a critical time. Their third child, to be named Mary Felicity, would be born in September. However, Mabel very much encour-aged him: after all, the life of the enlightened cotton magnate was a world she understood and had been brought up to. As if it were, say, a century later, Irvine was required to pitch for his salary. He pitched high: £2,600 and pension rights, and still they wanted him. His salary at that time as a professor in St Andrews was £750 per annum, plus £25 war bonus.

Jim then had to face the reality of his decision: 'It will be pioneer work right from the beginning . . . It will mean no more lab work for me & no more published papers – goodbye in fact to a scientific career and to a number of dreams such as filling Fischer's place in sugar chemistry, but it will be a position of power and influence, not to speak of a good salary.'[14]

The Lancashire firm of Kerfoots had made the cordite and novocain under Irvine's direction during the war. Ernest and Margaret Kerfoot were deeply attached to Mabel, and looked forward to the possibility of the two families being neighbours. Jim romanced about the happiness it could bring to his marriage: 'We'll take the best of the past and make it the worst of the future. I shall want help Mabs for there is much in me which has to be stamped out. I am not only too hasty and unmeasurable, but too critical of everybody. It's queer for it isn't as if I were unduly satisfied with myself. At heart I believe I'm rather a humble individual.'[15] His character analysis was true, and in some ways he was humble because there was nothing pompous or overblown in his more literal sense of his own abilities. When Irvine received the British Cotton Industry's confirmation of his appointment, however, he suddenly decided to turn away from the Manchester cotton industry. Might this change of heart have been caused by the terms of the agreement which, when finally drawn up, included the phrase 'shall serve for a term of five years'? Short tenure such as this was unlikely to appeal to a Scotsman with three children to bring up. In November 1919, Sir Arthur Crossley, another chemist brought into prominence by the war, was appointed in his stead.

Jim Irvine was not the only able chemist at that time to contemplate a move from a struggling university department to the directorship of one of these new industrial research stations. The war gave considerable importance to the several dye-producing chemical works that were so adaptable to the manufacture of chemical warfare. The Dalton Works and British Dyes in Huddersfield experienced a post-war amalgamation into British Dyestuffs Corporation, and in 1920 they appointed as director of research a man who would soon be linked more closely with Irvine and St Andrews: Robert Robinson. Robinson would later come to be regarded as the most distinguished British organic chemist of the century, and he was through and through an academic scientist. He had held the chair of organic chemistry at Liverpool since 1915, and during a somewhat restless period of his life had been tempted by those two sirens that were beckoning to Irvine in 1919: power and personal income.

When Irvine finally came to rest as Principal and Vice-Chancellor of St Andrews University, Robinson wrote to him cordially:

> Warmest congratulations on the very great honour which I see has now [been] conferred on you. It is very encouraging to have a chemist at the head of at least one of our universities. You will be very happy in now having a wider field for your executive ability whilst retaining full opportunities for research. It is a step you can never have cause to regret as I do my transference to this place. Unfortunately the promises made to me when I undertook this work have not been kept and I shall take the earliest opportunity of returning to the only environment which suits me. Put not your trust in Princes – more especially the merchant variety.[16]

The opportunity that came Robinson's way was Irvine's chair at St Andrews on Irvine's elevation to the principalship. However, Robinson's confession to Irvine that a move to the fleshpots of industry was not all it might seem may give a further clue as to why Irvine, in the previous year, had decided against moving his family to Manchester for the princely salary of £2,600 per annum, with pension rights.

Jim would not have been open to the temptation of a change of career if all had been well in St Andrews. He was always troubled by a sense of deep unease when he was unable to exercise power where he felt it was needed. And for Jim in 1919 that place was St Andrews. He noted: 'If St A had a good Principal – an impartial man of broad views – it would take more to make me leave, but St A is tied to a weak man whose ideas are not even provincial. They are parochial. The affairs of the village pump are big affairs to him.'[17]

At that time, the ecclesiastical historian Sir John Herkless was Principal, having slipped into the shoes of the far greater man, Sir James Donaldson, on Donaldson's death in 1915. It could hardly have been a more difficult time in which to establish a principalship, and Herkless soon showed signs of stumbling in his post. In 1916, Professor Scott Lang, the guardian of St Andrews' tradition, was obliged to bring to the attention of Andrew Bennett, the secretary to the university, the fact that Principal Herkless had introduced changes to the graduation ceremony without even mentioning it to the Senatus.[18]

In May 1919, Field-Marshal Lord Haig, elected in 1916, was belatedly installed as Rector of St Andrews. It was just the kind of event that Irvine loved: his emotions were stirred by the colour and pageantry of the recto-rial tradition, and he longed to put St Andrews in the public eye, 'but every-thing was spoiled to everybody by the fatuous pomposity of Herkless who excelled himself in his weakest aspects. I foresaw all this coming for months but my worst fears did not dream that "the asses ears" would show up so strongly.'[19]

At one time, when young, the Irvines had been close to the Herklesses. In 1911 Jim and Mabel, ever ambitious in university politics, had invited the then rising figure of the Rev. John Herkless to stand godfather at their daughter Veronica's baptism – and yet even then they were not blind to the fondness for self-importance that Herkless displayed at the quincentenary that same year. After the war, this now weakened and played-out man irked Jim Irvine, whose impatience knew no bounds.

The drama of the St Andrews principalship began to unfold during the first half of 1920, as Herkless's health failed. Before the death of Principal Herkless, however, Irvine was head-hunted once more, this time on behalf of the prime minister himself. Sir James Dobbie, the government chemist, was nearing the obligatory retirement age of sixty-five. Dobbie was a Glaswegian like Irvine, but of an earlier generation. He had been in a good position to observe well how, during the war, Irvine displayed those charac-teristics that should be found in a senior government scientific officer. In April 1920, Dobbie approached Irvine, suggesting that he put his name forward to succeed him in a post that was never advertised. The salary would be more than twice that of Irvine's current salary, and it carried with it security of tenure and a civil service pension: one that would extend to the widow. Senior St Andrews posts were still appointments '*ad vitam aut culpam*'; retirements were rare. Irvine often returned to the conviction that his wife and family would have a better life in London.

Jim Irvine replied promptly: he was interested. The government chemist, he was informed, could continue to keep his head up in the chemical community by examining and sitting on boards; a little private research might be possible, provided it did not conflict with the commercial work of the public analysts. Irvine calculated on the back of an envelope that his salary would be £2,010 per annum. He went to London to discuss the post with Dobbie. All summer, he held close to himself the thought that the well-paid job of writing reports and walking the corridors of power could be the fresh start he was looking for.[20]

He could not be unaware of all that he would be giving up. In May a young Japanese scientist visited him, and thanked him afterwards in an unaffected manner that would have appealed to Irvine. 'You are so kind to me took over me your laboratories and interesting places in St Andrews and also invite me to your tea. I have learned many things seeing your well-equipped laboratories and your experiments. I am pleasantly and strongly impressed by you and am same mind of you that there is no more satisfactory life than that of who devotes himself to scientific investigations.'[21]

Things in St Andrews were becoming more interesting. Principal Herkless had never fully recovered his health after an operation a couple of years previously, and he turned more and more to his energetic young colleague to act as his deputy. In May 1918 Irvine had been invited by Herkless to attend an important meeting convened at the Foreign Office by A.J. Balfour, the Foreign Secretary. The purpose of the meeting was to consider what facilities should be given to graduates of foreign and colonial universities to take higher studies and follow research in the 'Home Universities'. Irvine, who would in years to come take up the cause of higher education for the colonies with great distinction, was learning to play his future part. The fact that it was not Professor Burnet, the dean of the Faculty of Arts, who was invited to accompany the principal to discourse with the government was an indication of the role that science, as the pre-eminent faculty, was beginning to assume in St Andrews.

The meeting in the Foreign Office was followed by an inter-university conference with seventeen British universities participating. The subject under discussion was the PhD and a need for some consensus on the question of research degrees, and in particular doctorates that could be taken by visiting graduates. At this time St Andrews still had only the DSc to offer to scientists, and the PhD degree promoted by Irvine before the war had still to come into effect. Irvine, proudly defensive of his university, summed up as follows:

> The details submitted so far remove the impression that the new degree of PhD now contemplated will be a cheap degree. The conditions as to entrance qualifications laid down by Oxford are the same as those under which we admit research students under ord. 61 sec 23 (?)
>
> . . .
>
> By adopting . . . a distinction between original work carried out under direction on a topic provided to the candidate and that which is the issue of his independent thought and work, the value of the

existing doctorates will be enhanced considerably. On the other hand the Glasgow and London proposals would without doubt lower the standard. It was urged that the holding of such a degree as the proposed PhD would be considered essential for graduates entering manufacturing life and the scheme would prove of value to the community.[22]

In bullish mood, Irvine added that 'for a small university to abstain from assuming powers equal to those now being adopted by other and, in a sense, competing institutions may well prove to be fatal policy which might have the effect of keeping the university confined to undergraduate teaching in place of joining in what is evidently a serious and no light-hearted attempt to expand original work in this country'.

By March 1919 St Andrews, pushed by Irvine, had introduced Ordinance 16 of the University Court, concerning the institution of a degree of Doctor of Philosophy (PhD), and Ordinance 18 concerning regulations for degrees in Arts, Philosophy and Letters.

A clear mind for the legal details governing higher education in Scotland was not the only quality that earned for Irvine the admiration of his colleagues in St Andrews. Throughout the war years, and with a pretence at normality, the business of supplying education to undergraduates had gone on. Behind every committee, every meeting of the Court, every tussle with the Senatus, there was Irvine. A list of the standing committees of the University Court, 1915–16 shows Irvine sitting on *all* of the committees: the Finance and Land Committee, the Dundee Finance Committee, the University Grounds Committee, the University Chapel Committee, the Botanic Garden and Agriculture Committee, the Gatty Marine Laboratory Committee, the Gymnasium Committee, the Ordinance Committee, the Fire Prevention Committee, the University Hall Committee; he was also a member authorised to sign documents. Apart from the principal, none other of his colleagues was in such a position of power.[23] But the great power rested in Principal Herkless by virtue of his office lay dormant: Herkless was devoid of vision. Irvine alone impatiently wished to seize every opening that offered money, influence and development to St Andrews.

The first opportunity of this kind was on his doorstep, at the paper-manufacturing mills of Tullis Russell at Markinch. It had been during the war that Jim and Mabel first became friends with David and Alison Russell. The need for a scientific expert witness in a legal case had brought the Fife paper magnate and the chemist together. Throughout the war years, the Russells' home at Rothes represented an escape to the weary scientist, and in return the Irvine's house welcomed the Russells to the glamour of many a university function. Irvine, almost without realising it, through a friendship based on mutual sympathy, was laying the foundations for all the benefactions that were lavished by the Russell family on the university during the twentieth century. It was hard going, however, in December 1918 to push Russell's 'Spiritual Regeneration' scheme through the Court, and Irvine was defensive in presenting this potentially important friend to the university. Russell was a man to whom the spiritual life meant a great deal, and Russell's was but one of the many schemes spawned in the immediate post-war years that aimed at purifying the world and promoting peace among nations. He used the Walker Trust and St Andrews University to put into effect this essay competition, open to all, with the top prize set at £200.

> The Trustees, believing that the strife of nations is but the effect of continuous conflict arising from the domination of egotism, whether national or individual, consider the moment opportune for directing the attention to the study of world 'reconstruction' on spiritual lines. With this end in view they have decided to offer prizes for essays dealing with this subject.

The petty treatment of the idea by the Court, Irvine wrote to Russell,

> was highly characteristic of the men who are nominally my colleagues and in reality my hindrances in life. The Principal read out the document and would have approved of it but first Burnet and then Galloway took objection to some part of the wording, so that Herkless gradually changed his ground. It was a characteristic exhibition and I nearly lost my temper – which was doubtless characteristic too . . . a small committee was suggested and, much to my amusement Herkless nominated Burnet, Galloway and himself, deleting me as it was 'outside my subject'. To this I would not agree and finally the Court put me on as well.[24]

Mabel, who described Alison Russell as 'a lovely green valley, with rest and shade', also drew strength from their friendship with the Russells, who were kind and generous.[25] The Russells' Rolls Royce and their chauffeur, Binnie, were often made available to Jim and Mabel, who had no car. As Mabel's life developed so did her social position in St Andrews, and the Russells – Uncle David and Aunt Alison to the young Irvines – were invariably drawn into the excitement too. The Walker Trust next financed a series of important recitals of Schubert and Schumann that Mabel gave at the university, both in Dundee and in St Andrews.

By February 1919, David Russell appointed Irvine as the nominee of the Walker Trust, with full power to spend a grant for the Students' Union. Irvine was beginning to draw Russell in as a most willing collaborator and benefactor to the university. No wonder Jim Irvine felt at variance with Principal Herkless who, it has to be admitted, brought out all the younger man's self-righteous anger.

The several important contributions that Irvine, playing his part as dean of the Faculty of Science, had tried to make in St Andrews during the war years were not lost on the University Court, even if he had a characteristic inclination to support the case of the individualist in the face of the rather entrenched Senatus. One of the colleagues whose cause he fought was an interesting man called Wilson who, with Irvine's help, nearly succeeded in establishing the Scottish Agricultural Plant Breeding Research Station in St Andrews. John Wilson had provided lectures to the botany department for a pittance since the bad days of poor departmental funding, and he remained in post as lecturer in agriculture with precious little remuneration until his death in 1920. He had fought long and hard since the beginning of the century for the institution of a degree in agriculture, to include forestry, at the University of St Andrews. In the year before war broke out, he appealed to Irvine to assist him in setting up an agricultural research institute. St Andrews, situated as it is on the edge of the rich, mixed farming country of East Fife, was ideally suited to the development of a Treasury-funded research station of this kind. The local farming gentry were already familiar in St Andrews society and were willing to co-operate with trials of improved strains of wheat, potatoes and turnips on their land.

Dr Wilson's initiative appealed greatly to Irvine, who was already revealing his bias towards biochemistry and who relished an opportunity to wrestle with the mandarins in Edinburgh and Westminster. Believing that the scientific teaching in the university could contribute towards a practical end of national importance, in June 1913 Irvine had boldly instructed the Secretary to the University to send off the following to the Treasury:

> About a year ago a scheme was submitted to the Board of Agriculture for Scotland for research with a view to the improvement of the quality of potatoes and turnips. A considerable area of land has been taken for this work. Special laboratories have been fitted up for

the Biological and Chemical work involved . . . The University of St Andrews is provided with a very fully and thoroughly equipped series of Laboratories for the study of Practical Chemistry.[26]

Irvine, using his powers as dean of the Faculty of Science, siphoned off bursaries and scholarships towards this dual chemistry and plant research, and in this way provided Dr Wilson's experimental laboratory with workers fully trained on the scientific side. For its time it was an ingenious arrangement.

By the summer of 1916, grants totalling £555, via the Board of Agriculture for Scotland, had been awarded to St Andrews for scientific research into improving the quality not only of potatoes and turnips but also of oats. Towards the end of 1916 Dr Wilson was able to point out that St Andrews, with its unique confluence of research students seeking experience in chemical matters, could become a centre for the training of men who desired to specialise in plant improvement. This was followed up by Irvine with a further, stronger, defence of the scheme:

The gain to the economic wealth of the country will be very great. This work is not undertaken by the University with a view to profit. The results will accrue solely to the nation. The University as a foster-mother of science has indeed spent money for the purpose of promoting the scheme which it cannot expect to recover. But the main cost of the work has been borne by the Board of Agriculture for Scotland and the National Development Commissioners: grants amounting to upwards of £2,000 have been bestowed upon it.[27]

This is Irvine trying to sell a university development to the government with all the power of the advocate that he would become.

Sadly, Dr Wilson's life was soon to come to an end. When he died in 1920, his last assistant, William Robb, was transferred to the government scientific agricultural service in Edinburgh, with much of the experimental material. The lectureship in agriculture was at an end, and St Andrews University lost a chance to develop a national institute of research within its ordinance. Robb later became director of the Scottish Plant Breeding Station, based in Edinburgh.[28]

This episode, which developed despite the war, illustrates two important points of Irvine's character: the delight he took in challenging the Senatus, in an exercise to try and broaden his organic chemistry specialism by forming a partnership with botany; and the determined way in which he pursued the Treasury for funding.

Another botanist, Patrick Geddes, who held a personal chair in botany in Dundee at this time, came under Irvine's watch when he was dean of the Faculty of Science. A polymath scientist, Geddes was already building a bridge between the thinking of a biologist and that of a town planner. Irvine granted his colleague prolonged leave of absence in India in 1915–16 when all of his colleagues were labouring for the war, but Geddes proved his worth as just the sort of visionary that corresponded to Irvine's ideal: Geddes' Bombay Town Planning Act 1915 established him as the great twentieth-century innovator in town planning. St Andrews University would, however, see very little more of him as a botanist.

D'Arcy Thompson, whose *On Growth and Form* was first published in 1917, the same year that he was translated from the chair of biology in Dundee to the chair of natural history in St Andrews, was another original mind in a similar mould although, unlike Geddes, he never left St Andrews.

There were other ways by which Professor Irvine strengthened the university's power base. The University Court's business committee placed a high value on the way that Irvine brought in funds for the impoverished little university. During 1916, the payments received from the government and the Lister Institute for dulcitol alone produced a profit of over £200. Irvine proposed that, after the extraction of expenses for his workers, the surplus should be added to Purdie's original research endowment fund of the chemistry department. The same sum had been earned during 1915. The work on chlorhydrin brought in £500. That a university teacher could earn such sums for his university was something entirely new, and something that could not be imagined of the old-style theologian or classicist. Irvine came to be seen by the Court as something of an entrepreneur in obtaining Treasury funds.[29]

Twentieth-century university chemistry departments were not funded solely by a mixture of government and philanthropic financing. Industry played a generous part in enabling these departments to grow. It was not, however, merely keen business acumen on Irvine's part that brought the first small step in this direction into his chemistry research department. He always fervently believed that research in industry was led by pure research in the universities, and an interesting connection with industry came about unsought, as the direct outcome of one of Irvine's war activities. The Wilton Research Laboratories in Manchester, directed by a chemist called Atack in whom Irvine had much confidence, had been drawn into the production of chemical warfare under Irvine's direction. With the end of the war in sight, and with this experience, they sought to expand their original business: the manufacture of synthetic dye-stuffs and other organic chemicals. Atack wrote to the secretary of St Andrews University explaining that he had already consulted with Professor Irvine, and asking if a number of workers from the Wilton Laboratories could be admitted to the Chemical Research Laboratory of the United College to conduct chemical research and to receive training and experience in the methods of research. A fee of £45 15s was offered for each worker. This, possibly St Andrews' first opportunity to connect with industry, was approved.

> The proposal that these chemists should conduct research in the University of St Andrews is similar to the scheme now in operation under which chemists in the employment of British Dyes Ltd., and Messrs Levenstein Ltd work in the chemical laboratories of the Universities of Oxford, Cambridge, Manchester, Liverpool, and Leeds.
>
> . . .
>
> Professor Irvine and Dr Haworth have been good enough to express the view that the operation of this scheme will enable the University to take part in a movement of national importance and will have the effect of bringing the Research Laboratory of St Andrews into closer touch with scientific manufacturers. At the same time, it is expected that this association will open up a career for many graduates of the University.[30]

With his fast-growing reputation for getting what he wanted, Irvine assumed the role of Principal Herkless's 'Passepartout'. He begins to sound more cheerful. 'There has been . . . a lot of university work in connection with the Carnegie Trust Grants. As these affect science largely, our friend "John" has gone out of his way to be mighty civil to me so long as I can be of use to him! It's really very funny.'[31]

Poor Sir John Herkless had much need of Jim's assistance. His state of health was a cause of general concern, and the Scottish Office began considering who might succeed him, should he die. He chaired an exceptionally long meeting of the University Court (sixty-four items) on 1 May 1920, and attended a meeting of the University Grants Committee on 12 May. After undergoing a serious operation, he died on 11 June, having been in office for just under five years – years of great difficulty.

Although Principal Galloway, as Principal of St Mary's College, was acting principal during the interregnum, it was Irvine who made the arrangements for Herkless' funeral. Six months elapsed before a new principal could be appointed to the university, but the university continued to evolve, and Professor J.C. Irvine was invariably asked to serve as locum. He was appointed the representative of the University Court on the powerful Carnegie Trust for the Universities of Scotland, in place of the late principal. He soon began to make his presence felt with a far-reaching claim for a grant of £41,000 to be spent in this way: £4,000 on student hostels split equally between St Andrews and Dundee; £7,000 for the building and equipment of the chemistry laboratory; £7,080 for an extension to the Bute Medical School; £6,000 to endow a lectureship in medieval history; £5,000 for the two university libraries; and £11,000 for endowing lectureships in Dundee, in German and engineering. This was no longer the dean of the Faculty of Science staking a case for funding for the science departments. These are forward-looking claims for the endowment of the whole university, on both sides of the Tay. Here was a man who felt he was already running the university. He may have dominated the Senatus, but it was the University Court that most appreciated his persuasive power.[32]

A statistical and financial account of the university about 1922–3,[33] within the papers of the secretary of the university, is in a manner Irvine's Domesday Book. It demonstrates how during the last years of Herkless' life, it was Irvine who was instrumental in pulling the departments and their teaching programmes together, and in nudging St Andrews towards the spirit of a twentieth-century university.

It could not be of any surprise in St Andrews that in July 1920 Irvine, a man of vision, put his name forward for the position of Principal of St Andrews University. This move was strongly supported by the University Court and the Senatus. He was their chosen man. There was, however, a very grave difficulty. He was not the obvious choice in the eyes of Robert Munro, the Secretary for Scotland, who would have to advise the Prime Minister and ultimately the King, this being a Crown appointment. For a classicist, a historian or a divine at that date, elevation to a Scottish university's highest post was not a career change, but a natural reward for diligent service. The front-runner for the appointment was probably Dr Andrew Wallace Williamson, minister of St Giles' cathedral in Edinburgh, a somewhat elderly and frail divine, who was also Dean of the Thistle. His claim was anchored in Munro's mind well before the death of Principal Herkless.

The Secretary for Scotland and the Scottish Office thought that what St Andrews might need was a theologian who would be able to strengthen the position of St Mary's College, in the face of the complicated machinery of the final amalgamation of the United Free Church with the Church of Scotland. The Free Church owned specialist training colleges that in the past had reflected the teaching of the Free Church. St Mary's College in St Andrews was also a training ground for the Scottish ministry, and a question mark lay over how it could retain its life as an ancient seat of learning, with its established chairs, and still serve the Church of Scotland.

It was also rumoured that there were members of the government who favoured a man from the West of Scotland. Other candidates included – as well as several of Irvine's colleagues, one of them probably the classicist Professor Burnet – two government officials, two Church of Scotland ministers, a doctor and a United Free Church professor. A potential weakness around 1920 for St Andrews would lie in the inability of the civil servants in Edinburgh to grasp that there was a new vision for higher education thrusting forward in all corners of the United Kingdom. Competition among the universities in the new age might bring little St Andrews to its knees. The time had come to overturn something of the old order. St Andrews' only scientific principals had been Sir David Brewster, a physicist and co-founder of the British Association for the Advancement of Science, appointed in 1838; and his successor, J.D. Forbes, a glaciologist.

Although Irvine had other qualities attractive to the appointing powers, he decided that he should put himself forward as a scientist who could lead the university into a scientific age. His application was accompanied by a memorial drawn up by his friend, Alex Mackenzie, by then holding the chair of chemistry in Dundee. All the leading British chemists of the time signed it. It pleaded the case for appointing to the principalship of St Andrews an enlightened man who would promote the interests of research. It stated that Irvine shared with Emil Fischer the credit of discovery of the new types of reactive sugars, certainly one of the most important and far-reaching advances made in organic chemistry during the previous decade. It went on to say that if Professor Irvine were to be appointed to the principalship, the University of St Andrews would be guided by a man who was held in very high esteem indeed as a scientist. An investigator himself, he would have the outlook of an investigator.

Many of these scientists warned of the loss to chemistry that the appointment would make, but they also perceived that the appointment of Irvine to a vice-chancellorship would give voice and influence in support of scientific research in our universities. Arthur Smithells, who had so bravely and famously opposed Ostwald's attack in the Royal Institution on the value and meaning of organic chemistry, was spirited in his support for James Colquhoun Irvine: 'I don't know that I am right in conspiring to precipitate Irvine from his pleasant state into the awful business of Principalising. But I cannot honestly refrain from praising him if it is needed.' Robert Robinson expressed enormous regard for the value of Irvine's work. He could not have known that he would take up James Irvine's chair within the twelve months. W.H. Perkin wrote from Oxford: 'I have signed the document you sent me with some misgivings as I am afraid if this happens it will withdraw Irvine from the excellent research he is doing'. Percy Frankland felt that reference to the methylated sugars would be double-Dutch to the Secretary for Scotland. There were warnings that the Secretary might resent a memorial signed by chemists alone asking for one of their number to be made principal of a university with other faculties, despite the very great advantage to scientific instruction and research in Scotland, if he were appointed.[34]

The principalship of St Andrews was, of course, what Jim had wanted all along. All that summer and autumn, he kept the open offer of the post of government chemist in the top drawer of his desk, as an insurance measure against disappointment. Sir James Dobbie, aware of Jim's dilemma, privately supported him in both quarters. What ensued next was a secretive, almost cloak-and-dagger pursuit down every avenue of influence that occurred to him. Jim did not yet have a London or even an Edinburgh club, and he had few opportunities to enlist the help of the movers and shakers who could speak up for him in London. He engaged the help of David Russell, who had the ear of the MP Sir Alexander Sprot, Bart. Russell was to send copies of the application to any friend that he thought could help: the Chancellor of the University, Lord Balfour of Burleigh, and the Liberal peer Lord Haldane were thought to be the most important. Any connection with Lloyd George, the Prime Minister, 'would not come amiss'. 'As for the others, the Lord Lieutenant of Fife is officially connected with the university and might be enlisted. Mr Younger is working on the MP influence ... but it occurs to me that the university members: Sir William Watson Cheyne, Sir Henry Craik ... might be approached ... They could perhaps be neutralized if not enlisted.'[35]

At the beginning of August, David Russell, hard at work on Jim's behalf, wrote to him on holiday. He feared that Munro was not taking Irvine's case seriously. This was indeed so, but Russell did not have the necessary influence among the Tory grandees close to Westminster. If David Russell ever thought that he was the king-maker in the matter of the principalship of St Andrews, this was not so. The man who was actually pulling the strings was Sir George Younger, scion of the brewing dynasty and brother of James Younger, of Mount Melville near St Andrews. James Younger was an early twentieth-century philanthropist of St Andrews, and his brother George was Conservative party chairman and close to the Lord Privy Seal, Bonar Law. George knew how anxious his brother was that Irvine should be appointed.

Munro was not in a hurry to appoint, and the elderly Dr Williamson had become lukewarm on the matter. Although rumour was rife, there was still no word in St Andrews of how the interregnum would be resolved. Growing uneasy, in October Irvine wrote directly to George Younger. Any suspicion amongst his fellow dons that he might personally be lobbying for the principalship was fiercely rebuffed by Jim.

On 24 November, Jim received a letter on behalf of the Prime Minister in which he was told officially that he had been selected for the post of government chemist. The letter contained all the final details of the salary and pension, and concluded by saying that: 'As it is now some months since Sir James Dobbie retired, it would be convenient if you could take up the duties of Government Chemist at an early date.'[36] Young though they still were, Mabel stated that the first thing that counted in their lives was her husband's work, and she resigned herself to her husband's disappointment. Wherever they might live, she and the children would be happy and well.

The last act in the drama was kept secret from all but Jim's wife and his parents. On 28 November Irvine received a private letter from Sir George Younger, who had encountered Bonar Law at a shooting party of Conservative peers and politicians at Grimsthorpe, Lord Ancaster's Lincolnshire seat. Younger formed the distinct impression from Bonar Law that Robert Munro would never appoint Irvine. Munro was of the opinion that only an outsider could bring order to such a factious little place as St Andrews, seething with petty jealousies. It was rumoured that Robert Rait, the Historiographer Royal for Scotland, might be the favoured candidate. Jim could wait no longer, and resolved to go to London to speak to Munro face to face. He travelled on the night train on 30 November, but before he went he pressed into his wife's hands a scrap of paper: a used envelope on which he had written a code with which she could decipher the telegram that he would send her after the meeting.

The code was:

First Class – I've got it
Second Class – I'm likely to get it
Third Class – No impression
Fourth Class – I'm unlikely to get it
Fifth Class – I'm not to get it

The wire that Mabel received said: 'Rinman's process distinctly fourth class. Discussion most unsatisfactory. Jim.' And she telegrammed back: 'Re Rinman's process. I understand. Best love. Mab.'[37] There is a twist in this, in that she did not understand any chemistry, but she would at least have known that Jim advised David Russell on the application of the new Rinman's process in the preparation of pulp for the paper mills.

So depressed was Jim by his meeting with Munro that on 3 December he penned a letter to Andrew Bennett, secretary to St Andrews University, to resign his professorship. He wrote: 'I have been asked by the Prime Minister to accept the position of Chief Government Chemist in succession to Sir James Dobbie FRS and have to request you to intimate my resignation to the University Court.'[38]

Luckily, events overtook this move, and he never posted the letter. Later that same day he heard from Younger that actually Munro had been deeply impressed by him, particularly so because Irvine had stated that he would rather go to St Andrews than have the better-paid job of government chemist. All was resolved when, four days later, the Secretary for Scotland wrote to Irvine to tell him: 'I have pleasure in informing you that I have decided to recommend the King to appoint you to the vacant Principalship of St Andrews' University.'[39] All that remained was to decline the post of chief government chemist.

At the eleventh hour, it was Sir George Younger who dealt the coup de grâce to the one other man left in the game and tried, successfully as it happened, to force Munro's hand.[40] George Younger, with a canny reference to Dr Williamson of St Giles, wrote: 'I think I have killed any chance of a parson with Bonar.' Bonar Law was reported to be impressed with all that Jim had to say, and promised to push his case with Munro, who then finally came to see Younger on 6 December to tell him privately that he had decided to appoint Irvine.[41] Munro had need of courage and independence. Irvine's two attributes – his extreme youthfulness and the fact that he was a scientist – were not regarded by the establishment as qualities to recommend him. During those four intervening days, Sir George Younger had been at work, and Munro's mind had been changed in favour of Irvine. Younger found it rather amusing. He would have found it even more amusing if he had known then how St Andrews would be transformed under the hand of Principal Irvine.

St Andrews nearly didn't get Irvine. It has also to be admitted that the dénouement of these manoeuvres brought a lucky release for him. A life tied to the chemical analysts of London would have been grim. 'You have had a most notable escape from J.J. Dobbie's job,' wrote Purdie's old chemist, G.D. Lander. 'For a man of your brain to write annual reports on the collected results of milk analysis would have been pathetic.'[42]

The story of Irvine's elevation to one of the most coveted posts in Scottish education is an episode that has to be recounted in detail. It illustrates how a post-war battle over higher education was fought out at the highest level of political society, when within Lloyd George's coalition government the Conservatives controlled two thirds of the voting. It was widely regarded as a victory for a new enlightened order, whereby our British universities would become centres of excellence, stronger in the sciences, leaders of research and productive of the young men and women that the country most needed. Great things were expected of Irvine in that most conservative of academic societies situated in St Andrews.

All Jim Irvine's hopes were known to have been fulfilled when, on the morning of 13 December, the national newspapers published the news that St Andrews would have a scientist of forty-three years old to take it forward. Later, Lord Alness, who in 1920 was simple Mr Munro, wrote to Principal Irvine: 'I take more pride in your appointment than in any of the very many which it fell to me during my time of office.'[43] It was indeed an appointment made famous by the ensuing thirty-odd years of Irvine's life, in which he never escaped his love affair with St Andrews and never again, despite a flow of tempting offers, wavered from the essential truth that his life was indissolubly bound to an institution that 'had given [him] exactly the opportunity in life that [he] wanted'.

'I started on my task with this deep feeling of gratitude and a fervent desire to do my very best.'

NINE

The Young Principal

Irvine's appointment was gazetted in *The Times* on 13 December 1920, and his rule over St Andrews effectively commenced from this date.

NEW PRINCIPAL OF ST ANDREWS
LONG DELAY ENDED

The King, on the recommendation of the Secretary of State, has been pleased to approve of the appointment of James Colquhoun Irvine, Esq., CBE, PhD, DSc, Professor of Chemistry in the University of St Andrews, as Principal of the University of St Andrews, in succession to the late Rev. Sir John Herkless, DD.

The long delay in filling up this appointment is now ended. Sir John Herkless died as long ago as June 11 last.

It was a Crown appointment, but the King's departure for Sandringham at Christmastime meant that the royal commission was not signed for almost another three weeks. Irvine was appointed principal under the old ordinance, as with his professorship, *ad vitam aut culpam.*

During the early years of the twentieth century, the management structure of the University of St Andrews, along with that of the three other Scottish universities, was beginning to show signs of maturing into something that could perhaps be recognised today.[1] The Reformation, the religious struggles of the seventeenth century and, in St Andrews, the deep decline of the eighteenth century had finally necessitated two nineteenth-century acts of parliament (1858 and 1889) to arrest the decay that Dr Johnson had observed in 1773. Johnson remarked that it was a place 'eminently adapted to study and education', but he was distressed by its ruinous state and the struggle that it endured just to survive. Unlike Edinburgh and Glasgow, it had been starved of finance by parliament.

The Scottish Universities Act of 1889 incorporated amongst other things a heroic effort to make St Andrews viable.[2] This act also paved the way for the affiliation of Mary Ann Baxter's new college in Dundee with St Andrews south of the Tay. In 1897 this affiliation was transmuted, after much litigation and drafting, into a union, and University College Dundee came into being. It was a strangely ambiguous piece of compromise that in many ways continued to make both parties uneasy, until the Robbins Report of 1963 finally opened the door to Dundee's independence.

James Irvine, both as student and then in post in the University at St Andrews, had lived through his alma mater's late-Victorian struggles. He took the highest office there at a time when it could barely stand in comparison and competition with the English universities and thus claim the full support of the government in Westminster.

In terms of university governance, however, it could be held that the old Scottish universities had one great advantage over their sister institutions of Oxford and Cambridge. Under the titular head of each chancellor, they were simply governed by two bodies: the Senatus Academicus, consisting of all the professors, which was presided over by the Principal or his deputy and which exercised academic discipline and power over teaching and degrees; and the University Court, which had powers to regulate the composition and number of the faculties and exercised authority over finance, equipment and staff. After 1897, the University Court became also the legislative authority of these universities. The Court's nominal chairman was the Rector, elected for personal eminence rather than academic distinction every three years by the student body. The Rector's deputy was the Principal, and thus in nearly every instance the Principal also chaired the University Court, a Rector being seldom able to attend the meetings. In Scotland we find four ancient universities that were democratic in spirit but where the Principal and Vice-Chancellor was in a position of enormous power. On 1 January 1921, when James Irvine received the King's commission, he fell heir in essence to full control over the institution that he loved with his whole heart. It was that love that fired the whole of Irvine's life; the great power vested in him in 1921 met its match in this combination of deep affection, intellect and youthful energy.

The fact that in St Andrews Irvine could exercise such control over his university appealed to his self-confident nature. He disliked devolving power onto others, and small St Andrews was perfectly formed to submit to his full imaginative powers. In fact, by 1929 he had grown so much in command of his position that he could jocularly write to his wife:

No word awaited me at the Club from Mr Baldwin and I'm beginning to be seriously annoyed with that gentleman, as the only chance
of seeing him now on this trip is on my return to town on Thursday
night which is not a bit convenient. Well, well, I take worries less
seriously now than at one time – St Andrews can get along very well
without a Chancellor – or a Rector!![3]

Joking Mabel's 'Dimbie' may have been, but there is an underlying measure
of truth there, in that Principal Irvine much preferred having sole control.[4]
The next thirty years became a time of previously unprecedented and
undreamed-of growth and prestige for St Andrews University, despite the
dampening effect of worldwide economic depression followed by another
world war.

Irvine inherited the rumbling volcanic mass hidden within University
College Dundee; the larger the whole university grew, the larger grew the
destructive threat of the city of Dundee, with her desire for an independent
university. Until the end of his principalship, however, Irvine dealt an even
hand to these two forces comprising the Faculty of Medicine, the School
of Dental Surgery, and the Departments of Engineering, Education and
Jurisprudence found in the industrial city of Dundee on the one hand; and
on the other the faculties of Arts, Science and Divinity in the historic centre
of learning in St Andrews. The two factions were to be complementary
to each other, but the true picture was not so simple. The sciences were
provided with full and distinguished departments in both centres, but
within the one faculty, governing both sites. Fatally, a creeping doubling of
arts departments in Dundee and St Andrews would prove a further source
of discontent.[5]

However, development and endowment, on whichever side of the Tay it
was to be, was of prime importance to Irvine, provided it was on terms that
did not diminish the rising standing of the university. There was one thing
that he was clear about in his own mind. The St Andrews degree was an elite
distinction in which Dundee's Mary Ann Baxter's college was fortunate to
share by means of the union with St Andrews. Such hauteur also nourished
the seeds of Dundee's restlessness.

In January 1921, however, Irvine must have felt that he had at last won his
rightful inheritance, and one that was full of promise. Innumerable former
chemistry students and old friends wrote to say that they had predicted
this event many years previously, even if it came as a surprise to the civil
servants in London, who had planned otherwise. The whole chemical

community took Irvine's appointment as an indication of the beginning of a new scientific age. The voice of science would increasingly now be heard by the higher education policymakers. Whatever the disappointed candidates may have thought, the hundreds of letters of congratulation that were delivered to Jim and Mabel at home at Edgecliffe affirmed a sense of relief that the Secretary of State had been minded to bow to pressure from within the St Andrews University Court. Every letter was personally answered.[6]

In Scotland, Irvine most definitely was considered to be a prophet, and the Scottish newspapers reported on the appointment with marked and lengthy approbation. In St Salvator's College, he was met with a surge of joy and enthusiasm. It being Monday morning, the popular professor repaired to the chemistry department to lecture to his class. There, waiting for him, was a seething mass of excited students from every discipline. The student magazine, *College Echoes*, reported on this unusual sight.

> The inevitable reaction came on the morning of 13 December, when it was announced that the appointment had at last been made and the long period of waiting culminated in that wonderful outburst of enthusiasm which greeted our new Principal at his morning lecture. Never before had the precincts of the Chemistry Department been subject to such an invasion. In the lecture-room itself the Chemistry Class was submerged in cheering crowds of Arts Students, Medicals, and even Divines. Professor Irvine was obviously deeply moved by his reception, and the genius whose well-timed jocular remark discharged the electrical atmosphere must himself have felt no small astonishment at its effects.[7]

The jocular remark thrown out from the back of the room was: 'Hoo'd ye wrangle it, Jimmy?' To which came the Delphic reply: 'Twenty years ago I was sitting where you are.'[8] All which that answer implied gave Irvine his clue for how he would put his stamp on the principalship. The needs of the student would be highlighted in Irvine's programme for the next ten years. Ambitious young men and women from St Andrews could then be sent out as the ambassadors he needed. By addressing the life of the student he would achieve growth in student numbers and fee income, and thus justify rapid growth in faculty staffing and an ambitious building programme. From the moment of Irvine's first arrival in St Andrews as Professor Purdie's laboratory assistant he had shown an instinctive empathy with the professor's students; and once he had himself become the professor he developed this relationship. In 1921 his old students were eager to tell of the friendship they had enjoyed with their chief. His charm and powers of persuasion had drawn a whole generation of young scientists to a laboratory that the scientific world was beginning to recognise as pre-eminent in its field.

One, however, described early twentieth-century St Andrews as 'the shadow of a mighty name'. The truth was that its survival was very much in question, and Irvine faced up to the challenge. The difficulty of the new Principal's task was reflected at large in national affairs: in the need for retrenchment in some quarters and accelerated economic growth in others. The same edition of *The Times* that announced Irvine's appointment reported a speech made by Austen Chamberlain, at that time Chancellor of the Exchequer. He didn't pull his punches. Great Britain was experiencing the worst economic recession on record.

For a brief time after the war the universities were swollen with an unusual influx of ex-service students. Current economic factors in the United Kingdom threatened the normal balance of supply and demand in the universities: there was a general increase in salaries in the teaching profession; the depression in scientific industry, which raised the numbers in arts at the expense of pure science and medicine; and the increased popularity of professional degrees in engineering and industrial chemistry.

It had to be faced that the newer civic universities in England presented a competitive but dangerous alternative, feeding more directly as they did the regeneration of the economy. These sombre thoughts formed the substance of Irvine's inaugural address of 11 January 1921, which took as its subject 'The Place of a Small University in Reconstruction' and which *The Times* as well as the Scottish broadsheets published in full, with the publishers of the *St Andrews' Citizen* producing it in book form. In composing his address, Irvine looked into the coming difficult years, and he resolved to solve the problem by bucking the modern trend towards large universities.[9]

He decided to refrain from embarking on extensive building programmes during his first quinquennial of the University Grants Committee. His image of St Andrews recognised its special attributes, and these he selected for the foundation of its future. Because of its geographical position the university would never grow inordinately large, but it could be – in miniature – the very essence of academe. The handsome and historic buildings, and the quiet medieval streets and wynds, would enclose departments of disinterested learning and research, to which students would clamour for admission. Irvine would have to be bullish during these early years if he was to win the fight for anything so exquisite.

On this day of inauguration, Irvine described his vision of a university kept deliberately small, where he could strive to make perfect what he felt had been made good 500 years ago by its founding fathers. In St Andrews, Bishop Kennedy's College of St Salvator, now known as the United College, still survived, to give students the experience of intimacy with their fellows and a sharing of purpose with their teachers: a friendly comradeship that was recognised far and wide as the 'St Andrews Spirit'. Everything must be done to further the needs and fortunes of the individual: especially the scholars who would learn more than a utilitarian application of higher studies. The image of the medieval bishop, the devout patron of these buildings holding in the palm of his hand the very model of all he would create, floated in and out of Irvine's mind throughout his term of office. He would have this image of James Kennedy emblazoned in stained glass in his new men's residence once it came into being.[10] Irvine felt a spiritual connection with the medieval founders of his office, and in 1921 he dedicated himself to recreating in modern terms the university of Bishop Kennedy and Bishop Wardlaw.

His inaugural address did not dissemble. He needed at least £150,000 straight away from central funds in order to put right the lagging salary scales that could ultimately cause staff to leave; to continue the work of providing modern conditions for the laboratory teaching of the sciences; and to strengthen the number and value of scholarships. No man should be too good to occupy a chair at St Andrews. The address was gratifyingly prophetic. Irvine's tenure would show that this, his university, would possess chairs with emoluments sufficient to attract scholars away from the larger institutions. An initial policy not to increase staff numbers was attempted, and the existing staff coped with the post-war bulge with no apparent diminution of quality in teaching and research. This policy was soon overtaken by Irvine's proven skill in enlarging assistantships into lectureships.

Central to his plan was the realisation that he needed the co-operation of the students, the body corporate of the university. He flattered them that they would convey into every phase of national activity in the outside world something of the humanity and comradeship of St Andrews. Such men and women could, he felt, make the world a better place – a phrase that was on everyone's lips in those years of reconstruction after the brutality of war. He then played the card of the scarlet gown, a symbol of his commonality with all the members of the university, past and present. This common experience gave him a special insight into something that was lacking in the

still-primitive conditions of life of the Scottish student, and he embarked
on the redevelopment of the Men's Union.

On 20 January 1921, Irvine, a guest at the St Andrews University Conservative Association's annual dinner, introduced his plans for the students'
union. Predictably he spoke in praise of the charms and beauties of St
Andrews, and remarked on how the St Andrews spirit inspired the students
who had gone to war. In time these men came back – some of them. He also
remembered those fine men who had not come back. He threw down the
gauntlet: those who had returned had now to pick up the broken threads
and try to reconstruct a new world. Twisting the popular slogan, he raised
applause and laughter by stating that if this country was to be made a place
fit for heroes to live in, why should they not have a Students' Union fit for
students to live in?[11] In that year, the resources at the disposal of the Court
were appropriately increased by the allocation of a non-recurrent grant by
the Treasury for 'student and social needs'.

Irvine's life-long championship of the student would always stand in
contrast with the private scorn he bore towards many of his colleagues. To
take student welfare as his first arm of development might have seemed
perverse to his colleagues, who were conscious of the needs of their underfunded departments, but it was typical of Irvine's belief that higher education in St Andrews should educate the whole man. The normal development
of the university had of course been cut short by the war, but it had long
been felt that the need to provide for students' living conditions should be
the chief factor in arresting the impoverishment of their lives. St Andrews
would cultivate the social and civilised arts, and the 'new' union would be
more like a gentleman's club. The modest development of the union had
two further attractions in Irvine's eyes: it could attract private donations,
and it had picturesque qualities that would bring good press.[12]

Ever a pragmatist, Irvine seized the opportunity offered by the planned
new union to enlarge and restore the fine building that, 350 years previously,
had been the lodging house of the Admirable Crichton when a student.
This building on North Street, originally fitted by Lord Bute's benefaction
for the use of students living in 'bunks', had been requisitioned during the
war, and in 1921 it was dingy, dilapidated and almost unfurnished; to Irvine
it now offered a rather romantic fresh start. In 1921 there was very little
formal accommodation for the men students, who still lived for the most
part in lodgings. Irvine had lived in the same way during his student days:
he was only too aware of its shortcomings, and he wished to provide a
dimension to the student experience whereby students could benefit from

taking meals together and sharing their leisure hours. The facilities of the new union were a forerunner of the residential development to come.

Irvine attracted private donations to the union from his friend David Russell, and then most notably from the Chancellor's Assessor, Dr William Low, whom he described as the student's friend. Under a new ruling, Dr Low's gift of £6,500 was met pound for pound by the University Grants Committee. They were ready to engage the president of the Royal Institute of British Architects, Paul Waterhouse. This notable addition to the dignity of the university may have been Irvine's first development but, far from claiming a large-scale capital grant from the government, its cost was made up from several quarters, most of them philanthropic. Irvine's reputation for good housekeeping was beginning to shine forth, and so was his characteristic love of detail. With great relish, he could not resist involving himself even in the choice of club armchair from Maples, nor from insisting that the upholstery should be of a manly brown, rather than red. Dr Low finally added the gift of a specially sprung dance floor, and that pleased the Principal very much.

The *St Andrews Citizen* reported approvingly that

the interior of the building has undergone a thorough transformation and every provision had been made for the comfort and pleasure of the students during the hours of leisure they spend within its walls. No structural rearrangements were required in the old dining hall in the Butts Wynd part of the building, but it has been very tastefully redecorated. The new entrance hall in Butts Wynd has, however, undergone considerable alteration, and its fine domed ceiling is very effective. From this entrance hall one can pass through an old archway (which was originally part of the house of the famous Admirable Crichton) into the well-appointed coffee lounge. The old roundel in North Street has been preserved and made more picturesque with an attic window.

All was complete for that October day in 1923 when, as Rector, Rudyard Kipling, like Irvine a clubbable man, rededicated this student club 'in the service of mirth, fellowship and good will'.[13]

The architect Paul Waterhouse was also asked to give an opinion on how the chemistry and natural philosophy (physics) buildings could be enlarged with the addition of another storey. Mrs Purdie's large bequest continued to provide for the needs of chemistry in the university. Paul Waterhouse's scheme was estimated at £13,800 for these two contiguous buildings; it was, however, a local architect with offices in Dundee, Mr Donald Mills, who got the job on the sudden death of Mr Waterhouse, thereby cementing his future relationship with the university.[14]

This was but the beginning of a supremely happy period for Jim Irvine. He threw himself into his two worlds of St Andrews and London. London alone had the power to realise his hopes, and he enjoyed playing his part on the big stage. He would board the night sleeper at Leuchars, settle himself down in his usual first-class berth and, after a good night's sleep, be awakened by his friendly steward in time to prepare for a day of meetings. He jokingly branded himself the travelling salesman of education: education, in its broadest sense, was his vocation. He took an immense interest in the feeder secondary schools; he was never too busy to address speech days, to distribute prizes and to spread the word that St Andrews should be everyone's first choice of university.[15]

Many of the national committees that he sat on were still chemical and scientific, but there was now, additionally, the Standing Committee of Vice-Chancellors, which he had to impress. With no London club as yet, he put up at Cox's Hotel in Jermyn Street. A letter he wrote to Mabel in the spring of 1921 conveys the full flavour of his dynamic personality.

> Yesterday was a very very busy time but I enjoyed it hugely, was in good form and took part in all the business with a freshness and vigour which makes all the difference between happiness and misery. I chaired the Power Alcohol Board at 10, left at 11.45 for Russell Square to attend 'The Standing Committee of Vice-Chancellors', had lunch, another meeting & then back to the Fats and Oils. Met Robinson there & had tea with him.[16]

Irvine was contracted to carry on his duties as professor until September of that year, and the meeting with Robert Robinson was a prelude to drawing in the brilliant chemist to fill his place in the St Andrews chair of chemistry. Robinson's salary of £800 per annum, augmented by £200 per annum as director of the chemistry research laboratory, showed the increase from the Treasury that Irvine had promised to fight for, with the indication of annual increments to come.[17]

It was decided that the university should incur no debts, and no deficits should be allowed to accumulate. Post-war inflation added to the need to increase staff salaries, and pressure was being put on the government to make interim grants to cover these contingencies.

Even the fee to Messrs Munro of South Street, for winding the College Tower clock, had to go up, an increase that would bring the fee up to pre-war value.[18] Little by little, funds would come in, even if these were not initially the large-scale Treasury grants that Irvine needed.

In 1921, Irvine's reconstruction hopes for faculty and student accommodation were still waiting to be realised, but he was successful in bringing salary scales more in line with the rest of the country, and in gradually enlarging the existing departments, both in Dundee and in St Andrews, with new lectureships. Medicine in Dundee was richly treated at this time, with lectureships in clinical surgery, forensic medicine, anaesthetics and public health. It required the incisive mind of a new Principal to institute a Board of Studies in medicine, in uncomfortable partnership with the Board of Directors of the Dundee Infirmary. The powers of Scotland's first school of dental surgery, affiliated to the university, were, after a period of preparation, eventually enlarged with the granting of a degree in dentistry. In St Andrews, with provision for the sciences ever increasing, the Faculty of Arts was not neglected: English was given a lecturer and an assistant. The appointment of a new college organist and choir master, in the person of Mr Sawyer (known as 'Pop' to the members of the chapel choir), gave the opportunity to institute in 1925 a lectureship in music for the 'Singing University'.[19] Some of these introductions may seem insignificant today, but in the 1920s they were extraordinary.

Adding to the ranks of the professors was a more complex matter. The institution of new chairs had to go through due process and be submitted for the approval of His Majesty the King in council. New medical chairs – one, for example, in bacteriology – were given to Dundee, but the foundation of a chair in French in St Andrews proper was kept in abeyance. The Educational Institute of Scotland, of which Irvine was a fellow, backed St Andrews in its efforts to establish chairs in modern languages: only financial stringency held Irvine back.

Although it still retained many of the traditional characteristics of the Scottish university, St Andrews now increasingly embraced both the lecture system and the Oxbridge tutorial system; minor structural changes in the United College buildings were made in order to provide more tutorial rooms. The Faculty of Arts became more lively as the class libraries were brought up to date and class or departmental grants were enlarged. The composite effect of these developments meant that, when the large expansion in student numbers came with St Andrews' full espousal of the residential system, the university would be prepared on every front. An expansion in student numbers, for both financial and intellectual reasons, was of prime importance to the university, small and perfect though it might be. Irvine aspired to trawl for students from a far wider field than those previously served by the Scottish universities. He wanted St Andrews to be known for 'authentic scholarship'; for research. A letter he received at this time from Professor Burnet reflects the problem for young classicists who had never been away from Scotland: 'It is not easy for young men in Fife to realise the vast field that is open for investigation in the Mediterranean world if they have never seen it.'[20] Irvine had earlier fought against this tendency to parochialism; he was successful in staffing his chemistry department with research students and junior lecturers who came from all over the British Isles to study under him. With his fondness for the statistics that would illustrate St Andrews' attainments, he could say, even in 1921, that the ratio of research students to total numbers enormously exceeded the figure in Edinburgh, which was, overall, five or six times as large as St Andrews.[21]

In July 1921, a most unexpected event thrust the young principal into the limelight amongst the academic grandees of Oxford and Cambridge. The sudden death of Alexander Bruce, Lord Balfour of Burleigh, gave a platform to Irvine, who was attending the Congress of the Universities of the Empire in Oxford. He enjoyed any opportunity to show off his pride in St Andrews and its ancient ceremonial protocols. Lord Balfour, Chancellor of St Andrews, had been billed to address the congress in Oxford on the very day that he died. Irvine, as the acting Chancellor, became by Balfour's death both the youngest and the most senior of all the delegates, and he took the chair and delivered the substance of Balfour's speech. It was a stirring occasion. 'I was paraded as a kind of young lion who had been discovered lurking in the academic forests of the far North,' he wrote.[22] This proved to be the first of many occasions when he would broadcast his belief that this group of post-war vice-chancellors would be leaders of fresh ideals in education, and that they would 'carry into every phase of national activity and into the remote corners of the earth this spirit of sympathy, understanding and of mutual good-will'.

In time and in the same spirit, Irvine would chair the committee that ensured higher education in the West Indies, and head the Inter-University Council for Higher Education in the Colonies (1946), but on 7 July 1921 it was enough that he experienced the exhilaration of holding an audience of his senior peers in the palm of his hand, in the august surroundings of Oxford University's Examination Schools. It amused him to think that he had in this way held every position in his university, from bejant (first year student) to chancellor. Immediately, however, Irvine had an idea for Balfour's successor, and happily for Irvine his wish was not opposed. Field-Marshal Earl Haig's election as chancellor in February 1922 resolved the vacancy.

A vivid appreciation of an address given at the Royal Society of Arts in 1930 describes Irvine's oratorical style:

> It was perfect in every way – intensely interesting in matter, the purest poetry in style, and masterly in delivery. I have listened to a good many speakers in my day, from Gladstone and Rosebery downwards, and I can honestly say I never heard a more finished piece of oratory, nor one that moved me so profoundly.[23]

Irvine's power as an orator grew immeasurably from the early exposure of these years, and it added considerable grace and power to the manner in which he headed his university, despite the polymath D'Arcy Thompson's open mockery of his unease with Latin quantities. He wisely accepted D'Arcy's offer to coach him when the need to give an oration in Latin arose. In return, there is evidence that Irvine drafted correspondence in French for D'Arcy, whose education at the Edinburgh Academy had concentrated on the classics, unlike Irvine's 'modern' education at Allan Glen's, which provided the young technocrats with a smattering of modern languages for commercial purposes.[24] Beneath a superficial demonstration of mutual support, the two famous scientists somewhat despised each other: D'Arcy because Irvine, the new man, the charmer, the Glasgow scientist, was successful but lacked the Edinburgh polish of a classical education; Irvine because D'Arcy seemed to him to be a silly man, who must be tolerated and humoured for the reputation of *On Growth and Form* (1917), D'Arcy's seminal work, and for the originality and brilliance of his scientific thought, all of which added to St Andrews' international reputation.[25]

Irvine was a moderniser, with a business background. He got to work on the University Grants Committee, which was opening the door to university superannuation schemes; Irvine instantly offered these to the ranks of lecturers. The finance-starved early years were not wasted: there were more things he could put right without calling on capital funding from the Treasury. The Students' Representative Council petitioned Irvine's first Court meeting as Principal for the introduction of electric lighting to the library reading room, and a complete lighting scheme was authorised. By

1922 he was manipulating the library sub-committee, headed by D'Arcy, in its work to introduce a thoroughgoing index after the model of the American Library of Congress: an index that would be printed.[26] He could not be seen to promote his bookish brother-in-law Jack Williams, lecturer in history, but he persuaded D'Arcy to co-opt him onto the committee. The beautifying of Parliament Hall, the repository of the King James Library, with oak panelling, oak bookstands, central heating gratings in brass, a chimney piece of Cullaloe sandstone 8 feet high with three carved stone panels of the founders' heraldic coats of arms, was but the icing on a cake that included a large budget for steel shelving and strong-room provision. The modernising of the library is an aspect of Irvine's work that is very little known.

The two celebrated scientists, Irvine and D'Arcy Thompson, worked hard during these years to promote their common belief in the development of science in St Andrews. A threat to St Andrews' claim to supremacy in the field of marine biology soon came in 1923, in the form of the Development Commission's wish to develop the Millport station off the west coast of Scotland as the exclusive research station for marine biology. Jim Irvine's Glasgow contacts disclosed 'a plot that Millport is to be the one and only place where Biological Research is to be done in Scotland'.[27] Irvine grimly took on the fight to consolidate the development of the Gatty Marine Department under D'Arcy Thompson by whatever means he could, and St Andrews declined to contribute to the Millport laboratory. Little by little, Irvine siphoned off funds to support D'Arcy and the Gatty Marine Laboratory. St Andrews' friends, even as far afield as Baltimore, used their influence. It must be noted, however, that privately Irvine felt the Gatty would have a stronger future were it equipped for work in experimental biology and bio-chemistry.[28] But Irvine was sympathetic to D'Arcy's development of the University Museum's eclectic collection of scientific specimens. D'Arcy needed a boat: Irvine somehow found an obscure fund that he could pillage for a boat.[29] In conspiratorial tone, Irvine encouraged D'Arcy in his bid for prolonged leave of absence in 1929. The author of *On Growth and Form* was exactly the kind of personality and mind that Irvine knew would play the part he needed in putting St Andrews on the map. 'Naturally, you are having a specially busy year and the extra engagements thrust on you at this time, if not too tiring for you, shed luster on us . . . the University gains much by what you do.'[30]

To turn to Jim's cherished family life, Mabel and the three Irvine children – Veronica, Nigel and Felicity – could not help but enjoy the many things that their new life gave them. There was a honeymoon period of picnics in the garden of University House, the official residence that was being overhauled for the Principal's family, who moved in during the summer of 1921.[31] The University Court voted £1,000 to be spent on the refurbishment of University House for family use. Edgecliffe was let: it became a useful source of income with which to support their more expansive and expensive lives. Poor Lady Herkless tried to sell Mabel the drawing room's pink carpet, but Mabel had ideas of her own. She detested the Herkless's over-stuffed interiors, heavy with the sickly scent of hyacinths. She would allow the colours and the light of the sea beyond its windows to decorate her drawing room. The walls were painted pale ivory; her curtains were of sea-blue silk. The parquet floor would be revealed and simply covered with Persian rugs, ready for the many dances that Jim and Mabel would give: they were young and they loved dancing. The pretty mantelpiece, echoing the colour of the floor, was of honey coloured marble, and to its left, set into the wall, was a glazed cupboard, just waiting to be filled with Mabel's collection of pink lustre ceramics. When Veronica was still only five years old, David Foggie, Dundee artist and Scottish RA, had come to paint her portrait, and also that of her mother. These large, watercolour portraits hung on the walls of the drawing room at University House, much at home in that watery background of sea and weather. In pride of place was Mabel's Steinway grand piano, given to her by her father when she was a girl in Belfast.[32]

The dining room was richer: of gold silk and dark mahogany. Here was enacted all the solemnity of an Edwardian family's eating rituals. There were large sideboards bearing domed coverings, from beneath which would be revealed the kippers or devilled kidneys, or maybe a finnan haddie poached in milk. A hearty breakfast primed the morning comings and goings of the occupants of the house. The cook knew that the way to please the Principal was to provide herring roe, soft or hard. Porridge was, of course, as Scottish tradition demanded, taken standing, while the all-important question of the weather was pronounced upon by studying, from the tall windows, the outline of the hills of County Angus across St Andrews Bay. The formality of the dining room was put to work in the university's service: the student who read the lesson in chapel on Sundays was always invited to lunch, as was the preacher; Jim's guests to the university 'dined and slept' at University House, and at graduation time, distinguished company was invariably seated at formal dinners.[33] Early in 1922, the university's armorial bearings were proudly carved above the door to University House, in time for the press photographers that attended the arrival of J.M. Barrie as Rector, and Earl Haig as Chancellor.[34]

This was very much an upstairs–downstairs house, with an elaborate provision beyond the dining room for the servants that were always so hard to come by. 'Wee Nanny', as Jim always referred to the children's nurse, scampered up and down the two flights of the back stairs to the nurseries, while the children toiled alone up the handsome stair rising from the front hall. There was a night nursery for the baby, and bedrooms for Nigel and Veronica; and on beyond, far above the kitchens, were dormitories for the many maids that they should have had. The Irvines filled every corner of that handsome house. In the day nursery the children took their meals and played games on wet days. Here lived Michael Faraday – not the alarming demonstrator of the power of electricity, but the rocking horse. Veronica and Nigel, with one or two local friends, started their first schooling in this room under the instruction of a governess, Miss Lascelles. While they were still young, their father, who could not resist playing the part of the dominie, gave them lessons of his own imaginative devising. Soon, however, Jim, who had himself been an almost self-consciously manly little boy, had to persuade Mabel that Nigel must leave the family schoolroom and grow up with other boys in a boys' boarding school. He went to Craig-flower, a newly established preparatory school not far away at Torryburn, on the Fife shore of the Firth of Forth. The Irvines sought out fresh educational approaches for their son, because Mabel had a horror of muscular education in the Arnold mould. At thirteen, Nigel went on to Stowe which, under its first headmaster, J.F. Roxburgh, was considered the most interesting school of the age, despite being in its infancy.

The furnishing of University House was certainly daunting to the Irvines' purse, but within a few months they would be entertaining the constantly moving procession of famous guests that began with Sir James Barrie's rectorial installation of May 1922.

During the Edgecliffe years, Mabel's earnings from the *Glasgow Herald*, which published her verse and essays, had enabled her to buy antique furniture from sales and from shops in St Andrews. She never paid very much, and she had a good eye. Mabel found great solace in writing, and while Jim was absent from home, verse and essays flowed from her pen, coming to life in the newspapers and magazines of the day. A volume of her poetry, under the title *From a Nursery Window*, was published in 1922;[35] within its covers are to be found the secret thoughts and feelings of this woman, the wife of the Principal and mother of their children. It was well reviewed in the London press.

The new Principal's study, on the first floor, overlooked the college tower, which loomed over his every endeavour. Armchairs beside the study fire presented an open invitation to any colleague who wished to talk over university business privately. Even mere students seeking advice were welcome. True to his inaugural address, Principal Irvine ruled through his interest in the individual.

The fact that their daddy was the Principal might have had a dampening effect on the children's lives. Irvine required an orderly and quiet household that operated like clockwork, just as the night train to London was supposed to do. He was given to rages if this invariable rule was fractured. Mabel struggled, and the children played endlessly out of doors in the big garden, beyond the earshot of their father. This was an unusual father, however, who from their first babyhood had invented dramatised games for his children that he relished quite as much as did his young conspirators. The garden soon acquired many associations, growing out of the lives of the family that lived there for thirty years. All children are fascinated by kitchen gardens, and in the Irvine children's games this garden became Exmoor and was the imaginary location of R.D. Blackmore's *Lorna Doone*. They needed few friends other than each other, but Jo Grimond, the future leader of the Liberal party, was a childhood playmate, and with him they played at 'Jacobites and Hanoverians'. Unfortunately, Veronica had a red winter overcoat, and Jo firmly pronounced that she should cease to be a Jacobite and could only be one of the hated Hanoverians. The coat was quickly passed on to Nigel. One day he was chased all the way home by a drunk man who, shaking his fist, called out, 'Ah wan' yon wee laddie in the reid coat!'[36] Unlucky coat!

The Irvine children grew up with the roar of the sea in their ears, but this did not make strong swimmers of them. Veronica had been given early lessons in swimming using a Victorian bathing machine which was designed to impose modesty on the lady swimmers but which turned the process of learning to swim into something rather terrifying to the little girl. Their father was quite another kind of swimmer. He was a strong swimmer and throughout most of his life he habitually took a swim in sea-water from the Step-Rock all-male bathing pool. It released his pent-up adrenalin, and made him feel invigorated once more.

Mabel was too creative a personality to enjoy the role of housekeeper, but the sumptuous and natural beauty of the garden, with its backcloth of pale yellow sand and blue sea, gave her much joy. Their first gardener was called Doig, and with him she devised planting schemes that pleased her artistic sense. The path along the top of the cliff ended in a haze of foxgloves: 'Foxglove Corner' it became. 'The garden in June is like a dream – poppies and lupins banked against the blue of the bay. All these things are so good and so beautiful that one thanks God for them,' she wrote in her diary.[37] Soon Doig was proud to welcome the arrival of prize dahlias from America named Sir James Irvine and Lady Irvine, with ironic reference to the scientist who had turned dahlias into inulin and who seemed to be acquiring celebrity status in America. These ones would be spared the laboratory mincing machine, and were solemnly planted in the University House garden. When the Irvines moved into University House, they enjoyed the fact that the garden possessed a large conservatory, or winter garden as they called it.

After tea, often of crumpets toasted by Jim, a general exodus into the garden resulted in a romp that worked off any surplus energy, and the Principal became a boy again. A visitor to St Andrews peered through the gates of University House, and enquired who was the big lad playing with the Principal's children. 'Oh, that's the Principal,' was the reply. Jim needed that garden just much as the rest of his family. Seats were positioned in sheltered spots overlooking the sea, such as the paved circle that that they named Piccadilly, where he could read and rest. Here he would spin his dreams for the university for the benefit of visitors from America. A large window in the drawing room could be flung open, giving onto a handsome cast-iron flight of steps down to the garden beneath. On warm summer nights after dinner, guests would descend into the garden by this way. The lawn to the west of the house was maintained as a tennis court, and when he was not playing tennis Jim enjoyed keeping it free of weeds, by gouging out the daisies with his little penknife. He had the neat hands and fingers necessary to an experimental scientist, and the penknife was brought out to perform many fascinating tasks: tiny objects were made from wood, and the names of the family were carved on the trunks of trees.

If the Principal showed evidence of his scientific calling in his private life, how much more did he believe that the unfolding success of his public life owed everything to the fact that he was still essentially a scientist. Irvine was a philosophical sort of scientific man. Quite early on he felt it necessary to reflect on why he seemed to be good at his job, and he, a young, confident and thrusting public figure, argued that the best administrators are essentially scientists.

An orderly habit of mind was created in which something of the prophetic instinct can be discerned. A problem has to be solved, well what are the facts already known about it regarding it; next, what new methods can be devised to reach the goal; finally, what obstacles are likely to be encountered on the way and how can these be forestalled?

. . .

The best administrators, and incidentally, the best leaders are all endowed, irrespective of their training, with the basic scientific virtues.

To these qualities I must add another, and that is a sense of rigid accuracy.[38]

In these ways, he built up his towering reputation. Could such a paragon of virtue have possessed any faults? Alas, there was a fatal flaw, and paradoxically it was that he was always right. With some modesty he would try to modify this, but it was a strong characteristic of this driven man. Ultimately, it may have been the prime factor in the one devastating experience of his career: what he called the 'Dundee Fiasco'. The findings of the Royal Commission of 1952 that followed the failed Cooper Report on the relationship between University College Dundee and the University of St Andrews may be seen to have contributed to his death, but these disturbances could barely have been imagined in the new beginning of 1921. The effects on others of this supreme confidence grumbled away beneath the surface. His rages were often directed at his colleagues in Court or Senatus. Late in her life, his daughter Veronica would smile and say that it was not easy to grow up beside such a man for a father, no matter how loveable or how companionable he was when at play.

As a man of affairs, Irvine learned that he would have to acquire new skills on top of those of the laboratory. In St Andrews he was, under the university's constitution, lord of all he surveyed, but he had to learn quickly the art of getting his way in committee in London and Edinburgh. The lesson was soon observed by Irvine:

There is of course a vast difference between molecules and men – the former can be shaped and fashioned at will, they respond uniformly on all occasions when treated in the same way, but no-one can predict with any measure of accuracy the actions and reactions involved in human relationships. This at once introduces an element of uncertainty, which at first is inclined to bewilder or irritate the orderly scientific mind.[39]

Irvine lived under enormous pressure. He did not believe in delegation, and he imposed on his highly strung temperament a regime of long days and short nights. The financial strain was a further burden. His income was pushed to its limit. In those days, university principals and vice-chancellors were expected to live 'of their own': like medieval monarchs. There was no financial intervention or support from the university or the state for the expenses involved in running the official residence – although, in the case of University House in St Andrews, it was the university's secret asset. It was the means whereby the university could be shown off to all who would help St Andrews, and its door stood open to every visitor, both great and small.

Where Irvine's case differed from his fellow British vice-chancellors was that, as the youngest vice-chancellor, and of a university so small in terms of numbers, his salary was initially correspondingly lower. In 1921 it was £1,500 per annum, as compared to the £2,000 per annum given to the vice-chancellors of Edinburgh and Glasgow, and indeed to those of most of the English universities.[40] At first it was a relief to him that his scientific consultancies added to his means. However, such was the weight of entertaining Jim and Mabel took on that, when in 1923 an application was made to the Court for financial relief for heating and lighting University House, it was acceded to. At the very end of his life he could write to his wife that they could at last afford a few indulgences, since he was then the highest paid vice-chancellor in the country.

Many have spoken of the Irvine occupancy of University House as a golden age, and so it was. Mabel's diary, however, gives a picture of the reality.

> The Principal's income is absolutely inadequate to run this big house. The constant entertaining of all and sundry, from Princes, Peers and poets to professor and plain people, entails a staff of properly trained and expensive maids. It is impossible without a good cook with high wages, and a really good parlour-maid, housemaid, kitchen-maid and children's maid. This with the children's education swallows up every penny, and Jim is bound to add to his income by taking on scientific jobs of various sorts, adding to his labours.[41]

His wife despaired of her ability to manage the household budget, but Jim loved the generosity of his wife's form of warm, Irish welcome, the beauty of the home she had made and the lively conversations round the fireside, which drew the world to St Andrews and to their ever-open door.

The inimitable stamp of the grand and yet intimate that Mabel and her extended family of clever brothers placed on any occasion made their hospitality cherished by their important visitors. Luckily, her brother Jack, a historian of great promise and a brilliant conversationalist, was in post in St Andrews and proved to be of inestimable worth to his brother-in-law. If Irvine wanted his own way with any project of historic importance, Jack could be relied on to back him up with learned historical chapter and verse. If the dinner table needed enlivening, Jack was the ready guest. If the Principal was too busy to look after a visiting American, Jack was there to seduce them with a tour of the antiquities of the old town. And when on occasion Jim was in America at graduation time, Jack at least was on hand to help Mabel entertain the university's guests.

Irvine may have led two parallel lives – that of 'Jimmy the Princ', as the students irreverently dubbed him, evident to one and all in St Andrews; and James Irvine, soon to be Sir James, at the head of national educational development – but to Mabel there were also two Jims. She took pride in seeing her husband appreciated by men old enough to be his father; and in seeing her husband in a position of power and importance at such an early age, consulted on all kinds of appointments in the academic world. It was a great happiness to her to see him capture the attention of the public so vividly: he was a brilliant speaker, and yet quiet and dignified, simple and approachable, almost deliberately modest about his own achievements. She was also relieved that her Jim, as she knew him intimately, was not lost to her. He still played with the children and spent happy hours with her, planning and dreaming in the firelight of his study, and ever taking contentment from the little things, ever her rock of strength. 'Rather a wonderful Jim,' she observed wistfully in her diary, knowing very well that he had taken on the equivalent of many men's work, and that he lived under severe nervous strain in order to carry through his projects, to manage meetings and to keep up his voluminous correspondence.

This new life of theirs placed an enormous burden on her as well. The burden did not diminish. The weight of their surviving correspondence is ample proof of the degree to which they were apart. 'We were not made to live apart, darling, even for a week,' wrote Jim from an extended series of meetings in the south of England. Summer after summer, Jim embarked on long visits to North America, where he was fêted and handsomely remunerated for the speeches and lectures that his new friends commissioned from him. Jim's absences from home only added to his wife's responsibilities in St Andrews. By 1928, she was in a constant state of collapse.

Colitis was diagnosed. Finally she sought medical advice in London, and spent weeks on end holed up in a Knightsbridge hotel, under the care of a Harley Street osteopath. In an age of new therapies of every kind, Mabel's search for specialist relief from her sufferings led her to several of the alternative practitioners of the day. Her frequent and mysterious illnesses were the true cost, perhaps, of the Irvine success, and Jim never failed in his gratitude.[42]

The award of a knighthood to Jim in the New Year Honours List of 1925 was a reward for all that the Irvines' marriage had done for the university. People welcomed the fact that a knighthood so fittingly gave position and honour to Mabel as well. Many believed that it was six years overdue: they felt that others less worthy had been recognised in this way after the war. This, Baldwin's first honours list of his second term of office, followed immediately on the Conservatives' 1922 robust moral stand against Lloyd George and his 'money for honours'. In the year of 1925, Baldwin brought in the Prevention of Abuses to Honours Act, and the list of January 1925, described as 'small and select' was composed, to general approbation, of 'people of probity who had given high service to their country'. Stanley Baldwin, who first visited St Andrews University for the rectorial inauguration of his cousin Rudyard Kipling, became Chancellor of the university in 1929.

All of Jim's chemical friends claimed that the knighthood was a recognition of the part that chemistry was playing in this new world. The members of the wider St Andrews University community felt that a knighthood for their Principal brought honour to their alma mater. Friends of Jim's from his own student days emerged from the shadows to declare that they always knew this would happen sooner or later, and a chorus of his own students attested to the personality that had made him such a formative educator and that would now ensure St Andrews could be recognised in the wider world, stating: 'Your students would have knighted you long ago, had they been kings.' J.M. Barrie imagined himself young and a student: 'Bonfire tonight in St Andrews, or as soon as the students return.'[43] On Jim's next visit to London, having been witheringly told by the tailors that court dress was never hired, he had himself measured for a pair of breeches.

As Irvine drew near to the end of the first quinquennial term of his office, he estimated that a surplus of about £4,190 would be shown, something rare in higher education budgets. The university had reason to be thankful that Irvine had been appointed and, with this confidence in him, the Court sanctioned considerable investment in equipping the several scientific departments. In May 1924, Irvine faced his first visit from the University Grants Committee, prior to dispensing further university funding for the next five years. Under the pretence that there were not any vacancies in the hotels to accommodate visitors from London, the Irvines and Dr James Younger, at Mount Melville, put up Sir William McCormick, Sir Wilmot Herringham, Marjory Fry, Mr A.H. Kidd and Mr Chesterman in considerable comfort. This transgression of the rules under which the Grants Committee worked was never repeated, but the Principal prepared a meticulously conceived and printed programme for the visit, emphasising the current developments in the sciences and highlighting the restoration of the chapel. Like the producer of a play, he set the scene that he wanted his funders to see. The results were gratifyingly successful.[44] After the Second World War, the same technique would be successfully applied.

Most importantly, Sir William McCormick pointed out that the expansion in the number of students attending St Andrews would depend on the provision that the university might make for student residences. This was what Irvine wanted him to say and think; it would become one of Irvine's finest achievements. He must have been persuasive, because the Grants Committee came up with some non-recurrent capital. St Andrews received a substantial one-sixth share of the whole of the committee's additional capital funding of the universities of the United Kingdom for 1925–30.

In the same way, he prepared his submission to the Carnegie Trust for the Universities of Scotland, in earnest quest for money for buildings and endowments. The Carnegie Trust was of a mind to distribute large capital funds, and Irvine's claim for St Andrews recognised the need for better endowments for the new chairs in Dundee. The Trust's visitation enabled Irvine to make the acquaintance of Lord Sands, Lord Novar, Sir Francis Ogilvie and Mr H.P. Macmillan (later to be Lord Macmillan): all future dramatis personae in Irvine's life. The Trust complied with almost all he had asked for, including £20,000 for the ambitious new hall of residence for male students.[45]

The pawky old occupants of the Edinburgh New Club who, in 1920, had wanted to put a theologian at the head of St Andrews need not have feared for the university's well-being in the hands of a young scientist. By 1927 Irvine was heavily involved in the tangled business of church union in Scotland; the very future of St Andrews' theological college hung on his skill in bringing a committee round to his point of view.[46] The Conference on the Union of the Churches was given a day in St Andrews: 'We did our guests proud – gave them an excellent lunch, showed them how to conduct a meeting.' By showing tolerance, finding solutions to difficulties and topping it all off with a good tea in beautiful surroundings, Irvine and Principal Galloway of St Mary's College were sure they had secured the future of their pre-Reformation college. St Mary's continued to develop as central to the Church's training programme under the new union in the Church of Scotland.

Irvine was beginning to get a taste for the business of extracting capital funding, but it would be wrong to think that his growing importance in London led him away from his spiritual base. It was his old chemical colleague G.D. Lander who wrote to him with insight about his position: 'It is this spiritual aspect; this chance of leading plastic young minds to a glimpse of those things that far transcend pure reason, that appeals to me as the great opportunity of your honourable post.'[47] Everything in Irvine's life now led back to the lives of the students around him. At the beginning of the academic year 1925–6, the total number of matriculated students in the whole university, including the medical school and University College Dundee, had reached 643. It would require the building programme of the next years, in terms of halls of residence and faculty buildings, to show the real growth in numbers that St Andrews needed.

TEN

A Golden Age

To the generations that knew St Andrews at that time, the Irvine era was afterwards fondly remembered as a golden age, an impression which of course ignores the mundane reality of a principal's life: a life of tedious committees, petty politics, the constant search for money and the daily grind of too much work and too little time in which to do it. Irvine overcame his difficulties with a deeply rooted optimism and a belief that he had with St Andrews a concept of higher education that the whole world was capable of embracing, if he could but spread the word.

Throughout the three decades of his admittedly autocratic reign he stuck to the simple statement that St Andrews was the oldest and best survivor in the country of the medieval university, founded by the Church, with the elemental witness of cathedral and university buildings at the heart of what was still a late medieval town; that it was the smallest university in the country; and that, above all, it was the most romantic.[1] To this mast he pinned his colours, and it mattered not that the cathedral was in ruins. The remnants of the medieval collegiate university lay before him, ready to be brought to new life. How bitter he was that all that remained of Prior Hepburn's College of St Leonard was sold in the year of his birth to become a girls' public school.

The most romantic: Irvine was keenly susceptible to romance, but he also had something of the showman about him when it came to promoting the image of St Andrews. In the 1920s and 30s a series of brilliant rectorial installations, with which Irvine deliberately and personally identified, has left a colourful impression of the pageantry that Irvine hastened to put to his use. The office of rector in all four of the old Scottish universities is one which even to the present day is held most dear to each generation of students: 'The highest honour that we students of Scotland's oldest university can bestow,' as one student described it to Rudyard Kipling.[2] Although elected by the students to represent them in the courts of the university,[3] in the case of St Andrews the Rector in practice has often played a useful part as a confidential friend of the Principal, and as an adornment and ambassador of the university. Chosen by the students the rector might be, but these rectors could just as easily have been chosen by Irvine, so closely did they reflect his own interests and enthusiasms.

The traditions and stirring spirit of the St Andrews rectorial ceremonies offered to the young Principal an ideal subject for public relations, something that was not given full rein during Principal Herkless' wartime principalship. Herkless had grown to dread the high spirits of the students in rectorial mood, and when Haig came to take up his rectorship in May 1917, the students were given very little part to play in what was essentially their show. All of the customary high jinks that the students liked to use to make their rector welcome were forbidden. Instead of their torchlight procession and the drama of dragging the new Rector's carriage through the streets of St Andrews, the students were required to form 'rigid lines in the quad & like sheep without a shepherd marched to the volunteer hall'. Irvine would have agreed with the sentiments of this medical student, Clare Thomson, who described the ceremonies of Haig's installation as Rector in May 1917 as a 'wash-out'.[4] At that date Haig was regarded as a great leader in war, and his address took the classical model of Pericles' speech at the close of the first year of the Peloponnesian War. 'What,' he asked without irony, 'was the road by which we reached our position, what the form of Government under which our greatness grew, what the national habits out of which it sprang?' His message to the young of that time was that: 'The special value of education consists not merely in the cultivation of knowledge, but in laying the basis of noble and moral qualities.' 'We have won', he contested, 'because our national character is sound; because it is founded in honesty and love of justice.' In the peacetime of the 1920s Haig committed himself to an unbroken sequence of office, first as Rector and then as Chancellor of St Andrews. In 1917 Irvine had resented the fact that an opportunity was lost to show St Andrews to the world. It only made him ache to take up the reins of office himself.

In 1919, Haig was succeeded as Rector by Sir J.M. Barrie in the first contested election for twenty-three years. The war was still very much alive in the corporate mind of the university, and the rectorial committee, entirely composed of students, also considered the names of President Wilson, Marshal Foch and Clemenceau. The election of a playwright was considered something of a novelty; Principal Herkless regarded the imminent installation with horror. A sick man, he made it known that unless he could be guaranteed an absence of interruptions he would give no address, were there to be an installation, as is customary, in the early summer of the following year.[5] Fortunately for the history of the St Andrews rectorial, this depressing edict against a student tradition was unnecessary. Herkless died in June 1920. J.M. Barrie, who also dreaded the ordeal, breathed a sigh of relief at this excuse to defer his visit to St Andrews until May 1922.

With Barrie, Irvine fell heir to a most happy choice made by the students without any intervention from authority. It gave the signal for the first glittering occasion of Irvine's principalship. A rector's term of office is three years, and Barrie had left it to the eleventh hour to visit 'his' students. The date of 3 May was finally settled on, but still he prevaricated. A series of letters to Irvine, whom at that time he did not know, indicate his nervousness.

> I don't see why you should limit him [Haig, who was to be installed as Chancellor on the same day] to five minutes! The more of him, the less of me strikes me as a very fine writing arrangement.
>
> I trust the hall is not a large place, else I don't see how I can be heard. The smaller the better, I beg of you. (I conceive a deadly hatred of any outsiders who have applied for tickets.)[6]

What won him over were the letters that the Irvine children wrote to him: they were brimming over with welcome. This was a bookish family of natural thespians, and Nigel and Veronica could hardly contain their excitement at the thought of having the author of *Peter Pan* as a guest in their household. With Barrie came a royal progress of his friends from the theatre and the London literary scene. Ellen Terry, the actress, Squire Bancroft – the great actor–manager – John Galsworthy and E.V. Lucas all arrived as honorary graduands. Lady Cynthia Asquith, Barrie's secretary, was to describe Irvine as 'Scottish as peat', but Irvine, who was rapidly growing into the persona of a powerful academic leader, would have characteristically dismissed her as a conventional English type and lacking in imagination.

Field-Marshal Earl Haig had been elected Chancellor in January 1922, following the death of Lord Balfour of Burleigh, and Haig's introductions to the degree ceremony were servicemen, and colourful men at that: Lieutenant-Colonel Bernard Freyburg VC, the war hero, and: 'If it would not make the list too long I would also recommend Lord Wester Wemyss as a great sailor. He rendered very valuable service as First Sea Lord at a very critical period in the War; and of course is a famous Fifer.'[7] The arrival of these people alone created quite a stir in the little provincial town.

Barrie submitted with apparent good grace to the boisterous welcome that met him at the station, and the students played on Barrie's well-loved fictional rural tales of 'Thrums'. This Principal would positively encourage the students' holiday mood.

> As the train with the Rector steamed into the station, there was great commotion on the platform, 'Thrums Express' was noticed on the front of the engine ... A carriage from which the horses had been taken was in waiting at the station entrance, and when the Rector, the Principal and Dr Low had taken their seats in it, a large number of men students seized hold of the ropes and set off at a brisk pace to give the Rector a glimpse of the principal streets of the city before they took him to the Principal's residence ... Mrs Irvine and her daintily dressed little boy and girl were waiting at the door to welcome the Rector.[8]

Barrie's deep sense of foreboding was revealed in his 'au-revoir' to the students that afternoon: 'Bless you all. We shall meet at Philippi.'[9]

Principal Irvine, did not share Barrie's fear of the events ahead; on the contrary, in empathy with the students, he congratulated them on the splendid welcome they had given their Rector, on the good nature they had shown, and on their hauling powers.

That evening, however, began the close and trusting friendship that the two men enjoyed from that moment. Irvine has left a revealing account of the delicate situation he first found himself in on that day.

> By nature a retiring man, Barrie had not made many public appearances prior to 1922, nor had he experienced the exaltation which comes from successful public speaking. When he arrived in St Andrews as the rector-elect his anxiety at the ordeal confronting him gave no respite, and this nervousness increased as the fateful day approached. On the evening before his installation he asked me to accompany him on a walk out to the West Sands fringing St Andrews Bay. It was a superbly beautiful May evening, but Barrie was silent and obviously ill at ease. Suddenly he stopped and confronted me with the abrupt question: 'Tell me, will your students behave to-morrow when I am giving my address?' I wonder if you realize what that means to a Principal – what it means to the prestige of a university – to be able to give a confident answer to a question such as that. I assured him

that he would receive a respectful hearing from his constituents, but that in their exuberance there might be an occasional interjection of a harmless humorous nature. 'That is what I want to avoid,' he said.[10]

Jim and Mabel's evening party at University House was interrupted by a theatrical moment of instant appeal to the dramatist in their midst. A torchlight procession, a motley crowd of young people dressed as demons, policemen, fairies, clowns, fools in cap and bells and Red Indians, called out for their Rector to address them. It was the convention to demand to know the subject of the speech that would be given the next day. 'McConnachie,' they were given. Sir James, the darling of the fashionable theatre, informed them that he believed McConnachie had really been elected Rector, and not he himself; but nobody cared or understood that night that McConnachie was Barrie's other self. Only Mabel Irvine had the insight to see that the tragedy of the chameleon Barrie was that no one could know him, though he was loved by so many. When the mask lifted, there was a flash of reality, tired and sad.

Mabel was captivated by Ellen Terry, and wrote of her 'overwhelming charm and beauty'. 'She is enchanting, like a delightful excitable child'. Sitting by her bedroom fire and dressed for dinner in a gold silk gown, she reminisced with her hostess: 'Did you know [Henry] Irving? Ah, he was a wonderful man – so gentle, so good, so beautiful – yes, so gentle dear.' When the time came for her to try on her gown and doctor's hood, she was taken by how becoming it was: 'I could do Portia in this – I must do Portia again and wear this gown and cap, mustn't I?' Almost blind, deaf, and with a failing memory, the great actress showered love and loyalty on Barrie, and provided exactly the support that her old friend needed. Mabel's diary records their manner together as being 'full of a delicious, delicate raillery with her, all affection and tenderness'.[11] But Ellen Terry might have stolen the show were it not for Barrie's extraordinary performance when he came to deliver his rectorial address, later published as *Courage* (1922).

It was harder for Mabel to warm to the strange, rather puckish author of *Peter Pan*, but it was the Irvine children – and one might almost extend that to the Principal – who made this tiny man feel at home. As he prepared his speech, Felicity, who was two and a half, sat on the end of his bed, hearing his lines, which she would interject with 'hip, hip, hooay'. Barrie was very much taken with this child, and in receiving the Freedom of the Town of St Andrews he turned this encounter into a very pretty speech.

There is one lady, however, in St Andrews, not a student, who is certainly the most remarkable woman in St Andrews. I suppose you know whom I mean. But if you don't I will tell you. I mean Principal Irvine's baby. (laughter and applause) This speech would have been a very different affair if it had not been for that baby; and so I dare say would Lord Wester Wemyss' speech. This child, as soon as I arrived in St Andrews, obviously having been coached to say it (laughter) she made use of this remarkable expression – in fact she continued to say it for several hours. She said 'Hip, hip hoo-ay.' Since then when I have been sitting up in bed preparing speeches, she sits solemnly at the foot of the bed, and I pitch a little bit of the speech at her, and when I finish she says, 'Hip, hip hoo-ay.'[12]

The London newspapers picked this up, and photographs were captioned 'The hip, hip, hoo-ay Baby'.

Barrie's rectorial address to his constituents, the undergraduates, was a stirring appeal to the power of youth to remake the world. Published as *Courage*, it has entered the corpus of twentieth-century literature. The ceremonial began inauspiciously: the university did not yet possess any fine graduation hall, and the Volunteer Hall on the edge of the town had to be decorated for the occasion. '"Courage", didn't someone say (who did not have much of it himself)', wrote Barrie once.[13] His nervousness continuing, Barrie gazed at his audience, and fell silent. There was a long pause, during which he took a large paper- knife out of his pocket and played with it, drawing its blade across his cheek, until an anxious voice came from the back of the hall: 'Tak care, Jimmie, ye'll cut your throat.'[14] The ice was broken, and Barrie launched into his theme:

> I cannot provide you with that staff for your journey . . .You shall cut it – so it is ordained – every one of you for himself, and its name is Courage.
>
> . . .
>
> My own theme is Courage, as you should use it in the great fight that seems to me to be coming between Youth and their Betters; by Youth, meaning of course you, and by your Betters, us. I want you to take up this position – that Youth have for far too long left exclusively in our hands the decisions in national matters that are more vital to them than to us.[15]

The crowning point of an address full of paradox came when, fumbling first in one pocket and then the other, he pulled out the last letter written to him by his dying friend, Captain Scott of the Antarctic, and read to his young audience: 'It would do your heart good to be in our tent and hear our songs and cheery conversation.' The student audience was spellbound, and the Principal breathed a sigh of relief. At times it was hard to hear the hoarse whisper of their Rector, at others his voice swelled. Barrie allowed his sense of pathos to shine through. It was a piece of pure theatre, and his audience fell silent and then roared with approval. He called it his 'lucky day'.

More than a decade later, Barrie reflected on the magic of those days: 'St Andrews is the one place where I cannot make a speech again! The last time was the occasion of my only real appearance in public, when I somehow managed to reveal myself, and I want it to stand alone in St Andrews with none of the rest of me beside it.'[16]

The eyes of the whole academic world were turned to St Andrews that week. Even the popular press made the occasion fashionable. At last, St Andrews was in the limelight, with full reportage in *The Times*, the *Scotsman* and the *Glasgow Herald*. The new Chancellor, Field-Marshal Lord Haig, in uniform beneath his Chancellor's robes, stood in marked contrast to the diminutive Rector. Haig, serious and meticulous in performing his role, did not mind how much he was mobbed by crowds of students who carried him aloft and flocked to the chapel to witness his unveiling of the university's memorial to the fallen. Haig, the soldier, was approving of the Principal's ordered mind, his attention to detail and the meticulous preparation, which ensured that everything went off without a hitch.[17] Neither did the budget get out of hand: to the satisfaction of the university Court, the combined ceremonies for Chancellor and Rector cost a mere £438 7s 6d.

Irvine recognised that, from this time, St Andrews should be kept in the public eye. He himself subscribed to a press agency that sent him cuttings from any newspapers that quoted him or featured St Andrews. Recognising that books celebrating the old grey town made it better known, he recommended in 1922 that the old-fashioned anthology *Seekers After a City* (1911) should be reprinted at the university's expense.[18]

The University House visitor's book shows that Galsworthy, Barrie and Haig, and all the guests who were invited in all the years that followed, often returned to that house beside the sea, the hub of a university that now began to make its appeal to all corners of the globe.[19]

Jim and Mabel led busy 'town and gown' social lives. Long before the arrivals of Barrie or Kipling, they devoured modern literature. They were founder members of a play-reading club, called the St Andrews 1920 Club, whose aims included the promotion of new plays, with a focus on the plays of J.M. Barrie. Barrie had written a one-act mystery play for RADA in 1921, and it proved problematic to produce. The story goes that at a dinner with the Irvines in St Andrews, Barrie was discussing the difficulties that he had with staging *Shall we Join the Ladies?* It was often to be remarked that Principal Irvine was in many ways an actor–manager manqué in his management of university affairs, and he suggested to Barrie that they work it out around the dinner table in University House, and do a 'reading' of it there and then.[20] On 19 March 1924, the St Andrews 1920 Club attempted a semi-dramatised reading of the play. In the programme is the note: 'The Committee desire to express their indebtedness to the author for his kind permission to produce the play, for the use of his unpublished manuscript, and for much valuable advice. The play has not been produced outside London.'

The author sent notes to Mabel Irvine, and stated: 'The scene is at St Andrews and the people are the sort of people you meet there. Sam Smith, a sugar-refiner, is a little old bachelor who, for the last week has been entertaining a country house party. We choose to raise the curtain on them at dinner when the guests have that genial regard for each other which steals over really nice people who have eaten too much.' The part of Sam Smith was played by Jim Irvine.[21]

Mabel was from then on 'one of my actresses' to Barrie, though her doubts about him lingered. Perhaps she felt that Barrie failed to warm to her qualities as a wife and as a mother; his difficulties with 'motherhood' came to the surface in *Peter Pan*. Jim and Barrie shared a birthday, 9 May, and until Barrie's death the two friends would solemnly celebrate the occasion together in Barrie's Adelphi Terrace flat, with a cake sent to London by Mabel. Arrangements were made with Barrie for exchanges of visits to the various pretty country houses in the south-west of England that the Irvines would take for a holiday month. The west country and the Cotswolds seemed exotic in comparison with the Highlands, and Barrie would invariably be ensconced at Stanway, the childhood home of Lady Cynthia Asquith that he rented from Lady Cynthia's family, the Wemysses. Barrie, as sensitive to mood as was Mabel, tried to court her affection: 'You yourself were my delight and my chiefest joy, even with Jim in the field. He is now the "Vice-principal".'[22]

The social aspirations of the little town expanded in the 1920s. The good offices of Lord Haig brought the Prince of Wales to St Andrews in

September 1922. The prince had to 'play himself in' as Captain of the Royal and Ancient Golf Club, but the university took advantage of the royal visit and was proud to confer an honorary degree on him. Much was expected of this highlight of the autumn social scene. David and Alison Russell and the Irvines formed a foursome for the Royal and Ancient Ball that evening. The tickets were in great demand, the St Andrews 'court' dressmaker had been kept busy providing the ladies with new ball gowns, and there was much disappointment when the capricious prince did not attend the ball after all, having slipped away from St Andrews early.[23]

The next rectorial election was due that autumn and necessarily followed fast on the heels of Barrie's delayed installation. It was no less significant an event, not only for the man of letters who was elected, but also for the great man who came with him, who would become chancellor of the university in 1929. It was in the Michaelmas term of 1922 that Rudyard Kipling, yet another elderly man, was chosen over G.K. Chesterton and Lord Robert Cecil to be Rector. The man he brought with him as his nominee for an honorary LLD was his cousin, Stanley Baldwin (or Stan and Rud as they were to each other).[24]

Rudyard Kipling suited the rather conservative tastes of the under-graduates. Although at this date the odd politician still entered the electoral lists, this was on principle somewhat frowned upon, as being not St Andrews' style. Kipling appealed to the younger Irvines to a far greater extent than did Barrie. Imagine what it was like to have the arch-storyteller come to weave the stories of *Puck of Pook's Hill*, and Una and the centurion, all the ancient lore of the Sussex Downs, expressly for the Irvine nursery. Kipling was at the peak of his popularity, but he was a rather private man who sought every opportunity to escape the social throng in the University House drawing room. He quickly made friends with Veronica and Nigel.[25]

A national phenomenon of the inter-war decades was the pronounced growth and understanding of the forces of public relations. Irvine was robust about this, and rejoiced in any newspaper coverage of his university, or indeed of the activities of his family. But Kipling's early letters to Irvine reveal his own wish for caution:

And now will you let me know by return to Browns Hotel, Albemarle Street, Piccadilly.

What will be your arrangements about the Press covering the Rectorial Address? I ask because the papers are beginning to bother about it, and I purpose to follow my usual plan of treating them all alike. The University probably has a precedent in regard to date of issue and so forth, which I should like to know.[26]

Sure enough, two days later, Central News Limited of New Bridge Street, London EC4, wrote to Andrew Bennett, the Secretary of the University, to ask if they might cover, with their press photographer, the occasion when the honorary LLD would be conferred on Stanley Baldwin. Irvine endorsed the letter: 'Give permission and send Programme of functions.'[27]

Kipling had stated: 'I don't mind photographers – they are part of the work of the day – but I have no intention at any time of giving time to reporters.' With this in mind, he set off to motor to Edinburgh, remarking, somewhat desperately, that 'reporters are not yet trained to keep abreast of a motor'.

He chose 10 October 1923 for the ceremony of his installation, and at the station the previous day, amongst the great crowd of students, the receiving party included the prime minister, Principal Irvine and Dr Low of Blebo, the Rector's Assessor. Once again, an honorary graduand this time in the form of Stanley Baldwin, the man of the moment in Westminster, who was fast becoming the most important man in England, threatened to steal the show. That night the students stood outside University House, calling for the premier, who came forward, smoking his trademark pipe. 'Pipe out, pipe out, Bejant Baldwin,' they chanted, and he complied with the students, encouraging them in their game, until, remarking that he was only an undergraduate, he went in. 'Where's your gown, then,' they cried after him.[28]

Kipling's spirit had been broken by the death of his son at the Battle of Loos in 1915. He had been ill, and when he arrived in St Andrews he was not in a hurry to make impromptu speeches. On having to address the fancy-dress procession that evening, he was somewhat at a loss: 'Ladies and gentlemen and beasts,' he began, and 'your procession is a symbol of how you uphold and carry on the sacred torch of learning.' The students chanted 'We want Stanley.'

When Stanley Baldwin left the Imperial Conference in London for St Andrews in order to receive his honorary degree, tongues wagged. Was St Andrews so much more important than the affairs of the British empire? asked the national press. In this instance, the partisan Principal would have answered yes. Irvine drew closer to Baldwin during these years, and ensured that he became St Andrews' Chancellor and the first chairman of Edward Harkness's Pilgrim Trust, which was also Jim's baby.

Wednesday opened with a service in the partially restored chapel. The fifteenth-century chapel, the collegiate church of the College of St Salvator, was in a constant state of interesting restoration during the 1920s, and most of the leading Scottish church architects of the time had a hand in it.[29]

An Englishman through and through, even if an Anglo-Indian, Kipling was, nevertheless, at great pains to please his new friends north of the border. Unlike Barrie, he was an old hand at the business of giving speeches. He handed the address in advance to the Associated Press for distribution and publication in the morning papers of 11 October. 'No favouritism. Share and share alike.' As a compliment in addressing his young friends, he took as his subject Burns' refrain 'the glorious privilege of being independent', from his 'Epistle to a Young Friend' (1788), and his delivery was forthright, friendly and assured. Barrie's *Courage* and Kipling's rectorial address, *Independence* (1923), fell into a classic mould all of their own, and one with which St Andrews is now identified.

This rectorial inauguration developed an intensely familial flavour: an intermingling of wives and children, of the Kiplings, the Irvines and the Baldwins. Kipling, a man of the world, proved to be of real worth to Irvine: he did not replace Barrie – theirs would never be the rather quixotic relationship that Irvine had with Barrie – but as a constant, steady, manly friend, and one who took a penetrating and sympathetic interest in the administrative problems that Irvine faced, particularly with regard to the college in Dundee. Once again the Rector fell captive to the fascination of St Andrews, as his friend 'the king of critics', Sir George Saintsbury in Edinburgh, had warned him would happen.

When Irvine was elected early in 1924 to the Athenaeum, Kipling was quick to welcome him into the 'God-fearing, upright, and thoughtful' world of the 'best club in London', but he was at first puzzled by this man brought up on family charades and the Glasgow music hall, a Scottish vice-chancellor with a fondness for amateur dramatics. 'What the deuce ought to [be] a Rector's attitude to a Principal who – acts? The dead won't turn in their graves. They'll spin like turbines.' But he longed to get to know Jim and Mabel well, and pressed on them invitations to Batemans, his Sussex country house. When, late in 1924, Downing Street indicated to Jim that he would be awarded a knighthood in the next honours list, Jim must have felt assured of his friendship. He confided in Kipling, who may indeed have been given advance information by Baldwin. Kipling amused himself and Jim by proposing suitable heraldry for a scientist who had once been involved in devising chemical clouds: 'There is in Asiatic heraldry, a Thing called The Trator Cloud. Thus, *or on sable*, it might typify gas or research into the properties of gas.'[30] Jim was enchanted.

This rector's literary influence on the students of St Andrews was felt in several quarters. He was generous to the university, with the gift of a Rector's Essay Prize and the gift to the library of the bound manuscripts of the stories in *Actions and Reactions* (1909). He was generous and painstaking with his advice to a number of students. One of these, Donald Kennedy, a descendant on the cadet line of the founding bishop of the College of St Salvator, was an aspirant journalist and approached the Rector for advice. As a former editor himself, Kipling took an interest in the work of the editorial team of the student magazine, *College Echoes*. Irvine, remembering his own student days, cared about *College Echoes*, but he was concerned that it should adopt a business-like approach to its finances. Kipling urged its student editors to sharpen its rather juvenile style. It is not surprising therefore that Kipling devoted much thought to his gift of an essay prize; the subject, he stipulated, should be 'The Influence of the Democratic Idea on the Spirit, Work and Outlook of the Individual of a Generation Hence'. The sum of £50 was to be awarded as first prize, with £30 as second prize. Jim Irvine could never resist being in charge, and he was ready and willing when Kipling asked his new friend, the Principal, to use his own discretion as to who should judge the entries. Alas, the subject proved too tough for the young students, and the entries were too thin on the ground. Kipling was obliged to ask the Principal to 'hatch out some subject that would be within the capacity and interest of your present Young'.

With Kipling's assistance, Mabel Irvine was developing an idea of her own that revolved round producing an anthology of new writing exclusively devoted to the subject of St Andrews. Kipling warned her that such verses were difficult to write well, and he protected her from being cut up by the publisher, although he was willing to write something himself.[31]

On considering the Principal's acquisition of two such friendships – with Barrie and Kipling – the question must be asked as to what extent these rectors were Irvine's choices and not those of the students, as should properly be the case. A glance round Jim and Mabel's bookshelves would have shown the stories of Kipling and the plays of Barrie, all mostly acquired long before, when they were first published; Jim's study shelves reflected his interest in exploration, a further source of rectors between the wars.

It is also true that 'Jimmy the Princ' kept his finger on the intelligence pulse of student life, over which he cast a net, enabling him to work his influence amongst the students with great efficiency. Irvine found Barrie and Kipling serendipitous choices. Barrie remained very much around St Andrews during the 1920s, and it was Irvine, not the students, who asked him to try to persuade another playwright, George Bernard Shaw, to stand for election. Shaw stated, in Shavian fashion, that he was against universities, but still he was pursued right up to 1930. Unfortunately, he just could not take the matter seriously: 'I put my foot in over St Andrews. A letter came from them. I naturally took it for an undergraduate leg-pull and wrote back cheerfully enough telling them to try again. I appreciate the honour, which has knocked me by its unexpectedness . . . I think it is one of the jolliest things which has happened to me.'[32]

In the end, the students of 1925 chose a man of international statesmanship: a polar explorer who had become a diplomat and Commissioner of the League of Nations, a great humanitarian who fought for the desperate cause of the survivors of the Armenian genocide, and for the refugees cast up in their thousands by the international events of the previous decade. The Norwegian Fridtjof Nansen had been one of Irvine's heroes for many, many years; he was, in Irvine's eyes, the greatest rector of them all. The two men sat beside the study fire reminiscing and gossiping about events that Irvine could only know through his insatiable appetite for the accounts of *Farthest North* (1897) and the voyage of Nansen's ship, the *Fram*, through the ice and the uncharted polar waters in search of the North Pole. Nansen was an interesting choice for the students to make: he was an icon of his time, when the polar explorers were still sought out to grace the fashionable soirées and *conversaziones* of London. Both Irvine and Nansen were essentially scientists. Nansen's harsh experience of the struggle to survive had served to bring out the poet within him, and he exerted a deep fascination over others.

In Nansen's wake came Knud Rasmussen, the half-Eskimo explorer and anthropologist from Greenland who had taken the *Fram* to Antarctica. Nansen also brought to St Andrews Bjorn Helland-Hansen, the oceanographer, and Otto Sverdrup, his navigator on the *Fram*. They formed an impressive, strikingly different, list of graduands. Irvine recorded that: 'It made me tingle with excitement on the first night when I looked round the dinner table at the assembled guests. Nansen, looking like a Viking, old Captain Sverdrup of the *Fram*, Helland Hansen, Professor David, who reached the South Magnetic Pole, and Bruce of the Mount Everest Expedition – all men of action and lovers of adventure.'[33] Irvine and the university made a celebration of polar adventure out of the students' choice of rector. Irvine's appreciation of the picturesque responded to these blue-eyed giants coming to St Andrews out of the 'farthest north': in a truly literal sense in the case of Rasmussen, who had reached Aberdeen in a whaling boat, straight from an expedition to Greenland. Again, however, Irvine's wife did not share her husband's sympathies, and when Rasmussen returned the next summer with his wife, she remarked that he was a 'queer little man not to be thrilled by the antiquity and [the] old-worldness of St Andrews, yet as you say he's very practical. I suppose an explorer has to be practical yet look at Nansen.'[34]

Throughout the university today are to be found examples of Nansen's own lithographs of bleak northern scenes. These all originated as Christmas presents to his 'friends' – a word which had special meaning to him – Sir James and Lady Irvine. Following the success of Nansen's association with St Andrews, the students tried their hand at another polar explorer, Sir Wilfred Grenfell, the man who brought medical care to the people of Greenland. Unfortunately, although he was deeply touched by St Andrews, he failed to exert over his new university anything like Nansen's charm, and he was not a good speaker. He was a man whose wife was obliged to pass a note to him as he rambled on in his after-dinner speech: 'Stop,' the note said, and he stopped. Afterwards, and privately, the two Irvines discussed this illustration of perfect confidence between husband and wife, and Jim had to admit to Mabel that he could never possess the patient humility of the new rector.[35]

In 1925, Barrie had made a bold suggestion to Irvine: he tried to persuade Jim that Millicent Fawcett would be an inspired choice. 'Wouldn't it be in St A tradition of late years to have the first woman Rector? Mrs Fawcett stands out as the real head of the great woman movement. Too old, perhaps, yet I believe she would shoot into her proper prominence if chosen and be universally acclaimed, and St A for doing it.'[36]

Mrs Fawcett was not presented as a candidate for the 1925 rectorial election, but in June 1928 another leader of the women's suffrage movement, the composer Dame Ethel Smyth, was cajoled into coming north to receive an honorary degree. She was reluctant; she missed her train in Edinburgh; she lost her luggage on the way; she had no subfusc in which to be capped. Yet she managed to capture hearts. Nigel lent her his black patent pumps and, to everyone's amazement, told her where she could buy a hatpin. Considerably cheered up, she joined the ranks of her fellow graduands, humming 'The March of the Women', her anthem written for the suffragettes. When, finally, after a week she had to tear herself away from St Andrews – 'the place tugs at my heart' – she left a record of her visit in the

University House visitors' book, inscribing two bars from 'The March of the Women', together with the gloomy words from the fourth verse: 'Life and Strife, these Two are One.'[37] Reunited with her luggage, she appeared at the dinner in a very becoming black lace evening dress, but said to Mabel that if she had known there would be such a good party, she would have brought her best dress, and not the second best.

Although the flapper vote did not make itself fully felt until the 1928 Representation of the People Act brought the franchise to all women over twenty-one, Irvine felt throughout the 1920s, and for quite different reasons, that he was facing the 'march of the women' on home ground. In these years, women consistently outnumbered the men students. There is more than a trace of chauvinism in the pleasure he often took in referring to the 1544 statute of St Leonard's College: that no woman may enter the college save the laundress, and she must be more than fifty years old. He was afraid that St Andrews, for which he had such ambition, might be taken for a lightweight liberal arts college for female students, because far too often, when the world opened its newspaper, it saw photographs of crowds of winsome girls in red gowns mobbing the celebrities that were increasingly at large in St Andrews.

When in 1926 a group of men students came to see the Principal with a request to be allowed to revive the Kate Kennedy Procession, he seized this opportunity with enthusiasm. This student movement, whose name refers to the apocryphal niece of Bishop Kennedy, erupted in the nineteenth century as a form of satirical carnival, mocking the professors in rowdy and exaggerated caricature, and it had long been suppressed. Was it not strange that this twentieth-century disciplinarian was prepared to encourage its rebirth? But something of which Barrie had spoken reverberated in the students' minds: that each generation thrusts forward, guided by the shadows of those that had gone before. Irvine helped these boys to form a new society that would in a heroic sense celebrate the dramatis personae of St Andrews' past: this much fell in with Irvine's determination to make much of the romance of St Andrews. He made one firm condition that no women should take part in the club or its spring procession. More like a pageant than a carnival, the young men were solemnly to present the history of the university down the ages, dressed as religious men, as thinkers, as soldiers, as monarchs and, necessarily, as women. This pictur-esque cavalcade through the medieval streets would not escape the press photographers, but it would be an all-male society, engendering the manly qualities of comradeship, conviviality and mutual support, with the fine goal of honouring the romantic episodes that gave life to their alma mater.

The social mores of students before the Second World War were in many ways far removed from those of their counterparts today. The sexes were separated by rules and regulations, even in the lecture theatre. Dances and balls had to have chaperones present to ensure that nothing unseemly occurred. The girls would go home afterwards in cabs. It was still acceptable in referring to students generically to refer to the men of St Andrews. An all-male club purporting to represent the university would never be thought of as provocative in 1926, and the young men who portrayed Bishop Kennedy's niece, Kate, as well as Mary Queen of Scots and Elizabeth Garrett Anderson did so as if it were all an allegory. Historical knowledge of the principal figure of Kate Kennedy is shrouded in myth, and the honour of playing her, as a symbol of the arrival of spring and all that is young, is awarded to a bejant, or *bec jaune* ('yellow beak' or 'fledgling'), in his first year. Although there were members of the senate who carped and doubted, Mabel Irvine was skilful with her sewing machine and defied them all, making several of the first costumes. Irvine even enjoyed the irony implicit in an event that became absorbed into the traditions of the St Andrews calendar; subversive some may at first have felt it would be – a challenge to the statutes of the university – but Irvine was convinced that through the Kate Kennedy Procession he was bringing order to the natural desire of the male students to let off steam. He allowed them to think that it was all their own show, their responsibility. He presided at their dinners, chaffed at their jokes, cultivated those members like John Fewster, a biochemist and his last PhD candidate, whom he felt might reward him with loyalty and service to the university; and certainly he did feel their adulation.[38] He thought it was a great joke that the University Court found itself paying for the costume for the figure of Marat, the French revolutionary who had obtained, by purchase, a St Andrews degree.

After the Second World War, the Kate Kennedy Club celebrated its Jubilee; joyfully Irvine chose to reveal his puckish good humour in espousing a student society such as this.

> The Festival carries the full blessing of 'authority'. The ancient rules of St Salvator's College which prohibit sternly 'riding on horseback, the wearing of masks or costumes, assembling in crowds or walking in procession' do not apply on Kate Kennedy's Day. The Principal's Lady, who does not stand in awe of any member of Senatus, aided and abetted the students' efforts by making the costume worn by the

central figure twenty-five years ago when Kate emerged from a retirement lasting half a Century. Even the University Court showed its good will by providing funds to acquire a costume for an additional character to be selected by them. These young gentlemen, with a fine sense of what is appropriate, promptly clothed Marat in garments paid for by the custodians of law and order, a gesture much enjoyed by the elder statesmen of the university who gave full marks to this answer.[39]

At the end of Irvine's first decade as Principal, the 'Quinquennial Report' to the University Grants Committee included a special reference to the rediscovered spirit of St Andrews: 'No better indication . . . can be found of the growth of a new pride in the University than the recent revival by men students of Kate Kennedy's Day.'

The new life of the Kate Kennedy Club sprang up at a time of fresh optimism. Prosperity was beginning to return to East Fife: sugar beet production had increased, and unemployment in Dundee was down. Yet hot on the heels of this latest student success, and only a few days later, came a bombshell: at midnight on Monday 1 May 1926, the railway employees at Cupar, the county town, downed tools, and work at the sugar beet factory in Cupar was suspended. On 1 May the King issued a proclamation of a state of emergency. The General Strike was on. With no railway, and no products coming out of the Fife and Angus mills and factories, the docks would close down and hundreds of east coast men and women, the mill workers, factory workers and dockers, would be out of work. In Edinburgh a train left on the line caused a serious accident. A leader in the *St Andrews Citizen* on 8 May commented that the anxiety felt over the trades unions' efforts to stop the vital industries of the country was comparable only to the opening stages of the Great War.

Once again, it was the students who brought St Andrews into the news. Through the Students' Representative Council, students volunteered to run the essential services of the country. Despite the scant public transport, about 150 students (50 per cent of the matriculated men) were drafted off to various employments such as unloading cargoes at Dundee docks, and at Leuchars and Perth railway stations acting as firemen, drivers and signalmen. The press was fulsome in its praise of the students' public spirit, and was even pleased to remark that no profiteering took place![40]

The University Court decided that the university would not close, classes would carry on as far as possible, and the majority of citizens and local workers supported Stanley Baldwin's government. Rather shamefully, the university printers, Henderson's, went out on strike. Members of staff were given authority to enrol as special constables, to ensure law and order.

By 13 May the strike had come to an end, and the examinations were reinstated in June. The civil commissioner wrote in glowing terms to the Secretary of the University. The students had loaded 1,000 tons of manufactured goods onto the steamer SS *Hoosac*, bound for New York, and thus enabled the mills of eastern Scotland to keep running. The students had enormously mitigated the effects of the strike. Irvine could feel that his belief in the student body was being repaid.

Barrie, no longer Rector, counted himself amongst the red-gowned cohorts of 'his university', and wrote to Jim Irvine: 'Good for the red gowns of St Andrews. I am very glad to hear of this sporting behaviour but not surprised. One good thing out of this darkness is the exhilaration of feeling that youth can turn from its own jobs when need be and run the country. With a little guidance they ought probably to take it on permanently. (Of course they would have to strike first.)'[41]

The General Strike had issued a shot across the government's bows; perhaps this was not such a golden age after all. A small university town may not have felt the full economic extremes of the 1920s, but folk there learned in the years ahead to buy only empire produce, to pull in their belts, and to do their bit in the effort to overcome the Depression, which had an almost mortal effect on neighbouring Dundee. In Fife the prosperity so briefly felt would not return until the mid-1930s. Mabel's family business in Belfast, Williams and McBride, collapsed, exposing the families of two of her brothers to great hardship and anxiety. University teachers were cushioned against the failure of business and manufacture, but Jim Irvine was a good man: he undertook to pay the premiums of his brothers-in-law's life insurance policies, and he and Mabel did their best to console and assist the bewildered brothers.[42]

Irvine's detractors were always there. He suspected that the celebrated D'Arcy Thompson disliked him, and he felt that the Principal of St Mary's College was a thorn in his side, but generally the whole body of the university basked in the good he brought to their lives. In February 1928 Mabel heard privately that the university wished to show its pleasure in his achievements by means of a gift: it might be a motor car, or perhaps a portrait. 'I feel the rank and file of the University respect us and feel something like affection for us. I don't look for gratitude but am human enough to feel happy when it does come – it adds "a sort of bloom" to a Principal's life.'[43]

Irvine preferred a portrait, thinking that it might savour of conceit were he to commission his own portrait, whereas he might buy himself a car at some point.

The most fashionable portrait painter of the age was selected, and Oswald Birley put himself to the task of painting two portraits: one would hang in the university, but the other was a personal gift to the Principal. Oswald Birley's studio was in the colony of well-known artists in St John's Wood, in North London; during the sittings there he and 'Sir James' settled down into easy companionship. In working on the replica, he wrote: 'I will try and conjure up your friendly presence in the studio and hope for a good result . . . By the bye a highly critical painter friend of mine thinks your portrait one of my *very* best – was most enthusiastic.'[44] This enjoyable process had the merit of producing an image of extraordinary likeness of character.

On 1 February 1928, Irvine was chairing a meeting of the Forest Products Research Board of the Department of Scientific and Industrial Research at their laboratories at Princes Risborough in Buckinghamshire, when his attention was distracted by an urgent telephone call from Bennett, Secretary of the University. The Chancellor, Earl Haig, with whom Irvine had been corresponding only a few days earlier about the chemical problem of preserving the leaves on the Remembrance Day wreaths of poppies, had died. He was to have a state, but military, funeral in Westminster Abbey. Would not the university have to be represented, and should the bedellus be sent down on the train with the university's priceless medieval mace? Irvine rose from the committee table, made several telephone calls, in particular to the Ministry of Defence, where his overtures met a stone wall: the funeral procession would not require the presence of Haig's university. Irvine protested in the strongest terms. He forced an entrance to room 114 at the War Office. He felt righteous indignation, not for his own sake (and there were those who thought he was becoming too 'grand') but on behalf of the institution he loved.[45]

Irvine negotiated unwaveringly with the army bigwigs in charge, and the mace, the mace bearer, Principal Galloway of St Mary's College, James Younger and the Vice-Chancellor's academic dress all arrived off the train. In the end, three seats in the abbey were designated for the office bearers of St Andrews University. In ceremonial academic dress, they must have struck an interesting note amongst the regiments: Irvine, short of stature, somehow always commanded attention. He had a strong sense of history and a strong sense of theatre: these prompted the tribute that he paid to his

Chancellor that day. As official mourners of their much-loved Chancellor, Irvine, Younger and their mace bearer joined the company of three royal princes in the national procession to the abbey from St Columba's, Pont Street, where Haig had lain in state on the gun-carriage that had carried the Unknown Warrior to his grave, and had also borne the gun that fired the first British shot in World War I. The French marshals Pétain and Foch were Haig's pall-bearers.

Lady Haig was deeply conscious of the honour paid to her late husband: that the mace, which had not crossed the border for 500 years, had been brought to London, to symbolise the high office that he valued so much.

Haig's successor as Chancellor, Lord Haldane, did not live long to enjoy his office. A new Chancellor would have to be chosen, and Irvine was again enthused by an idea of his own: one that only Rudyard and Carrie Kipling knew about. He was, by this time, well known to Stanley Baldwin, and when late in December 1928, in impenetrable fog, he crossed Horse Guards Parade to chat informally to the prime minister about becoming Chancellor of St Andrews, he found that Baldwin was delighted with the idea. Their confidential conversation that afternoon revealed that Baldwin had received several similar offers, all of which he had turned down. For the St Andrews chancellorship he was willing to submit to anything, even a poll. Baldwin felt that to be Chancellor of St Andrews was 'a tremendous honour', and chivalrously he committed himself 'in devotion to that ancient foundation over which you so happily preside'.[46]

There was one glaring omission in St Andrews, where ceremony symbolised so much of its rightful stature as a medieval university. Since long before the Great War, the university had desperately lacked a fine hall in which to confer degrees. So many famous people now came to St Andrews to receive honorary degrees. At the time of the quinquennial, there was a move amongst the members of the Senatus to set up an endowment fund to provide for a graduation hall. Relief to this – it must be admitted – hopeless aspiration came in the person of James Younger, whose great wealth was secured from brewing. He was the Chancellor's Assessor, and had been the key to getting Irvine appointed as principal. It was in Herkless' time that Younger came forward and offered to give a graduation hall outright.

Dr and Mrs Younger lived but a short distance from St Andrews, and they had already done much good for the social structure of the town: they were the patrons of All Saints Episcopalian church, that served the needs of the fisherfolk down by the harbour. Cynics might say that this interest in building had a further purpose: their daughter's father-in-law was the

London architect Paul Waterhouse, who had inherited the family firm that his father, the architect of the Natural History Museum, had made famous. It was a dynasty of architects. Paul Waterhouse had made such a success of the restoration of the fine Scottish Renaissance building that was the Students' Union; he had also been invited by James Younger, on behalf of the university, to submit ideas for a graduation hall. During the first year of Irvine's principalship, the matter was being very seriously developed, and Dr and Mrs Younger responded patiently with yet more money as the costs escalated.

The quinquennial endowment fund that stood at £9,000 was made available to the Court for the general purpose of the hall. Dr and Mrs Younger's total gift amounted to £82,977, but the building, both aesthetically and in the detail of all it provided, was of an elaboration that did not please the Principal. His efforts to influence the design so that it would become something that would enhance the intimate collegiate atmosphere he so much wanted to reinforce were all in vain. However, when the foundation stone of the Younger Hall was laid, the names of the Chancellor, the Rector and the Principal – Haig, Nansen and Irvine – were inscribed on its rather grandiose façade, which Irvine ensured would be mercifully recessed from the medieval street line. In its name it celebrates the two good people who gave it. Younger provided his architect with a complex brief for a building that would have to perform many functions, and the best possible attention was given to its acoustic qualities. The services of the leading acoustic architect in the United Kingdom, Hope Bagenel, were engaged so that the new building could double as a concert hall. Younger thought that it should also provide a large dining hall, with kitchens in the basement. The land lying between North Street and the Scores was purchased by negotiation from the Thoms family, a family of local builders. More of this land would be added to the university's holding at this time for further purposes.[47] Irvine started to dream that the whole of North Street could become an avenue of university buildings.

In 1927, the popular Duchess of York had visited St Leonard's School, the St Andrews girls' public school, for its golden jubilee. The event had been much photographed, but in 1929 the university invited her to return to St Andrews to receive an honorary degree, and to inaugurate the Younger Graduation Hall. Elizabeth Bowes-Lyon, as Fifers and Forfars thought of her, did not take much persuasion to undertake engagements in Scotland, so close to her childhood home at Glamis just across the Tay. Irvine, who had recently received his knighthood and took seriously all that he imagined an

order of chivalry implied, was enchanted to renew his youthful acquaintance with her: her infectious femininity worked its charm on them all, but
mostly on the Principal, as the photographs testify. The Irvine children had
been well drilled in the stultifying conversation that one should have with
royalty. Gazing far down onto the rocks and the surging tides beyond the
garden of University House, the future Queen asked Veronica and Felicity:
'Do you bathe down there?' 'Oh yes, Ma'am,' they dutifully and untruthfully
replied.[48] Irvine's oration was predictably that of a courtier:

> You are of our race and know that in the north we often shrink from
> the display of our deepest feelings, but you must also be conscious of
> the fact that today you have broken down that barrier of reserve and
> won our hearts . . . today here you have unfolded another romantic
> page in the history of St Andrews.[49]

The Duchess of York had endured a gruelling six month's visit to Austral-
asia in 1927 and had shown a pronounced sense of duty during the King's
recent serious illness; she had indeed earned her spurs in the nation's eyes,
and yet St Andrews wanted to claim her for its own. 'She has endeared
herself to an Empire, yet nowhere is she held in more loyal affection than
in this corner of her native land,' proclaimed the oration in the hall that she
had just opened. On 28 June 1929 she joined the small band of interesting
women who had received the St Andrews degree of LLD.

Haig's last letter to Irvine contributes a fitting comment to a decade of
growth in the university: 'I am delighted to hear from you how well things
are going in the University, and I congratulate you with all my heart on
the great success which has characterized your work since you became
Principal and Vice-Chancellor.'[50]

When in elegiac mood, and in high spirits when in a mood of celebration,
such occasions were how Irvine brought what he felt was the rich heritage
of St Andrews before the public gaze. These events of Irvine's golden age
were but the icing on the gingerbread. As his life unfolded, both he and the
university to which he was bound were beginning to show development
and recognition of considerable import.

ELEVEN

A Citizen of a Scientific Age

James Irvine's life is certainly divisible into two parts: that of the research chemist and that of the university administrator, and they ran concurrently for a long time. He would even have it that there were three sides to him: the career scientist, the vice-chancellor and the public figure. He left a legacy in the field of higher education development that has overshadowed the fact that, as a young man, he was forging a reputation as a carbohydrate chemist, a reputation that placed him at the head of his peers. After his death it was remarked by the Cambridge chemist D.J. Bell that 'modern knowledge of the structures of the carbohydrates stems wholly from the pioneer work on methylation by Purdie and Irvine.'[1] Irvine's methylated sugars were essential to carbohydrate chemistry as 'reference compounds'. As 'Sugars Irvine', he is still remembered by science schoolmasters and research chemists alike, and Oxford biochemist Dr Michael Barry was pleased not long ago to pronounce him second only to Emil Fischer in his field. In 1926 Professor Hauser, a chemist of German origin but working at McGill, hailed him as 'the greatest sugar chemist of our time.'[2] For the first twenty years as St Andrews' thirty-fourth principal, he continued to exert his influence as a teacher and explorer of science, and as a senior advisor to scientific institutions. He was arguably at his most vital on long summer sessions in North America, where he was in demand for his courses in advanced and even not so advanced carbohydrate chemistry. These encounters with eager minds in the New World thrilled him, and exhausted him in their insatiable appetite for the lively way in which he revealed his complex subject. With the progress of time, his lecture tours in North America became increasingly a platform for Irvine the elder statesman, the citizen of the world, but one operating in a scientific age.

Irvine, whose almost annual visits to North America invariably included engagements to give public lectures, chose to speak on 'Citizenship in a Scientific Age' when he was invited to give the Josiah Wood Lectures at

Mount Allison University, New Brunswick, in November 1935.[3] It was a subject that he returned to on other occasions and, as a churchman who liked to give everything a moral dimension, it pleased him to reflect on science and its ultimate meaning, within the context of society. By the mid-1930s Irvine was celebrated and successful in a worldly sense and was as much a professional citizen as a professional scientist. Irvine's subject suited the philosophic phase that his thinking as a scientist had passed into, and in Sackville, New Brunswick he revealed that he found spiritual growth through the unfolding of scientific knowledge of the material universe. Senator Wood's gift of these lectures to the people of Sackville had a serious purpose: appalled by what he saw as moral dissipation, a sliding away from the integrity of earlier generations, he wished to impress on his fellow citizens the lessons in citizenship that men of the highest standing could give. Irvine rose to the challenge by stating his belief in the character-building power of scientific research and then daring to touch on the world of the metaphysical, which he arrived at by studying the riddle of nature: 'Whence came this world; what is its relationship to other worlds; what are the forces and mechanisms which envelop us – and the penultimate question, whence came man?' Note that Irvine uses the word 'penultimate'. These lectures mark a shift in Irvine's life, and they were given when his original work in the St Andrews laboratory had almost drawn to a close.

But to what extent did Irvine's scientific career survive his elevation to the principalship of St Andrews University fifteen years before he gave the Josiah Wood Lectures? His daily life during the 1920s demonstrated that he could, to a certain extent, sustain his two lives: that of the administrator of higher education and that of the patient investigator at the laboratory bench – and certainly that of the informed scientific advisor. Irvine carried in the forefront of his mind his lifelong conviction that he was a scientist of the new age and that thereby he was called to effect change. He was aware that his scientific training brought clarity and reason to his administrative work. This was much valued and remarked on by the trusts and government bodies for whom he served: they often required from him long and penetrating reports.

At the time that Irvine was appointed Principal of St Andrews, there was much hope on both his part and that of other chemists that he would at least keep up his research. His active life as a scientist, leading his own field of research, can be traced through his published papers. Often in collaboration with his research students, between January 1921 and 1938 he published forty-four papers of original scientific research, for the most part concerning the challenging polysaccharide group of the carbohydrates.[4] His wife noted in her diary in February 1926: 'During all this time of organization & hard work in the university his research work in his beloved lab has run steadily on – increasing in importance – & at the same time his work in London on boards and committees has multiplied.'[5]

In December 1920, when the news of Irvine's impending appointment was announced in the press, his fellow principal, Principal Senter of Birkbeck College, an inorganic chemist who had taken the same career path, warned Irvine that his chemical work would slip away, and his chemical colleagues on the whole mourned what they believed would be a grave loss to chemistry.[6] When he allowed himself to do so, he did admit that he had made a great personal sacrifice in order to lead St Andrews out of almost certain annihilation. He was nominated for election to the presidency of the Chemical Society of London in 1924, which he then had to decline, owing to pressure of work: the only perceptible casualty of his new position.[7]

The Department of Scientific and Industrial Research, with which Irvine had been associated from its very beginning, issued this warning from its secretary: 'Your elevation to the Vice-Chancellorship raises questions as to the continuity of the work on power alcohol which you are directing for Sir F. Nathan & the latter wishes me to talk matters over with you.'[8] In August 1922, however, he was appointed by the Privy Council to be a member of the advisory council that informed the Privy Council on DSIR matters.[9] Irvine continued to serve the DSIR to the end of his life. He took the concerns of the Forest Products Board, of Oils and Fats, of Power Alcohol and the Building Research Station seriously, studying their scientific papers carefully and visiting their laboratories. In 1934, he was asked to extend this work by agreeing to represent both the Colonial Office and the Forestry Commission on the Oxford University Imperial Forestry Institute Committee. It refreshed him to talk to scientists whose laboratories acted as a bridge between academic research and the nation's future in industry. There was no falling off there.

'I am off to London tonight to be a chemist again for one busy day and deal with the Governments [sic] specifications of cements! A strange bypath for one whose real interest lies in young students and the molecular architecture of sugars,' breezed Irvine to Kipling.[10]

Irvine, generous with his knowledge, offered a sympathetic approach to some of the DSIR's problems, which were at their most manifest in the Applications Committee, which gave grants to science graduate students to pursue research. His knighthood was interpreted by Sir Frank Heath as being a reward for his work for the Department of Scientific and Industrial Research: 'Clearly Irvine is working very hard for the DSIR.'[11]

Perhaps where he felt the sacrifice of his change of career most keenly was in no longer being the 'Prof'. His close relationship with the chemistry department was by no means at an end, and the business of easing Irvine out of the chair of chemistry was played out over the next two years. At the time of his induction to the principalship in January 1921, he generously kept up his chemistry classes until the end of the academic year. In the meantime, his chair would be advertised, and it was much to the credit of the department's reputation that Robert Robinson, who would become Wayneflete Professor of Chemistry at Oxford, was appointed. Irvine afterwards described Robinson as 'one of the greatest organic chemists of our time' and 'a genius'.[12] The students found Robinson rather an unsympathetic character – 'not a Scot, doesn't play golf'[13] – and were struck by the contrast he made with their old professor. Smoothness of handover, however, was reflected in Robinson's willingness to seek advice from Irvine. Irvine got on well with his successor, who made no objection to his predecessor keeping his collaborative work with his own research students.

Unfortunately, Professor Robinson was offered the chair of chemistry at Manchester University in 1922, and he resigned his chair in St Andrews on 1 April 1923, after only eighteen months in the department for which Irvine had such high hopes. Irvine made a virtue out of this rather shabby departure, and at the end of April 1923, he proposed a solution to the enforced interregnum of five months before his successor could begin. Robinson had so overspent the funds available from the Purdie Bequest for equipment and materials that these sums would have to be carried over as a charge on the next academic year, but Irvine now put forward a better budget, using the funds at the department's disposal: in fact he proposed a saving of £500, thus leaving an unencumbered department for the new professor.

A note of relish creeps in when Irvine suggests to the University Court that he should at this time supervise the research students who found themselves without a supervisor, including John Oldham, a PhD candidate formed in the classic mould of the Irvine organic chemist. Oldham became one of his most trusted and brilliant young collaborators. During the Whitsunday term the Principal offered a course of lectures on the carbohydrates. At the same time, he suggested a reorganisation of the department, using the existing staff. The degree examinations would be allowed to proceed in the normal way. For a time, he could pretend that he had not sacrificed his beloved department to the high office which demanded so much of him. For a total of fourteen months during the years 1921–3, Irvine performed the two roles of Principal of the university and head of the department of chemistry.[14] Quite how satisfactory this was for the honours students has been questioned, but for his chosen band of researchers life went on very satisfactorily.

Irvine formed an enduring personal friendship with the man who was finally appointed to the vacant chair. John Read (professor with effect from 1 October 1923) came from a period of time spent at the head of the large-scale department of chemistry at Sydney University. He had been a student of Mendola and his chemical background was impressive. The Principal must have exercised great charm in persuading him to come to St Andrews, which at first glance was still impoverished in terms of capital funding and student numbers. However, John Read joined a department that already had shown it was at the cutting edge of stereochemistry. To this he brought his own stereochemical specialism in the essential oils and, to Irvine's delight, he built up chemistry in St Andrews to the level that Irvine must have hoped for while watching his department mark time during the difficult years of the war. They shared an interest in the achievements of the great men of the past who had made their discipline possible. Read's enlargement of the departmental library with treasures of a chemical bibliophile resonated with Jim, for whom the history of chemistry and even alchemy also held an enduring fascination. Irvine had a private collection of old chemical pewter pestles and mortars on which he could play a tune, to the amusement of visiting grandchildren. When the time came to mark 100 years of the chair of chemistry in St Andrews, Irvine paid tribute to his fellow chemist, John Read, who had slipped into his shoes but who never excluded him from the department of which 'every stone was dear'.

When Read arrived in 1923, he was welcomed with warmth and generosity. The sum of £1,500 earned by Professor Irvine and his team in the research laboratories during the war had been set apart, and was now made available to provide the equipment needed by the new professor, whose chemistry brought something fresh to St Andrews. Acting as professor during the interregnum, the Principal prepared the way for Professor Read by submitting claims for extraordinarily large class grants for the chemistry department – claims that he made sure would be passed. Professor Read proved to be an asset just after the Principal's heart. Behind his West Country voice, there lay deep-seated imagination and strength of purpose. He remained bilingual in the old south Somerset dialect that he had used as a boy on his father's farm. He could have had a literary career, and he wrote with feeling for the romance of the past. As a young man he had known Thomas Hardy, who encouraged him to write a cycle of dialect plays and to set up a touring company to stage them. The range of his published books displays something of his eclectic knowledge, which extended far beyond chemistry and the history of chemistry. His little history of St Andrews did much to convey an image of this ancient town that was in tune with that of his friend Jim Irvine.[15]

The first indication of Irvine's continuing life as a chemist is to be observed in the 1922 meeting of the British Association for the Advancement of Science (BA), to which he was elected president of Section B (chemistry). The BA was always held in fond and high regard by Irvine: one of his St Andrews predecessors, Principal Brewster, known to every well-informed St Andrews child as the inventor of the kaleidoscope, was its founding spirit. The BA had, furthermore, given young Jim Irvine, freshly returned from Leipzig, his first platform when 'The Alkylation of Sugars' was presented at the Belfast meeting in 1902. With his keynote address ten years later, Irvine could enjoy some professional freedom from the compunction to publish a new paper: 'The Organisation of Research' was an overview of the powers of his own new position as a vice-chancellor.[16] Using the access to the press that the British Association offered, he made a lengthy and well-exposed argument for the supremacy of research in our universities, and spelled out exactly how the higher education of the future should be organised to give structure and room for his values. The details of the address are illuminated by his belief in the role of the individual gifted young research scientist. His own experience within the microcosm of university life that little St Andrews represented was used to show that, provided the impulse of the individual scientist was given room to be original, any research position would be pregnant with opportunity. This much was to the future health of our universities and could, he suggested, be writ large. The prospect of the conveyor-belt principle of chemical research remained anathema to him.

Having presented a vision of his work as a vice-chancellor – to develop research along enlightened lines – he then delivered to the BA an important paper on the polysaccharides, 'Cellulose, Starch and Inulin', and it is worth remarking that here he speaks as a chemist *in medias res*. This paper reflects a confluence of collaboration between his most valued colleagues and protégés: W.S. Denham, who was his chosen assistant; John Macdonald, the research student who had written to him from the trenches; Ettie Steele, his early student who became his loyal secretary; E.S. Hirst, his new protégé; and John Oldham, one of his last PhD candidates. This paper brought him closer to his ultimate goal: the synthesising of sucrose, an aspiration that continued to engage him to the end of his life. At the 1922 meeting of the British Association for the Advancement of Science, he is both the undiminished scientist and the new vice-chancellor who feels that he is in a position to shape the universities of the future.

The University Court in St Andrews acknowledged the honour brought to the university by the conspicuous part their Principal played in these proceedings.

Two years later the BA convened a gathering of its members in Canada, and this took Irvine for the second time of his life across the Atlantic. He had already discovered the therapeutic benefit of the Atlantic crossing when, as one of the few who were not prostrate with sea-sickness, he could rest, read and relax. His gift for telling a tale that Mabel had discovered when they were students in Leipzig could always be brought into play, and he didn't mind when he was called upon to give an impromptu lecture to the motley collection of scientists on board the SS *Montlaurier*. He spoke on the 'Romance of Chemistry', and in writing home he excused himself to his wife: 'Isn't it awful to be a public man and a speaker Mabs, but then I don't mind it a bit when I am rested.'

The hub of the meeting was Toronto, and although Jim found the formal programme of the trip a trifle tedious he seized with both hands the opportunity of meeting a large number of American and Canadian chemists. Rather mischievously, Irvine makes a caricature for his wife of his St Andrews colleague, D'Arcy Thompson, who 'runs round all day tuft-hunting and kow-towing to an extent which nauseates those who know what a sheer humbug the man is. It amuses me and yet it is irritating too for, despised thoroughly by those who know him, he is pushing himself in this crowd just as he does at your parties.'

Irvine's personal form of networking was probably to more effect. 'Today I've slacked off a bit – went down late to the meetings and was then taken to a Rotarian lunch where I had to make a speech along with Sir E. Rutherford and Sir Wm Bragg.' These were men that were at the top of British research: at the Cavendish and the Royal Institution. Irvine was often at his best when he made social connection with influences that would help his work as a vice-chancellor. The Rotarian lunch was timely: the key to success in St Andrews lay in building up student numbers, and Rotary International's sponsorship scheme for American students to study in the UK would soon be extended to St Andrews. This was to be the beginning of the web of international student exchange cultivated by Irvine.

To read the little diary that he kept of the British Association's event in Canada is to be overwhelmed by his stamina. A small band of the scientists were given the opportunity of an escorted tour of the western provinces of Canada, primarily to inspect its mines and raw materials. With some precision, he calculated that he travelled about 16,000 miles in a train with an observation car. There is something of the schoolboy in the diary that clocks up various trophies: sunrise and sunset on the Pacific, the Indian chief whom he meets on top of a glacier, the memorials to Edith Cavell (the heroic First World War nurse of recent memory), and a swim in the hot springs of Banff.[17]

Irvine was able to extend this 1924 visit into the US, where he continued forging the scientific friendships that for the next ten years brought him fame and the scientific lecturing that he craved. At Cornell he was the guest of the eccentric American physical chemist Wilder Dwight Bancroft, and the cellulose division of Cornell's Ithaca campus gave him an 'uproarious reception' as he commenced to lecture on all his pet subjects: cellulose, dextrins, photosynthesis and even 'education'. Here he was made an honorary member.

The gazetting of his knighthood in January 1925 was proof enough that his own country felt that he should be honoured for his science. He earned a leader in a Scottish newspaper:

> His contributions to the chemistry of the methylated sugars – a branch of research which he himself created, his difficult work on glucosamine, of immense interest to the biochemist, and his researches on the polysaccharides may be described as of fundamental importance. In the world of science the name of Irvine is indissolubly linked with carbohydrates, and Sir James is justly regarded as the greatest living authority in this branch of study.[18]

That same year brought the recognition of the cream of his peers. The award of the Royal Society's Davy Medal in November 1925 was to him the high-water mark of his impact on the chemical world. It was remarked in the press that the honour fell on a 'singularly attractive personality'. The Royal Society's Davy Medal is an annual award given by some of the most eminent of the world's scientists for the most important discovery in chemistry made in Europe or in Anglo-America. Irvine's predecessors in a rank of chemists whose work had opened up new worlds included Marie Curie. The esteemed older Scottish chemist, Professor Walker from Edinburgh, was now a familiar friend, but he only expressed what many at the time felt:

> I am very pleased indeed to see from the *Scotsman* that the Royal Society have awarded you the Davy Medal. It is a fit recognition of the excellence of your work, and I send my heartiest congratulations. Honours now fall fast upon you. To save correspondence I think I had better congratulate you by anticipation on the Nobel Chemistry Prize, a baronetcy, the presidency of the Royal Society and ultimately a peerage in the reformed House of Lords . . . I can't help thinking of the pleasure it would have given dear old Purdie had he been alive to know of your success.[19]

None of these further honours did in fact come Jim's way, and he was almost ashamed of his pride in the Davy Medal. The only speech at the award dinner described him in rather flowery style as the new 'Wizard of the North', making reference to another Fife worthy, Michael Scot, the alchemist and necromancer of the thirteenth century. In 1925, the Davy Medal was given in two forms: both a gold medal and a silver one, and so he returned to his club 'with a bulky medal case in each tail-coat bumping into me symmetrically at every step. I would have known in a moment if anybody had pinched one of them.' That night came a further endorsement of Irvine's work: Lord Inchcape, who had been awarded the St Andrews' honorary degree of LLD in 1924, pressed into his hands a cheque for £5,000 for the men's residence scheme that Irvine could now allow himself to plan for.

Jim had given an illustrated evening lecture in February at the Royal Institution on 'Sugars from the Standpoint of the Organic Chemist';[20] it was no coincidence that Sir William Bragg, director of the Faraday Research Laboratory and Fullerton Professor at the Royal Institution, should appear in St Andrews at the beginning of December that year to open the enlarged and rebuilt physics and chemistry laboratories, and to deliver a paper. Far more than ever before, Jim Irvine was a force to be reckoned with in London scientific circles, and he lured many chemical luminaries up to St Andrews.

Marie Curie was also among the previous recipients of Irvine's next distinction, the Willard Gibbs Medal of the American Society of Chemists. It was America that for the next ten years continued to shower rewards and distinctions on him. Jim admitted that in America he was privileged: he had even received honours denied to American scientists. In March 1926 Irvine received a letter from Dr Charles Parsons, the secretary of the American Society of Chemists, informing him that he had been selected to receive the society's medal. The letter explained that the main stipulation of the award was that the recipient should deliver an address upon a chemical subject before the society.[21] The award of the Willard Gibbs Medal as well as the Davy Medal are strong indicators of the fact that, for many years after Irvine took up the principalship of St Andrews, the reputation of his achievements as a chemist grew, both internationally and at home.

There were never any sabbaticals for him: these extensive trips to America were his sabbaticals, and like a boy he threw himself into everything, including life on board ship, which he found so restful. He could pretend that he was born to the sea, as if he were one of his sea-going Colquhoun forefathers. Crossing on the *Metagama* in 1926, his letters home give a picture of the St Andrews Principal in holiday mood. He got on well with the captain of the ship, who gave him 'the freedom of the bridge':

> I have used it freely . . . A lesson on the use of the sextant and sure enough at 12 noon I joined the officers in 'shooting the sun' and calculating the latitude . . . The journey, darling, has been a great success. I'm slept out, clear in the head, brown as a berry, and, I'm certain, a little heavier. Walking on a swaying deck and climbing up and down ladders have restored something of my muscularity. . . it's only now that I realize how necessary it [a break from work] was, for only now I am conscious of what it means to be a normal idle human being for these few blessed days of rest.[22]

In 1926 he would be away from home for nine long weeks, and the Willard Gibbs medal and its lectures were but part of an overwhelmingly busy visit. As was usual with Irvine, his trip had several strings to its bow, and he arrived well in advance of the other 'Masters of Chemistry' who flocked to Philadelphia that summer to participate in the September Golden Jubilee meeting of the American Chemical Society. First, Jim Irvine, in evocation of Purdie's summer advanced chemistry tuition, would be conducting classes for Columbia University's summer school. His image headed a profusion of newspaper articles when he set foot on New York soil that July, one even going so far as to caption the photograph 'Lord Irvine', and several, comically, making him 'Lord Colquhoun'.[23]

At the end of the first century of its life the American Chemical Society was three times as large as any other chemical organisation in the world, and hundreds of scientific papers would be given at the meeting. America, so inclined to introversion, was opening up. The New York and Philadelphia newspapers went wild and reported that 'every civilized country in the world' would send representatives. Irvine had been elected an honorary member of the society, one of only fourteen prominent chemists from throughout the world to have been honoured in this way during the previous fifty years. Some three or four thousand chemical delegates were there to hear his Willard Gibbs lectures. Jim was now conscious of the vast force of American science and American scientists. Although, in general terms, Irvine made no secret of his war work as a chemist, it was not for this that he was singled out for a Willard Gibbs Medal. It was his most recent work on starch and cellulose that interested the Americans. In North America he was regarded as a scientist at the top of his game; his research was of critical importance to the booming industries of Canada and the US, in particular the North American pulp and paper industry. The Scots scientist was drawn to the company of his American counterparts, whom he found engagingly approachable and companionable.

The long visit of 1926 was his third exposure to what he jokingly referred to his wife as 'the land of well-appointed bathrooms'. His first visit to North America was in April and May 1923, the year before the British Association gathering. He and the London physical chemist Fred Donnan, a childhood friend of Mabel's, were the two British chemists invited to attend the opening of the Sterling Chemistry Laboratories at Yale. When Irvine stood up to make his address, the whole audience rose to receive him. Rather bewildered, he began to speak, and they would not let him stop. The paradoxes inherent in the visit of a British scientist to the New World were paramount. The British scientist learned this much from his huge audience: that even the smallest of British universities possessed a quality of achievement that still escaped the American, that there could still be *magnum in parvo*. 'Funny little St Andrews with its wee labs and simple Scottish students to do work which has made a real impression on this great country . . . The St Andrews sugars were the star turn.' But Irvine was astute enough to know that the old world was in danger of destroying itself. 'I can certainly say that America is a much finer country than I imagined . . . the educated American is in earnest and is going to be a hard man to beat. The centre of civilization must in time shift to the New World unless Europe stops all this scrapping and fighting.'[24]

To his surprise, Jim found it a small world in America; at every turn, there was someone with a connection to his life in the UK. 'The smallness of the world is illustrated again by an experience in the train when an elderly gentleman came up the Pullman car to me and said "are you by any chance Principal Irvine from Scotland?" I said I was, and he produced a letter from Rose asking him to show me some kindness in Boston. At once he offered to put his car at my disposal, but this I could not accept as the Harvard people had made all arrangements.' Of course, Rose was Robert Rose, or Cabbage, Jim's old friend from his student days in Leipzig and now a research scientist at Pittsburgh.

He was obliged to observe that the trip 'had developed into a kind of triumphal tour . . . we are fêted as the outstanding physical and organic chemists of Britain. It's almost embarrassing'. In this vast country Jim Irvine and Fred Donnan would soon discover that 'American kindness almost kills you while it stimulates and invigorates. They forget that they are different people at almost every party but I am the constant factor.' Speeches and lectures were required of him at every turn, but he acquired on this first of so many visits to America a considerable knowledge of a number of American universities of the Ivy League. He was struck with the simplicity of their ceremonies and the elaborateness of their dinners and luncheons. When called upon to read the lesson on Sunday morning in the chapel at Yale, he observed that the chapel was rather modest compared with everything else: it was more like a Methodist chapel. Where he came from, it would often be the other way round, with the chapel a fine building at the heart of the university. The presidents of these universities – President Sargent of Harvard, President Angell of Yale, and President Richmond of Union College, Schenectady – were rich men, but they felt that the lavishness of their hospitality was well repaid when, with their wives, they were received into the urbane understated elegance of the Irvines' lives in the old-world calm of St Andrews, even if they were dismayed at how few bathrooms Scottish households possessed at that time.

In analysis, despite the evident luxury of these lives before the Wall Street crash, it was America's freshness, energy and perhaps even simplicity that Jim found so beguiling. Still wearing his chemist's hat, he was taken to visit Princeton for the first time in 1923, and of course he lectured on his sugars. Afterwards he recounted to Mabel what he called, in mock reference to Conan Doyle, 'The Incident of the Key'. On returning to his rooms after lecturing and then dinner, he realised that his key had been left locked inside his room. From the group of admiring students with whom he had chummed up, one broke away and, to Irvine's admiration and horror, began climbing up the ivy on the wall outside his room. Once he had gained entry, Jim instructed his new friends boisterously in the game of rugger, which they played within the confines of the room with an impromptu ball made out of paper salvaged from the wastepaper basket. Perhaps it was not known to many that there was an anti-authoritarian streak deep within the autocratic Jim Irvine.[25] Incidentally, for holiday reading, right up to the end of his life, Jim liked to read and reread the adventures of Sherlock Holmes.

His reactions to the elite college at Princeton, founded in 1756, were wistful:

Can you imagine Oxford stripped of its houses and streets, leaving nothing but the colleges. Place these colleges amongst groves of trees and consider them built of new stone and you get an idea of the place. No factions, no industries – rather like what St A might have been and should have been . . . off for a round of the Colleges and Labs and so to my rooms at this College which is modelled on Magdalen Oxford. My quarters are beautiful, luxurious and artistic to a degree.[26]

The irony in this impression is to be perceived when in 1932 his good friend Willard Connely, the director of the American University Union in London sounded him out on behalf of Princeton to take the helm of this fine New World institution, perhaps the beau ideal of academe that Jim Irvine was searching for all his life.

President Hibben of Princeton was in the office this morning. He told me both he and his university as a whole would like very much to have you as President of Princeton. But he told me at the same time he feared there was no chance of luring you away from such a place as St Andrews. Knowing your own feelings as I do, I took it upon myself rather to agree with those fears. Nevertheless, I thought you might like to know the 'views' held at Princeton.[27]

It was no novel idea on the part of Princeton to bring over a Scotsman to be their chief: the first president of Princeton was the Rev. John Witherspoon, who left his charge as a minister in Paisley to head the new College of New Jersey at Princeton. Irvine showed that he was open to the idea of running an American university, and even took part in informal conversations. However, it was his enduring love for the old grey town, with its very houses and streets, old and worn, and its venerable university buildings perched on an unparalleled site, and the university itself, still needy for him, that continued to exert such a strong pull. He may also have suspected that his wife and his three children would not have been so happy to be uprooted. Jim Irvine turned Princeton down.

Jim was an impressionable man, open to new experiences and keen to learn. He was bowled over by the landscapes of America and the scale of her natural forces.

He would soon discover, of course, that not all of North America was virginal and sweet to the eye, and that the laboratories and industries of Buffalo, for instance, and the town of Niagara, linked by the hydro-electric power resource of the falls, imposed on their inhabitants an ugly way of life in shanty towns polluted by chemical fumes. He was forced to spend a morning with Dr Carey, the millionaire director of the Cancer Research Institute of Buffalo, famous because it possessed more radium than any other installation of its kind. Dr Carey insisted on boring his scientific guest with an ignorant and faulty understanding of the science that had made him rich. Jim Irvine's low boredom threshold and impatience with humbug and pretence nearly got the better of him. In Buffalo, an accidental encounter made up for the discomforts of get-rich-quick America and brought him to a Mr Franklin B. Locke, father-in-law of President Richmond of Union College Schenectady. Irvine recognised in his host a strong resemblance to his famous ancestor, the English philosopher. Being a well-read man, Jim loved unravelling the thread of history, and in the 1920s these links with the old world were still to be found in the fine houses and gentlemanly libraries of old American families, such as that of Mr Locke.[28]

In 1923, while still feeling his way among these enthusiastic hosts, there emerged an experience that would continue to nourish his needs and ideas. It lay waiting for him at McGill, over the border in Montreal, 'a fine place beautifully situated under the mountain'. Once over the 'frontier' (as he liked to call it), with the pleasing sight of the Union Jack flying over a school to remind him who he was, Irvine found himself amongst friends: the organic chemists of McGill were, like him, specialists in the 'γ' sugars, and they hung on his every word: 'The keenest audience imaginable.' McGill impressed him greatly and he found the Canadian scientists, so many of them Scotsmen, real kindred spirits. His visit to the physiological laboratories gave him further knowledge of an aspect of his own subject. Professor Macleod's patent of the control of the manufacture of insulin had been greatly criticised, but here, in the laboratory, Irvine was distressed to see the dire results of overdosing on insulin, and how necessary it was to manufacture insulin under control. The model of McGill University, with its medical faculty and its laboratories designed to advance the application of the knowledge of cellulose to the raw materials all around, would come to the forefront of his mind twenty years later, when he was called upon to create the University of the West Indies. Irvine would return to McGill.

Irvine felt that, with the 1923 North American trip, he had had 'under the best conditions an experience which will be of great service to me'.

There would be other strictly scientific invitations to him from the United States. During three weeks in July and August 1928, Irvine was the chief speaker at the meeting of the Institute of Chemistry of the American Chemical Society, taking place at Evanston. It was not a happy experience, and it took off on a bad footing: for the first and only time in his life he was sea-sick:

> There was once a wee Scottish Principal
> Who thought his sea-legs were invincible
> But the Atlantic overcame him
> (So we'd better not name him)
> And now the wee fellow's more 'sinsible'.[29]

He begrudged the fact that at Evanston he was expected to work day and night. He conducted a week-by-week series of lectures and seminars on carbohydrate chemistry. The exhausting programme was delivered to an ill-informed crowd of chemistry students of Northwestern University, which is situated in a privileged position on the shore of Lake Michigan; it was largely undertaken because of the enormous fee.

Chicago in summer, even on the shoreline, is unbearably humid. Irvine's quarters were disappointing, but by the second week he had worked out a solution to his discomfort that was characteristic of the cheerful resource-fulness that he had enjoyed since his youth.

> This week has been more pleasant, largely through my own doing for I have given some of my lectures out of doors. You would have laughed to see the little crowd, ranging from graduates to grand-fathers, clustering round me whilst expounding the sugars to them. My blotter takes the place of a blackboard and the sheets are passed round from hand to hand. Then at the close, I autograph them and they are kept as souvenirs. To add to this my 'class' has attached itself to me for morning bathing and two broiling afternoons were spent on the beach, in bathing suits; in fact they follow me about like sheep.[30]

He soon discovered that a lakeside fashionable dress of swimming costume and a kimono was de rigueur.

He was able to escape the department at Evanston from time to time; once, memorably, to join a weekend house party given by George Eastman, of the Kodak Company. Jim was not averse to seeking out the company of famous men. Here he met a strange collection of American inventors and philanthropists, including Thomas Edison, of electric light bulb fame. He described this trophy in a letter for his son: 'He really is a wonderful man with a grandfatherly air about him – a kind of mixture of Napoleon and Sir James Donaldson.' (Donaldson having been the venerable Principal of Irvine's youth in St Andrews.)

As a souvenir he preserved for his son, Nigel, some of Edison's observations:

> One of the strange thing[s] to me is that sugar is an acid sufficient to dissolve Ca Hydroxide.
> In my rubber experiments we are bothered by starch and sugar.
> All living things seem to use sugar as a food but store it as starch.
> I think sugars are definite compounds but starch granules look as if they were not organized on definite lines, they vary so much in shape.[31]

Frank Whitmore, of the American National Research Council, thought of writing to Mabel afterwards to tell her how much Jim had been appreciated, and quoting another chemist: 'Before I came, I thought that Sir James was overemphasized, but I haven't recovered yet, marveling that one person can be so truly and so kindly human'[32] – suggesting that contemporary appraisals of him must not be taken as hyperbole. Irvine was so much in demand as a speaker at this time that he had to fall back on speaking without notes.

His public addresses were now extending beyond the American departments of chemistry and deeper into the foreign affairs of his time. He had spoken on Anglo-American relations to the English Speaking Union in Chicago in 1926, in an attempt to heal the wrong he felt Kipling had done America in attacking her tardy entry into the war:

> At the eleventh hour he came
> But his wages were the same
> As ours who all day long had trod
> The winepress of the wrath of God.[33]

He was horrified to learn from one old lady that she had travelled 500 miles to hear him, but he felt that he had an important message, and one that he would be called upon increasingly by governments and universities alike to convey: Great Britain and the US needed each other and should stand together. He was mobbed by his audience but even more by the press, which, of course, picked up his off-record remarks and gave them an exaggerated political slant. 'The worst of it is that this country is so over-ridden by the Press that in place of speaking from a few notes it is necessary to write out a synopsis for the reporters and this takes time and annoys me for when all is said and done their newspapers are infamously poor things.' He who had loved the fame that the press in his own country gave to his university was finally learning Kipling's lesson: that reporters are to be avoided and speeches are to be given for publication to a responsible body. He recorded: 'There is a scramble for the publication of my lectures and this I have solved by presenting them to the American Chemical Society.'

These were years when many scientific honours and medals were awarded to Irvine: in 1929 the Elliot Cresson Medal, the highest award given by the Franklin Institute, crowned his reputation in America. Finally, in 1941 in his homeland he was elected Gunning Victoria Jubilee Prizeman of the Royal Society of Edinburgh.

Privately, Jim Irvine did not disguise the fact that one reason for under-taking the transatlantic engagements was financial. The lectures and speeches he gave in the United States were attractively well paid. His letters to his wife show that, in gratitude to her for being willing to let him spend these long weeks away from home, he wanted her to indulge herself. His account books show that during the inter-war period he built up a private income from fees and consultancies that doubled his salary. Thanks to this bulwark against her husband's inadequate stipend, Mabel now had more freedom to take holidays and to visit London, with its concerts and theatres. Her wardrobe now included an array of fine evening dresses made for her to wear at the now widely reported functions of rectorial installation and the installation of Baldwin as chancellor.

The education of their three children would make considerable demands on their purse. Running the official residence in St Andrews cost far more than the Principal's salary would allow for – although the reason for this may have lain in Jim's gift for friendship, and the stream of visitors who lunched, dined and slept at University House. The Principal's now fabled friendships were a constant drain on his domestic budget. For many years he believed that he had 'expectations' from the estate of the rich, childless aunt, the widow of Captain James Colquhoun. Agnes McNeil Colquhoun finally died in 1929, leaving the residue of her considerable estate to found a lifeboat to serve North Berwick and to be called the *James Colquhoun*: her late husband's family were left small mementos of her, but nothing of her fortune. Jim and Mabel had to bite back their disappointment. Jim's father died in 1926, and left his four children over £4,000, an impressive achievement for one who had really started out in life with nothing.[34] Unfortunately, the division of John Irvine's estate caused a family rift which was not healed until shortly before the Second World War. The death of his father occurred while Jim was in America. It grieved him deeply to have been prevented from attending his father's death. He had a close bond with his father, with whom he had enjoyed the companionship of so many boyhood activities. Jim paid a price for his pursuit of the New World.

He neatly entered in his 'log' his American income and expenditure over these years. Over the four early American trips, which he undertook primarily as a scientist, he showed a final profit of £250. The real necessity of America to him, however, lay in the complete refreshment that he drew from the open, athletic life that he lived there.

It would be wrong to suggest that Irvine was overlooked as a scientist in his own country once he had begun his administrative life. It was by no means only in America that he was honoured with honorary scientific degrees. He noted with approval that his degree from Cambridge (1932) was to be an honorary DSc, unlike the Oxford DCL that he received the next year. When Liverpool gave him an honorary DSc in 1925, he rewarded them with much valuable advice on the development of their chemistry department, and made a confidential friend of the Liverpool chemist Professor Baly. In March 1933, together with W.N. Haworth, he was awarded the Longstaff Medal of the Chemical Society of London. He served as a trustee of the Ramsay Memorial Fellowship, to which he was ever willing to contribute a speech about Ramsay, whom he had emulated when young. In 1931 he became a member of the prime minister's committee on the training of biologists, and on 21 September 1931 he was an honoured guest at the Faraday celebrations of the Royal Institution, whose cause at that time he was promoting.[35] None of the speeches, he felt, did justice to Faraday, one of his heroes. The occasion was redeemed for him by meeting up with the Leipzig molecular chemist Professor Rassow, whose lectures he had attended long ago.

Irvine's was the busy life of a public figure who still described himself as a chemist, and it was for his chemical life as well his acute performance in committee that he was in 1934 invited to become a commissioner of the Royal Commission for the 1851 Exhibition, the very body that had awarded him those two significant years in Leipzig. It is in his role as president of the Lancastrian Frankland Society that we find him promoting the need in chemistry for the same flights of sheer imagination that might more properly belong to a literary man. These positions were to him but the adornment of a man of science, but he knew he had the power to promote the well-being of his profession in the world at large, just as he knew that graceful speeches extolling the antiquity of St Andrews would bring fame and fortune to his university. He was more than a public figure: he became increasingly valued as a publicist.

Over a long period, his account book records his annual retainer of £131 as chemical consultant to the Tullis Russell papers mills at Markinch in Fife. This was not a sinecure because, as a specialist much interested in cellulose, he was of great use to the Markinch paper mills. Back at his laboratory bench in St Andrews, and throughout the early years of the Principalship, in 1923, 1924 and 1925 Irvine was in receipt of a personal grant of £75 per annum from the Carnegie Trust to continue his chemical research.[36] In these years his daily pattern of life, when not travelling, had not changed since he was an undergraduate: every afternoon he would don his lab coat and set to work in the chemical laboratory. It was in the 1920s that his nurturing of the ultimately distinguished careers of a handful of graduate students, including E.L. Hirst, John Oldham and David Traill, was perhaps at its most fruitful. From his post with ICI, Traill would continue to carry the torch for Irvine and St Andrews. Hirst had been cultivated by Irvine since he was not much more than a boy, and his early years were as a carbohydrate chemist in the tradition that Irvine had carved out. He left St Andrews to develop his distinguished career, and for a time his name was linked with that of W.N. Haworth, who had left St Andrews after a blazing row with Irvine. Irvine's misgivings about Haworth, whom he felt was too hasty in publishing results, were aired in the pages of Nature. Irvine did not share the contemporary admiration of Haworth's quality of 'conclusiveness' that attached to his work.

It must be admitted that John Oldham was a particular favourite of Irvine's, and in collaboration with this student and with Eric Stiller, Irvine came as close as he would get to synthesising the important sugar, sucrose.[37] Many angles were attempted, but not even Irvine's clarity of thought, meticulousness – the 'Scotch caution' and 'sheer dogged perseverance' that he ascribed to his Scottish scientific heroes from the past – quite achieved the aim of producing synthetic sugar that had all the same stereochemical arrangement as cane sugar. They produced a new isomeric disaccharide, which they termed iso-sucrose. In 1928 a Swiss chemist, Amé Pictet, working in Geneva with Vogel, published his claim to having synthesised sugar employing a method that, in Irvine's hands, had failed to give the desired result.[38] Irvine was a man of high probity, and he found Pictet's work questionable. He was, in any case, intrigued. He thought of John Buchan's novels. These tales of international conspiracies, mysterious clinics in the Alps and chases across grouse moors were Jim's favourite holiday reading. John Oldham's widowed mother was comfortably off. Why should not the young chemist take his mother for a beneficial holiday in the Swiss Alps, to a hotel near the Geneva laboratory of Dr Pictet? While there, and unannounced, John should visit Pictet's laboratory and try to find out what were the bases for Pictet's claims. The story is that what he found confirmed Irvine's suspicions.[39]

Jim Irvine remained deeply attached to the chemistry departmental buildings that his mentor Professor Purdie had given to the cause of chemistry in St Andrews. Within the first ten years of his office as Principal he looked on as his successor, Professor Read, faced two major building extensions undertaken to what became known, many years afterwards, as the Irvine Building. The late 1920s saw the enlargement of the teaching laboratories, made possible by Irvine's negotiations with the Carnegie Trust, but in November 1931 the new building was severely damaged by a fire originating in the adjacent physics department. Only swift action prevented the loss of the entire Chemistry Institute.

The continuance of Irvine's scientific thought can be traced in *Nature*, to which he was a frequent correspondent – as, for example, on 28 July 1934, where he shows that he was still at work in his laboratory seeking to prove that iso-sucrose was a stereoisomeride of sucrose. Perhaps it could be said that his originality of thought, so often remarked on by his peers, could never be fully repressed, or perhaps it was that spirit of adventure that Irvine himself singled out as a mark of the chemistry department at St Andrews: the department's 'virtues of accuracy, honesty, endeavour and adventure'[40] were Irvine's virtues, and these he had culled the hard way from Henderson and Purdie. In believing that his life's work at the chemical research bench 'will lead to the understanding of the mystery of material living', he was merely stating what he believed to be the truth.[41]

There is something of nostalgia in how he regarded himself as a scientist twenty years after he had hung up his lab coat: 'I used to be a scientist – and at heart . . . I am one still . . . like all scientists I have a constant desire to get at the origin of things.'[42] To the end, Irvine remained deeply interested in the application of carbohydrate derivatives to modern problems.

TWELVE

America's Favourite Britisher

Jim Irvine enjoyed something of a love affair with America, and it was reciprocated. He had to admit, however, that it was primarily to the charms of the New Englanders that he was drawn. Irvine was too deeply rooted in Scotland for America to be any more than a flirtation, but the friendships he made there were deep and real enough. These friendships, especially his friendship with Edward Harkness, were productive of a significant union between the New World and the mother country.

The first and longest of these American connections was with the family of W.J. Matheson, a successful chemical industrialist. Although an American, Dr Matheson nurtured an affection for St Andrews, to which in the 1860s he had been sent to be educated. Furthermore, he had then spent two years studying chemistry there, as a non-graduating student during the period when Heddle was professor, and this made rather an appealing connection for Jim, whose initial link with Matheson was in so many ways ready-made. Matheson had already commenced his giving to St Andrews at the time that Irvine became Principal, and Irvine loved him for this early generosity. There were donations from 'a friend to St Andrews', to the growing fund for the building of student residence halls; there were the Matheson Bursaries, and then from Matheson's legacy the Matheson Scholarships. Truly William Matheson merited his place in the 'founders' window of St Salvator's Hall.

Dr Matheson and the family of his daughter, Mrs Willis Wood, gave Jim something of even greater personal worth: they gave him his American vacations. The Wood family's house became Jim's second home and the New York apartment a comfortable base from which to do business. For a few weeks in the summer, they virtually adopted him. Their holiday shack, deep in the primeval forest of the Adirondacks, reminded Jim of Glen Affric, only it was more rugged. They slept under the stars by night, and fished in the lake by day. This was a wonderful escape from the grind of work: sailing off Long Island in the *Corisande* and later in William Matheson's *Seaforth*, or swimming from the beaches of the Lloyd Neck properties of Matheson's extended family; tennis matches and deep-sea fishing completed the cure. None of this would have been Mabel's idea of a holiday, but the sunshine and open air restored her husband to life. They were both acting a part: it suited him to be for a while the sporty, clubbable Yale graduate; and Mabel, who lived in a 'tied cottage', became the literary lady in possession of a house in the country, from which she developed the Irvines' joint friendships with writers such as Walter de la Mare. Mabel loved the gentle pace of the country vicarages they rented for the summers, where her house parties included all her favourite Irish relations. She had the imagination to assume for a short while the character of each house as if it were hers. From folds in the Cotswolds, she, Veronica, Nigel and Felicity explored country churches, discovered the byways of 2,000 years of English history and were asked out and about by the local gentry. While Jim was crewing the racing schooner of a rich American – 'Sailed across the Sound in *Laverock* in a full gale. Situation serious for a short time, arrived home soaked through,' he noted in his 'log' – Mabel was seated at her watercolour easel in a rectory garden. Although the business of getting a maiden aunt, a delicate sister, two maids, two dogs and three children across the length and breadth of England cannot have been easy, this was the reward she wanted for the life of endless entertaining and being 'on show' in St Andrews, yoked to her husband's job. It was a lonely reward, but the array of interesting old houses that she and the children took for their month in the country was satisfying. Sometimes Jim joined them for part of the holiday, especially if there was fishing with Nigel to be had in the still, limestone pools of the Gloucestershire rivers, or the more challenging fishing of Somerset or the Welsh Marches.

However, although Jim and Mabel had to endure long separations in their life together, their marriage remained like a rock, just as firm and loving as it had always been. Mabel wrote of the strong telepathic communication between them, and whether it was because of this, or Jim's vivid letter-writing style, she was able to follow in her imagination all the details of his wanderings in America precisely as if she had been there. Mabel was a remarkably strong character, and she drew hard on this strength when these long absences of Jim's required her to be the university's hostess without her husband at her side. Many a student invited to lunch at University House on Sundays found her even more intimidating than the Principal. What a pity she never revealed to these nervous young things what a rich and creative personality she was, and how sensitive and skilled she was at looking after people. J.M. Barrie once bumped into her as she came out of her painting studio in University House's old coach house, and saw for the first time a woman at peace with herself: no longer wearing the mask she put on when serving the university as her husband's wife, or addressing meetings on behalf of women's education, or children's literature or even the Unionist Party. 'The real you begins when the doors are shut and you emerge as the imaginative artistic dreamer of dreams, far from sure of yourself, indeed very humble.'[1]

Jim never lost the hot-headed, determined side to him that drove him relentlessly in pursuit of a public career and in fulfilment of what he saw as his duty: sometimes it was to the exclusion of his wife and family, and certainly to the destruction of his health. A different wife might have been broken by it, and Mabel suffered illnesses, which became more acute during the years that Jim was so often far away from home. The life they led nearly destroyed her.

The years between the two twentieth-century wars have been described as a new capitalist age: a rebirth of nineteenth-century capitalism, but with more interest in taste and style. Jim Irvine's tastes were uncomplicated, and he enjoyed the fine things of life without feeling in the least guilty. On the transatlantic liners he danced and dined as a VIP passenger, and he spent his days swimming and reading. In America he rode on the crest of the wave of all that was new, and yet luxurious. In order to earn his dollars in Chicago, he crossed half of America in the *Twentieth Century*, a long journey in the most sumptuous train in the world. More like a liner, it had a Pullman dining car for meals and a 'club' car for those who wished to catch up with their work, and Jim's first-class accommodation provided him with a 'state-room'. He wrote admiringly of his 'own "nigger" manservant', who with great charm foresaw his every need, including a quiet place to work and write, for how else could he catch up with the avalanche of requests to make public addresses? He was certainly intrigued by his experience of America. And as he checked in at the hotel in Chicago, he noticed that the name above his in the book was Al Capone. At the railway station, his diary notes that he took his breakfast at a 'counter', a novel enough experience for one whose breakfasts normally were taken in the rather more decorous surroundings of University House or the Athenaeum Club in London. The enthusiastic students would drag him off to a 'drug-store' to eat ice-cream sundaes. He wrote home to his daughter, Veronica, extolling the glamour of the 'soda-fountain'. In the open air arena at Ravinia, on the fashionable north shore of Chicago, he had the pleasure of hearing *Lohengrin* for the first time since his student days in Leipzig.

The rich socialites of Long Island – and these included the Marshall Fields, the Tiffanys and the Lloyd Smiths – wanted more than anything to give him a good time, and to introduce him to the good and the great of Manhattan. In accepting a 'lift' to New York in Wilton Lloyd Smith's private aircraft, he felt he had to justify himself to Mabel, who would have been horrified.

> I flew back from Long Island to New York in a seaplane!
> Lloyd Smith, the Woods' nearest neighbour has a private plane and he telephoned after breakfast inviting me to travel to NY by air and see the City from aloft. It seemed
> (a) silly to refuse such a chance
> (b) silly to risk air-travel when there was no necessity
> but being always keen on new experiences I went along. Mab, it was glorious and I really enjoyed it immensely: at the finish of the trip we circled round New York looking down on the skyscrapers and at one stage being right above the Carnegie mansion with all the familiar land-marks beneath us. We landed on the East River.'

Always a celebrity as soon as he stepped on board ship, he became extremely well-known on the other side of the 'pond'.

His description of 'a special party, given in my honour at Forthill', Matheson's Long Island estate, reveals his incredulous reaction at finding himself thrown into such a crowd. 'Such a performance Mabs, 140 people to dinner with dancing afterwards, the grounds illuminated with fairy lamps, search-lights playing through the trees and the elite of Long Island present. The dinner was out of doors, ten people to a table, and I had a niece of Mary Harkness' next me. The Roosevelts were there, also the Pages, the Doubledays and old Mr Colgate (of soap fame) who knew Pat Playfair well.' Pat Playfair, the minister of the town kirk in St Andrews, was of course a prominent citizen there, but it was a surprise to hear his name in this far-away stylish world of the American super-rich.

There would be many more of these parties, extending deep into the hot nights: 'swell parties' he would say. Lifts in hotels would always be 'elevators' to him. The novelty of it all was very far removed from St Andrews, but when he returned he would enjoy gathering up his family on a Saturday night, to go to 'the movies'. He had adopted something, even if superficially, of America. It was Philip Levine, a chemist at the Rockefeller Institute who described him as 'the most popular Englishman in the United States',[3] and Jim used his position with Americans to great effect during these years.

James Irvine had only been three years in office when an important development in educational philanthropy came onto the scene, through the American Edward Harkness. Edward's father Stephen, a saddler by trade who became an investment manager, had lent John D. Rockefeller half a million dollars to start what eventually became Standard Oil; he made his son a billionaire. With modesty and wisdom Edward Harkness devoted his life to giving away his father's fortune in an enlightened and system-atic continuation of what the father had begun. Harkness, whose legacy marks him out as a world-class philanthropist, was a penetrating reformer of education. He was of the same generation as Irvine, and like Irvine he was not afraid to be an idealist. During the early 1920s, he was enlarging the scope of the Commonwealth Fund, formed by his mother before her death. In Edward Harkness's hands, the fund became a multi-million dollar trust that would approach the needs of education in a rounded sense, rather than fall into the trap of piece-meal giving. Irvine described Harkness's life-work as 'the practice of the science of giving'. Thus, within the United States, the Commonwealth Fund enabled Yale and Harvard to adopt a collegiate form; it funded medical research centres and hospitals; it brought the spirit of family relationship into schools and local medical care.

Edward Harkness's belief in the essential goodness of his fellow man was already making itself felt through his investment in American educa-tion and research when he turned his mind to the whole Anglo-American world of the future. He began to extend his influence across the Atlantic. The Harkness family was probably of Scottish Covenanting extraction, but although Edward Harkness's ancestor arrived on American soil long ago, in the first years of the eighteenth century, Ed was a sympathetic admirer of the culture of his roots. He had a strongly held desire to nurture Anglo-American friendship: he felt that the future of civilisation hung on the understanding engendered in this way. By January 1925 he was ready to launch his scheme of Commonwealth Fellowships, as a trust reflective of the Rhodes Trust, but which would bring British graduates in the other direction to experience the universities of the United States. These fellow-ships were to be for a period of two years, and each carried the valuable award of £600 per annum.[4]

A board of trustees in the UK had to be established in order to handle the considerable administration that the Commonwealth Fellowships would

entail. British vice-chancellors were invited to meet Harkness's representative, Max Farrand, in London on 27 January 1925, and Irvine was there. Jim
and Max Farrand had plenty of mutual friends in the good Americans who
brought Irvine over to speak in the States. Farrand and Irvine were at ease
with each other.

Irvine encountered a powerful cartel in that Oxford and Cambridge were
determined to control the show. He knew he was up against it when Oxford's
representative spoke up, stating that he thought that out of twenty annual
fellowships, Oxford could safely lay claim to six. Naturally, the Cambridge
delegate felt that the same figure could be apportioned to his university, and
London, not to be outdone, put in for a third allowance of six scholarships.
Irvine, who was representing the four Scottish universities, rose to his feet,
saying: 'Gentlemen, I see that the number to be assigned to Scotland is
minus four.' This brilliant stroke no doubt owed much to Irvine's competitive streak, and to his natural determination to see that his best students
would stand a chance. Max Farrand was clearly impressed and slipped
Irvine a note: would he have lunch with him after the meeting? Farrand
immediately wanted to place Irvine as chairman of the British Committee,
but Irvine had a better, more subtle, suggestion. The chairman should be
the neutral chairman of the University Grants Committee, but he, Irvine,
would agree to be permanent vice-chairman. The other members would be
appointed from the other universities for short terms in rotation.[5] Irvine's
future control of the British board of trustees was assured. To start off with,
however, he was the only non-Oxford or Cambridge man on the board,
and he would face many battles. Soon he would impart to the candidates
an impression of the living presence of his friend Edward Harkness, and
he made it his special care to ensure that the fellows took with them to
America something of his own commitment to Anglo-American relations.[6]

The Commonwealth Fellowships offered exactly the kind of broadening
experience that English complacency at that time needed; but Irvine felt
that his Scottish students had the right mix of freshness and ambition to
benefit most from this enterprise. Edward Harkness, the most discreet of
men, needed a friend he could trust on the British side, and in Jim Irvine
he found one. In June 1926, Edward Harkness and his wife Mary visited the
Irvines in St Andrews for the first time.

The scheme required an immense amount of work by the British universities who put forward young men for interview, but the prize was great. The
London interviews, in which Irvine invariably took a leading part, required
two or more gruelling days every year to accomplish. Irvine, whose concept

of higher education was wide-ranging, espoused Harkness's idea with all his heart. His boys needed post-graduate experience, and he would make sure they obtained it. He personally drilled his candidates, feeding them with the technique and the knowledge of the world required to excel at interview. Within a year, both men and women from St Andrews were dominating the scheme.

Mabel noted in her diary that

> There is a force and character about the best men St Andrews turns out that makes them outstanding – as has been proved by the six men appointed to Commonwealth Scholarships last year. Reports are now beginning to come in from all the Fellows, & Jim tells me it is most striking the way our St Andrews men are grasping the academic situation in America, utilizing it to the very best advantage, enjoying the experience & finding the best in everything; while the six Oxford Fellows are cavilling & finding difficulties & comparing all the American universities with Oxford, naturally to their disadvantage, instead of laying hold on the vital & youthful characteristics of the younger universities & appropriating some of their keenness and zest.[7]

The board found that the St Andrews students who had followed a four-year course were interesting in interview, because of their broad intellectual experience.

In return, Harvard and Yale came to play a conspicuous part in Anglo-American relations by offering the Harkness Fellows a taste of the vaster, more modern political, economic and industrial machine that was America. The deal was that at the end of two privileged years, during which they would travel in the States, the fellows must return to the United Kingdom to put their new experience to good use. As with the Rhodes scholarships, the Commonwealth Fellowships aspired to the creation of a 'Common-wealth' of leaders for the English-speaking world. The only one who could be said to have flaunted the rules by remaining in America was, inciden-tally, Alistair Cooke, whose *Letter from America* broadcasts did so much to further Harkness's aspirations.

It gave Irvine pleasure to observe how a Commonwealth Fellowship could change a young man's life, particularly one whom he knew, and this is how it was for the son of his friend, John Read, the professor of chemistry. When young, Jan Read had shown an interest in photography, and he hankered after a life in film-making rather than following his father and becoming a scientist. It was a time when every young thing – even the University House maids, whom the Irvines called the glamour girls – dreamed of going to Hollywood. Jan's interest, however, was serious, although he eschewed the academic path to studying film; he wanted to learn directly from those making the iconic films in America. He has recounted how shrewd Principal Irvine, 'with his puckish smile', coached him for the interview, observing that documentary film-making was the up-and-coming thing in America. When Jan Read won a Commonwealth Fellowship it took him to California, where he joined the genius Fritz Lang, and from this followed a successful career in British film-making.[8]

There was to be no visit to America for Irvine in 1925, the first year of what he called the Comfund. It was not until 1926 that Irvine was able to visit Harkness at Eolia, his Connecticut estate on the ocean. Harkness's fascination with Irvine had begun. As the faster *Berengaria*, with the Harknesses on board, passed Jim crossing to Montreal on the *Metagama*, a 'Marconigram' of good wishes was dispatched to the Scotsman, who was already sending to America exactly the kind of scholar that the fund was seeking, and in excess of the St Andrews numerical ratio. When Jim finally reached Eolia, the long weekend consisted of talks with Harkness deep into the night. Mabel would collect her letters from a village post office somewhere in the west of England and read about the multi-millionaire's house that bore an air of studied simplicity. The party was of Harkness's inner circle: Max Farrand, Samuel Fisher, Mac Aldrich and Sir Walter Riddell, the chairman of the University Grants Commission and chairman of the Commonwealth Fellowship Board, with the new addition of Irvine, who was now clearly a force on both sides of the Atlantic in Harkness's great scheme. His visits to North America from this time on would in some measure be financed by the Commonwealth Fund, and justifiably, because he would undertake considerable work for it in its New York offices.

Harkness had so recently been in St Andrews to receive an honorary LLD: a cunning move on Principal Irvine's part. Edward and Mary Harkness would have seen its beauty through Jim's and Mabel's eyes. Jim Irvine must have felt secure in his new friendship with Ed even as early as that first summer's encounter, because that August, in the car driving from Eolia, at Goschen Point on the Connecticut seaboard, to Yale at New Haven, he began to unfold to Harkness's sympathetic ear something of the very great problems that still threatened St Andrews' survival.[9] When he returned home he did as Harkness asked, and sent him a memorandum on the university's financial situation, with an analysis of the non-recurrent expenditure that he felt was urgent. The whole document reads as a litany of the university's failings: laboratories, lecture rooms, scientific museum, salaries, student comforts – all of these needed an instant injection of cash, and yet what Irvine wanted most of all was a large residential hall that would build up the student numbers and attract boys from the English public schools. He wanted the chapel of St Salvator's to be at the heart of student life.[10]

Irvine used the phrase 'new-poor' to describe his alma mater. The only funds that St Andrews had, independent of the Treasury and the Carnegie Trust for Scotland, came from a small annual surplus from the fee income, accruing to £6,464 by 1926, and with this it had been resolved to buy land adjacent to the United College, to be ready for the desired expansion. True, there was a fund for the new residence hall, which was growing too slowly for the eager Principal. The shadow of competition from south of the border loomed darker and darker, and Irvine was desperate to expand his small university. Of course, expansion to him meant expansion of everything: of all teaching and living facilities, rather than merely a crude influx of student numbers. He would, however, be content for the time being with an addition of 350 students.[11] Irvine chose to present himself to his new friend as a visionary who had pondered St Andrews' difficulties long before he became Principal. He laid a complex plan before Harkness, rather than a single aspect of expansion. There were other dangers that threatened St Andrews. The degree of state control in British universities, even at that date, was alien to Harkness's way of thought, and Irvine could see that if the government's contribution, which stood at 47 per cent, crept up any further, St Andrews would lose its independence and he his autonomy. He was noticeably alarmed at the possibility of a Labour government. These were powerful arguments to an American, and they aroused Harkness's interest.[12]

Harkness liked the lucid, straightforward manner of his friend's memorandum; even more, Jim's conversation in the car, driving across Connecticut in August 1926, had been seductive. Early in 1927 came Harkness's reply: he would make a gift to St Andrews of £100,000, to be spent in ways that he knew coincided with Jim Irvine's ideas. He would support nothing that was the business of government to provide. He wished his gift to have the effect of civilising the student's whole life. Initially, in any press announcement of this, the first of Harkness's donations to Irvine's university, his name was to be withheld. He stated that his interest in St Andrews was largely personal and that, therefore, he wanted to feel assured that Irvine's connection with the university was not likely to be discontinued in the immediate future. Irvine could not have made this promise, given his lingering restlessness.

The gift was to be ring-fenced for St Andrews, as distinct from Dundee, for it was to the ancient institutions and collegiate buildings of St Andrews that Harkness was drawn. St Andrews has always enjoyed the intimacy of its small scale: something that was lacking in early twentieth-century Yale. Much of Harkness's educational work in the States promoted his belief that education succeeded better if students lived and worked nurtured in small social groups, rather than being cast adrift in the large and bewildering world that otherwise made up a university. St Andrews' new residence would have dignified dining; Yale students dined in cafeteria style. He was embroiled in a tussle on this issue with Yale, his old college. Its governing body prevaricated when Harkness offered a multi million dollar gift for the building and endowment of residential quadrangles in the collegiate manner.

While Yale paused and questioned the idea, Harkness turned his giving to Harvard, a move guaranteed to make Yale realise its loss and return cap-in-hand to Harkness.[13] Perhaps what was happening in St Andrews would, he thought, illustrate his point. As Harkness himself said: 'Little by little you see, we are growing up and taking over the best you can show us.'[14]

In St Andrews, £29,000 would be allocated to complete the sum needed to build St Salvator's Hall, the long-awaited hall of residence. The amount of £8,000 was to be spent on finally completing the restoration of the fifteenth-century chapel; while £40,000 was to be kept as an endowment fund for the residential experiment – for an experiment at first it was, with many features new to higher education, and designed to break down university life into a closer and more fertile association of teachers and pupils. The income from the Harkness Bequest was to be directed towards scholarships to enable poor students to participate fully in all that the residence had to offer: formal meals, with a high table, presided over by a Warden; spacious rooms for living and studying; fine architectural details; memorials in stained glass to the great men of St Andrews' past and present, including Harkness and Lord Inchcape. Irvine planned to have the founders' armorial bearings displayed in the windows of the dining hall. He was not put off by the fact that Harkness, an American, had no coat of arms. With Harkness's compliance, he corresponded with the College of Arms. Eventually, thanks to Irvine's persistence, Harkness's arms were matriculated.[15] The balance of the Harkness Bequest was left to Irvine's discretion to spend. In the years of the Depression ahead, there were often students whose source of income had dried up, and those who confided in the Principal found that he was in a position to help by digging into the Harkness gift, or often into his own bank account.

Following hot on the heels of the developments in St Andrews, Yale announced it was ready to accept the Harkness Quadrangle, and the eventual addition of further residential quadrangles, each a social group of its own. Harkness built into the Yale bequest a scheme similar to the St Andrews' model of the scholarship endowment fund. No-one who merited a place at Yale should be excluded from the social privileges of the rich Yale student: all would dine together and play together, just as they studied together. This democracy was already freely available in St Andrews.

Edward Harkness was, like Irvine, a man of plain Presbyterian faith, and he took a particular interest in the two medieval college chapels that had survived in St Andrews. He indicated that if Irvine wanted more for the chapels, he had only to ask. The larger, more central chapel of St Salvator's would be fully restored and made fit for use. Then, in 1930, Harkness made it clear that he wished to restore the little chapel of St Leonard, regardless of cost. It was all that remained to the university after the sale in 1877 of the site and residual buildings of St Leonard's College to St Leonard's girls public school. St Leonard's Chapel had suffered many indignities since the time of Prior Hepburn, its sixteenth-century builder, but most shocking of all was the sacrilege committed by Principal Sir David Brewster, who fitted out the sacristy to provide himself with a wine cellar, complete with wine bins. Whether it was because of the pathos of St Leonard's Chapel, or whether it was just that it had charmed Principal Irvine many years before, Harkness had caught something of Irvine's feeling for the little chapel. He called for plans to be drawn up. Harkness did not give blindly to Irvine: his approach was always business-like and fastidious. Unfortunately, he laid down a condition that the stability of the fabric should be examined by the Scottish architect Sir Robert Lorimer, whose National War Memorial in Edinburgh Castle had just been unveiled. He was the most prominent restoration architect in Scotland. Lorimer condemned St Leonard's Chapel as beyond repair – something that was shown later to be untrue – and pressed strongly the counter-proposal that the ancient building should be demolished, and that he himself should design an entirely new chapel on the site – a quite disgraceful line for an architect to take in this case. This was far from what either Harkness, or – above all – the university, wanted: the hope had been for restoration or nothing.

Harkness withdrew his offer, and for almost twenty years the project had to be abandoned.[16]

Encouraged by Harkness's open manner with him, early in 1929 Irvine asked for more. He now despaired of ever being able to build up the teaching faculties. A chair of civil history, instituted in 1747, had been lost to history by its conversion to a chair of natural history at the end of the nineteenth century. This odd logic had to be put right. Irvine knew very well that a provision for the enlargement of the department of history had hopefully been put into every quinquennial plan for the last twenty years, and it was certainly an area where the English universities were outstripping anything that St Andrews could offer. Irvine could bear it no longer. Mabel's brother, Jack Williams, had held a post in the university in medieval history since just before the First World War. In 1929 this had been elevated to a readership in history at St Andrews, but there was no further prospect of advancement for Jack Williams there. Irvine confided his frustration to Harkness, who responded that he was happy to make up the £20,000 required to endow the chair, particularly since the amiable 'Williams', whose beguiling company he remembered with pleasure, would be the first to occupy the chair. Once again, the whole transaction was conducted in a personal and anonymous way, from a 'friend of St Andrews': 'friend of Jim Irvine' would be closer to the mark. They were by now Ed and Jim to each other. The banker's draft stated that it was for the establishment of a chair of American history in the University of St Andrews. This minor difficulty seems to have been just ignored and forgotten about, and the Harkness Chair of American History became the chair of history – but from this date came the teaching of colonial and American history as part of the St Andrews curriculum.[17] Eighty years after the foundation of the 'Harkness' chair, the teaching of history has become a very strong suit at St Andrews.

Jim felt that, with Harkness's gifts, a turning point in the history of St Andrews had been reached, and he was profoundly grateful that this much had been achieved during his principalship. He promised his friend that he would have no cause to regret his generosity, which eventually amounted in all to $200,000. On the contrary, he made sure that the gratitude of the university was expressed in every conceivable way: the honorary degree, Harkness's figure in the windows of St Salvator's Hall, and a window in the restored chapel. 'I very much doubt if such a thing would have occurred in any other institution,' was how Harkness reacted to the university's acknowledgement of his generosity.[18]

Finally, Irvine's talent for extolling St Andrews brought to the university Sir Frank Salisbury's portrait of Harkness. Salisbury, the establishment portrait painter who had a thriving practice on both sides of the Atlantic, had just completed Harkness's portrait for Harvard when Irvine met him at a private dinner party in New York given by Mrs Carnegie. By some good fortune, Salisbury had chosen to paint Harkness in the glowing red gown of the St Andrews LLD: it is a flattering portrait of a man who was described as 'parched, mysterious and looking rather like a frog'.[19] Irvine told Salisbury the whole story of all that his friend was doing for St Andrews and beyond, and the result was that, as 'a token of gratitude for Mr Harkness's benefactions to our beloved country', Salisbury gave a replica portrait of their benefactor to St Andrews University.[20]

Jim Irvine's first American friends may have felt that in the late 1920s he was beginning to shun them. The truth was that Ed Harkness was monopolising him, and wearily Jim had to decline many of the invitations that greeted his arrival in the States from 1928 onwards. Irvine was touched by the simplicity of this rich man, for whom he devised little presents: a St Andrews University badge for his blazer, and a present of black bun at Christmas. The Scottish delicacy black bun[21] mystified Ed and Mary, who pronounced it 'the doctor's friend' and sent it down to the servants' hall. Jim noticed that, to achieve his aims, Harkness preferred to give rather than take a lead, and he relied on his close associates to put his ideas into effect.[22] It was satisfying for Jim to work with this thoughtful man, whose great schemes seemed so needful of the kind of painstaking assistance that Jim was prepared to contribute.

America was still living a confident life, and the stock markets were thriving. Ed began to turn over in his mind a further idea – 'something big', as he thought, and a gift to Great Britain. Irvine loved to recount the tale of the birth of The Pilgrim Trust,[23] one of the UK's most valued and influential trusts today. In the autumn of 1928, the two friends lay on the sands after bathing at Long Island, and Ed began to speak of the growing number of appeals for help that were reaching him from English sources. The aftermath of the General Strike lent a special urgency. Jim could see the direction in which his friend's thoughts were travelling, but it was on the Eolia estate in Connecticut on 13 September 1929, after a round of golf called off by rain, that Harkness finally felt ready to lay before Jim the essence of his thoughts. The two friends sat by the study fire and, in visionary mood, Ed began to speak of his feelings of indebtedness to Britain for a heritage and a tradition that had not yet been submerged by the post-machine age.

Although an American, he was keenly aware that the mother country had borne the brunt of the Great War; he had observed that Britain had endured difficult succeeding years, whereas America had not yet suffered in this way. On his visits to England he had seen with his own eyes the signs of poverty and of a crumbling infrastructure: a nation struggling to surmount the post-war economic slump. His gift was to be an act of thanksgiving for all that Great Britain meant to him, and of gratitude for his own lineage. During these days, he returned over and again to the subject, and finally the outline of what would be The Pilgrim Trust was complete: a trust to give to the land of his fathers the means to preserve its cultural identity and social institutions. It should have a compact body of trustees, and it should be run independently of America: a trust for Britain run by Britons, was how he first conceived it.

This kind of plotting was something that Irvine was good at, and before the visit was out he had put forward the names of those he thought would be good trustees. Harkness wanted to know who the most important man in England at that time was: a man who could command the respect and confidence of all classes and opinions. Irvine, who was developing a confidential relationship with Stanley Baldwin, had no hesitation at giving his name. He was out of office at this time, and that suited Harkness, who was averse to having a politician in government. Baldwin would be chairman. John Buchan was the next name put forward: typically up-to-date, Irvine felt that Buchan's power with words could be masterly in preparing the trust document and in directing publicity. To these names was added Lord Macmillan, a Lord of Appeal and at one time Lord Advocate under Ramsay Macdonald.[24] Irvine suggested that they should complete the five foundation trustees with Montagu Norman, the governor of the Bank of England, to advise on investments of the fund. Interestingly, Harkness vetoed this on the flimsy grounds of his being a banker. Then Irvine lit on Josiah Stamp, reputed to be the richest man in England; he was, in fact, a banker of sorts, and became a director of the Bank of England in 1928. Harkness must have glossed over this, and liked to think that with Baldwin, whose mother was Scottish, they had a board of trustees that was overwhelmingly Scottish by birth.

Then, as Jim told, a few days later and in Biblical manner, his friend took him to a height overlooking the waters of the sound: a place dear to his mother. A concrete policy for the trust emerged, and the amount was settled. The task of obtaining consents from these prospective trustees was imposed on the willing Jim Irvine.

Only one thing remained: to give the trust a name. The 'Pilgrim Trust' was the idea of gentle Mrs Harkness, and so it was adopted: a confusing name perhaps, amongst several Anglo-American organisations that use the word 'pilgrim'.

Irvine was very busy in May 1930 on Harkness's behalf, running between Westminster and Claridges, where Ed and Mary Harkness stayed when in London. A private meeting with Baldwin was essential, and it went well: Baldwin 'was absolutely delightful in his reception of Ed and his scheme. So the Trustees of the new foundation are practically fixed now and the general plans adjusted.' To the surprise of the five British trustees, the world at large regarded the foundation as a historic occasion. The foundation gift of £2 million was deposited with Farrer's, who were to be the trust's legal representatives in London. It all leaked out in the *Daily Herald*, the official organ of the Trades Union Congress, which claimed that the gift was £10 million; this was then copied by all of the New York papers. Harkness became alarmed; he felt nervous of the English fourth estate, and the English establishment. Irvine was his bulwark against these imagined dangers. There would, however, be no more money, despite these rumours or perhaps because of them, but Irvine's letters to his Mabel reveal that originally the sum of £2 million was to be just a beginning. Max Farrand believed that it was enlarged to £10 million. Harkness encouraged The Pilgrim Trust to spend all his capital sum, if they wished to do so.[25]

This was a most attractive way of doing public work, and the 'little brotherhood', as Baldwin called the original trustees, genuinely enjoyed the opportunity it gave them to scan the United Kingdom for suitable subjects. It was not enough to pay for the repair for an old building or the conservation of a historic library. Always there was before them the requirement to achieve public good. Increasingly, Harkness quizzed Irvine: 'And how is this going to help Britain?'

Irvine's personal dilemma had always been that, although St Andrews was all and everything he wanted, his personality cried out for a wider, more worldly, stage on which he could play out his talents. The Pilgrim Trust, of which he remained a trustee for the rest of his life, gave him a sphere in which to operate that was not primarily concerned with higher education. With The Pilgrim Trust, he was connected with the world of the arts, and of social service. As a trustee of a valuable trust, he found himself a sought-after commodity. The trust came to Britain's aid at a period of great social unrest, when the pervasive sense of hopelessness had created a sort of moral stupor. Lord Macmillan has described how they were sustained by the thought that they might effect a reawakening of the nation. The new presence of The Pilgrim Trust really did make Britishers feel that life was worth living again.

Their attention was drawn by Jim Irvine's friend, Bishop Hensley Henson, to the plight of Durham Castle, the great Norman edifice that was 'half Church of God, half Castle 'gainst the Scot', which was found to be slipping.[26] The massive job of underpinning could only be undertaken once The Pilgrim Trust gave its assistance. It was restored to the University of Durham as a ceremonial and residential centre, thus achieving an educational as well as a heritage good. The press publicity was seen as an encouragement, and this spectacular work of repair at Durham became a model for all future restoration projects of the trust, whether large or small.

The threatened beauty of English parish churches was an obsession of the trust in those early days, and Jim Irvine, who throughout the 1930s more and more took his holidays in England 'en famille', found many deserving causes in provincial highways and byways for his colleagues to consider. A grant to a remote church at Westonzoyland in Somerset, the scene in 1685 of the battle of Sedgemoor, elicited such thankfulness towards the American benefactor and the trust that it was plain that the Harkness ideal had done more than repair the carved timber roof; it had achieved a mutuality of Anglo-American feeling for history.

The pattern whereby The Pilgrim Trust would define its area of benefit was to a great extent set in those early days by its first trustees. Jim Irvine pleaded the case of the Royal Institution in London, which as a historic scientific research institute represented all that he cared about in his own profession. The Pilgrim Trust enabled the Royal Institution to embark on a significant programme of modernisation in 1931, the year of the Faraday celebrations. In the chaos of the poverty of the late 1920s, there were libraries and archives rich in our history that lay neglected by previous generations. The muniments of Westminster Abbey were given the attention that was desperately needed, and the salary of an archivist was endowed for generations to come. It was heady work for these early trustees. Irvine remained the link with Harkness, who had difficulty in understanding the British psyche and the committee of powerful men, the trustees. Harkness desperately wanted to establish some sort of friendship with Baldwin's 'band of brothers', but dreaded the Anglo-Saxon froideur.

It was important to maintain this link with their benefactor, despite the essential autonomy of the trust, and the board paid Harkness a pretty compliment in preserving for him the first cheque issued by the trust after it had been cashed, and bearing the signatures of all the trustees. At the beginning, Harkness felt strongly attached to 'his baby'. He thrilled to the writing of the preamble to the trust; this was in large measure Buchan's input. The preamble struck a deep chord with public opinion, but today it seems larded with purple passages. Harkness was the man of the moment in London; he addressed a parliamentary sub-committee; he and his wife attended a royal garden party; and in 1936 they were given seats in Westminster Abbey for the coronation of George VI and Queen Elizabeth.

Very little time had elapsed, however, before Harkness confided in Irvine his unhappiness about The Pilgrim Trust. It had unleashed a flood of appeals made directly to him from England, where he felt he lacked knowledge of our social mores: 'I wish they wouldn't cover up an appeal with an apparent social affair.'[27] His American advisors fed his mind with the idea that the Pilgrim trustees were neglectful of medical needs. He fretted that The Pilgrim Trust seemed to be drifting away from his grasp, despite the fact that he must have known this possibility was always there. When Harkness was in London, Jim would go round to Claridges after a trustee meeting and privately brief their benefactor on the meeting. It was Irvine's firm intervention, and his combating of the views of the London-oriented trustees, that prevented the early profligate dispensing of their capital. London University's claim was put to one side, and Jim was successful in keeping their initial spending to about £25,000, rather than the £200,000 pressed for by his colleagues.

Having at first thought that it was a brilliant choice to appoint the former cabinet office civil servant Thomas Jones as the first secretary of the trust, Harkness started to feel bitter towards him for apparently excluding him from meetings. He found Jones inappropriately manipulative. He was critical of Baldwin, who wanted to retain the chairmanship after becoming acting prime minister in 1931. Irvine also began to resent the way things were going, and thought that Harkness should have appointed him chairman if he wanted a man who was close to him and would do things to his liking.[28] Jim forgot for a moment the original crystalline simplicity of the trust, which Harkness wanted to be headed by a man known and respected by the whole country. Irvine, whatever his opinion of himself might have been, was not prominent in public life in the same sense as a popular politician. He tended to suspect that one or two of the others were acting independently of the whole. Perhaps this was the cause of Irvine's burst of temper against Baldwin in 1933. It was the same with all his committees: he would prefer to be in control of them. He could, however, be graceful in defeat, as in the case of the Pilgrim trustees' presentation of Newton's Library to Trinity College Cambridge: Irvine had ardently wanted it to go to the Royal Society. Whether or not it was out of loyalty to his old friend, Ed, he remained to the end of his life critical and impatient with Dr Jones, secretary and then chairman of the trust, who had a tendency to misrepresent Harkness. After Baldwin's death, however, Jones's diary makes it plain that Irvine was a hot contender to succeed as chairman.

Edward Harkness died at the relatively young age of sixty-six in 1940, but he would have felt that the opportunities and needs that opened up with the 1939–45 war gave increased justification to The Pilgrim Trust. His work did not die with him. A fresh and desperate demand for exactly the kind of vision that the trust enshrined came with the Second World War. Just as the trust had been conceived at a time of adversity in the British Isles, so it was able to mend the British spirit and confirm Great Britain in her culture, when all around feared that her values and tradition would be the first things to go, if we lost the war.

Irvine struck Harkness from the beginning as an astute man of considerable influence in his own country, but one who was also companionable and easy to get on with: a bridge between the old world and the new. They gave each other mutual support. Harkness's view of Irvine seems to have been general within that sector of American life. From as early as 1926, Irvine was in demand as a political commentator on the affairs of the world, and a series of four lectures, ostensibly on chemistry, which he gave in August 1926 at the Institute of Politics at 'Williams' College, at Williamstown in Massachusetts, thrust Irvine the statesman into the limelight. His lively report of the manner in which he introduced his own black view of German intentions to intellectual American minds is valuable evidence of the thoughts of the Anglo-American opinion-makers. In 1926, the Weimar Republic was becoming dangerously dependent on American money, and Irvine disliked the distinctly pro-German feeling that he detected amongst his American colleagues.

My penultimate lecture at Williamstown was a kind of triumph. German influence has been strong at the Institute this year and I shifted my lecture to make it a direct attack on Germany. I had only notes but words came easily and when I finished the house 'rose at me' and there were shouts of 'Amen' . . . They called and called for me to come back, but I couldn't . . . I am not sure I like the feeling of raising an audience to frenzy – at least I prefer to slip away afterwards by myself.[29]

These lectures were published in the *New York Times*, and a stranger to Irvine, Emily de Forrest, read them: 'Your wonderful lecture as published in the New York Times, 21 August 1926 on future conflicts . . . only the blind cannot see all as you depict it and so vividly too and the fact that navy reductions will not ensure peace.'[30]

The chemical lecturer first brought over in 1923 had emerged as a most surprising Cassandra. Some Americans began to talk of him as an 'ambassador' to their shores. His conviction was that the chemist touches every phase of civilisation, and he never forgot the experience as a young chemist of being brought face to face with the dark side of the complex German mind.

Unfortunately, Irvine found that American politicians and the American press were only too inclined to be blind to what was happening on the other side of the Atlantic. They had grave concerns of their own, of which perhaps Irvine, himself, had only partially been made aware. When he crossed to America during the first week of September 1929, he thought it strange that the SS *Transylvania* was so crowded. Hosts of Americans who had blithely spent the summer months in Europe were unaccountably desperate to return home. First-class passengers gladly accepted any berth, even in second class. Jim was put out that the usually calm smoking rooms, writing rooms and saloon, where he was in the habit of resting and reading, were full of the agitated chatter of American matrons and their daughters, writing up their journals and frantically sending cables. One month later came the Wall Street Crash. Yet the chemist turned ambassador continued in the following years to visit for Harkness's sake and also for the fees: 'Despite hard times, they pay well and they certainly have shown me much kindness and attention.' He marked how commendably the subdued Americans faced their ordeal. It was ironic that only in February 1929 he had observed to a friend that: 'If only they know it, Americans are living in a Golden Age.'

It was with serious intent, however, that he continued to promote Anglo-American solidarity as the fascist decade unfolded. Germany's solution to the hyperinflation of the Weimar Republic and then the Great Depression was one of totalitarianism: *ein volk, ein reich* – and now *ein Führer*. In Germany, 1933 was the year of no return: with the burning of the Reichstag in February, Adolf Hitler was at the head of his one-party nation. In horror, Great Britain looked on. The Principal of St Andrews may have given all the appearance of a Scottish dominie presiding over his university in cap and gown, or at rest in plus-fours, but in London he mixed with civil

servants, industrialists and the movers and shakers he met in his club or at
meetings. In London, he was an establishment figure, in sombre short black
coat and striped trousers, and grey suede spats on his shoes, a monocle in
his waistcoat pocket: just like a senior civil servant. It was with the mission
of international friendship in mind that he gladly accepted an invitation in
December 1933 to address the English Speaking Union in New York, where
he pleaded that 'we cannot act alone'. Speaking as an educator, and still
dealing with Utopian ideals, he demolished the vulgarity of the notion that
the peaceful relationship of nations is based on trading agreements, and he
turned instead to the Anglo-Saxon axis created by Rhodes' and Harkness's
schemes for international understanding through higher education.[31] His
plea that 'we cannot act alone' grew louder as the years drew on. Relying on
his popularity in America, many would be the speeches he would undertake in this vein.

THIRTEEN

This Dear Wee Gossipy Place

The Irvines never left St Andrews so long as Principal Irvine was alive. What really was it that thirled James Irvine to the 'dear wee gossipy place', as he referred to St Andrews? The University of St Andrews was the springboard from which he pursued the cause of higher education all over the world; the university itself was ultimately the great cause of his life, but its insularity often drove him to despair. His way was to form a clear and, to his eyes, totally correct view, from which he would refuse to be deflected by anyone. Frustrations often threatened his attachment to St Andrews.

Perhaps at the heart of the matter was the beauty of the medieval city; even its ruins cast a spell over the Irvines. Quite early on, Jim and Mabel were forced to learn an expensive lesson that brought home how much St Andrews meant to them. Not all the holiday houses that they rented were a success and one, a damp cottage knee-deep in nettles, up in Banffshire, was so much the obverse of Mabel's dreams of a romantic rose-filled garden, old oak furniture and chintz curtains at the windows, that they decided to cut their losses and they turned for home the very next day after their arrival. It had been advertised with fishing to be had in the river and Nigel, nine years old, was bitterly disappointed to be deprived of taking his new rod out with his father; but an earth floor, a cooking pot hanging above a peat fire, the walls dripping and green with damp were more than Nanny and Kate, the cook, could cope with. The next evening, and once more at peace, Jim and Mabel sat on the low wall that edges the cliff at University House in St Andrews. As they watched the sun go down behind the hills of Angus beyond the Bay, Jim said: 'I don't know why we ever go away from St Andrews.'[1]

Unfortunately for his peace of mind, attempts to lure Irvine away from 'this dear wee gossipy place' came fast and thick from other, more amply financed, universities. It was in this same year, 1925, that Liverpool University was facing the possible early need to fill the post of vice-chancellor, owing to the fragile state of health of John Adami, their pathologist head. Informally, Liverpool began to court Irvine's interest. Against a gently persuasive letter from his friend, Professor Eric Baly of the chemistry department at Liverpool, Irvine wrote a set of figures, which added up to 2,650; this was the salary that he could expect to receive if he went to Liverpool: a considerably greater amount than that which he received at St Andrews in 1925. Liverpool University was what one of Jim's chemical colleagues called a 'plasticine university': it was ready to be moulded by a strong and high-minded man into something big. They were looking for growth not so much in numbers but, as Irvine was told, 'in greatness'. This type of appeal was difficult for Irvine to resist: when he could put his dreams for St Andrews aside, he knew that he craved a really big challenge, and he knew that an avowedly scientific university would give him scope to exercise his experience.[2]

In June of that year, Liverpool conferred on him the honorary degree of Doctor of Science. Liverpool's oration came straight to the point when defining his reputation: 'The pages of modern chemistry bear few names as great as that of Irvine, who by his investigations, has solved the mystery of the carbohydrates and made the way clear to those who follow him.' The Liverpool students were less high-flown but none the less graphic in their tribute to Irvine's stereochemistry. They sang to the tune of 'Comin' through the Rye':

> If a body takes a body, tests it by the smell,
> If a body says it's sugar – can a body tell.

In October 1926, Liverpool's President of the Council wrote to Irvine, inviting him to put his name forward as a candidate for their vice-chancellorship. But Jim was caught up in St Andrews' still-desperate financial situation, and he was a leading player in some of the most colourful pageantry the little place had ever known. He did Liverpool the honour of thinking about the idea, but it was never a serious thought.

Earlier that very year had come an approach that was at first glance even more difficult for Irvine to reject. The University of London was the next to face the certainty of an interregnum. When, at the end of the 1926 session, Principal Sir George Perry's post was advertised, none of the applicants was considered suitable by the Senate. The Senate committee came to the conclusion that the best man might not answer an advertisement, but might be willing to accept if approached privately. Irvine was considered by several members of the committee as the pre-eminently best man for the position. Knowing that the principalship of London University would give Irvine wider influence and greater scope than did St Andrews, the required informal approach was made to him on behalf of London by his fellow chemist George Senter, Principal of Birkbeck College.[3] The truth of the matter was that, after only four or five years in office, Irvine's skill at manipulating committees and fund-giving bodies in favour of his university was being observed in the wider world, and the other universities looked on enviously at St Andrews.

Irvine's wartime scientific career had put him on intimate terms with London University, which was arguably the most powerful of all the British universities owing to its size, its geographical position and the facilities of its departments. By 1926, its scientific reputation was formidable, and contemporaneously Irvine was beginning to think that St Andrews was perhaps too small, too precious a place from which to launch his family on the world. He knew that if he accepted London's overtures, Mabel's aching need for the stimuli of London's concert halls and theatres could be assuaged, and the lives of Veronica, Nigel and Felicity would be enlarged by living in the metropolis. He and Mabel would have like-minded friends. He already found the public life of influence that he led on visits to London invigorating, even essential to his well-being. And yet, and yet . . . London was too big, too amorphous. St Andrews was perfectly formed for his attentions, and Jim turned away from the principalship of London University, which would not give him the complete control that he continued to enjoy in St Andrews.

Once more he resolved to settle down, but he was not entirely happy. For him, 1928 was to prove curiously difficult in St Andrews. Owing to pressure of work, he reluctantly had to relinquish some of his government committees. He was aware of carping and back-biting in his little university, and he was restless once again. To Mabel, who had been away with the family, he wrote: 'By the time you are back in St Andrews which place, darling mine, we must regard as a happy place – let's ignore other people's criticisms and I'll try to be less critical of myself.' Nevertheless, he complained bitterly to his friends that he was overworked and under-regarded. He was often inclined to think of himself as 'a kind of human parcel consigned, carriage-paid, from place to place'.[4]

With rising numbers, St Andrews began to reap the harvest of the early Irvine years: as 1929 came in, it could be seen that before the year was out the university would have a large graduation hall, would be well advanced with the building of its pioneering hall of residence, and that its departments were expanding. Harkness was behind the new endowment of the chair of history, and he continued to back most of Irvine's needs. 'The university is going great guns at present. Mr Baldwin, the Prime Minister, has been elected Chancellor in succession to the late Lord Haldane . . . This is a splendid appointment for us and a great score to get such a man. American students are simply flocking to St Andrews and the latest arrivals are a very good lot indeed.'[5]

Neither Liverpool nor London had been serious contenders for Irvine's service, but just at the time that the Harkness benefaction enabled him to open a new chapter in St Andrews, an even greater temptation to lure him away from Andrew Lang's haunted town appeared in the form of an offer from Edinburgh University. This hung over Irvine's renewed happiness in St Andrews like a dark cloud, but there were moral constraints on him. Baldwin had to affirm that in accepting the chancellorship of St Andrews, one of the inducements was having Irvine at the helm, and Harkness's great gifts had been granted on condition that Jim remained Principal.

Sir Alfred Ewing would retire as Principal of Edinburgh University in October 1929, and the feelers that were being put out in Irvine's direction felt to him like a 'suction'. Edinburgh people spoke of his duty to give his experience to the larger interest. The truth was that Edinburgh University had lost its sense of direction, it was in financial difficulties, and it desperately needed a strong man at the helm.[6] Edinburgh was considered the jewel of the four Scottish principalships, and Edinburgh was avowedly a real city of noble proportions and great beauty whose sole purpose in life in 1929 seemed to be to serve the law, the Church and learning. Jim and Mabel had many friends in Edinburgh: cultivated people of their own standing in life. A Scotsman like Jim Irvine would consider that Edinburgh, the capital of Scotland, would be the perfect place in which his young family could grow up: they would have as a home the Principal's official residence in Moray Place, surely one of the most desirable addresses in the world.

On 21 February, Sir Alfred Ewing wrote to Irvine on behalf of the 'curators', whose decision had been unanimous, offering him the post of Vice-Chancellor of Edinburgh University. The practical details were as follows:

> The stipend offered is £2,500 plus the rent of an official residence (at present £170) which the Principal does not live in. Of the £2,500, £1,800 is treated as the formal stipend on which (as well as on the house rent) income-tax and super-tax are charged. The excess above

£1,800 has in my time escaped tax, being regarded as a 'hospitality' allowance. The age limit is 75, which gives you time for a long and effective reign.

Ewing added his own gentle pressure to that of many other Edinburgh luminaries: he begged Irvine to follow in the footsteps of Principal Sir David Brewster, who had moved from St Andrews to Edinburgh in 1859.[7]

For about a fortnight, in the face of what was a momentous decision for them, Jim and Mabel immured themselves in University House, not daring to show their faces or wanting to encounter questions or receive calls. Fortunately, Principal Irvine's cultivation of the press worked in his favour this time: Sir Robert Bruce, the powerful editor of the *Glasgow Herald*, knew perfectly well what was going on, but out of respect for Irvine he put an embargo on any reportage of the Edinburgh question until his friend had made up his mind.

The legal grandees, Lord Sands (Christopher Johnston) and Lord Alness, the Lord Justice Clerk in the Court of Session (who as Robert Munro had appointed Irvine to St Andrews), easily assumed that Irvine would soon be amongst them in Edinburgh. Jim and Mabel's old friend, Robert Kerr Hannay, the Historiographer Royal for Scotland, whom they had known since they were first married, remarked that perhaps the ugliness of the Younger Hall would persuade them to leave St Andrews. He wrote almost petulantly to Mabel: 'It would be glorious to have him here – & you – & the children. But that is my selfish point of view – & the selfish point view of a University which is so big & so shapeless, & which needs a human man so badly! There are so few Jims! – & several Universities! That is the trouble!! And of the Jims – St Andrews holds the only one.'[8]

But Irvine's London colleagues understood him best. Wise Dr Armstrong, a man of high repute amongst the chemists, who himself had never left Lewisham, paid Jim the perfect compliment: 'I venture again to urge you to stick to the good ship, which already owes so much to you but is not yet equipped up to the point of efficiency which you can give it. I am so impressed both by the way in which Oxford and Cambridge are falling off – owing to their size – and the need of a small compact school such as St Andrews & here seems to me to be a corporate influence at work which is to be found nowhere else.'[9]

Jim, who didn't want change, and who still wanted to make St Andrews perfect, felt his decision to remain in St Andrews was the right one. In the shadows, Barrie quietly commended Mabel for lovingly supporting

PLATE 28. Principal Irvine working on his papers in the garden of University House. This shows him very characteristically, cigarette in his right hand, working out of doors.

PLATE 29. Nigel, Veronica and Mabel in University House, in about 1923.

PLATE 30. Fishing on Fionn Loch, Wester Ross, 1925. Fishing in the Highlands gave Jim the escape from pressure of work that he needed.

PLATE 31. Principal Irvine playing with Nigel and Felicity. A stranger, peering through the open gate to University House, enquired who the big boy was, playing with the Principal's children.

PLATE 32. The Irvine family with the family of Professor Read. John Read, FRS, became professor of chemistry in St Andrews not long after Irvine became Principal; he was a close and much loved friend of all the Irvines.

PLATE 33. Irvine with the editor of *Nature*, graduation June 1927. This photograph was captioned by the photographer: the V.C. turns his back on 'Nature'.

PLATE 34. The Duchess of York (later Queen Elizabeth, the Queen Mother), who received an honorary degree from St Andrews in 1929, is greeted by Jim and Mabel at University House (1929).

PLATE 35. The Duchess of York opens the Younger Graduation Hall, 28 June 1929.

PLATE 36. Irvine with Herbert Hoover, President of the United States, October 1932. At this time, Irvine gave the Carnegie Oration at Pittsburgh.

PLATE 37. Harkness window in St Salvator's Hall. St Salvator's Hall, opened in 1929, was St Andrews' first modern hall of residence; Edward Harkness, the American philanthropist, endowed it with residential scholarships. This window in the dining hall shows the coats of arms of the hall's chief benefactors, with Harkness represented in the middle.

PLATE 38. The first trustees of The Pilgrim Trust, Edward Harkness's gift to the British nation. From top left: John Buchan, Sir James Irvine, Dr Tom Jones; and, seated, Lord Macmillan, Stanley Baldwin (Chairman) and Josiah Stamp

PLATE 39. Irvine Committee of Inspection of the Indian Institute of Science, 1936. Irvine was called by the Viceroy, Lord Willingdon, to advise on how to stiffen the administration of this important research station, in the light of the Government of India Act (1935) and the process of indianisation.

PLATE 40. Bishop James Kennedy's tomb in St Salvator's College Chapel, drawn by R. W. Billings and engraved by G.B. Smith: originally prepared for *The Baronial and Ecclesiastical Antiquities of Scotland*, first published 1845–52. Irvine felt a mystical connection with Kennedy, the founder of St Salvator's College.

PLATE 41. Irvine with Jan Christian Smuts in the Cathedral ruins in St Andrews. Smuts, the Prime Minister of South Africa, was installed as Rector of St Andrews in 1931.

PLATE 42. Sir James Colquhoun Irvine, portrait by Bassano, c.1938.

PLATE 43. Lady Irvine, portrait by Bassano, c.1938.

PLATE 44. Conferring Honorary LLD on General Sikorski of Poland, 1941. The Free Polish Army was stationed in Fife and Forfar during the Second World War, and Irvine opened the resources of his university to these exiled Poles, many of whom took degrees in St Andrews.

PLATE 45. Irvine Committee for Higher Education in the West Indies, 1944. Left to right, standing: Raymond Priestley, Hugh Springer, Thomas Rowell (Secretary), Philip Sherlock; and seated, Margery Perham, Sir James Irvine and Miss de Verteuil. Through the agency of the Asquith Commission on Higher Education in the Colonies, Irvine and his colleagues steered through the development of higher education in the British colonies in the Caribbean.

PLATE 46. Jim and Mabel in Kingston, Jamaica, 1950. Jim took Mabel and their daughter Felicity to Jamaica for the installation of Princess Alice, Countess of Athlone, as Chancellor of the University of the West Indies.

PLATE 47. *Above.*
Quincentenary of St
Salvator's College, 1950:
in conversation with the
Duke of Hamilton. HM
Queen Elizabeth (later
the Queen Mother) in the
procession.

PLATE 48. *Right.* Principal
and Lady Irvine at a student
ball, 1950. Principal Irvine
and his wife loved dancing
when they were younger, but
on this occasion, not long
before the Principal's death,
they sat and watched.

her husband's unworldly choice, and Baldwin simply wrote: 'On personal grounds and for the University, I rejoice and remain your grateful Chancellor.' Sir William McCormick, former chairman of the University Grants Committee, was in complete sympathy with Principal Irvine, who had great work on hand in St Andrews, but one and all begged him to tell them who on earth, if not him, might be chosen for Edinburgh's next principal.

And there were other vacancies: Irvine must at some time have made it an open secret that he had the principalship of Glasgow University in his sights. Therefore, it is hardly surprising that the usual informal approach was made in August of that same year, 1929, when Sir Donald McAlister, whom Irvine thought of as a rather empty-headed man and who was manifestly not good with money, made it plain that he would like to be elevated from principal to chancellor in Glasgow. It is easy to imagine that there had been a time, soon after the end of the war, when Irvine nurtured the thought of coming home to Glasgow in a post that would put him at the apex of Glasgow society. In 1921, the university gave him an honorary LLD. Glasgow never forgets its sons, and in the course of his life he received many honours and acknowledgements from the city of his birth. However, by August 1929, and with neither parent still alive in Glasgow, Jim understood himself enough to be able to respond that St Andrews would now always hold his heart. Speculation about a successor to Sir Donald McAlister was not suppressed this time, and Jim, crossing the Atlantic in the *Transylvania*, was amused to read in the *Daily Mail* that 'the name of a Scottish scientist who has a world-wide reputation has also been mentioned in certain quarters'. But the Scottish press this time painted him as cynical for playing with the idea of these posts. Jim, who was the most sincere of men, wrote angrily to Mabel: 'What right have these penny-a-liners to bandy about people's names!'[10] To say that Jim Irvine played with the idea of taking up another post would be a gross distortion of the truth: he considered all these posts with the seriousness they deserved, and he was flattered, but in the end they only served the purpose of confirming him in his commitment to St Andrews.

Even their Edinburgh friends knew that nothing would ever equal the beauty of the setting of Jim's and Mabel's lives. Hannay, who had come over to St Andrews in the forlorn hope of being able to help them choose Edinburgh, admitted: 'I saw the community which Jim is making into the only real university in Scotland. Can I be so selfish as to wish him and you to leave that?'

The approach during the years 1932 and 1933 on behalf of Princeton, the last of these prestigious universities to try to claim Irvine, in the end fizzled out like a damp squib. Princeton had had every opportunity to size Irvine up: he gave the prestigious Vanuxem Lectures there in 1929, in which he displayed himself as a statesman by advocating a liberal policy towards the funding of research that then gives something back to the body politic. The university sent a representative over to London to put the idea into Jim's head, they interviewed him in America, they dangled the post in front of him for a period of eight months, but no real invitation was forthcoming. The Americans expected Jim to put himself forward for the post, but the days when Jim would contemplate throwing himself into the job market were long gone. He preferred the patrician ways of his own country.

A letter written to one of his American friends says it all. 'As for Princeton, my mind is made up: if they offer me the post I shall refuse it for although the idea of being on your side of the water and part of your country is most attractive I am not accustomed to have people hesitate in selecting me for any position. Sounds conceited possibly, but you know I'm not conceited a bit and am only expressing the fact that the time has long since passed when I had to *ask* for a job – now people ask me!'[11] In the years to come, there would be visits to Princeton, and he would look fondly at its exquisite form and think that it might have been his, but in reality he was by now deeply embedded in an acceleration of development in St Andrews, and in the demanding roller-coaster of a double-dip financial recession. These required all his intellectual powers, and in this sense even the consequences of world financial markets were to him deeply fascinating. What is of real significance to Irvine's life is not perhaps to ask how it was that he was courted by so many senior universities: the reason lay most clearly in how he was perceived as a man of influence; rather, the real question is what was it about St Andrews that made it impossible for him to draw away from it.

By 1930 James Irvine's commitment to St Andrews was absolute. In this year he received the Freedom of the Royal Burgh of St Andrews, and in publicly allying himself to the cause of the town, he made a speech that was to have an impact for generations to come. From his pious prayer on that occasion – 'that St Andrews be preserved before it was too late'[12] – the St Andrews Preservation Trust was formed in 1938 to take up the challenge. Irvine's 1930 speech was prompted by the threat posed by the 1930 Housing (Scotland) Act. The housing acts of the Labour government were designed to improve accommodation for the working classes by first demolishing swathes of slum dwelling in the inner cities. Irvine had reason to know that Fife County Council had aspirations for applying the act to St Andrews, and initially seventy-eight old properties were to be cleared, including along the shoreline beside the harbour. Irvine was the first president of the St Andrews Preservation Trust, giving him the opportunity to become loved as a townsman by Church and trade as well as university. His feeling for his alma mater was indissolubly linked with the romance of the scale and details of the medieval town that had first supported a seat of learning. Which was it: town or university that bound him to this place?

The St Andrews Preservation Trust, under the eagle eyes of the painter Miss Annabel Kidston and the historian Ronald Cant, was in the vanguard of preservation trusts, and it devised an enlightened approach. Its small capital should at all times be sufficient to buy any threatened group of buildings, restore them and then return them to the housing market. The small medieval and eighteenth-century houses that had escaped the Playfair town planning reforms of the nineteenth century were their chief concern. One of the trust's first successes was with Louden's Close, a complete burgher tenement of semi-derelict eighteenth- and early nineteenth-century houses off South Street,[13] for which Irvine engaged in a fight with the Fife planning authorities and spoke up at the public enquiry in Cupar on behalf of the Preservation Trust.[14] He lined up his political friends, including Baldwin, to support him with legal advice. Finally, he obtained a large emergency grant of £1,000 from The Pilgrim Trust, and the close was saved. When he was a student almost fifty years before, his first lodgings had been in the area known as Southfield, and picturesque Louden's Close offered a short cut every morning to the chemistry student on his walk into college, so it contributed to his early romantic attachment to the town. The final outcome of Irvine entering the lists at the enquiry was the transference of power in town planning matters from Fife County Council to the Burgh of St Andrews under the St Andrews town council.

Irvine continued to work in the interests of preserving the town throughout the war and during the post-war period, and his own words best describe how he continued to fight for his vision of St Andrews against his *bête noire*, the Fife County Council.

Now you see why I have as a burning enthusiasm the preservation of St Andrews, of Old St Andrews, of the mediaeval town, because in the University we have the last surviving example. Founded by the

Church with the Cathedral and the University cheek by jowl, and the houses of the people clustering round – there you have a true democratic system of education which has grown up naturally, and that is one reason why the Scottish Universities are democratic to this day, and why St Andrews is essentially democratic in its methods. Do not let us break through that romance. We are the last survivor of an old type.[15]

Within these thirty years of Jim and Mabel's married lives, enormous changes to their town had already crept in like a thief in the night. The fisher-folk's community at the east end of North Street had died out: no more did women in their voluminous petticoats and colourful skirts sit outside their doors mending nets, as they had done even twenty years before. You would no longer be likely to encounter a dancing bear in the street, nor to attend a performance of Shakespeare from a barnstorming troupe touring remote parts of Scotland. The ironmonger, Mr Bridges, would no more travel to St Petersburg on business with the Baltic trade. But in Irvine, the trust had a man who could command national interest in the future preservation of this little place, and in 1939 Principal Irvine broadcast to the nation on behalf of the St Andrews Preservation Trust.

What the good townsfolk did not know was that, in private, the Irvine family, and especially Jim, made St Andrews the butt of their gentle satire. The Irvine children half-lived in a country of their own imagining called Antipassio, a childish version of St Andrews that had its own dialect, and their father entered into this make-believe with delight. Conveying something of the town they lived in, he wrote up the Spring 1927 edition of the *Antipassian Gazette* in the style of *Cranford*:

THE FASHIONS
(By our Paris Correspondent . . . Madame Moffatt)

We have all been wondering if the kilt was going to be quite the thing this spring, but there can be no longer any doubt on this important point. Only this morning I saw Lady Irvine and her daughter (how difficult it is to tell them apart, for the one grows so sweetly mature and the other so maturely sweet) and one of them was wearing the family tartan. I really couldn't tell which of the pair was thus adorned, but I think it was Miss Véronique for she put out her tongue at the cab-man.

Miss Moffatt was of course the actual proprietress of a St Andrews ladies' dress shop that had pretensions to knowledge of the latest fashion; the Irvine children submitted, sometimes unwillingly, to being dressed in kilts when they were not in school uniform. In those days kilts were passed on from child to child, and this introduced a modicum of economy into the household.[16]

Principal Irvine became an elder of the parish of Holy Trinity, the town kirk in St Andrews; the fact that Mabel said that she was more proud of him for this distinction than for all his honorary degrees together says something about her affection for the Church of Scotland. She, herself, liked to emphasise that she was more town than gown. Their involvement in the civic life of St Andrews provided for Jim and Mabel an escape valve from the frustrations of university life. Mabel was a founder member of the St Andrews Chamber Music Society, and she was responsible for bringing guest ensembles and soloists of international renown to the little town. Of course, the visiting musicians stayed at University House, but to fill the house with the members of the Griller Quartet, or to make a friend of Myra Hess,[17] imposed nothing of the usual burden on Mabel. She was a regular delegate to the conferences of the National Federation of Music Societies and took her position seriously.

Despite the grave financial crisis that shook the funding of higher education, and despite several serious illnesses that struck both Mabel and Jim at the beginning of the decade, the 'thirties' were a time of happiness and settled commitment in the Irvine household. The growing maturity of their children had something to do with it: Jim was naturally drawn to the stimulus of young minds and personalities. He found a congenial golfing partner in Nigel, and any of the three – Veronica, Nigel or Felicity – could provide companionship and conversation if a walk along the sands was called for.

Jim and Mabel's life together expanded to include return visits to some of the more interesting of their St Andrews visitors, and amongst these was the feminist Elizabeth Haldane, whose brother, Lord Haldane, was all too briefly Chancellor of the university. Cloan, the Haldane's country house in Perthshire, seemed a gently hospitable place: 'That peace of body and mind which Cloan and you provide.' Kindly Miss Haldane even gave a dance there, to which Veronica was invited.[18] Principal Irvine was camping in the wilds of the Adirondacks when St Andrews suffered the death of their Chancellor, Lord Haldane, in 1928, but Jim's letter of condolence to Elizabeth Haldane reflected his happy connection with the great man:

It made me thrill with pride when he asked my opinion on anything and although always conscious of being in the presence of a great intellect I always felt the warmth of a fatherly friendship to a younger man. It is a consolation to know that he learned of the tribute paid to him by St Andrews before his strength faded. In the last letters we exchanged we spoke of the personal pleasure we felt in the closer association which we thought lay before us.[19]

Veronica, the eldest Irvine child, who had completed her education at St Leonard's School, entered the university in 1929 to read for a history degree. Jim Irvine was close and sympathetic to his gentle eldest daughter, although Felicity, the boisterous tomboy with the golden curls, had much of his personality. Veronica's inclination was for the stage, and initially she agreed to take a degree just to please her father. She did not live in a student residence, but rather submitted to the economical choice of remaining at home and under the eagle eye of her parents. This, in practice, was not easy, but her student life intensified her interest in the theatre. Her clear, pretty features and dark curly hair were a strong point, as was her intelligent and sensitive interest in the texts. She was quite vain of having inherited from the Colquhouns the Highland feature of a 'lantern jaw'. The student dramatic society, the Mermaids, which continues to flourish generations later, was at that time fresh and new, and it promoted the latest plays, as it even promoted playwrights from amongst its student members. Veronica became a leading light, both as the author of a one-act play and as the female lead in a play by the Hungarian dramatist Ferenc Molnar, *The Swan*: fashionable and 'of the moment'. The review in *College Echoes* of her performance praised her cool, detached manner as being appropriate to this sophisticated exposé of the manners of a ridiculous group of Ruritanians.

Her father's great delight was to step across to college of an evening to attend a performance given by the Mermaids. His heart was also with the stage, to such an extent that Barrie liked to call him a co-author of his last play, *The Boy David*, for an acute structural suggestion that he gave the playwright.[20] Interestingly, however, what most impressed her father was the strength of character that Veronica demonstrated in applying herself to the tricky business of passing in Latin, a requirement for even a General Degree in those days. He liked to see a young person getting the most out of their talents, no matter whether they were great or small. Beneath the simple adage of one of his most spine-chilling sayings, 'that no man do more than his best', there lies the possible interpretation that it is very difficult to do one's best. He suspected that the 'English' public school education that his children were receiving did not really teach them how to work, and his hope was that a degree at St Andrews would do just that for Nigel. In 1932, Nigel also entered the university to take his first degree, in science.

It was during one of Mabel's severe bouts of illness, in 1930, that Veronica was called upon to take her mother's place as the university's hostess. Veronica looked absurdly young as she sat at the head of her father's table, but how proud he was of her poise and beauty. Veronica's parents were in a mild way socially ambitious for her. Mabel next threw herself into the preparations for presenting her daughter at court, although Veronica was still a student at the university. As she sat in the chauffeured car in the queue that filled the Mall with debutantes, she swotted for her degree finals: she had no wish to 'do the season'. When she took her degree from her father, the national press picked up the telling image of the notable principal 'capping' his daughter as she knelt before him.

Jim and Mabel had to employ a succession of nurses during the early years of this decade. Irvine's own life was dogged by severe illness. In the spring of 1933, he was at a trustees meeting of The Pilgrim Trust when he started to feel hot and unwell. This was made worse by the fact that, being perhaps not quite 'himself', he launched into an attack on Baldwin. Irvine had experienced the discomfiture of being turned down by his fellow trustees when he applied for a large subvention for St Andrews, and he thought that Baldwin had become too high-handed. Afterwards he felt shocked that he should have been unmannerly towards his prime minister, but when he got back to the Athenaeum, his temperature was 105 degrees. He lay in bed battling influenza for inside of a week. Mabel came to London to her usual hotel, the Knightsbridge, but the rules of the Athenaeum concerning ladies barred her entry. They could only begin to put their minds at rest when Jim was strong enough to leave his club in a taxi en route for Mabel's hotel. Here she looked after him until he could manage the journey north to St Andrews where, comfortable in his own home, he completed his recovery.

They felt that their joint feeble health deserved a good holiday, and in August of that year they rented a beautiful Georgian house in Herefordshire, complete with the owner's silver, for their month in the country. It had been Sir Rowland Hill's house, and framed examples of his archive hung on the wall of the study that Jim used. The business of the university did not abate during the vacations. Jim's fondness for writing letters prompted the ironic thought that even Rowland Hill's original introduction of a penny post could not save him from the particular personal expense of using the post. The real pleasure of the holiday lay in the outdoor life they led together: walks, picnics and expeditions to local places of interest were crowned for Jim by the opportunity to fish. He had instilled in Nigel a love of this sporting skill, but Nigel had gone off to experience the Passion Play at Oberammergau.

Jim fished indomitably; all sorts of waters shunned by the rest of his house party were for him fair game. In fishing stagnant sections of the river he, alone of their house party, must have absorbed the bacteria from which he developed paratyphoid fever. By the autumn he was ill once again, this time with a sharp bout of enteric fever that nearly killed him. A team of day- and night-nurses in University House pulled him through in time for Baldwin's presentation to him on behalf of the university of his Oswald Birley portrait in November. He remarked ruefully that 'St Andrews had not had much for his salary during the past year'.[21] His illness was suffi-cient to bring Veronica home from RADA, where she had tried out her aptitude for the stage. Was it the charmed life that the Irvines wove round themselves in St Andrews that drew her back, never to return to RADA, or simply her recognition that, in the old-fashioned way, she rather liked keeping her mother and father company at home? Her father questioned whether she was really cut out for the rather rackety life of an actress, and he resolved to enlarge her social life in more conventional ways.

When he was invited to lecture on the Hellenic Travellers' Club's cruise on the Donaldson Line, Mabel and Veronica were given the treat of accom-panying him. Jim liked to refer to this threesome as 'The Three Musket-eers'. The concept of the Hellenic cruise was in its infancy, and this one was exhaustive and exclusive. Sir James Irvine, who chose for the subject of his lecture 'Are we Greeks or Romans?', was billed to speak almost at the halfway mark on the map of the Mediterranean, and he picked up on this, giving a well-exposed, graceful argument that, as a scientist, he brought to rest on the side of the Greeks. The British and the French, he argued, were the Greeks of modern science; he apportioned Roman characteristics to the practical scientific mind of the Germans and the Americans. What started as caprice concluded with a stern warning that the world, in marching forward so fast, should be arrested from tumbling into chaos.[22] In thirty years he had not changed, and once again he recommended that weight should be applied to scientific foresight and anticipation. He knew only too well that his country would soon need these qualities. His audience was thin, the Mediterranean was not kind to his fellow passengers, but this mattered not. He was there to share this holiday of discovery with his two companions. It was an extended trip that included almost every point of the history of the Mediterranean, not confining them to the ancient world: from Gibraltar to Istanbul, they took in a pilgrimage to Gallipoli. From Palma, they went to Cairo and Athens; from Naples to Nice, they included Corsica – and in Nice they left their boat and went overland via Provence to Paris. Jim was insistent that they pay a pious pilgrimage to Avignon, the seat of the schismatic Pope Benedict XIII, whose Papal Bulls set the seal of the Church on the infant university of St Andrews. For once, however, even his colourful imagination failed to find in the gloomy Palais des Papes any suggestiveness with which to connect it with St Andrews. In Paris, Mabel and Veronica were amused to find that Jim, with his usual boyish enthu-siasm and remembering his boyhood holiday with his father forty years earlier, unerringly took them from place to place.

This exploration of old European civilisation was such a success that, despite the need to be careful about money, Jim felt that Mabel and Veronica were ready for a longer voyage – although Mabel was adamant that she travelled badly, just as her husband travelled with ease. For their intro-duction to the New World, a fitting excuse was offered by the centenary celebrations of Andrew Carnegie that were held in New York in November 1935, and the personal hospitality offered by Mrs Carnegie.

Irvine was the chief guest of honour at a dinner to which he gave the memorial address on behalf of the four Scottish universities. He was better qualified for the task than anyone of his generation, for he was on his own admittance the doyen of Carnegie's Trust for the Universities of Scotland. He was its first fellow, and had been a trustee for over fifteen years. He was felicitous with words, and he painted a romantic picture of the circum-stances of Carnegie's birth in 'a city of kings' and within bowshot of the national shrine to Robert the Bruce in Dunfermline Abbey. But Irvine's association with Carnegie's work was not confined to his native Scotland. It came naturally to him to appreciate the benefit to mankind of not just the technical Carnegie Institute in Pittsburgh, but that rather more disinter-ested 'temple' of scientific research, the Carnegie Institute of Washington. Within the context of the universities of Scotland, Irvine could speak from the heart of all that Carnegie saved when the Scottish Universities Trust came into being. It was not enough to save these crumbling institutions for the generations to come: Carnegie's gift had the effect of intensifying the natural democracy that was inherent in Scottish higher education.[23]

The Carnegie dinner was like something out of a Hollywood film: at each lady's place was a jewel box containing a diamond watch from Tiffany's. The dinner service was in the latest American style: each guest's plate was of a different design from the others. Jim, Mabel and Veronica were Mrs Carnegie's guests at the Carnegie Mansion at 2 East 91st Street, and kind Mrs Carnegie insisted that this should be their base for a holiday in America. Everything they needed – the transatlantic crossing, railway journeys and hotel bills, together with a handsome fee of $1,000 – was paid for by the Carnegie Foundation.

Jim had so many times dreamed of sharing his enthusiasm for America with his wife. This time he would take them to Quebec and Montreal, to Washington and Mount Vernon. He called it their 'Second Crusade'. It was autumn when they arrived in Canada, and the St Lawrence Seaway, as they sailed deeper into French Canada, made a deep impression. However, from the citadel of the Carnegie Mansion they had a disappointing experience of Jim's beloved New York. Mrs Carnegie insisted that it was not safe to go out alone: they must always travel in a closed car, or with a bodyguard. One evening they ventured out with their elderly hostess who took them to hear one of the first performances of Gershwin's 'negro' opera *Porgy and Bess*.

The stamp was finally put on Veronica and Felicity's education the next year, when their father agreed to let Felicity leave school and attend a finishing school in Switzerland, on Lake Lucerne, with Veronica chaperoning her. Veronica attended classes at Lucerne University, while Felicity acquired the usual veneer of French conversation, cookery and sewing skills. It was a frivolous experience, but it gave them a first-hand glimpse of Europe in the 1930s. Their father was in India at the time on government business, but he worried whether it was wise for them to be in central Europe in 1936. In their mother's eyes, it was a step up the social ladder for her daughters, who were expected to marry well. On their return to St Andrews, Veronica and Felicity became known as the 'Velocity'.

Mabel's hope was that St Andrews would cast a spell over her family, binding them to her and to this corner of East Fife. Perhaps initially she drew this golden cord round her children to compensate herself for the long periods when Jim was in America. Although the early years of the 1930s were dogged by their ill-health, Jim and Mabel and the three young members of the family flourished during the Fascist decade, owing in great measure to the fact that Jim's talents were so satisfactorily stretched in his own country. Jim's happiness with his family continued to find increasing expression in their summer holidays. His visits to America would now be strictly business trips, and he no longer felt the need to seek vacation refreshment on the other side of the Atlantic. The Irvines' tied cottage had the drawback of being an official residence, while the houses that he rented for the month of August were family houses, even if they grew more and more distinguished with the succeeding years. One of these houses, the romantic Ashley Combe near Porlock Weir in Somerset, was a great prize. In 1932, during the Great Depression, Jim had skilfully obtained a summer's lease of this magical house at a knockdown price. Here the complete family threw themselves into the never-to-be forgotten experience of discovering the secret, overgrown world of the house that had belonged to Lord Byron's brilliant daughter, Ada Lovelace. With terraced gardens and a loggia with far, blue views over the Bristol Channel, it was Italianate in both appearance and position. It came to represent to the Irvine family the 'Land of Lost Content': an idyll of the heady 1930s, when the young Irvines had smart aristocratic friends and rushed about in Nigel's little car. The life they led in this house, they saw in retrospect, was the end of an era. Lodged in their memories, all that was left to them was an elegy of lost beauty and gaiety. In the years to follow the Second World War, Ashley Combe was finally demolished.

Principal Irvine's wife and children were barely affected by the Depression, although Mabel, Felicity and Veronica put up a united but hilarious effort to put only empire or British goods on their Christmas shopping lists. Did a pencil case, normally an acceptable offering from Felicity to her father, come from Shanghai, or had it been made in India? However, the Principal was only too aware of the need for careful retrenchment. In 1931, when the political–financial storm burst, Irvine cut his holiday in Devon short and returned to St Andrews to recast the university's budget, make cuts and introduce economies. This both bruised his expansionist hopes and pleased his liking for finance. He made an informed calculation that he would suffer an effective reduction of £600 to his own income, but he reassured his wife that with a little care their lives would go on as comfortably as before, without selling any investments.

The country went off the gold standard on 21 September 1931 and the stock exchange closed down for a day. Principal Irvine was in London, and he was hounded to return to St Andrews, which was infected with panic. The Chancellor's Assessor, James Younger, was all for the Principal going round to a stockbroker's in the City, to instruct in the sale of all the university's investment stock. Irvine, who had come to London to attend the Faraday Centenary celebrations as a privileged guest of the Royal Institution, was predisposed to take a long view of the emergency, and to stay where he was.

His calm common sense was, in any case, needed not only by St Andrews but also by the Department of Scientific and Industrial Research. He was required to go down to the DSIR's Princes Risborough laboratories to chair an important meeting to address the continued funding, even in time of crisis, of this essential feeder of British industry.

In the end, it was well that Irvine fulfilled his engagements in London, where he had developed the skill of keeping his ear to the ground. The information that he obtained there from his friend Josiah Stamp was that, contrary to expectation, the value of the pound would not drop below 17s: a tenable position, Stamp advised. This was of real worth to St Andrews, and Irvine refused to countenance selling any of the university's investments. When he bumped into the editor of the *Glasgow Herald*, Sir Robert Bruce, in the Athenaeum, he was able to glean from him the latest cabinet gossip: the two like-minded Scotsmen agreed that if 'Labour had been kicked out a year ago the country's finances would have been saved'. The return of the Conservatives under Baldwin to some semblance of power in the October general election, Irvine wrote triumphantly, 'has given the most wonderful result in British history. What a relief it is to have that noisy, vulgar spendthrift gang of Socialists thrown out so decisively.'[24] It was of course a coalition government, and Ramsay Macdonald invited Baldwin to serve in it with him.

Irvine enjoyed flexing his intellectual muscle on the budgeting of his university. He was a powerful combatant with the University Grants Committee, and he could see grave danger for the funding of the Scottish universities when Walter Moberley came into office as Riddell's successor. In March 1934 he received private information that Moberley, as chairman of the University's Grants Committee, would seek to withdraw some of the usual UGC funding from the Scottish universities, believing that they should get more local financing, like the civic universities in England. Jim was incensed that St Andrews should be spoken of in the same breath as the new 'civic' universities. Apart from the possible devastation to higher education in Scotland that Moberley's plans would cause, Irvine's anger was stirred by the injustice and lack of understanding that would lie behind the move to push the ancient universities of Scotland off their pedestal. His feeling always was that St Andrews deserved special treatment, being in the same league as Oxford and Cambridge: of ancient foundation and appropriate to the pursuit of pure research. With gusto, he constructed a defence made up of a bewildering command of figures, both large and small. Perhaps few men would have had the patience to expose the UGC's threadbare position in this way. Of course, in observing that Scotland paid 3s per head more for education rating than England, he enjoyed pointing out that St Andrews already received £4,500 from local authorities. He knew that he also had the prospect of a fight on his hands with the County of Fife Educational Trust Scheme: the county was provocative in demanding more jurisdiction over the awards of bursaries to local students. Just when he thought he deserved some spin-off from the development of his new residence hall, the county might take away from him the power to select the students he felt worthy of St Andrews. 'THIS IS APPROPRIATION,' was Irvine's marginal note to the working document.[25]

In 1934 the British economy was at rock bottom, and the only non-recurrent Treasury grants claimed by the university within that difficult quinquennial were for Dundee. Irvine argued that the Carnegie Trust's annual capital grant of £45,000 could be regarded as a local contribution, since the trust only applied to Scotland. Looked at in this light, the Scottish universities' ratio of local funding to Treasury funding further contradicted the case of the UGC in wishing to impose on the Scottish universities the requirement to raise more money locally. Irvine's coup de grâce was delivered with the rather arcane argument that although, under the Scottish Education Act of 1908, the grant for higher education became lumped as a Treasury grant, the 1929 rating reform had rendered the grant local money.

Irvine was already experiencing the gratifying effect on the university of the Harkness benefaction, and his instinct was to keep public funding at bay for as long as he dared. He continued to develop other ways of 'putting St Andrews on the map'. In 1937, St Mary's College celebrated its 400th year, and the Duke of Kent brought lustre to the functions with his presence – but the brilliance of the historic occasion was deflected onto the Vice-Chancellor who had ensured hope in the college's future.

Irvine continued to feel that St Andrews suffered from a similar insularity to the one he had found in the United States. With his friend David Russell, whose Walker Trust backed the scheme, he launched on both town and gown a remarkable series of public lectures on aspects of leadership: they were intended to be an intellectual and even a moral strengthener against the significant events taking place in mainland Europe. The speakers were all men who could command national attention; the lectures were all published. Even the King and Queen read them. John Buchan opened the concept with a lecture using his hero, Montrose, as an exemplar, but later came an 'Analysis of Leadership' given by the Bishop of Durham, who underlined the original intention of the lectures by stating that modern civilisation was suffering from a weakening of the sense of individual responsibility: the National Socialism of the Nazi party had no place for the moral code that was still so British and had been ingrained in Irvine since boyhood. The lectures brought St Andrews face to face with the consequences to civilisation of creeping fascism, and when they were reissued in 1950, Irvine wrote of their enduring significance: 'The claim is unlikely to be disputed that there have been few periods in recorded history when the world has stood in greater need of Leaders than is the case today.'[26]

Unlike their counterparts at the beginning of the century, the students of St Andrews in the 1930s were more engaged in the issues of the day. When they chose Jan Christian Smuts as their Rector, the corporate mind of the university had shifted from the old admiration of literary glamour, or even from its rather Edwardian heroes of polar exploration. Smuts was chosen as a statesman for their time. At his installation as Rector of the university in 1934, his address adhered closely to a theme not unrelated to the Walker lectures on leadership. He spoke on 'Liberty'. Prophetically, his message to the receptive minds of his young and still predominantly Scottish students, brought up on the ethic of hard work, was that 'freedom is bought with a price and preserved only through self-sacrifice'. Irvine was at heart a peace-maker; he was president of the local branch of the League of Nations, and on this occasion he chose to symbolise peace by flying the Boer flag over St Andrews. 'The new Rector is General Smuts of South African fame, a great fighter, a great Statesman, a great Imperialist and a fine man,' he proclaimed. 'Thirty-five years ago the University sent out a battery of guns to fight the Boers: now we welcome a Boer General to our position of honour.'[27] The two staunchly British students of the Boer War period in Leipzig in 1899 had come a long way, but in 1934, while enjoying the fruits of his labours for his university, Irvine knew that this peace could only be the lull before the storm. To the students of this generation, in the presence of the honorary graduands for 1932: Albert Schweizer, Herbert Hensley Henson, the controversialist Bishop of Durham, and the Moderator of the General Assembly of the Church of Scotland – he warned that 'the fate of civilized mankind hangs on the moral forces which it is able to call forth'.[28]

The Gifford Lectures, the gift to St Andrews, as to each of the universities of Scotland, in the will of Lord Gifford, have contributed an almost unbroken flow of edification and stimulus on moral theology and ethics since 1887 – not only to the University of St Andrews but also to the town itself. It was Adam Gifford's wish that the lectureships should promote, advance and diffuse 'the study of Natural Theology in the widest sense of that term, ... and that they should be both public and popular ... open not only to students of the universities but to the whole community'.[29] They were richly endowed, and Principal Irvine referred to them as 'a kind of Nobel Prize'. In 1933, observing with regret the recent tendency of the series to lecture 'to dwindling and mystified audiences on the dreariest of philosophies' – 'We have heard more about Plotinus than of the teaching of Jesus Christ' – Irvine resolved to reach St Andrews' town and gown with a Gifford lecturer of wide and deep Christian experience. Such a man would surely address the spiritual needs of his time.

This reinterpretation of the Gifford lectures would go deeper than the Walker Lectures. Irvine wrote persuasively to his friend the Bishop of Durham, who was at first consumed with doubt as to whether he would undertake what would be a painful discipline to him: 'A restless night, haunted miserably by the menacing ghost of Lord Gifford!' The elderly Hensley Henson knew that he was expected to make a *Confessio Fidei*, a confrontation of himself. Hensley Henson had received the St Andrews' honorary DD in June 1932, and he was no stranger to the Irvine clan. Luckily for St Andrews, Jim Irvine and William Temple combined to reassure the good bishop in the matter of Lord Gifford's inheritance, and his lectures on 'Christian Morality' were given in St Andrews in 1935–6 to an audience that no longer had any need to feel isolated from the debates of the day.[30]

The cry for British moral values, for the native sense of self-individuation and responsibility for self, was brought home to St Andrews over and over again in the lectures and addresses that Irvine and his distinguished friends gave during these years. Domestically, the country yearned for family values in their monarch, and at the same time the country tip-toed around the delicate issue of rearming. The views of Irvine, which were cautious like Baldwin's, echoed these of his fellow countrymen, except that he was now a figure of the establishment. A ticket for the thanksgiving of George V's Silver Jubilee was followed later that summer by an invitation to Jim and Mabel to dine with the King and Queen at Holyrood on 22 May 1935. The position that he had reached afforded him much respect in public life. It was while chairing a meeting in London that he was given the courtesy of advance news of the abdication of Edward VIII. 'Few people on our side are likely to shed tears on that decision,' he wrote to an American friend.[31] St Andrews sent their Chancellor a telegram of congratulation on his handling of the abdication crisis. On the day of the coronation of George VI and Queen Elizabeth, he strolled across Horse Guards, in the company of his friend the Bishop of Durham, to take up his seat in the abbey for the coronation of his monarch. To his intense joy, Oxford gave him the DCL in 1938: 'I have always had a sneaking desire to have a degree from both Oxford and Cambridge'.[32]

Finance from those wishing to impose their influence on St Andrews, in the disguise of gifts to fund university development, were sometimes declined by Irvine. Earlier in the first year of the Irvine principalship, a Dundee businessman, George Bonar, made it known that he wished to munificently endow the university with £30,000 in order to fund a university 'qualification' in commerce. The sticking point was the standard of entry, and after a six-year probationary period even Mr Bonar had to admit that the terms of the preliminary entrance examinations did not correspond to his ideas for commercial training in Dundee. George Bonar withdrew his offer of a fund now amounting to £40,000, and the Court gave the Principal permission to use the press to explain matters. Nevertheless, for many years the people of Dundee believed that Irvine had done them down in the matter of Mr Bonar and his commercial degree.

Perhaps we should not be surprised that a man of such rectitude and independence as Jim Irvine turned down an approach from Antonin Besse in the 1930s. Besse tried to oil his way into the position of philanthropist to St Andrews, and he offered positions to St Andrews men in a graduate training scheme in his company.[33] Besse, whose Aden-based global trading empire extended to shipowning and the manufacture of gum arabic, was a mysterious and rather sinister figure who claimed French antecedence; as a merchant and industrialist, he dominated European business during the inter-war years. For a couple of years in the mid-1930s, Irvine was amused by Besse's attempts to draw near to him, and an opportunity to visit the industrialist in Aden occurred when, en route for India, his ship passed through the Suez Canal. 'Mr Besse, being Mr Besse, was determined that we should see everything and indeed we did, including a long run out into the desert to see a rather wonderful garden,' he reported. Three St Andrews graduates were already there, working for Besse in his web of businesses, all in Aden.

Besse had intense aspirations to be an educational philanthropist, and at the end of his life he endowed St Anthony's College, Oxford; but when he visited St Andrews in 1935 he was still tainted with the British government's wartime, unproven suspicions that he was involved in illegal arms trading. At this date, this was enough to persuade Irvine to give him little encouragement. Irvine, who in these years just before the Second World War was regarded as an authority on higher education development, and who was a trustee of the lofty policies of The Pilgrim Trust, had been drawn into a circle of intellectual politicians and moral thinkers. His own interest had by then extended from the needs of St Andrews to similar but international projects. In October 1938, Irvine, who would lend his influence with The Pilgrim Trust, was invited to speak on the same platform as the Foreign Secretary, Lord Halifax,[34] on behalf of the development of International Student House in London. He was flattered to have new friends like Lord Halifax. Irvine felt that he would do harm to his cause by consorting with men like Besse: he preferred idealists like Harkness – idealists who gave him a free hand – and he was attracted to ascetics like Halifax.

FOURTEEN

The Residential System

When Principal Irvine came into office in January 1921, the *Scots Pictorial* couthily observed that 'he will be keenly interested in the pleasures as well as in the labours of the students, and on their occasional frolics his eye will be indulgent'. Irvine's vision for St Andrews panned over every aspect of the student's life; he was concerned with everything that could amplify the development of the young men and women in his charge: the roof over their heads, the stimulus of the company they kept, their health and – yes – their frolics. He went further: he wanted to make men of his male students. His chief vehicle for this would be a fine purpose-built hall of residence for them.

Today, in April, the student who portrays Irvine in the Kate Kennedy Procession[1] clasps in his hand a scroll that is reputed to contain the architect's plans for St Salvator's Hall, the hall of residence that is often rather loosely regarded as Irvine's greatest achievement in St Andrews. This rather superficial belief ignores, for example, that although Irvine achieved the great enlargement of St Andrews by means of the development of halls of residence, his own value system required him to think first of the spiritual life of his charges, and the attention that he lavished on the restoration of the chapel was of equal importance to him. The institution of the residential system was but one phase of Irvine's new order.

In the Kate Kennedy Club's annual spring celebration of the men and women of the past who made St Andrews, James Colquhoun Irvine walks in the same company as the other James: Bishop James Kennedy, who was the founder of St Salvator's College (1450).[2] Principal Irvine liked to consider himself as being charged in a mystical sense with the role of James Kennedy's successor. He wore a replica of Kennedy's signet ring, which his wife had had made for him for a Christmas present. With St Salvator's Hall, Irvine wanted to set the seal on bringing the collegiate university of the fifteenth century, with its chapel at its heart, to a new beginning.

St Salvator's Hall, which opened at the start of the academic year of 1930–1, was designed to be a hall of residence in the fullest twentieth-century sense. It found an early place in a world-wide movement to launch fine and peaceable citizens on a new world by means of fashioning their social order as students. The Cité Universitaire in Paris, established in the hope of creating peace and harmony among nations, was built at this same time, and it owed much of its appearance to the campus designs of North America, as did St Salvator's Hall. Certainly, Irvine had in his mind some of the east coast Ivy League universities of North America, as well as the colleges of Oxford and Cambridge, because he admired their buildings and the possibilities for a corporate life that he felt they encouraged. He was proud that St Andrews, by virtue of its age, belonged to the same elite group as Oxford and Cambridge. But he also knew that what had survived from St Andrews' medieval past, although but a shred of the dreaming spires of Oxbridge, made it different from its English counterparts.

In the Scottish universities could still be found a genial democratic structure whereby dons, and administrators, and even in a limited sense students, contributed their mutual support to the easy workings of a simple constitution: colleges in St Andrews, such as they were, had no separation of government from the university, over which Irvine had almost absolute command. Or that was the idea. Irvine placed his trust in this simple formula; the fact that, later, University College Dundee caused some disintegration did not concern him at this date. Irvine, known in the Scottish way as Principal Irvine, was both Principal and Vice-Chancellor of the university, and Principal of the United College. Irvine's purpose in developing St Salvator's Hall, Dean's Court (the post-graduate hall of residence) and then all the others, was not to ape the Oxford colleges such as New College or All Souls, but rather to reinterpret for our time something of the medieval duty of care, the master–disciple relationship that was, as he thought, prevalent in fifteenth-century St Andrews: this Irvine identified as Kennedy's 'desire to enrich the studious life with the spirit of family life'. The concept of these twentieth-century halls does not go so far as to include the attachment of a fellowship of tutoring dons, as with Oxford and Cambridge. The appointment of staff to St Andrews was to remain entirely a matter for the Senatus and the Court, with the powerful Vice-Chancellor in charge of a university that would become residential: a new quality for Scottish universities. Remember that Irvine, when a student, had constantly to be looking for digs in the town; he was now determined to give St Andrews the corporate spirit that he believed would come with the residential system.

A glowing leading article about St Salvator's Hall, written by Principal Irvine's brother-in-law 'Jack' Williams, who the previous year had had the good fortune of appointment to the new Harkness Chair of History, appeared in the *Scotsman* during the week that the new hall opened. 'The policy of Principal Sir James Irvine, modern in the best sense as it is – energetic, enterprising, and far-seeing – has always been informed by a sympathy with, and devotion to, the ancient traditions and ideals of the ancient University.'[3]

It was not enough that 'Sallies', with its public rooms, its handsome purpose-made furniture, its fine dining hall and its well thought-out study bedrooms, should be up-to-date. It should also make gentlemen of its residents. These young men must be cared for in a mature way. Irvine revived the medieval Scottish and European tradition of the regent, after an abeyance of nearly three centuries. Every awardee scholar, and any student by request, would have a regent assigned to befriend him, and to counsel him when in difficulty; also to encourage him in the widening of his intellectual life and to stretch his thought, but never to supervise his work. The nearest analogy may be the Eton College 'tutor'. The warden would preside over the formal running of the hall; guests of the university would be invited to dine in hall; and the Principal of the university would himself dine in hall once a week. This whole concept aroused the enthusiasm of the best dons, who pressed to be appointed to the role of regent, a position that was to carry no emolument.

The Principal sought endowments from his friends to provide foundation scholarships, and although the Harkness scholarships of £100 per annum were the most highly regarded, other donors soon followed Harkness's example. No boy worthy and needful of a scholarship should be turned away from entry to St Salvator's Hall, and a responsible scholarship board was set up. It is worth noticing that St Salvator's Hall was begun in the same month that the Wall Street Crash occurred, but there was no dearth of interest from local businessmen, who found it fulfilling to take part in such an inspiring development on their doorstep. There was the Montrose Scholarship given by the jute fortune of the Boase family, and there was a scholarship given by the Russells of Tullis Russell Paper Mills. The banker Robert Fleming gave a residential scholarship. Lord Inchcape was one of the larger donors to the building fund, and his image and coat of arms were placed in the dining room's embellishment of stained glass, together with those of David Russell, W.J. Matheson of New York and Edward Harkness, whose large benefaction finally enabled Irvine to realise the ideas he had been putting together throughout the 1920s.[4] Irvine's report to the University Grants Committee in 1929 reflects something of the ideals of a Cecil Rhodes: 'It is already evident that these selected students, endowed with qualities in which scholarship is the outstanding but not the only feature, will form a nucleus of men who, in time, will occupy prominent positions in student affairs.'

So what was it like to be one of those first students in Sallies? Eugene Melville was one of the first to be awarded a Harkness Scholarship. He was not only a leading light among the students of his generation, but he rose afterwards through a distinguished career in the diplomatic service to become British ambassador in Bonn. He took up residence in Sallies on the day it opened, and he was exactly the kind of young man that Irvine was targeting. He spent six years studying in St Andrews; he acted with the Mermaids; and he played a mean trumpet in the Sallies dance band. He was a great favourite with Veronica and Nigel Irvine, who were his contemporaries as students. But at this distance in time, it must be emphasised that he and his contemporaries, who were in the main rather earnest Scots with little money to throw about, had many restrictions placed on their freedom. They were forbidden to receive ladies in Sallies; they might not let alcohol pass their lips in their hall of residence; it was strictly against the rules to wear plus-fours in the dining room; and they were expected to be in the residence by ten o'clock on most nights. There were few Englishmen among them. Despite his friendship with the young Irvines, Eugene found the Principal rather a remote figure, difficult to get to know but with already a reputation for skill in diplomacy and administration. Beneath this he discerned a determined, terrier-like character that would fight to the death for St Andrews. These students thought of their disciplinarian Principal as rather like many a dictator, right down to his short stature, but they knew that the comparative luxury in which they lived was all due to 'Jimmy the Princ's' deep concern for the welfare of his students.[5] Their Principal had style.

Sallies was the cornerstone of Irvine's design for St Andrews. Principal Irvine walked a tightrope that has remained a conundrum for his successors: to make his fine, perfect university valid, he had to enlarge its numbers; to make it desirable, he had to retain something of its exclusivity. The critical problem that he first faced on becoming Principal in 1921 was, however, entirely a question of numbers, and soon he could put figures to his aspirations. A men's hall of residence should be capable of lodging more than 100 students, with features that were unique in Great Britain, and it should be collegiate in form and in spirit. It should be beautifully finished, so as to attract the very best students from throughout the British Isles. In 1922 student numbers were temporarily inflated by the returning servicemen; nevertheless, of the 782 full-time students, 585 lived within a radius of 30 miles of the university, and only 145 came from other parts of the United Kingdom. In an effort to break down the established pattern of trawling for students who lived a mere bus ride away from St Andrews, the Principal commissioned photographs of the university to form a booklet which, from 1929, was sent round to all the English public schools; these were known for a breadth of education that was perhaps still lacking in the Scottish schools. An expansion in student numbers, with St Salvator's Hall setting the pace for further development, would permit rapid growth in the teaching faculties; it would permit that apex of university endeavour – research – to become more powerful. It would also permit the large development of the sports grounds and athletics tracks, and the gymnasia; and it would justify encouraging an expansion in music and the theatre. At this date, the fee income was a significant element in the university's annual budget.

Self-assured though he was, Irvine ran a risk in flooding St Andrews with so many places for men students in 1930, on the eve of international financial collapse. There were plenty of Job's Counsellors on the University Court, who warned him that he may have taken a disastrous step in providing for so large an influx; they were sure that he would bankrupt the university.[6] Luckily, Irvine's gamble paid off. From the day it opened its doors, St Salvator's Hall was oversubscribed, and the way was open for Irvine to embark on the equally important development of the teaching departments.

A decade of cautious preparation had been necessary before the university could be assured of this success. The forward planning of St Andrews just after the end of the First World War included consideration of a men's hostel. Although not yet himself Principal, it was Irvine who in 1919 was driving forward the 'Men's Hostel Scheme', and displaying his flair for the procurement of finance. But the Scottish student, Irvine felt, would benefit from a less rough-and-ready environment than a mere hostel could offer. He argued that the Scottish student needed to be released from a slavish dependency on the lecture system. The corporate life that Irvine began to envisage would give the socially inexperienced Scottish student a chance to develop, and it would engender a sense of responsibility towards their university amongst the students.[7] Or so Irvine dreamed. Part of Abbotsford Crescent was leased from Professor M'Intosh, and from 1921 Chattan House, as it was known, accommodated some two dozen male students. Irvine slowly began to accrue the funds he would need for his more ambitious development. At his first quinquennial meeting with the University Grants Committee, Irvine obtained the support of the powerful committee members, who unwittingly played into his hand and pronounced their preference for a purpose-built hall of residence. Their report recognised that young men and women of the post-war generation expected a far greater corporate life than had been enjoyed before the war, and it expressed the opinion that the conversion of existing houses could only be a temporary expedient.[8] The members of the UGC, whose privilege it was to dispense Treasury grants, optimistically hoped that aspirational schemes for student accommodation would have strong appeal to private benefactors.

It was felt that women had been provided for handsomely when University Hall was built around the beginning of the century (1896). There has never been a shortage of young women applying for entry to St Andrews; Irvine felt he constantly had to fight off an onslaught of headmistresses staking their pupils' claims to study at St Andrews, and he worked the speech-day platforms of boys' schools in his campaign to redress the balance of the sexes at his university. When Edinburgh walked away with most of the medals at the Scottish Inter-Universities' Athletics Meeting in St Andrews in 1925, Irvine remarked that until St Andrews had more male students it would continue to do badly in these competitions, and he was still enough of the athlete he had been as a boy to feel that this diminished the university.

In fact there was another reason for Edinburgh to succeed in athletics at this time: their star was Eric Liddell (whose story was told in the 1981 film *Chariots of Fire*). In 1925 Liddell competed for Edinburgh University in the 100 yards and the 220 yards races in St Andrews, as he had done the year before.[9] In 1924, Mabel Irvine presented Eric Liddell with what is believed to have been his first medal. It was later in the summer of 1924 that, at the Paris Olympics, Liddell, a principled Christian, was forced to withdraw from the 100 metres race, because the heats took place on a Sunday. However, he established a world record in the 400 metres in Paris, and brought home a gold medal. Irvine was intrigued by this earnest, unassuming, but brilliant young Scot – Scotland's first Olympic medalist – and struck up a conversation with him after the chapel service. 'I had a talk with him – a charming fellow this "Flying Scotsman".[10]

Principal Irvine grew increasingly worried about St Andrews' female image. He began to learn how the students of Harvard, of Yale and of

Princeton lived. He toyed with the idea of bringing over to Scotland James Gamble Rogers, the architect of much of Yale. He spoke at length with Edward Harkness, who himself wished to repair the shortcomings of the American system. In America, Irvine looked closely at the more cohesive way of working and living that quadrangle developments offered to the American student.

The analogy with Bishop Kennedy continues. Kennedy endowed his college richly, and Irvine charmed rich gifts for his hall out of local donors. William Carstairs, a manufacturer of sou'westers from the fishing burgh of Anstruther, greatly enjoyed a morning spent in St Andrews with the Principal, and took considerable trouble with his gift of a silver bowl for the high table of the new hall. 'I had no idea – not in the least – that your work was so varied in its complexion and extent. I am so pleased to see the social and human side means so much to you too,' wrote Carstairs in appreciation.[11] Such was the success of St Salvator's Hall that it very soon justified the enlargement of the university's athletics grounds.

Irvine's legacy shows that as a 'building bishop', no other figure since Kennedy in St Andrews' history can hold a candle to him. But Kennedy was literally a building bishop. Ronald Cant, the historian of the university, has described the magnificent scale of Kennedy's plan, to which nothing was denied. The finest medieval church in Scotland, St Salvator's Collegiate Church, was fitted out with vestments and furnishings. A silver-gilt mace for the College, rich in symbolism, was commissioned from Paris.

Irvine approached the provision for St Salvator's Hall in the same spirit. Nothing should be denied. No detail was too small for him, and every detail had to be of the finest. The dining furniture, of Scottish oak, was commissioned through Justice's of Dundee, who had a fine reputation for their Arts and Crafts furniture. It cost £450, which was a very large sum in 1930 and a measure of the importance that was ascribed to getting the tone exactly right. Armchairs were bought from Maples, in London, but Jim Irvine, as with the Students' Union restoration, fussed over even the choice of armchair to exemplify the manly ethos he was looking for. It was perhaps fortunate that the architect of the hall, Donald Mills, who practised in Dundee in the partnership of Mills and Shepherd, was a neighbour of the Irvines in St Andrews. The Irvine and the Mills families were on social terms, and the appointment of Mills was a fortunate one. His well-mannered hall is built in a Scottish country house style, but following a gentle three-sided collegiate plan, capable of extension.

St Salvator's Hall is situated on a prime site, adjacent on the east to the main quadrangle of the United College and set privately behind North Street, with the Younger Graduation Hall as its neighbour. To the north, its study bedrooms look over the villas on the Scores, with wide views across the bay. The process of canny acquisition from the Thoms family of this site absorbed all the years of the 1920s: years when the capital needed to advance with building works was still lacking.

Rich James Younger had put much pressure on the University Court to engage Michael Waterhouse, the architect who was working on the Younger Hall, to build the residence, and Irvine found himself having to write a difficult letter turning the London architect down. It was the Treasury, who – strongly critical of Waterhouse's extravagant design – settled the matter for Irvine by threatening to withdraw its offer of a non-recurrent Treasury grant of £12,000 for the hall of residence. Irvine felt a sense of merciful release and, once again in a position of command, he settled down to a pleasing relationship with Donald Mills.

Amiably, Mr Mills submitted to the Principal's almost daily suggestions. As chairman of the Forest Products Board for the Department of Scientific and Industrial Research, Irvine had access to its associated research laboratory, the Building Research Station, and he took it upon himself to research building materials. Samples of reinforced glass for the service areas of the hall, for example, were sent up to St Andrews from the south of England, as was a sample of Indian Laurel for a decorative wood to panel a 'senior common room'. Unlike his father and brother, Irvine was no draughtsman, but the backs of envelopes and the margins of committee papers were freely covered with his drawings and sketch plans. The picturesque impact that the hall could have on the corporate body of the university was enough to engage a disproportionate amount of the Principal's time. This was particularly so when it came to the stained glass for the dining room windows, which Irvine had set his heart on. They were to celebrate the figures of the university's past as well as the donors of the present. Notes flew between him, the architect and Mr Burns, the sympathetic designer in stained glass of the Edinburgh firm Donaldson and Burns, who had to deal with questions such as what a sixteenth-century archbishop, who may have been armed, would have worn under his vestments;[12] and was 'Bonny Dundee', who was never Claverhouse to Irvine, wearing boots that looked like boots, or did they look more like silk stockings?

Once Sallies was opened, Irvine encountered strong criticism from the committee ranks of the Carnegie Trust, which had provided £20,000 of the £46,000 required. They carped that the Hall would 'train young men to a luxurious style of living'. Irvine suspected Lord Novar. He defended himself by pointing out that he had devoted ten years to collecting information regarding the design and management of residence halls from all over the country and from the United States. Never admitting that it was he who had invited these gifts for St Andrews, he replied that it would have been folly to have refused gifts which in the words of one donor were designed to 'elevate and refine student life'.[13] Lord Aberdeen, one of a diminishing band that had known the privately run but ultimately unsuccessful St Leonard's Hall before the turn of the century, made a good point when he congratulated the Principal on a development that showed every sign of being a lasting and vital element in the modernised university. Sallies avoided the drawbacks that led to the demise of the old St Leonard's Hall, which was too small to be economic and was confined to well-heeled students whose fathers could keep them in what operated as a semi-private institution for young gentlemen.

The building of Sallies invigorated Irvine; it sparked a renewed interest in St Andrews for him, and it came in time to save him from accepting the principalship of Edinburgh University: 'Fresh hope for the place has stirred within me,' he wrote to Mabel, 'and it doesn't tire me a bit when I can spend my time doing things which are really effective.'[14] He looked to a time when the whole of North Street in St Andrews would be a fine avenue of university buildings, perhaps not unlike Leipzig's Liebig Strasse, to which he had repaired every day as a PhD student at the turn of the century. The first fine residential development gave confidence to donors, even to those who had once carped at its splendour; right at the heart of these donors was the backbone of higher education in Scotland, the Carnegie Trust, which pledged another £20,000 towards the extension of St Salvator's Hall. By the spring of 1937, St Andrews was ready financially and otherwise to begin building the second phase. Urgent action to contain costs had to be taken. Seaview, the villa previously on the site, was to be demolished, and salvage retained: large masonry would go to University House for garden walls. Windows were saved for garden frames. Flagstones were be set aside. Irvine, armed with advance information from the DSIR on wartime rationing of steel and timber for building, moved quickly to complete it in 1940.

Fine dining halls alone were not enough, nor even the system of regents. The spiritual life of the student was of pre-eminent importance to Irvine's scheme of things. It has already been demonstrated how, with little capital to spend but right from the start, Irvine's projects slowly pushed forward, always putting the students in the foreground. First came the Union, then the implementation of the residential system – 'the social purposes movement' as he termed it. As he built the new, he pledged to restore the old. Before his very personal crusade for the residences, he picked up on a wish amongst his colleagues to embark on work to the chapel, as a means of remembering the university's losses in the Great War. They little realised what an enormous sum of money would have to be found for it during the next ten years.

The evidence of Mabel's diary gives an impression of what it was like to live with Jim during these years. 'But all the bigness of it, the development in every department, the making sure & safe, financially, old & shaky foundations that he discovered full of holes, the rebuilding of new laboratories, the rebuilding of the men's Union, the restoration of the chapel, the smooth and business-like working of the whole university that used to be run on such parochial domestic lines, all this, so wide, so full & so satisfactory, has filled Jim's life day & night, & has taken every ounce of his marvellous powers of organization, energy, courage, foresight, patience.'[5]

Chapel observance and a consciousness of a metaphysical dimension to all he did were inseparable from James Irvine's life. He clung to Bishop Kennedy's adage that 'learning without God is but husky provender', and it is hardly surprising that he needed to see the chapel fully restored in beauty but, even more, to be 'the very soul of our university life'.[16] Throughout these busy early years of his principalship, he oversaw a protracted series of works of restoration of this important collegiate church: Kennedy's College Chapel.

Today we can little imagine the state of the fifteenth-century chapel of St Salvator in 1921. Serious structural defects had first been noticed c.1760 by James Craig, the architect of Edinburgh's New Town, and it is thought that Bishop Kennedy's tomb was damaged when, under Craig, the old stone roof was replaced with one of timber. The works of succeeding generations of principals, though worthy, had the effect of leaving a flawed building to the twentieth century. Irvine's memory of St Andrews was a long one, and he remembered with horror the heroic efforts of Principal Donaldson to modernise the chapel, employing the university janitor as electrician. The north cloister had been enclosed since 1861 with glass screens, and in this uncomfortable space degree examinations took place and societies held their meetings. Macgregor Chalmers, the leading Scottish restoration architect, had made a sound start in Principal Irvine's first years, but then his death intervened. What Craig had noticed 100 years before, that the weight of the medieval stone roof had eventually thrust the walls out from the vertical, had never been fully addressed.

Irvine wrestled with defect after defect. As a chemist he could not resist taking a professional interest in whether it was the use of proprietary chemicals that had damaged the stonework, or whether the cause was environmental and could be attributed to the seaside town's salty atmosphere and the ultimately corrosive use of sea-water during earlier repairs to the building.

In the spring of 1930, during the work of altering the floor level of the chapel, workmen revealed an old passage leading far underground to the tomb of Bishop Kennedy. Deep in the vault, at the first breath of air, the coffin burst open and there lay the mortal remains of the founder of the college. Principal Irvine bent, and in act of dedication he raised up the skull of the man whose work he vowed to complete. Later that evening he and his college colleagues reverently gathered in the chapel by candlelight for a service to re-inter the coffin of Bishop Kennedy in his great tomb. Above the doorway of the screen of the restored chapel, Irvine instructed to be inscribed:

SCIMUS ENIM QUONIAM SI TERRESTRIS DOMUS NOSTRA HUIUS HABITATIONIS DISSOLVATUR QUOD AEDIFICATIONEM EX DEO HABEMUS DOMUM NON MANUFACTAM AETERNAM IN COELIS

Only his wife, who like him was curiously stirred by the events surrounding the restoration of the chapel, can give the authentic explanation of this, the finishing touch, and of Jim Irvine's visionary reaction to this episode. As the date for the university's service of rededication drew near, his mind was intensely full of all that it meant to him. He was much disturbed by a dream he had experienced, and Mabel recounted that he told her:

I dreamed I was reading the Second Lesson at the opening service, as of course I shall be doing before long. I had gone up to the lectern when suddenly I saw that Professor Duncan was in the pulpit instead of remaining at his prayer desk. A wave of annoyance swept over me as he went on to announce the chapter which I was to read – the second chapter of Fifth Corinthians – and there at the first verse I turned a few pages of the Bible helplessly and then looked at Duncan and said, 'Where am I to find it?' He pointed an accusing finger at me and now he looked like John Knox. 'You ought to know. You will find it after the Apocrypha.' I turned over the pages confusedly, wondering at these new books which I had not heard about. At last Fifth Corinthians, second chapter, first verse – I drew a breath of relief, and it was in cypher. It looked as if a compositor's box had been spilt over the page, question marks, asterisks, brackets, dots and dashes. Cold perspiration broke out on my forehead. I turned to John Knox and said 'How am I to read this?' He replied sternly, 'Read it as it stands'. The effort to give voice to this jumble of signs, the dismay I felt at the want of dignity and reverence in the service, wakened me.[17]

Of course, St Paul did not write five epistles to the Corinthians, but if we turn to his second epistle to the Corinthians, at chapter 5 we read: 'For we know that if our earthly house of this tabernacle were dissolved, we have a building of God, an house not made with hands, eternal in the Heavens.'

'What more beautiful text could there be for a restored chapel,' was Jim's relieved answer to his dream. Those words in the Vulgate are those of the carved inscription on the screen.

Annie Dunlop's *Life* of Kennedy states that 'St Salvator's is truly more than [James Kennedy's] monument in stone and lime; it is the embodiment of his aspirations and endeavours, the foundation to which he committed his dust and bequeathed his personal treasures'.[18] James Irvine, the romantic, committed himself to take the spirit of Kennedy's work and make it live again, vital and organic, in our time. It was by these means that he achieved the mission he was entrusted with on his appointment as Principal: to save St Andrews University. With an understanding of these events – the restoration of the chapel and the foundation of the residential halls – we can better comprehend the claim in his obituaries that James Colquhoun Irvine was St Andrews' Second Founder.

Jim Irvine was such an enthusiast for the power of tradition to oil the wheels of his much-loved alma mater that where he did not find tradition, he invented it. The restoration of the chapel opened up an opportunity that, as the years went on, acquired the patina of age and the rhythm of tradition. His chapel addresses, which were given at a special service held on the last Sunday night of the summer term, only dated from 1926, but he regarded them as grafted to St Andrews' calendar. He speaks through them as a scientist who walked the Christian way of life, and who ardently believed his students would follow him, as he had tried to follow his academic forbears.[19]

For St Salvator's Chapel, Ed Harkness never refused Jim the funds he required to see through to the end this work that was probably closest to his heart. First came £20,000, but silently and unquestioning came as much again: enough to complete the stained glass after the Second World War and to commission from Hew Lorimer the little sculpted shrine to those of the university who lost their lives in the war, among whom numbered Nigel Irvine, Jim and Mabel Irvine's only son. Soon Reginald Fairlie's beautiful stalls and the ante-chapel, with its reminders of past cives, were full of the red gowns and the black gowns of the university's community, and Principal Irvine was content. A visitor in 1932 found in St Andrews 'an academic dignity and decency with a pride in the traditions and prestige of the place'. After the Principal's death, the windows of the east end were completed and the arms of James Irvine, three holly leaves taken from the Irvine crest and a crucible to represent his scientific calling, glow in stained glass beside the arms of James Kennedy.[20]

Because of Sallies, the enlarged student body of the late 1930s was diverse. They were a febrile, stylish, talented and often idle generation. Some were monied, some were not. With students now coming to St Andrews from not only all over the British Isles but also from America, the colonies, South Africa and the continent of Europe, Irvine had opened Pandora's box. It would be difficult to exercise moral control over these young people. Irvine, who liked to feel that he was connected to each new generation of students by an unbroken thread from the days when he wore the scarlet gown, grew out of touch in the 1930s with the Students' Representative Council and with the young men and women whom he wanted to know and understand as well as if he were in their shoes. He returned to St Andrews after an absence on government business in India to find that the students to whom he was so devoted were now ready to betray his trust.

To his sadness, the congenial array of famous rectors, who had been as much a support to him as to the students, became briefly a thing of the past, and all the students could think of was electing a 'working Rector', a man who no matter how inconsequential would attend and chair every meeting of the University Court. In 1937 they elected a local man, Robert MacGregor Mitchell who, although not undistinguished in the legal profession, did nothing to bring St Andrews into the public eye. It is true that he made it his business to attend every Court meeting, thus displacing his accustomed deputy, Principal Irvine, from the chair. It was during one of these meetings in 1938 that MacGregor Mitchell suddenly died; and furthermore, through no fault of his own, his period of office is now associated with student scandal.

The president of the SRC, although solemnly present at Rector Mac-Gregor Mitchell's memorial service, was reported in the local press for his involvement in scenes and drunken quarrels worthy of a Victorian penny shocker. This student, a showman with a fondness for fast cars, seems to have invented himself: *College Echoes* described him as 'the corporate life of the University'.[21] Irvine's attention was finally drawn to the extent of this student's disgraceful activity by a St Andrews bunk wife (or landlady), who in great distress called on the Principal to whom she made a statement. She had unwisely let the top floor of her house to a strange ménage à trois that consisted of the student in question and a woman and her daughter. In a case involving breach of promise, fights in the street and embezzlement of the SRC charities account, much harm was done to the university. Jim Irvine found that the student was supposed to be reading divinity but had never been seen in St Mary's College, and that he had demurely played the part of Bishop Kennedy in the Kate Kennedy Procession, but that he had also obtained a motor car from Central Motors without ever paying for it. It emerged that the individual was a mystery, without any of the funds that he pretended to possess, but his creditors came to the Principal's door.

In this same year there were five other cases of misappropriation of money: a Dundee student collected subscriptions for a dance but vanished without settling the corresponding accounts; another case concerned a student regatta which incurred a debt to the local boatmen; two SRC officers were forced to confess to the Principal that legal proceedings had been instigated against the SRC charities account; the balance in the Mermaids Dramatic Society Account had vanished; and the accumulated profit of *College Echoes* did not exist. Numerous unpaid accounts from tradespeople of all kinds appeared on the Principal's desk and, rather than see the university brought into disrepute, he discharged the debts, which could not be allowed to appear in the university's books.[22]

This temporary dislocation between the Principal and his students disappeared during the Second World War period. Those who were students as war broke out, and on their return to St Andrews after the end of war, remember how Principal Irvine was watchful of their comings and goings from the windows of his office over the porter's lodge and overlooking the quadrangle of St Salvator's College. But they also speak of his humanity: the student who came to resign his place at St Andrews because of his father's financial collapse was given the means to continue when the Principal pulled his chequebook out of the drawer in his desk. That student paid every penny back and became a distinguished physician. There was also the student who became a leading historian of his generation and who had been awarded a Bruce Scholarship to attend St Andrews: he and his wife-to-be met as students. Their wish to marry in College Chapel was debarred by some local difficulty but, on hearing of their dilemma, kindly Principal Irvine immediately suggested that they be married in St Leonard's Chapel, the last work of restoration of the old Principal. During these last years, the student body of the university reached the 2,000 mark that Irvine envisaged, but this body was somehow, to Jim Irvine, composed of individuals whom he liked to think he knew, and who – of course – must be in want of a residential scholarship to St Salvator's Hall.

There was never any diminution of Irvine's interest in helping a student's career, and after the Second World War he was acutely aware of the difficulties they would face in seeking a job. A local boy, whose father ran the St Andrews taxi service, took a scientific degree at this time, and luckily for him the Principal had kept his friendships in ICI and Procter & Gamble in good repair; in this way, the door to a career in industry was opened for this student and for many others. In a letter to Mabel a few days before he died, he reveals how much pleasure the personal touch with students actually gave him: 'This has been a very busy week, no meetings but much routine work and many interviews with students regarding their careers, a matter on which they will not confide in Duncan or Knox.'[23] Old and weary though he was, he just could not resist it: to be ever available to a student was essential to him.

The residential development in St Andrews that began with Sallies was continued throughout his office without any abatement, except perhaps during war. A claim for a large extension to the early trailblazer – the women's residence, University Hall – featured in the 1930 quinquennial application to the University Grants Committee, and it too, with the Carnegie Trust 1935 quinquennial, was awarded capital funding. Other buildings had, admittedly, to be converted from private dwellings to provide student residences. Not all the residential provision, for which there was a tidal wave of demand, could be custom-built. Abbotsford Crescent, the focal point of the nineteenth-century classical suburb, had been almost entirely owned by Professor M'Intosh, the first director of the Gatty Marine Laboratory, whose family had originally been in business as builders in St Andrews. Despite the Principal's dislike of uneconomic conversions, it became a women's residence. St Regulus Hall, a men's residence which started out life as a club for the schoolteachers at St Leonard's School, also dates from immediately before the Second World War period.[24] Annexes to St Salvator's Hall offered a more intimate life to the student by reason of their small size, and the Swallowgate, Mrs Bell-Pettigrew's expansive villa, was soon added to the stock of residences. Jim Irvine grew to accept that it was popular precisely because it was small and more relaxed than Sallies. Contrary though these annexes were to the grand gesture of collegiate life that he favoured, he added this residence, his neighbour on the Scores, to his list of dining fixtures.

Irvine continued to address the needs of the 'compleat student', and under a speech of that title he put forward a picture of the university he was building that has a certain period interest today.[25] In defense of his wish to introduce a physical training institute in St Andrews, and with more than a backward glance at the transformation in the German student that obligatory physical fitness had brought about, he argued that by introducing physical training he could create an academic institution of truth and beauty.[26]

Sadly, the residential developments in St Andrews were yet another cause of Dundee's jealousy, and the mid-1930s saw the first fiery outbursts in the Dundee press against what they chose to regard as their unfair deal. University College Dundee underwent expansion and development, just as much as old St Andrews. Residential accommodation, even if of a plainer variety, was also built up there from the early 1920s, although many students at University College Dundee were Dundonians and still lived at home. Dundee was also given gymnasia and sports facilities. Although Jim Irvine could never bring himself to feel for Dundee as he felt for the life that permeated the medieval town of St Andrews, he tried to convince himself that he was doing the right thing for Dundee. Faculty development generally in Dundee was, if anything, more lavishly funded than in St Andrews, and although this was for the most part directed at medicine – the medical school was independent of University College Dundee – new chairs were instituted more numerously north of the Tay than in Fife.

Believing that Dundee was essential to the worth of his university, Irvine was much admired before the Second World War in the commercial city for his wily skill in claiming funding from Treasury and trust alike. Romance, he was sure, was wasted on Dundee: 'The compassionate feeling for the needy student has pushed into the background the more pressing, if less romantic, necessity of giving the really brilliant student the facilities he deserves.' He was no advocate of piece-meal development for Dundee; he was a visionary there just as much as he was for the city of St Andrews. He gave to Dundee something that he was uniquely able to give at that time: the broad sweep of far-ranging, comprehensive growth in the applied sciences and the encouragement of government-funded scholarship in engineering, which he saw as having a vast future. From a Whitehall perspective, and as chairman of the government committee charged with providing research training in engineering, he knew that the supply of DSIR research scholarships in engineering exceeded the demand. This was an opportunity with which he knew could make something enviable in Dundee.[27]

Irvine's early plans for a post-graduate hall of residence with something of the intellectual allure of Oxford's All Souls were soon on the road to being realised. Architecturally, Deans Court, a fine sixteenth-century town house, is a jewel in the university's portfolio, and it was well that it could be absorbed into the residential life of St Andrews so soon. By May 1932, it was being prepared for its temporary use as a necessary annex to Sallies.

Intriguingly, in May 1932, there were two German students who had to be accommodated in Deans Court; these were probably the two German scientific research students who left as mysteriously as they had arrived. Between the estuaries of the river Eden, to the north of St Andrews, and the river Tay lies the moorland of Tentsmuir. Here Nigel Irvine had built for himself a hide for bird watching, in which one day he found a map of the whole area that surrounds RAF Leuchars. On it, marked up in German, were flight paths and minute details of a corner of Fife little known outside the East Neuk.

The restoration of residential life to old St Andrews was a statement of Irvine's faith in what has been known as the 'St Andrews spirit' and, after the last war, Clement Attlee woke up to Irvine's unabating efforts: 'Unlike most northern universities, there are residential colleges, the result, I gather, of the energetic efforts of the Vice-Chancellor Irvine, with whom I had much talk at lunch.'[28] The pleasure that the Principal took in observing how well Sallies worked for him was in evidence after the war. A visit to St Andrews of five Scandinavian rectors, who were rectors in the medieval European sense, prompted this observation:

> St Andrews certainly did them proud, beginning with a delightful dinner in Sally's (Salmond does these things extremely well) on Monday night. A special collection of Regents was invited, also a selected group of students had coffee with us in the Regents Room – the first time I had seen scarlet gowns in that room. Like many others, I felt myself asking how did we get on when there was no St Salvator's? and the answer is that we didn't get on at all.[29]

It was fortunate that Irvine's plan to bring growth to St Andrews through the restoration of residential collegiate life could be completed to the extent that it was, and within his lifetime. With what satisfaction, but with a tinge of romance, did he deliver the Dow Lecture during the quincentenary celebrations of St Salvator's College, 1950:

> It is an arresting thought that the Collegiate system which sprang into being so long ago should have survived essentially unchanged throughout the changing centuries, and that the model carried forward from the Middle Ages by Oxford and Cambridge should have persisted in Scotland and in our own time should have been considered worthy of adoption by the most famous Universities of the New World. Beyond question the Collegiate system has been of great advantage to St Andrews, giving the university a characteristic quality denied to her younger sisters, and binding her sons, now her daughters also, in a corporate life which strengthens their allegiance to the University.[30]

FIFTEEN

'Here am I, send me':[1]
A Traveller in Education

James Irvine's visiting card bore the usual chaste inscription:

Principal Sir James Irvine
The Athenaeum The University
St Andrews

However, he frequently joked that instead it should read:

Young Man
Traveller in Education

And indeed in his earlier, more straitened days, when called to London on university business he would put up at a high-grade commercial travellers' hotel.

Jim loved the anecdote told of him that, at a Holyrood House garden party given by Queen Elizabeth and King George VI early in their reign, the Queen exclaimed: 'Oh there's Sir James. My husband and I call him our unofficial ambassador.' He was already known for the way in which he, as a trustee of the Carnegie Trust for Scotland and spokesman for the Scottish universities in Whitehall, had broadened and developed the whole course of higher education in Scotland,[2] and the Colonial Office mandarins became interested in what he might do for the cause of higher education in other parts of the British empire.

It was no accident that during the last twenty years of his life he was selected to lead a number of important delegations to the colonies to investigate and report on their higher education and research potential. As chairman of the Forest Products Board of the DSIR, he was already intimate with the vital importance of the colonies' natural resources to the economic well-being of the mother country. An impressive and charismatic Scot, he intrigued his colleagues south of the border: this served to cut through the Oxbridge axis that otherwise prevailed in the civil service.

His qualities were those that had pushed through St Andrews' remarkable renaissance: he was still a scientist with a lucid and penetrating mind, and he was held somewhat in awe as an administrator for his capacity to put vision into effect. A man like him, with a pronounced sense of service, would suit the government's purposes. The broad thinking of the Colonial Office had to encompass the many strands of a vast problem, which boiled down to one thing: how to restore national confidence to the many nations that made up the vast spread of the British empire. Great Britain bore a heavy responsibility towards its colonies; they had been so loyal in war, and yet remained neglected and underdeveloped. Even more, the process of independence had begun, and the winds of change were blowing long before the Macmillan governments of the 1950s and early 1960s. Much development in the colonies had still to be undertaken, and it was urgently required before they could attain independence. The development of indigenous higher education was one solution.

Late in 1928, Irvine was appointed by the India Office to inspect Indian scientific research stations. The prospect clearly gripped him. 'I start on or about Christmas Day, and beat it as far as possible over-land to Aden, pick up a fast boat there and so to Bombay and the Himalayan Frontier. From thence I go to Simla and Dehra Dun where I write my report. The homeward journey will include Delhi, Lucknow, Agra and Calcutta, but dates and addresses are all fluid and, indeed, unknown to me . . . My chief worry is that Mabel is not at all well.'[3]

In the end, despite his thirst for travel, Jim decided not go to India in 1929, and Mabel's relief was palpable. For him to turn down this first opportunity to serve his country in a wider way was a significant indication that he was taking Mabel's ill-health very seriously indeed. Jim was a personality whom no-one could ignore, and he felt compelled to make the whole world see things through his eyes, experience things through the magic of his pen, and dance to his tune. Mabel, at his side, as she struggled to keep up with her husband, and even more as she struggled to be the university's hostess, became listless and dyspeptic, no longer gay and lighthearted. All her considerable artistic talents were sublimated in the needs of St Andrews University. What was hardest to bear was that she knew she owed her children and her husband more than she had the strength to give, and yet Jim was so overworked that she shrank from unburdening herself to him. 'Something has gone out of me that made life worth living. Something has dulled my sense of beauty – something has numbed the sort of romantic joy in which I have lived for forty-eight years. – Something has made my mind a forgetful, slow-moving hazy thing that wants to go to sleep & forget, forget, forget.'[4] The painful battle to recover her old spirits and youthfulness persisted for two or three years, and always the needs of her busy husband came between them and their plans to seek the warmth of the French Riviera for her recovery. Jim certainly did not ignore all that his wife did to ease and facilitate his life; it only made him love her all the more.

Her cure was finally sought and found in London, in the hands of the fashionable American osteopath Wilfrid Streeter. Osteopathy was at that time regarded as something even more than 'alternative' – it certainly did not come within the compass of the General Medical Council, but although Jim was a research chemist with a biomedical interest, he did not dismiss the possibility that Mr Streeter's 'laying-on of hands' could succeed where medical colleagues in Dundee had failed. He settled the fee of £100 without question, and he interviewed Mr Streeter with approbation, only drawing the line at some of the more extreme treatments that the osteopath proposed for his poor wife.

Ironically, given that Jim had turned away from the principalship of London University, it was London itself that gave Mabel back her life. While Jim stayed at home and was a good companion to the children in her stead, she spent her days being pummelled in Harley Street; and in the evenings she saw every play and dined with their London friends. This, her London life of going to the theatre, of exploring quaint London streets, of doing a little shopping and of meeting up with literary friends, had much of Bloomsbury about it. Her brother Dick, the managing director of the failing family firm, Williams and McBride in Belfast, led a double life in London. As a minor poet, and under the name of Richard Rowley, he associated with the Bloomsbury group. He gave Mabel a taste of this fascinating world.

Mr Streeter practised his healing holistically, but Mabel had to submit to starvation diets, the extraction of teeth and colonic irrigation, as well as manipulation to remove the toxins that were supposed to have built up in her body and to loosen the tension in her spine. It was a lonely hard experience without her dark-haired, dark-eyed, merry husband at her side, but something of her enjoyment of London can be understood in her description of a dinner party in Woburn Square. Her host was Fred Donnan, a shy Irishman, a bachelor don, professor of chemistry at University College London, who was close to Jim as a chemical colleague and close to Mabel as a friend from her Ulster childhood.

I went by tube to Russell Square & dined with the Donnans. A delicious dinner. The only other guest a completely inarticulate North of Ireland rough diamond (if diamond he be at all!) of the name Jimmy O'Neill! The conversation once more of food, food, food, varied by drink, drink, drink – in neither of these absorbing topics am I the least interested. Fred is nervously anxious somehow with me & after the talk of pure gourmandise he lends me the most delicious spiritual lovely appreciation of Shelley by Francis Thomson. Then at midnight I went home in a taxi with Mr Jimmy O'Neill, now distinctly friendly, almost affectionate, after so many drinks of every sort and description! Pouf! I can't bear these men with their minds on material things, & their poor blind souls restlessly asleep, or stirring unhappily in the darkness. I can't believe that however solidly built you are, square in the jaw, small in the eye, stubby in the nose, short in the neck, there isn't some imagination somewhere struggling to the light. On the other hand Fred is like a nervous sensitive thoroughbred – shying away from every bit of white paper on the road because he thinks its going to contain an emotion or a thought that he doesn't want to think, so he fills his outer personality with 'mushrooms à la something or other, pêches flambées', cocktails, wines. Queerer and queerer & all the time his mouth looks as if he needed comforting or like a naughty little boy that wants to be kissed.[5]

It could only be the unworldly imaginative Jim who in her mind suggested the obverse of her dinner companion.

Mabel came back to St Andrews, and the sun shone on her life again. Gradually – very gradually – she recovered. She felt confidence in Mr Streeter, whom she would visit again for occasional treatments. She would no more feel separated from the beauty all around her by the black pall of illness. She would return to London again and again, with Jim and without him, and when she became a widow she left St Andrews and went to live in a little house in Mayfair.

Late in the year of 1935, however, the call came again from the India Office, seeking Irvine's intervention in India: this time to investigate the failing Indian Institute of Science, under the guise of conducting its quinquennial inspection. He was to be responsible to the viceroy, Lord Willingdon, whose sway over India came at an intensely delicate time of transition. The Colonial Office had already good cause to know Irvine for the painstaking work he had recently contributed as a member of Ramsay

MacDonald's Economic Advisory Council on the post-graduate training of biologists (1931), with particular application to securing trained biologists for the colonial service. India optimistically believed that it would soon be able to train all of her own specialist forestry, veterinary and agricultural officers, but the British government was concerned about the current hiatus in the supply of trained biologists throughout the British empire.[6]

Acquainted thus far with the needs of the imperial service, Jim Irvine boarded the P&O mail ship the *Strathnaver* on 1 February 1936 at Marseilles. The voyage struck him forcibly as something quite different from the glitzy experience of the transatlantic liners: the contrast being between a crowd of 'people who could buy the world and those to whom the world belonged as of right'. He thought of Kipling, and he sat at the captain's table along with 'old Brown of the 41st Sikhs and old Jones of the Punjabis. Very decent old birds but very limited I'm afraid.' He attended divine service ('kirk' to him) and again he, who was so used to the crossing to New York, seemed surprised to discover his own culture: 'An immense congregation and very good singing, altogether inspiring and another contrast with the N. Atlantic methods.' Already the experience of travelling east began to play on his imagination, and his consciousness of the great divide between East and West would play a large part in the findings of his report on the Indian Institute of Science when it finally saw the light of day later in 1936.

Irvine's powers of observation were not reserved solely for the laboratory; he must be seen in the round as one who expressed in his life something of a chronicle of the age. He lived his times. He even admitted of himself that 'the feeling of power, of being in the inner circle of the affairs of Empire, is flattering to a man's vanity'. Very little of current affairs of state passed him by, he was well read in political and economic commentaries, and he never missed an opportunity to perceive at first hand the political undertones of the dangerous 1930s. His ship slipped in to Malta, where he noticed that 'the Navy is very busy in these waters and that if Brother Benito tries any monkey tricks he will find himself in trouble'. First-hand knowledge of the 'gathering storm' would at least prepare him mentally for the demanding task of leading a university in time of war.

On arrival in Bombay, he was looked after by the governor, Lord Brabourne, and dined by Sir Dorabjee Tata, the wealthy Bombay merchant who funded Bangalore's scientific research institute. The four days he spent in Delhi, as the guest of the viceroy at Viceregal Lodge, he considered to be an immense experience: the pageant of regal life, the guard of honour formed by turbaned, bearded warriors, the blaze of colour in the parks, and the whole vast composition of New Delhi. It was only five years since Lutyens' New Delhi had been inaugurated, and it presented an exquisite and overwhelming sight. New Delhi was already perceived by Irvine as Britain's legacy to India. The time he spent in Delhi interviewing ministers of state and civil servants was the prelude to the task that lay ahead of him in Bangalore. He would chair a committee of three in total, with a secretary, Mr Edmonds, a man of the old-fashioned public-school type. But before arriving in Bangalore, Irvine and Edmonds went about interviewing as many people close to the government as possible. This commission was sensitive politically and of first importance to India's future. A 'royal' car with a pennant, defying all traffic rules, enabled him to fit much into the short time at his disposal. The brief committed to him by Lord Willingdon was not just confined to the quinquennial inspection of the Institute of Science: there were many privately financed scientific research stations in India, and at a time of what was known in government circles as the period of 'Indianisation', the viceroy was concerned to impose standards and wipe out corruption. In the light of the new Government of India Act (1935) Irvine's work was to serve the task of Lord Willingdon and his counterpart in London, the Secretary of State for India, in formulating the principles whereby the central government would support with funds these several Indian research laboratories.[7] Already, as the exercise to replace European staff with Indian scientists progressed, the Bangalore scientific institute was showing signs of systemic financial and administrative failure, and Irvine's visit was overshadowed by the considerable difficulties of implementing the 1935 act. Willingdon wanted to pick Irvine's brains, and to use his special experience as one who had both built up a distinguished institute of chemical research in Scotland and who was carving out a sound financial base for his university.

Irvine travelled the 1,500 miles between Delhi and Bangalore by train: he was shocked by the insanitary and uncomfortable conditions of the ordinary Indian's mode of travel, and he was disturbed by this country of contrasts, where the lush suburbs of British civil servants and successful Indian businessmen stood close by squalid and fetid slums. As the train rattled along, mosques gave way to the brooding temples and little shrines of Hinduism. Mud villages peopled a landscape where, in medieval style, animals lived under the same shelter as the farmers. The depth of poverty was quite unlike anything he had ever encountered before.[8] Jim Irvine had left St Andrews in the spirit of the little Scotsman who had been called to serve God and the empire under a tropical sky. He managed to cling to his cheerfulness, but he was shaken by this country. He had already been apprised in Delhi that his job in Bangalore would not be straightforward.

Bangalore, when they finally arrived, bore all the appearance of an oasis in the desert. Handsome avenues, and fine houses set in gardens full of flowering shrubs and trees were evidence of a prosperity brought to it by the reforms of the enlightened Maharaja of Mysore and the hydro-electric plant at Shivanasamadra. At its heart was established the premier institute for scientific research and study in India. The Institute of Science, which had been munificently provided by two generations of the Tata family, was no more than thirty years old at this time, and its early years were stamped with the success brought to it by its founding director, the British chemist Morris Travers, who was Sir William Ramsay's collaborator in the isolation of the 'noble' gases. In 1933, Professor Sir Chandrasekhara Venkata Raman was appointed the first Indian director, after the resignation of Sir Martin Forster, an old friend of Irvine's. Other resignations from the ranks of the professors had followed when they found their departments neglected under the new regime.

Built on a vast campus, the institute attempted to provide for all the daily needs of its staff and students. All were housed within its grounds at Kumara Park, but Irvine's first impressions were of a web of intrigue and discontent. He set about things in the manner typical of a scientist: meetings in the morning, evidence taken in the afternoon, and writing up in the evening. The financial problems that lay at the heart of the malaise were exacerbated by decisions taken at the time of its foundation: the gift of a great benefactor and a national institution, the institute was, nevertheless, sited somewhat remotely in the independent state of Mysore. However, the British government wished to see research in India efficiently carried out in the service of developing India's industrial resources: therefore it had weighed in with large financial contributions, and to this, not to be outdone, the provincial governments had added their bit. The result was too many paymasters and an institution that was straying too far from the intention of its founder to promote Indian industry.

Once he began to take evidence, a sort of double-dealing faced Irvine: 'Patience is severely taxed in the cross-examination of very voluble gentlemen who are masters of the art of suppressing the truth without telling lies. If hard pressed, however, they don't hesitate to tell lies.' He grew used to what he called 'the shirt and trousers existence' of his work, but he never could grow used to the 'perpetual service, of having someone at your elbow all the time to fetch and carry', which he found demoralising to master and servant. The only exception was his charming bearer, Abdul, whom he longed to take back to Scotland with him. He mused that if Abdul were to settle in St Andrews and marry their parlourmaid, Thomson, all of their servant problems would be solved.

The hot weather of southern India came upon them early that year, but Irvine deplored the need for a siesta: it was a gross interruption of his work, he thought, but the heat made the ink in his fountain pen dry up. All the time he felt he was skating on thin diplomatic ice. Countless invitations from states and potentates had to be refused. But having innocently accepted an invitation to dine with the British Resident, the little committee could not then avoid the Maharaja of Mysore, who had to go one better and invite them for the weekend. It was a distraction from their work, but there, up in the hills, they saw many sacred places. They shopped in the bazaar and wandered through the gorgeous but empty halls of Tipu Sultan's summer palace, once plundered by the British. India began to grow on Irvine, and once he had returned to St Andrews it was the rich sunsets behind the silhouette of these hills that he remembered.

Jim was not eager to protract the work, having been lucky enough to procure for his return journey a first-class cabin on a P&O ship sailing on 28 March: such berths were in very short supply. That year of the Italo-Ethiopian war, no Britisher would sail on the Italian Lloyd-Trestino line, whose boats ran empty from Bombay. The stiff work of drawing up the report fell on his shoulders; and the day began an hour or two before breakfast – he and his colleagues working in their pyjamas – and continued until nightfall. The result was something exhaustive and condemning.

Within the five years since the previous quinquennial, very meagre work had been done at Bangalore to support India's industrial needs. The director, Sir C.V. Raman, was a brilliant physicist, FRS and Nobel prizewinner. In pursuing his own ambitions, he had quite patently ignored all applications and requests from industry for chemical and biochemical research; he had refused to conduct correspondence with any interest that challenged the physics and mathematics bias that he was developing. After resignations, two of the most important chairs – those of general and organic chemistry – had been vacant for three years, thereby weakening the authority of the institute. The director, who plundered other sections of the institute in order to expand his own department, had depleted the chemistry and biochemistry departments' laboratory equipment. Irvine's inspection strongly recommended that confidence and a degree of autonomy must be given to those of professorial rank and to their departments. There was, furthermore, no mechanism at the institute for bridging the gap between laboratory research into potential industrial applications, and the application of this knowledge in an industrial context. The report recommended there should be far less intellectual isolation, and it prescribed future co-operation with government bodies such as the Industrial Intelligence and Research Bureau and the Imperial Council of Agricultural Research. Research, in future, should be vetted by the institute's senate, and it should not be carried out at the director's whim.[9]

Raman immediately set up an attack on the Irvine Committee via the willing propaganda of the local newspapers, but there were further warnings from Irvine. Transparency of financial administration was insisted on for the future: the intellectual life of the institute had been undermined by a total lack of financial control, and it would soon have to draw on its reserves. A proper finance committee of seven was proposed, on which the director would have but one vote. There should be fair representation of all the universities of India at the institute. Particular emphasis was placed on building up the department of biochemistry, whose researches into food science and drugs were essential. In 1936, all of the indicators were that the departments of biochemistry and biology should be the lead departments.

The conditions provided for the student body were found to be ideal for the development of a happy and contented life within the institute, even if it was rather too lavish, but the students too were depressed and anxiously aware of the bad relations existing between the director and his staff. The committee laboured to make suggestions that would help the institute to attain a position where, without challenge, it could operate for 'the benefit of India', according to the wishes of its founder.

The official report, though damning, was thus constructive, but it carefully concealed Irvine's full opinion of all that he observed, and for that he wrote a private memorandum to the viceroy, to be handed to him by special messenger. As he recounted it to David Russell, the work could be described as 'classifying our witnesses into the two categories: half liars and complete liars, and finally writing two reports – one for use and the other for publication'.[10]

Only to Mabel did Jim tell the true story, 'which has proved to be quite different from what anybody expected and we have found ourselves in a maze of intrigue and political rivalry. As a result, our report is of so serious a nature that it is doubtful if it can be published.' 'East is East and West is West,' he reiterated despairingly. His report was published in May 1936 in its more measured form. In India it received a mixed reception; many had the common sense to admire this earnest attempt to unravel the problems that dogged a key element of the new India, but a long leading article in the Indian Academy of Science's journal was defensive and hurt.[11] Much was made by Raman's supporters of a feeling that Irvine's mind had been made up long before he arrived in Bangalore, and that this confident, experienced scientist from Scotland, who admitted that he had difficulty in understanding the Indian mind, wanted to impose his own construct on the resentful director, without paying enough deference to the Indian scientists.

However, several of the report's recommendations were adopted and a registrar was appointed to be the chief administrator. At the end of the year, the work of the Irvine Committee earned a leading article in *Nature*, and by 1937 Professor Sir Venkata Raman had ceased to be director. 'I have been fully paid for the India trip and so feel quite opulent,' Jim was able to note in April 1936.

This was not quite the last that Irvine heard of India. The students, all post-graduate scientists of India's new generation and highly regarded by Irvine, continued to feel nervous of the effect of Indianisation at the institute. Fearing political repercussions against themselves, they entrusted the professor of electrical technology, Kenneth Aston, to write to Irvine to urge him to return as the new director of their institute. Perhaps this was the last invitation of this sort that he would receive but, believing that what Bangalore needed was a director with a biological interest, he spoke to his colleague D'Arcy Thompson about the problem: 'What they need most is ... a man who can restore some happiness into a place which had become a Hell.'[12] Could Irvine have been thinking that he could send his attention-seeking colleague to southern India?

Jim Irvine looked back on his visit to India as an adventure, and he wrote to his friend David Russell: 'Our mission was both difficult and delicate, I am looking forward to telling you all about it and it's rather a thrilling story of a pilgrimage which took me into queer places and into the company of queer people.' It was, however, an adventure of serious import, and after seventy years the work in India of Jim Irvine, the Traveller in Education, has acquired a gloss from the technological and economic boom in Bangalore in our time. Irvine's final word is full of meaning for us today: perhaps he did play a part in the development of India's well-being. 'The whole experience left a deep impression on me and I can well understand the attitude of the Indian civilian who feels he is pledged to the service of India. The people are a strange mixture of good and bad, cunning and simplicity, culture and savagery, but the good predominates and some day in the far future India may lead the world.'[13]

The concept of colonialism was increasingly fostered in the 1930s in the West: an important exhibition devoted to the subject and conducted jointly by the governments of Great Britain and France took place in Paris in 1931. But the reality of life in the West Indies, West Africa, the protectorate of the Sudan and in Malaya was still largely ignored. Those who could surmount poverty and claim higher education came to Great Britain from these colonies: some were Rhodes scholars, but they were few in number. It was not an arrangement designed to develop the colonies from within, where illiteracy prevailed.

The fractured society of the West Indian islands of the Caribbean – multi-racial, insular and jealous of each other, ridden with disease, lacking in drive, and with no provision for higher education to set the institutional standard necessary to the West Indians' aspirations of government – was a dangerous case in point. In 1928, Dr Arbour Stephens, a retired chairman of Swansea Education Committee, took it upon himself to visit the West Indies armed with an introduction from the MP and president of the Board of Education, Lord Eustace Percy. Although self-appointed, Dr Stephens reported back to Baldwin, warning the government of the danger of allowing these countries, so rich in natural resources, but with a North American frontier, to remain cut off from the mother country. Open to the overtures of American big business, their loyalty could not be assumed in the future if nothing was done by the central government to address their medical and educational needs. He urged that what was required was an indigenous system of higher education in the West Indies, and that Great Britain should be connected to the West Indies by means of wireless communication – that twentieth-century channel of education, which was already supplied between the islands of the Caribbean and the US.[14]

In 1938, despite the imminence of war, a commission with a broad brief under Lord Moyne was sent out to the Caribbean to bring news of the British government's intention to address social conditions, labour, education, health and agriculture in the West Indies. Yet another rogue correspondent, the well-known broadcaster Arthur Calder-Marshall, wrote to Moyne's commission warning about the state of deprivation in the West Indies.[15] This time, concern was with the inadequacy of the medical facilities, which cried out for a teaching hospital and a university medical faculty to take the lead. The Moyne Commission recognised the key role that institutions of education should play in the West Indies, and Lord Moyne visited

Irvine in St Andrews. Rapid development of air transport and the growth of federalist tendencies provided the right opportunity. Yet nothing was done.

It was nevertheless an astounding demonstration of faith and liberality when, in August 1943, the wartorn British government set up another commission under the lawyer Sir Cyril Asquith, to take the matter further and to inquire into higher education in the colonies, including the West Indies. The advisory Asquith Commission comprised sixteen members, of whom Irvine, already sixty-six years of age and past normal retirement age, was one. On 21 September 1943, he began the committee work of Asquith's general remit, which was more concerned with principles than the application of those principles to any colony.

Jim, who by this time considered his continued wartime correspondence with friends in the US to be something of a patriotic duty, wrote to one saying: 'For my sins I have been appointed to a Royal Commission on the Colonies, hence a weekly trip to London under difficult travel conditions and much hard work – all this due to the fact that St Andrews has become a strong recruiting centre for officers in the Colonial Services.'[16] The visit to India in 1936 had made an impression on Jim Irvine's mind, and he retained a deep sympathy for the work of expatriate administrators, many of them young men who had so recently left his charge in Scotland.[17]

From the start, however, he made it plain that he would not be content to play the part of the elder statesman, appearing at meetings in London and then hastening back to Scotland. Two satellite committees of the commission were appointed to make enquiry on the spot as to how solutions might be applied to the local need: one would inquire into the West African problem, and one was to be sent to the West Indies, which was safe from the theatre of war. When the chairmanship of the latter was offered to Irvine in November 1943, he seized it with all the eagerness of a young man, and the composition of his delegation was announced on the BBC: Sir James Irvine as chairman, with Miss Margery Perham, Raymond Priestley, Philip Sherlock, Hugh Springer and T. Rowell as secretary. Once again Jim Irvine had been offered a mission, even an adventure, full of possibilities. Strictly speaking, he had no business to contemplate leaving his desk in Scotland, where the universities had been unexpectedly asked to prepare forecast budgets for the first quinquennia since war began of the Carnegie Trust and the University Grants Committee. These were to reflect putative university structures for a post-war Britain, and Irvine immediately set about burning the midnight oil in early preparation for his university's submission. It meant that for over a week, with little sleep, he laboured at structuring facts and figures to ensure his university's future.

In December 1943 he fell seriously ill on the eve of his son Nigel's marriage in London to Cecilia Banister, daughter of a naval officer. Neither he nor Mabel could attend their son's wedding, and they would never see Nigel again, for he was tragically drowned in May of the next year, while on active service. For some time, it looked as if Jim would be cheated of his great opportunity to be an ambassador for education in the West Indies. His doctor was most insistent that it was not a stroke, but it had all the symptoms of a stroke: he lost his speech and the use of his limbs. Medical opinion was that it was an extreme nervous spasm brought on by overwork. Guarded by the starchy authority of a permanent nurse, he calmly devoted himself to his recovery, and by mid-January he could walk about the house and in the furthest reach of the garden, where he was safe from the prying eyes of visitors. The Secretary of State for the Colonies in Churchill's wartime government, Oliver Stanley, pressed him to go ahead with the expedition, and his doctor also urged him to accept. Wisely, Dr McKerrow thought that his patient would have a better chance of recovery in the tropics, where he would be well fed and where, removed from the worst of the war, he could enjoy sunshine and something of outdoor life. Jim determined therefore to go to the West Indies, although it took much courage on his part to go ahead. Rowell, the devoted and capable civil servant appointed secretary of the Irvine Committee, travelled up to Scotland to go over every detail with him. Irvine was by then so much the grand old man of higher education that invariably people came to see him, rather than the other way round.[18]

The complexities of a mission briefed to bring unity and progress to an immensely diverse set of peoples not educationally well served were, at first glance, insuperably difficult and could only be regarded as an adventure by the Irvine Committee. The sense of adventure was heightened by the danger of the journey itself, which proved to be a real test of the courage and commitment of the participants. Irvine, although seemingly old and ill, was very much the ringleader of the 'Three Musketeers' – the three men of the party – as they set off in the blackout and the darkness of early morning on a sleety day in February 1944, at the height of the doodlebug attacks on London. The band of cheerful charwomen – 'plenty o'room, dearie' – who were their companions on a crowded bus to the Victoria air terminal were, in retrospect, the one bright spot on a journey of four days of sheer misery.

Before mounting the special train from Victoria to Poole, where a flying-boat was waiting for them, Irvine, Rowell and Raymond Priestley,

Vice-Chancellor of Birmingham University, were joined by the only female member of the group, Margery Perham, who was suffering from flu. Margery Perham, as an academic specialist in colonial administration, was an original member of the Asquith Commission. She was an Oxford blue-stocking, and her instinct was to be argumentative and opinionated; she would use this opportunity of visiting a part of the world new to her to collect data for her department back in Oxford. She was at that time more a specialist in African affairs, and her West Indian experience became a fresh perspective on her view of the interlocking roles of the 'white man' and the native populations of the British colonies. Irvine was afraid that she would prove to be an awkward member of his committee. Irvine and Priestley were, of course, experts in university administration, which was the real point of their visit. Priestley's past, as a polar explorer, endeared him still further to Jim: 'It is a safe guess that a distinguished Antarctic explorer will be a reliable travelling companion,' he noted. Jim Irvine, or Sir J., as Margery Perham called him, came in time to be fond of her, and theirs developed into a friendship of affectionate mutual admiration,[19] but in 1944 Irvine was what he had always been: a man's man, more at ease with male colleagues, comfortable in his male club, and used to doing business with a male dominated establishment. He liked women to be intelligent, gentle, decorative and at home. Some of his colleagues in Scotland had already felt that an element of chauvinism lay behind his initial reluctance to appoint the brilliant Margaret Fairlie to the St Andrews chair of obstetrics and gynaecology. However, Margaret Fairlie was eventually appointed in 1940, and was the first woman in Scotland to hold a chair. Margery Perham was a different matter. On the Asquith Commission, she had perplexed Irvine, and in the West Indies she became rather detached from the group, owing to the serious turn her illness took.

They were to fly – secretly of course – to Foynes on the Shannon, and then on by Pan Am Airways sea-plane via Lisbon, on an unannounced route that they discovered took in Dakar in West Africa, Natal and Belem in Brazil, and so on to Trinidad. The plane immediately before theirs, on the Foynes–Lisbon route, had been shot down by the Germans. Lisbon, their first port of call in the American aircraft, dazzled them with unaccustomed bright lights, even in the middle of the night. It was seething with a brittle, monied international set; for the first time since he left Leipzig, Jim found himself 'disagreeably conscious of German being spoken all around us' – 'a nest of spies,' he pronounced. Already, thrown into the challenges of a kaleidoscope of impressions, his cure from illness had begun.

Trinidad was their first Caribbean land-fall, and it would ultimately prove to be a happy but critical element in achieving their solution. When the group arrived, however, their reception was almost hostile, and the Irvine Committee met a wall of cynicism. After all, the West Indies had been bombarded by a wave of British government commissions, all of which had sailed away and done nothing, leaving the West Indians fed up with the mother country's good intentions. The recent Moyne Commission, with its enormous, self-defeating remit, had been the final straw.[20] The Irvine Committee faced a desperate situation, which Whitehall had barely begun to understand.

Irvine soon found that its strength would lie in the two West Indian members appointed to their committee: Philip Sherlock, an educator from Jamaica, and Hugh Springer, a Rhodes scholar lawyer, who had read for the English Bar but who had returned to his native Barbados to become a politician. Irvine was not initially told that the inclusion of two indigenous committee members was an innovation, and that he had been put in charge of a test experiment in human relations. Luckily, Irvine was not pompous; he had furthermore put an embargo on any discussion of their mission until the two West Indians could join the party. This policy helped to establish the open democracy of their group. The presence of Sherlock and Springer on the Irvine Committee was much more than a nod to local interest: both men would become to Irvine in particular warm friends and allies, who guided and supported him in the even more difficult years ahead, when Irvine pushed the cause of the University College of the West Indies through the prevarications of Whitehall, successfully bringing it into existence.

Jim Irvine, whose personal style was to be reserved, never admitted to a perhaps even more vital reason behind their collective success. One and all on the Irvine Committee fell for him: he was, in Raymond Priestley's words, 'their ideal as a Chairman'. They knew at once that his genial personality and active mind gave them a weapon well fitted to their exacting task.[21] His sense of theatre and even farce were never far away, and with these attributes he made some success of the interviews with their voluble West Indian informants, who had only to pause for breath whereupon he would leap in firmly: 'Dr X, the Committee are very glad to hear you end on that note.' This trick had often to be repeated.

The London contingent's warm appreciation of the parts played by Sherlock and Springer, not to forget the excellent Creole stenographer Miss de Verteuil, was, however, decisive for the smooth running of their enquiry; and the West Indians assured the Irvine Committee of a warm welcome wherever they went. In Trinidad they were joined by a Trinidadian, and in British Guiana by a native of that country. If ever the committee members met with an alien point of view, these West Indian colleagues mediated for them and helped to marry theory with reality on the ground. Once started, this mission met none of the resentment directed at Irvine when he visited India in 1936. In return, and by private agreement with his original colleagues, Irvine devised a way of breaking the ubiquitous colour bar. The group would refuse to go anywhere where all the members of the committee were not welcome, whether it was a dinner at a Government House or the necessity to stay at a hotel or country club.

Trinidad, where the Irvine Committee spent three weeks gathering evidence, was already the home of the Imperial College of Tropical Agri culture, and was also the would-be site of a projected Central Teacher Training Institute and a proposed medical school. The territory had some wealth and maturity, and it had to be admitted that it was a strong contender for the site of a new university. But, keeping open minds, Irvine and his colleagues assumed a policy of taking evidence from all levels of society: from archbishops to ordinary witnesses with a child to educate, they ignored nobody. The worth of the procedure they followed became clearer as they drew out answers to the two simple questions that Irvine had mulled over as he lay in his bunk on the Pan Am clipper, 'Is a university in the West Indies necessary? And if necessary, what kind of university ought it to be?' Some witnesses argued forcefully that the most that was required was a series of polytechnics – something that Irvine actually despised: 'semi-technical bazaars', he liked to call them. Others thought that a long drawn-out process of educational development should concentrate on primary education. Irvine's conviction was for a challenging education system led from the top by the privilege of research departments in a first-class university.

The colonial governors played a strong part in the process of acquiring information, and in this way the outfit moved from one island state to another: from Trinidad to British Guiana, to Jamaica and then Barbados, with a visit to Puerto Rico at the invitation of the US government to observe the university there. Puerto Rico prompted Jim to quote his hero, Liebig on visiting England: 'I saw much and learned little.' All the states of the British Caribbean were to be included, from British Honduras to the Windward and Leeward Islands: a triangular line equivalent to that which could be drawn between London, Moscow and Cairo. No-one could accuse the Irvine Committee of superficiality.

Irvine's early determination to give a research-led university to the West Indies must have been fed by his informed interest in all he could see of the region's under-capitalised, half-understood natural resources. In his free time he visited sugar plantations decimated by the British government's investment in home-grown sugar beet in places such as Fife; he visited the extraordinary pitch lake in British Guiana, from which Walter Raleigh had re-caulked his ship, and the bauxite mines on the banks of the river Essequibo; his scientist's eye took in the source of rubber in the tropical forests that they flew over, and he visited marine oil wells, yet barely exploited. These countries had resources rich beyond anything possessed by Europeans, and Irvine had always advocated the importance to industry of a lead given by the pure research departments of university faculties of science. The committee's report to the British government would place great emphasis on the value of a university in promoting specialised research associated with the Caribbean area. Ultimately, this approach was much commended by the British government.[22]

Irvine delighted in his team, whom he drove hard and charmed; he was eager for the others to share in his vision. In reality, a synthesis of the views of a committee composed of individuals used to getting their own way was not always easy to obtain. They continued their debate on the principles of education deep into the tropical nights, and in these private sessions his fellow committee members learned something of Irvine's ability to put his point of view so forcefully that none could deny him. One night he challenged his colleagues with the claim that the educational ladder was a Scottish invention. 'I am keenly interested in Toynbee's historical doctrine of "Challenge and Response",' he declared.[23] This dictum expresses Irvine's determined policy for the West Indies.

His diary expresses his satisfaction: 'With such a team it was no wonder that what we used to call "the university of our dreams" quickly took place.' Emotionally, this was of deep significance to him. In his beloved St Andrews, he was beginning to feel that the attack from the Dundee press was eroding all that he so dearly believed in. Here, in these beautiful tropical islands, he met gentle people who warmed to his character and were learning to appreciate all that his committee could do for them. Jim Irvine could feel as he had twenty-five years before: that he had the makings of the perfect university in the palm of his hand. 'The interviews with witnesses began to take a more definite form and we found ourselves engaged in the daily task of explaining the advantages of a unified university, the benefits of residence and our desire to produce a university of the first rank.' These, his beliefs, were rooted in St Andrews, and he set about applying them in the West Indies. He insisted that the plan should allow for a university chapel, despite the derision of local church leaders, who thought that the Students' Christian Movement would be sufficient. He insisted on the university being fully residential, to encourage the inclusion of all West Indians. The committee could appreciate the acute importance of establishing residential life in the new university, whose students would come from so far and from such diverse social backgrounds. In fact, the West Indies committee found that they were formulating a university exactly on the lines that Irvine had nurtured so personally in St Andrews. His experience with Dundee made him detest affiliated colleges, and he strongly argued that there should be no pandering to the island nationalism that clamoured for faculty colleges in each of the main islands.

On this, the vexed question of whether or not they dared choose a single site for the university in a loose collection of islands rent with jealousy, Irvine brought his fellow workers round to possibly having to resort to the blunt threat that they were prepared to recommend a unified university or no university at all. Jamaica offered the gift of an incomparable site: not far from Kingston, at Mona. The committee's originally icy reception in Trinidad had melted, and even the proud Trinidadians willingly accepted that unity was everything and that, rightly, the new university, complete with an initial three faculties – medicine, science and arts – should be sited in Jamaica, with distances of up to 2,000 miles separating the furthest-flung islands from the Jamaican site.

When Irvine and his committee finally retired to write up their report, they chose a sequestered spot – Sam Lord's Castle, a private club on the tip of Barbados – and there they worked solidly for a fortnight. Five more typists came to assist Miss de V., as they called their stenographer. As they thrashed out their views, Irvine's colleagues could not escape the steely streak that lay beneath his genial exterior.

Controversial elements in their proposal had to be resolved; the most glaring of these was Irvine's determination to see the Medical Faculty affiliated to McGill University in Canada, rather than to the more cumbersome mechanism of London University. Like some new British universities, the university in the West Indies would need an established tertiary institution to nurture it through its infancy and act as the degree-awarding power. Canada had strong diplomatic links with the West Indies, and McGill was well known to Irvine, who felt that he could factor a speedy and advantageous deal for the West Indies. Convinced of the political urgency, and perhaps blinded by his own friendship with McGill, Irvine stubbornly chose to ignore the fact that McGill was not allied to the British General Medical Council. It was Sherlock and Springer, and then the British Colonial Office, who ultimately persuaded him to drop the idea.

Miss Perham quarrelled violently with their chief over curricula. 'I have my doubts about Miss Perham,' Jim recorded, 'who has some queer views on curricula and doesn't seem to realize that the West Indies is not Oxford, or that Oxford is not perfect. What we don't want is to have a minority report submitted exhibitionally, by one woman.'[24] He took Miss Perham for long walks, they swam together, and he recounted stories to her – most tellingly, about Smuts and the evolution of European rule in South Africa. Priestley admiringly admitted that Irvine's urbanity ultimately won them all round.

The political aspect of their mission drove Irvine forward in his determination to see the report complete before they left the islands. He had arrived at the conviction that a single university for the whole British Caribbean, but on one site, and to which each state would contribute, would give the whole area a powerful but unified cultural identity. During these weeks, he and his committee had immersed themselves deeply in the whole question, and unlike so many earlier commissions and reports, their committee was ready to present an expert and forward-looking recommendation. Irvine did not want a moment to be lost by the British government in taking their proposal to the next stage. Every detail of the grand plan was put in place at Sam Lord's Castle. The budget was impressive: a detailed capital cost to include the endowment of chairs, and the staffing of every department and of the administration; the construction costs of the first buildings – faculties, library, chapel and residences – were also calculated. These capital costs would be a foundation gift from Britain. They placed an informed sum of £1.6 million against this. In return, the West Indian states would be responsible for the running costs. Providing for the cost of travel expenses for all West Indian students who had to journey from their home states to Jamaica was seen as a priority.

The committee's draft report was submitted to the Secretary of State on their return to London. As the months went by and the civil service sat on it, waiting for Walter Elliot's West African report to come in, Irvine began to fret.[25] He was conscious of a certain political danger in leaving the West Indians without a response; he felt committed to their cause. When Walter Elliot's report was eventually submitted, it had attached to it a minority report; a minority report could nullify, or at best weaken,

Elliot's recommendations. Irvine had to stifle his impatience and submit to
the due process of the civil service while his report was passed from hand
to hand. Christopher Cox, a specialist at the Colonial Office, contributed
his opinion: he was impressed by Irvine's note of urgency and added his
own plea that delay would imperil the West Indian unanimity that was the
committee's greatest achievement.

> The Committee know their own minds and have set out their case in
> a refreshingly lucid, direct and forceful document . . . The Commit-
> tee's achievement in apparently carrying West Indian opinion with
> them on the major question of a single university and in reaching
> unanimity among themselves as to its site, is all the more remarkable
> when one bears in mind the great difficulty which the Elliot Commis-
> sion is rumoured to have experienced in tackling similar problems in
> West Africa.[26]

Irvine had to contain his impatience for eighteen months. The West Indian
legislatures, in varying degrees, all eventually arrived at a commitment to
support the university. The Senate of London University met, and welcomed
the scheme into their care. Only then did the Asquith Commission feel
free to encourage the initiative, and the Colonial Office published Irvine's
report at the end of 1945.

It would be a University College affiliated to London University for a
space of years, after which it would go forward as a degree-awarding institution in its own right. This would be the rule applied to most of the seats of
higher education considered by the post-war Inter-University Council for
Higher Education in the Colonies, chaired by Irvine, although Malta, Hong
Kong and Malaya were given autonomy within two years.

As for the West Indies, Sir Raymond Priestley cheerfully admitted that
Sir James Irvine was the mainspring and chief driving force of this blueprint
for a colonial university. The Irvine Report was widely regarded as the Bible
of the colonial university world. Both Priestley and Irvine were prominent
in discussions within the Colonial Office concerning the appointments of
a principal designate and a director of extra-mural studies. The Royal Institute of British Architects and Sir William Holford were consulted on the
appointment of an architect, since it was felt that an architectural competition would introduce too much delay.[27] The plan for the buildings, by
Graham Dawbarn, was published in the *Times Educational Supplement* on
October 4 1947; and in this way the Medical Faculty opened its doors in

October 1948 to thirty-three medical undergraduates, with a teaching staff of fifteen, to be followed by the Faculty of Science in 1949 and the Faculty of Arts in 1950.[28] Irvine, in memory of his son, gave from his own library over 2,000 scientific journals to form the basis of a scientific library. The University College of the West Indies was granted a Royal Charter in 1949, and the occasion was marked by a leader in *The Times*.[29]

Irvine proved himself in the West Indies, and the Colonial Office did not let him go. He had been at home but a few months when Oliver Stanley, the Colonial Secretary, approached him with a request to join a commission to enquire into constitutional reform in Ceylon, as Sri Lanka was known at that time. This time, he was importuned not in his role as an academic, but for the wide range of his experience, his drive and his outstanding intellectual ability. But it would have been a distraction from his work in the cause of higher education, which was not by any means over, and Irvine did not go to Ceylon. The Asquith Commission had identified several other British colonial dependencies where it was desirable to have a national university. In the early spring of 1948 he flew to Khartoum in the Sudan, where the Gordon Memorial College on the bank of the Blue Nile was the object of his investigations. His only fellow delegate was Miss Penson, professor of modern history at London University. It was an intense visit of hard work, without the expansive experience that his committee had so much enjoyed in the West Indies. His brief was to report on how the Sudan could have a university with a scientific bias, using the already existing Gordon Memorial College as its foundation.[30] Jim absorbed experiences like blotting paper, and he was fascinated by this oasis of civilisation on the border fringe of Africa. Every morning Jim greeted the statue of Gordon of Khartoum, seated on a camel, which stood at that date outside Gordon College, and he thought of a family joke. The Irvine children had grown up on the amusing story told to them by some friends of their parents. Their son had wished to bid goodbye to 'Gordon' before going home to England. As an afterthought, the little boy, not realising that Gordon was not an animal, enquired who was the man on 'Gordon's' back. When Jim returned to England, yet another colonial university in the making could be added to Cyril Asquith's tally, and he could assure his younger daughter, the tomboy Felicity, that he had paid his respects to the mounted figure of General Gordon.

If the University College in Jamaica, later to become the University of the West Indies, was modelled on St Andrews University, the compliment was returned when the first hall of residence was named Irvine Hall. As a tribute to Sir James Irvine, their university's founding father, the West

Indian students enquired if they could adopt the scarlet gown, but made of cotton rather than the thick woollen fabric appropriate to the east winds of Fife. The deep significance of this gesture was cherished by Irvine, and the West Indians asked him when they should wear their gowns. 'I could do no more than tell them the custom of our St Andrews students, impressing on them that the wearing of the gown was a symbol of their adoption into the brotherhood of learning.' His last visit to the college in Jamaica was in 1950, to attend the installation of Princess Alice, Countess of Athlone, as Chancellor. She would be sworn in with the same oath that was used in St Andrews, and which had been heard there not long before at the installation of the Duke of Hamilton as Chancellor. Mabel and their unmarried daughter, Felicity, accompanied him for this special occasion. For the St Andrews *Alumnus Chronicle*, he affectionately described a quiet Sunday morning's drive in the vicinity of Kingston: 'Round a corner emerged a group of cyclists each with a Scarlet Gown slung over his shoulder. They were students of the University who had been to church in Kingston and were now making their way back to the Residences in College. It was exactly the kind of thing we see every day in the Double Dykes or in Market Street, and it warmed my heart.'[31] St Andrews' foster-child was coming of age.

SIXTEEN

The Second World War

The prospect of war hung like a dark cloud over the households of all classes of the British empire during the decade leading up to September 1939: it was an anxiety that was felt no less in the quiet backwater of St Andrews and within the old-fashioned family that Mabel Irvine ruled in the house on the Scores. Always bitterly critical of the pacifist socialist government, and with her mind fed by her husband's old distrust of Germany, she noted in 1930 that Ramsay MacDonald was determined to cut off aid to school cadet corps, the training ground for troops in the Great War. 'It seems shutting the stable door when the steed is stolen,' she wrote.[1] The sight of her teenage son in his OTC khaki uniform, however, did not at that date have too much significance for her. It was a boyhood rite of passage. Jim, increasingly anxious for the future safety of his son, as well as for the social fabric of his life's work, watched and warned: he spoke publicly on both sides of the Atlantic of the very real dangers of disarmament, but he was gentle by nature and he loathed the means by which he had helped to bring an end to the hostilities of only twenty years earlier. Once a 'new man', now the senior figure in Scottish higher education, he liked to stand by values of more worth than the shifting sands of trade alliances and economic greed: 'We are told that the relationships of nations are ultimately based on trade . . . that treacherous function on which man so pathetically pins his faith.'[2]

Through the minds of Principal Irvine and many like him flitted that vexed question of whether their country should arm or disarm, and to Mabel he wrote from America: 'I must say I don't like this situation a bit – poor Britain has tried to be a peacemaker and to disarm, with the result that these savage Germans and greedy French get the whole world at logger-heads.'[3]

As a scientist, Jim maintained an international life of friendships and collaborations, which gave him the privilege of knowing something from the inside about current scientific development in Germany; he had long felt that he had an insight into the German political mind. He responded positively – 'your timely action has my warm support'[4] – when the Fabian-esque William Beveridge wrote to him in May 1933 to ask if he would contribute his name to a select list, mainly of scientists, who were heading an appeal on behalf of displaced university teachers from Germany and other parts of central Europe in which persecution was taking place. This, the Academic Assistance Council, under the chairmanship of Lord Ruther-ford at the Cavendish Laboratory in Cambridge, grew into the Society for the Protection of Science and Learning (SPSL). Irvine, as a founder member of its council, joined a mainly London- and Cambridge-oriented group that included John Maynard Keynes and Sir Frederick Kenyon, who would become chairman of the society after the death of Rutherford. Bever-idge was surprised to find from men like Irvine how international natural science was.[5] The stated aim of the Academic Assistance Council in 1935 was to be non-sectarian, although the many refugees whom they helped with grants over the following ten or twelve years were almost exclusively Jewish. It was partially funded by a small sum taken from the salaries of British academics. Out of the thousands of cases submitted to them, the names of many well-known Jewish scholars appear, and to those on the council, like Irvine, the SPSL served as a personal wake up call, if one was in fact needed.

Irvine's membership of Rutherford's council was not just an empty gesture. Although it remained the fact that St Andrews' departments were not flush with either staff or money, and positions there remained hard-fought-for, already in 1934 and ahead of any action taken by the Academic Assistance Council, the students and citizens of St Andrews subscribed to produce two post-graduate scholarships to the university to support a Jewish student from Germany and a political refugee.[6] When Walter Leder-mann, a mathematician from Berlin, was awarded the scholarship for a Jewish student, a certain formal difficulty had to be overcome: his qualifica-tion in Germany was a diploma and not a degree. The St Andrews PhD is a post-graduate degree, and Irvine was proud to chair the meeting of the St Andrews Senatus Academicus that 'for the first time in five hundred years' permitted a student with only the German state diploma to be admitted to study for a post-graduate research degree. Irvine got a taste for bending his university's rules to enable displaced persons to study in St Andrews, and the years ahead would see a remarkable scheme flourish that allowed Poles, Norwegians and Czechs to pursue their studies there. A modest but comfortable arrangement, typical of Irvine's sensitive handling of student welfare, was made for the otherwise destitute young German. Ledermann wore the scarlet gown, took lunch as the guest of the Students' Union and dined formally every night in St Salvator's Hall.

Walter Ledermann discovered that he had fallen into a musical university. When Mabel Irvine's Musical Society brought the famed Griller Quartet to perform there, the young Berliner felt he had witnessed one of the finest performances of chamber music he had ever heard. Ledermann had a considerable talent as a violinist to add to his distinction as an algebraist, but despite these attractive skills in a donnish young man, he encountered small jealousies in the town and at the university. Not all of the professor class were as well-informed as the Principal, and on successfully completing his PhD, Ledermann was told by a professor of philosophy that he would, of course, have to go back home to Germany. Others in St Andrews, including Turnbull, the professor of mathematics, were more caring, and luckily a post in the mathematics department fell vacant in the summer of 1938, and the professor was pleased to offer this to his former PhD student. Turnbull's kindness and Irvine's action were not ill-conceived: Ledermann was a brilliant mathematician and he brought honour to St Andrews, but Turnbull was severely criticised by some of his colleagues, who jealously guarded such posts for 'our own people'. Such was the confused corporate spirit of the old grey town. When Ledermann proposed the novel idea of publishing a series of pocket books on mathematics, he was firmly told that his own name, being German, could not be associated with the little books, and two of his colleagues in the mathematics department had to assume editorship. Safe in his St Andrews post, however, Ledermann avoided internment, and in 1940 he took British citizenship.[7]

Of course, Irvine had unbendingly to put the needs of his university first. His nurturing of the delicate social and economic balance that existed in St Andrews was put to the test at this time, and despite the considerable pressure that was put on Irvine by Beveridge and refugee groups to take further deserving cases onto the St Andrews' staff, the only other refugee who found a post there before war broke out was Erwin Freundlich. To Irvine's pleasure he came through a purely personal and scientific connection, and not an official channel. Freundlich was an outstanding man; the friend and collaborator of Einstein, he had carved for himself an international reputation as a mathematician-turned-astronomer who had built two observatories: one in Istanbul and the other at the Charles University in Prague, from which he had been obliged to flee.

A.S. Eddington, the Cambridge mathematician and astronomer, knew of Freundlich's position and felt he could confide in Irvine, whose path crossed with his on a number of occasions. Freundlich, although not a Jew himself, was married to a Jew and was devotedly the adoptive father of his wife's sister's children, Hans and Renate. His tall frame and kindly manner soon became well known in his adopted city: St Andrews took pride in ranking him among its characters, and the 'Herr Professor' seemed to be loved by one and all, and by none more than the Irvines. He established a personal niche for himself as he built up St Andrews' distinguished astronomy department, where he would come to be appointed to the new Napier Chair of Astronomy. This important chair was endowed by the daughter of the late Professor Sir Peter Scott Lang, in fulfilment of her father's difficult testamentary wishes of February 1927 that his family would found the Napier lectureship in astronomy in St Andrews, provided that the university built an observatory with the necessary instruments, 'so that [Napier's] genius and the very great benefits which it conferred on the Human race may be kept fresh.'[8]

Just after the outbreak of war, in the Gatty Marine Laboratory, Professor D'Arcy Thompson had to be encouraged by Irvine to be stony-hearted when he was begged to take in a German scholar, a Dr Friedmann, whose particular line of work was already being competently explored at St Andrews.[9]

To return to the Irvine family, in 1936 Nigel Irvine took his honours science degree from St Andrews. He could well feel that he was satisfying one of his father's ambitions, but he also grew to realise that he simply did not want to follow his father into a career in science. Later that summer he felt able to admit that he wished to go to Oxford to read law and then enter the English Bar as a member of the Middle Temple. Jim hid from his son his disappointment in him. As a specialist practitioner at the Patent Bar, Nigel argued, his science could never be lost, and he found to his pleasure that his father determined to trust him absolutely. This open trust between father and son gave rise to a mature period in their relationship, when Jim seized on many reasons to spend time in Oxford in the company of Nigel and his talkative friends. Nigel's contemporaries at Oxford formed an interesting generation, and among his year in Corpus Christi College was a most engaging scientific Rhodes scholar from Tasmania, with whom he shared rooms and a scout – whom they called 'Alph', with an obscure nod to Coleridge's 'Kubla Khan'. Dick Gandy and Nigel became firm friends; they shared a fondness for walking in the Tyrol and exploring central Europe which, despite the rise of Hitler, exerted a certain charm over almost all of these young people. Dick was invited to spend the Christmas vacation at University House in St Andrews, and Nigel thought that this cultivated and good-looking Australian might hit it off with his gentle elder sister, whom he regarded as something rather special.

Christmas with the Irvines in those years just before war broke out was a very jolly affair, with a round of private dances to fill the calendar. They tried to be lighthearted; Mabel booked a band, but unbeknownst to her Nigel had also booked a band. One had to be paid off, and Nigel was scolded, but Dick Gandy danced his way into their hearts: he sang German Lieder, and Mabel accompanied his fine tenor voice. He and Veronica fell in love, and settled down to that delicious thing: a deepening affection conducted between Oxford and St Andrews by means of letters.

The Principal of St Andrews University now had a future son-in-law to add to all the others about whom he worried. He lent a willing ear to government ministers whom he met in the Athenaeum and even on the train to King's Cross, and he acquired much information with which he tried to protect the two guiding forces of his life: his university and his family. A letter to Mabel written in London in 1939 is extraordinarily revealing of how a Scottish principal put himself behind the scenes of Westminster's policy-forming debates. He was, of course, a member of the Vice-Chancellors' Committee: a large body not without influence, and comprising all the leaders of higher education in Britain. Jim privately considered it prolix and vapid. On 29 April 1939, he attended one of their meetings. He had words beforehand with the Secretary of State for Scotland.

We had before us an advance confidential draft of the new Military Service Act and were asked to advise on the framing of Regulations which will be added to the Bill at the Committee stage in the House. Everything had to be done in a hurry for our recommendations had to be in print by the evening and it was disconcerting to observe the failure to grasp at the first essentials and to see valuable time taken up with secondary details. Actually I found my talk with the Secy for Scotland at once a great help and a serious embarrassment for he told me more than I could possibly disclose and I had to be mighty careful to keep clear of the suspicion that I had been in touch with a Cabinet Minister who had given, in confidence, more information than he was expected to divulge. I have a shrewd suspicion that Lord Eustace Percy[10] was in exactly the same position and in the end we had a considerable effect on the findings. We have recommended that every student already embarked on a course should be allowed to finish it before taking their Military Service and that all professional students should have an uninterrupted run of 4 years from the date of their first beginning . . . nothing emerged which throws any new light on Nigel's case or Dick's, but of course I'm keeping a careful look-out.[11]

Jim grew more and more irritable: he could only depend on his extraordinary ability to sleep refreshingly. To sleep deeply and dreamlessly at any time and in any place remained his greatest physical asset in a life in which he imposed such demands on himself. Very occasionally his sleep was violently disturbed by a dream, and only in this way did he allow his inner fears to come to the surface; only then did his vulnerability ever show itself, so carefully had he built up a protective carapace around his family and St Andrews. On the train going south on the night of 28 April 1939, his disturbed dreams revealed fears that what he loved would be destroyed. He dreamed that St Andrews was shattered by an earthquake so violent that his house rocked to its foundations and that, with a roar, a chunk of the cliff broke away and fell into the sea, while mortar oozed out of the structure of University House. In his dream he, Mabel and their two daughters leaned out of his study window, watching the world disintegrate around them, and to their horror they saw that the tower of the chapel had been rent in two: the tower that had for so long been the moral guardian of his thoughts and guide of his life.

On reaching the Athenaeum for breakfast, he opened *The Times*, and there he read in full the speech that Hitler had delivered to the Reichstag exactly at the time when his train was roaring through the night and he had tossed and turned, tormented by his dread of another war.[12] No-one could now deceive themselves about Hitler's intentions: his move into Poland could only be weeks away. Principal Irvine's work for St Andrews grew heavy as extraordinary measures were imposed. He decided that he must spend his long vacation within easy reach of St Andrews; and Synton, a country house in the Scottish Borders, thirty-four miles from Edinburgh, was taken for their holiday. Here, Mabel and Jim consciously and deliberately drew around themselves a gathering of family and their good friends. Veronica had become engaged to Dick, and Dick and several others of Nigel's special circle visited. At first, Jim allowed himself to be boyish again in the daylight hours, but at night he worked late, and as the end of August drew near the tennis racket and the fishing rod were forgotten, and the family crept back to St Andrews early. Germany invaded Poland on 1 September 1939.

Nigel, although in a protected profession, volunteered for the Royal Naval Volunteer Reserve (RNVR). Veronica and Mabel worked for the Red Cross, and Felicity, with her fair curls pushed under a cap, worked as a driver for the RAF, driving a bus of air force workers to Leuchars and back, day in, day out. Dick, who was an aeronautical physicist, applied to join the RAF, but he had to swallow his pride and settle down to his war work of designing aircraft at the National Physical Laboratory in Teddington and in Manchester: his was unquestionably a reserved occupation. He worked with Barnes Wallis, the designer of the bouncing bomb made famous by the raid carried out by 617 Squadron, 'The Dambusters', in 1943; he was collaborating with a strange collection of mathematical boffins. His future father-in-law knew that this would be a physicists' war, but the chemist principal was once again sent by the government to his laboratory in St Andrews to do war work in the field of chemical weaponry.

Principal Irvine clung to the common conviction that this was a holy war, and his letters to America spoke of how 'Britain with a clear knowledge of what it means has taken up the challenge on behalf of the oppressed'. His immediate responsibility lay in keeping his university going, in good heart and holding firm to a belief in a better future. Above all, an arrangement for funding the universities during wartime had to be worked out. As a trustee of the Carnegie Trust for the Universities of Scotland, he was party to the trust's special arrangements for providing capital funding to the Scottish universities at this time: not by quinquennia, but by annual distribution of one fifth of what might be deemed a quinquennial grant. Student beneficiaries of the Carnegie Trust whose studies were to be interrupted by the war would have their places and the fees held in credit by St Andrews University until they could return to their degrees.[13] This was all most reasonable, one might think, but it was a laborious arrangement to put into effect; nevertheless, Irvine fought hard for it in his committee deliberations. This form of funding could never lend itself to any forward management of the universities. It was hand-to-mouth, and it was a hand-to-mouth existence that took place in every home. In the Principal's residence, all but three small rooms on the first floor were for most of the war put under dust sheets. They were eventually left with one part-time worker, an old man who carried in the coals. Mabel and Felicity took charge in the kitchen, while Jim lunched in college. The maids, who could get better wages in a munitions factory, left them; the fine cast-iron gates and railings that had furnished the drive and gardens of the Principal's residence also went: the iron – they were told – was to make tanks for Russia.[14]

Jim and Mabel had persuaded Dick that he and Veronica should marry soon: long wartime engagements, they felt, were invidious affairs, but it would be a wedding without champagne, and the guests on 16 March 1940 were for the most part in uniform. Despite this, their friends flocked to St Andrews to attend the service, which was conducted by the Dean of the Thistle, Charlie Warr. Veronica's wedding dress was reputedly made from the last bolt of French silk satin to come out of France, jealously kept by her dressmaker for an important occasion. In St Andrews, attractive pieces of old furniture could still be picked up at the local roups, or auctions, to furnish the couple's first home; and in Dundee a couture dressmaker was found who would make a trousseau. Nigel was granted leave, and the wedding of Principal Irvine's 'popular daughter' was widely reported in the press. The family's many friends raided their attics for acceptable presents: an antique mirror, perhaps, or some old Spode, or a fine carved chair.[15] It was a good way to set up Veronica and Dick in the little flat in the south-west suburbs of London that became the hub of 'the London section' of the Irvine family, as Jim would refer to Veronica's married home. During the war years Nigel, on twenty-four hours' leave, would often find his way out to Dick and Veronica at Hampton Wick in the blackout, braving the bombs to make a surprise visit; or Jim, whose meetings in London seemed to multiply under the prevailing conditions, would appear at tea-time out of the London fog. Dick's salary would be for many years considerably less than his princely Rhodes scholarship, and Jim and Mabel gave them much help. The wartime marriage of their elder daughter was an occasion of happy resolution for them. War, however, had broken the golden thread that Mabel had drawn around her family in St Andrews, and Jim and Mabel lived out every day with dread in their hearts: both Nigel and Veronica were now far from home and in danger.

Nigel was offered the opportunity of attending a course in radar in 1941. With his legal practice put to the back of his mind, and a renewed interest in science, he could now engage in long scientific discussions when at home, going some way to overcome Irvine's secret disappointment that his son was not a chemist. Nigel was appointed radar officer to the heavy cruiser HMS *Berwick*, on the dangerous Murmansk convoy in the North Atlantic. While waiting impatiently to join his ship at Scapa, he was sent to Glasgow to fit a gunboat on the Clyde with radar. It was in a gloomy Glasgow hotel that he noticed an exceptionally pretty girl, the daughter of Captain Banister, under whom he had worked in the admiralty at the beginning of the war. The conversation that they struck up revealed Cecilia Banister as sensitive and musical, and destined to be special to Nigel. She was very young, and Nigel's leaves were unpredictable, but she soon became close to both the London and the St Andrews branches of the Irvine family.

Principal Irvine's university job in these years was a strange one: the projected changes in education made him reflect deeply. As a philosopher of education, he considered that what Scotland would need after the war was a post-graduate technical university that attracted advanced students from the other universities. He became a strong advocate of the 'gap year'.[16] He found himself in the role of counsellor and friend to a student generation that, on graduating, would find not a gateway to the life that they deserved but chaos, disorder and uncertainty. He tried to send them out into the world with a special mission, for these students would be called upon to restore a broken world. With fluctuating numbers and staffing, and with the usual Treasury grants suspended, the Principal had to keep the show on the road with as much maturity and vision as could be mustered.[17] As junior staff were called up, Jim seized the chance to rediscover his old self: the lecturer in chemistry.

The Workers' Educational Association, as an extra-mural arm of his work in higher education, was a branch of education to which Principal Irvine readily turned during the war. In some senses, it picked up on the unsuccessful University Extension Lecture Scheme that had been set up in Dundee in 1874. Characteristically, from the time of its fresh start in 1927, Irvine took a lead in the WEA and made a plea that it should be professionally administered. The opportunity to use it to provide educational stimulus to members of the forces gave a new purpose to the Joint Regional Committee for Adult Education, and Irvine lined up some of his best staff to conduct talks. These included literature, of course, but they ranged from wood engraving to a well-planned course on the integration of the sciences. Admittedly, some of the titles suggest the forced jokes of the after-dinner speech rather than higher education, but alongside Professor Dickie's 'Nonsense in Life and Literature' we have Principal Irvine talking about 'Science and War' and – his latest fascination – 'Oil'. On the whole, the topics offered were of a deeply serious and current nature, and a report on the scope of the wartime classes is endorsed by Irvine as being 'very remarkable'. A scheme that brought to the lives of ordinary men and women something of the confidence that education could give displayed a certain similarity to the spirit of adult education in Glasgow that had been so valuable to James Irvine's father eighty years before.[18]

In fact the war gave Jim Irvine a greater opportunity than he had enjoyed for a long time to relate to students. Fifteen years earlier, and in response to student request, he had instituted the tradition of the chapel address at the end of each academic year. His wartime chapel addresses were heavy with meaning: he might have been a theologian, and he certainly was not afraid to make a confession of his own faith; but he also, for a space of time, stood as one with them, his students.[19] As the moral leader of his university, even in 1940 he knew that he was already playing an important part in fashioning the new social order of the post-war world – a world to which his student soldiers would return, and to which his wartime students must somehow look forward. Irvine used these years to prepare for the extraordinary challenges that would face him when the war ended: the universities would be vastly inflated in numbers, and there would be a demand for new departments but, above all, the Medical School in Dundee would face a complex reordering and fresh approach to funding, if teaching hospitals were to be nationalised.

Through the work of the SPSL, William Beveridge, known of now as the author of the post-war welfare state, had become fascinated by Irvine, whose advice he sought while the 1942 Beveridge Report on Social Insurance and Allied Service was being put into effect. As a man successful in administration, Irvine's value to the mandarins was perceived as considerably greater than might be suggested by the size of the small institution that he governed. Alas for Jim and Mabel, because this conceited man invited himself so often to University House, and without his ration book, that jokingly they felt the Principal's official residence in St Andrews should change its name to the Beveridge B&B.

Seven days a week Jim kept up his necessary but monotonous war work, keeping fit by means of his morning swim in the North Sea and the occasional game of tennis. Late in 1940 St Andrews was bombed: two laboratories at the Bute medical department to the west of the university library suffered in the attack, and there was considerable damage to books in the library. Such setbacks would have been keenly felt in peacetime, but in 1940 Jim shrugged off the worry, thankful that it was not worse. When things were black, he cultivated the skill of living in the past. His mind reverted to America constantly, sometimes just to call up the memory of happy times: surely these congenial people, whose friendship he had grown to rely on, would not desert him or Britain. His old friend, 'Ed' Harkness, was too set on American neutrality. In March 1940, Lord Halifax had spoken publicly about a 'special relationship' that existed between Britain and the US (perhaps the first time that this phrase had been used), and Jim

Irvine, who was held in such respect by Americans, resolved to do what he could to turn America around and bring her into the war. His friends, Nan and Willis Wood, with their estates on Long Island and property in New York, had close friends in high places; they would be well placed to assist him, and in June 1940 he wrote a letter to Nan that she copied several times to show to like-minded Americans who were in the opposite camp to Lindbergh, the isolationist.

> Your letter and the news that France has thrown in her hand arrived together today, and the comfort afforded by the one was sorely needed by the stunning blow of the other. Poor old Britain, the country which went to war without thought of gain (and with the certainty of loss) so that freedom might live in this world has had to stand so many treacheries that faith in God can scarce survive. Faith in man has long since gone by the board – first the perfidy of Russia in August 1939, then the betrayal of Norway, the unspeakably cowardly action of King Leopold, the perfidy of Italy and finally the panic collapse of France with all that will entail for the Second British Expeditionary Force to be left high and dry through desertion of Allies. In this gloomy recital I have said nothing about America's attitude about which one hears precious little criticism – only a vast disappointment that the champion of Liberty should stand aside when tyranny is hammering down all that is dear to free people. America surely had a great opportunity to give a lead and take the lead; in these days of 'Blitzkreig' the opportunity passes and does not come again.
>
> So Britain fights on alone after carrying the heavy end of the burden for ten months, for, without the British Navy and Air Force, France would not have survived the autumn. The losses of France have been concentrated into a few days, while ours have been continuous and therefore less spectacular though none-the-less heavy. Now we are an island fortress and have to stand the greatest siege in history; may we be worthy of our fathers.[20]

Perhaps Irvine's long practice in the art of persuasion had been noted in Whitehall, and during August 1941 the sort of strange commission that only war could throw up was offered to him: he was asked by the British government to lead a British cultural mission to the South American countries. The temptation to accept the new experience of a diplomatic post extending for the greater part of a year was great, but he refused on sound grounds: he did not speak either Spanish or Portuguese, he had no previous experience of Latin America, and 'the fact that I am a successful chemist in English does not fit me to become a successful diplomat in Spanish'. Had the invitation been to head a mission to the United States, which he knew and felt that he partially understood, he would have gone like a shot. Halifax, whom he continued to admire, had recently gone to Washington as British ambassador, and Irvine would have liked to work with him. Harkness had once felt that the only job Irvine might take in preference to his principalship would be to head the British Embassy in Washington. Jim kept up the pressure on his American friends:

> The America I know is too proud to be content to leave it to others to fight for freedom; equally, the America I know is not a selfish country which can be stirred to action only when her own immediate security is threatened. The chivalrous America would fight to the death for a principle and count not the cost. But there is an America I do not know, with its Wheelers and Lindberghs[21] who preach the forlorn gospel of isolationism and it is heart-breaking to see how their influence is holding back the country from a step which I believe to be inevitable and which, if taken now, will shorten the war and be for the benefit of the whole world. And now is the time to act without a doubt.[22]

The Japanese attacked Pearl Harbour on 7 December 1941, at last bringing America into the war in support of its allies. It was with great personal relief Jim could write that the Union Jack and the Stars and Stripes were then flying from the same masthead; he looked to a day when there would be a great family of the English-speaking nations.

Principal Irvine didn't have too long to wait before he could once more put to the test his new skill at bending the university ordinances governing matriculation and the awarding of degrees. He who, earlier in his life, had taken pride in being the architect of new ordinances of this kind now took impish pleasure in persuading his stickier colleagues that the university could even be enriched by bending the rules and accepting for entry to the university scores of young Poles, all servicemen, many of whom had had to abandon their higher studies in Poland without obtaining a degree. On the fall of France in June 1940, over 20,000 Polish troops – all that remained of the Polish fighting formations that had defended France – were evacuated and reformed in Scotland under their commander-in-chief and prime minister, General Sikorski, to continue their stand against barbarism. In

the autumn of 1940, the 1st, 2nd and 3rd Rifle Battalions of the Free Poles
arrived in St Andrews to be billeted in small hotels all over the town. With
headquarters in Cupar, the county town of Fife, and in Forfar, they mounted
guard on the shores of Fife and County Angus. They were anxious to learn
as much as they could of this new country.

The people of St Andrews were deeply touched by the brave band of
exiles who had lost everything, most of all their country, and yet who sang
through the streets on Sunday mornings on their way to mass at the little
Roman Catholic church overlooking the sea on the Scores. Something of
a welcome culture shock shook up the rather dour society of this town;
nothing like it had been seen in St Andrews before, especially on a Sunday
morning. People responded with warmth and hospitality: the gallant Poles
brought colour and music into the grim monochrome world of Britain
during the war, and the Scots loved it.

The hospitality that Principal Irvine offered to these young men was of
a different order – he offered the hospitality of his university. Not only did
he bend the rules of admission, he ignored them. He opened his libraries,
laboratories and lecture rooms to Poles, who would then be able to study
towards a St Andrews degree. They arrived, bewildered by the language
spoken around them, and they responded so well to the opportunity that
was offered that in March 1942 a law school, bringing a qualification in
Polish constitutional law, was inaugurated in the university's beautiful
seventeenth-century Parliament Hall, to prepare the Polish soldier students
for a future time of peace in which they could return to Poland and govern.
With such idealism, Jim Irvine tried to infuse their spirits with hope, and
the Poles described his action as a ray of light in dark and gloomy days.
Over seventy degrees were conferred on Poles in St Andrews during these
years. In 1941, General Sikorski was invested with the honorary degree of
LLD in a fine ceremony that took place not in the detested, overblown
Younger Hall, but in the romantic Parliament Hall, a public mark of the
friendship between St Andrews and the Polish people. The colours of his
LLD hood picked up the colours of Poland: red and white.[23]

Strange encounters happen in war, as Jim Irvine had discovered during
the 1914–18 conflict. One such was thrown up by a lecture that he gave to
the Scottish Polish Society in 1942. Resuming the mantle of scientist, he
lectured on Marie Curie, the Polish Nobel prizewinner, and in so doing he
revealed his old mistrust of German scientists in possession of dangerous
materials. At the end of the Great War, Marie Curie, who had been given
$50,000 by the women of America, bought 1 gram of Belgian radium, and

this, he told his audience, she had given to her native Poland. Irvine threw out to the audience the grave but rhetorical question of whether or not it was safe. He was staggered to be answered by a Pole in the audience. He was Marie Curie's nephew, he said – and yes, it was safe.

Ultimately, the intellectual breadth of the university was widened by the wartime Scottish–Polish friendship. In collaboration with the Polish Minister of Education in London, the university introduced lectures in Polish history and literature as one of the subjects leading to a St Andrews MA degree, and this lectureship was renewed on Principal Irvine's initiative in 1949.[24]

St Andrews took to its unusual wartime multi-nationalism with spirit. The circumstances of war brought, in the wake of the Poles, many high-ranking Norwegians, Yugoslavs and Czechs to a university town that had never entirely lost the medieval sense of what Irvine valued as 'the brotherhood of learning'. A dinner had to be given to five American congressmen who wanted to observe the presence of the Poles in Scotland: a silly business, thought Jim; but on the other hand, King Peter of Yugoslavia was given the by then well-tried Irvine treatment of a conducted tour round the historical landmarks of the university. Mabel opened up the fine rooms of University House for what could be described as '*salons des refugiés*', and with a pretence at pre-war gaiety, a luncheon for General Sikorski became a table of the generals, with General Rasckiewicz, the president of Poland in exile, and General Pasckiewicz as guests of the Irvines. At an evening party Jan Masaryk, the Czech nationalist, could be discerned. The Irvine's little granddaughter had been given a lady's bracelet to play with, and she screamed when it was taken away from her. 'Ah, she has only lost a temporary possession,' the Czech could be heard darkly to say.

Academic hospitality was a fine thing, but very early on Felicity Irvine, who had inherited a great deal of her father's vitality and staying power, saw that the welfare of the servicemen in St Andrews – British as well as Polish – should be addressed. She, Anne Sutherland and Avril Moir-Gray led a group of townswomen in a campaign to provide a servicemen's club. A local solicitor, Charlie Grace, who had moved out of his large house in South Street for the period of the war, came forward and offered 'No. 60' to Felicity. Number 60 South Street stands in a row of sixteenth- and seventeenth-century houses that has been described by Ronald Cant, the historian of St Andrews, as 'almost unique among Scottish townscapes'.[25] It became the Number 60 Club, and in August 1940, aided with gifts and loans of furniture and furnishings, Felicity opened its doors. Her father, who had been given a sum of money to spend on war charities by a sympathetic American, presented a cheque for £50 with which to equip Number 60. From then on, when Felicity wasn't driving for the RAF, she was running a club: a comfortable home from home where a new spirit of understanding and friendship between British and Polish soldiers could flourish, and where the men could find rest and recreation. Her father, newly installed in the role of grandparent, self-deprecatingly remarked that if asked, 'Grand-Daddy, what did you do in the Second Great War?', he would reply, 'I did a little to start Number Sixty, St Andrews.'

Jim's espousal of the Polish cause had been prompted by a chance encounter. One day, when the Poles had first arrived in Scotland, a dispatch rider on a motorcycle roared into the quadrangle of St Salvator's College, bringing a letter for the Vice-Chancellor from Sikorski. Having taken the reply, the Pole clicked his heels together sharply, and said 'cheerio'. The Principal's heart was touched: it was probably the only word of English the lad knew, and Jim Irvine resolved then and there to do all he could for the Polish army in Scotland.[26] The Poles embraced Principal Irvine in their traditions: he walked in procession with them along the West Sands in a mass celebrated on 26 August, the feast day of their national icon, the Madonna of Czestochowa, revered for having granted her protection to the Poles. They presented him with a valuable enamel icon of the Black Madonna, and invested him with the Order of Polonia Restituta.

The war was ageing Jim Irvine. In his shaving mirror he saw the signs of advancing years: the once-curly locks gradually disappeared, his hair became rapidly white, and he lost weight. Two of his closest friends, John Buchan and Edward Harkness, died in 1940, and he felt their loss deeply. The war prompted The Pilgrim Trust to take up work that was in itself a return to something of Harkness's original impulse. Harkness, in founding the trust, had been moved by the extent to which Britain had been bled dry by the Great War, and he had hoped that his largesse might be spent in sustaining and restoring Great Britain's cultural identity and social infrastructure. With the outbreak of a new war, Harkness's trust found an intensification of purpose in supporting war charities and backing heritage projects, and Jim became adept at claiming funds for the many excellent appeals that were made to him. He was much in demand in London at the trust's deliberations. His usual first-class sleeping compartment, in a slow and cold wartime train on the LNER line, was not as comfortable as it should have been; taxis at King's Cross had to be shared with strangers, and the Athenaeum could not always put him up.

Irvine and the trustees of The Pilgrim Trust were already, in 1939, contributing to the birth of the Council for the Encouragement of Music and the Arts (CEMA), later the Arts Council, with advice and a large grant of £25,000. At the same time, one of the first appeals of any size and significance to reach the offices of The Pilgrim Trust in the first autumn of the war concerned the employment of artists in wartime. The Ministry of Labour and National Service had called in Herbert Llewellyn Smith to chair a committee to consider how to use artists in the national interest. It was proposed that a collection of topographical watercolour drawings of places and buildings of significance to Britain should be commissioned. Certain places would necessarily be exposed to the destruction of war; there was also an awareness that much of rural England was already changing in the hands of social improvers and developers. The Pilgrim Trust responded generously, and in England and Wales a small committee of painters and authorities on art handled their grant and its responsibilities.

The case for recording Scotland was treated separately. If anything, the prevailing conditions in Scotland made it even more difficult to provide access for the artists to coastal areas and sensitive places; Irvine, as a Scot, was appointed chairman of the committee for Scotland, to operate on behalf of The Pilgrim Trust. With his own fiefdom, Irvine was able to form a small band of congenial committee members to see the project through. It was exactly the sort of show that he most enjoyed, and in Scotland he could promote his own ideas; it gave him the opportunity to express his deep feeling for his native land.

Scotland was just as vulnerable as England to destruction by enemy action. A scheme to preserve architects' drawings already existed. By March 1942 Irvine was ready to make a statement of his approach.[27] In order not to duplicate the work of other organisations, such as the National Buildings Record (which dated from early in the war), he wanted more than documentary evidence of buildings: he felt it was important to convey the character and even the atmosphere of a place as seen through the eyes of an artist. He would include oils as well as watercolours, because colour was more suggestive of the quality of place than black and white. It made Jim's competitive spirit rise when he observed how, initially in 1940, the English committee of purely art experts had bungled its relationship with The Pilgrim Trust. Perhaps in Scotland they could do better.

Between the wars, Jim and Mabel had formed friendships with several painters. They were on good terms with Muirhead Bone, Laura Knight and the colourist Francis Cadell, as well as the establishment portrait painters Salisbury and Birley. Mabel exhibited at the Royal Scottish Academy. With the country at war, Irvine made sure that his university was used as a civilising force. St Andrews took the lead in welcoming 'Art for the People', CEMA's project to bring travelling exhibitions to groups of people to whom such things were unfamiliar. It came to St Andrews in the summer of 1942, with an exhibition in old Parliament Hall for the August seaside visitors. Irvine's taste in art was conservative, but he could certainly justify his position in leading the Scottish Committee of Recording Scotland.

The idea took root in his mind when on a visit to a recent exhibition of the Royal Scottish Society of Painters in Watercolour (RSW): several of its exhibits would give them a good start if they could negotiate a fair price. The Scottish committee under Irvine comprised an architect, Reginald Fairlie, who had of course already worked for St Andrews University; a painter, Captain A.E. Borthwick, past president of the Society of Scottish Artists and of the Royal Society of Painters in Watercolours; David Russell, who was a businessman, with an interest in art – he was Irvine's closest friend; and Kenneth Sanderson, a collector. David Russell made available his own secretary, Miss Bell, to assist with much of the administration, and with her support the Scottish team set about the business of acquiring pictures, either by purchase or gift.[28] One hundred and forty-five pictures in all eventually comprised the Scottish collection, and these were exhibited in galleries and schools – and even in Draffens, the Dundee department store, as well as in a new Youth Hostel. It was a subtle way of responding to the country's elegiac mood, and the committee was right to feel that it had made an effective contribution to Scottish art. Once again, art was brought to the people by means of travelling exhibitions. Forty-seven Scottish artists were represented, including Keith Henderson, who had recently painted Principal Irvine's portrait for St Salvator's Hall. Jim disliked both the portrait and Henderson's rather effeminate manners, but both Keith and Helen Henderson were much loved by Mabel Irvine.

The Scottish committee was frugal; it did not need to spend more than £1,600 of The Pilgrim Trust's money. Borthwick, who himself contributed several pictures to the Recording Scotland scheme, got on with Irvine rather well and they both gained a friendship out of this episode. He persuaded Jim to obtain a grant of £500 from The Pilgrim Trust, to be expended in providing prizes for the schoolchildren's art competition held in conjunction with the council of the RSW. In 1945 Borthwick offered to paint his friend's portrait, and so another portrait was added to the iconography of

Principal Irvine. A version hangs in Deans Court, the post-graduate hall of St Andrews University.

Out of this response to Sir Herbert Llewellyn Smith's appeal to The Pilgrim Trust to support his work for artists, a permanent form in five volumes, *Recording Britain*, was published during the years just after the war. The fifth and final volume of the series was devoted to Scotland, and once again it had the stamp of Irvine's hand all over it. The eighty plates in *Recording Scotland* include a greater preponderance of colour illustrations than did its English counterparts, and each plate is accompanied by an essay written by J.B. Salmond, who was a protégé of Irvine's. Having cut his teeth with the Thomson Press as a journalist on the *Scots Magazine*, Salmond found his true home back in St Andrews, where he had been a student. As warden of St Salvator's Hall, and as university archivist, he was the ideal servant of his Principal; it was his belles-lettres style that endeared him to Irvine, who made of him something of an amanuensis. Salmond, the editor of *Recording Scotland*, endeavoured to re-people the pictures with the folk who, at one time or another, lived, moved and saw out their existence in the places portrayed. It was published in March 1952, just before Irvine's death in June of that year.

Nine months later, the secretary of The Pilgrim Trust wrote to St Andrews University offering the gift of all the pictures commissioned for *Recording Scotland* in memory of Sir James Irvine, who had conceived the scheme. Just as the touring exhibitions of these pictures to schools and halls throughout Scotland had brought something refined and beautiful into the lives of many young Scots, so it was hoped that the pictures would continue to delight young men and women by hanging in Irvine's halls of residence. It was a valuable gift – more, perhaps, than was fully realised. It was fortunate that Irvine had not excluded oils from the series, because amongst others in this collection that have considerably grown in value is a delightful Peploe oil of Ceres, a village not far from St Andrews. This painting, now too valuable to hang in a hall of residence, can be seen in the university's excellent museum, MUSA.

To return to the war, Mabel bore her wartime work with enormous equanimity. Deans Court was requisitioned by the Red Cross, and, as vice-president of the Red Cross for Fife, she ran a busy depot there. At first, the fact that she was needed for her own self invigorated her. Soon, however, her anxiety about Nigel wore away at her spirits, and her family felt that she worked much too hard at Deans Court. The acquisition of a very simple rural property just outside Blebo Craigs, about six or seven miles from

St Andrews, was perhaps what she had needed all along, and never again would they take over somebody else's place in the country for the month of August. South Flisk, once a quarrier's settlement, is in a beautiful position, the epitome of East Fife's undulating wooded landscape but with views on a clear day to the peak of Schiehallion in the Highlands. For the first time since they had moved so blithely out of Edgecliffe, she was in her own home. Jim gave it to her for her birthday in June 1942.[29]

The historian Caroline Ketelbey, whom the Irvines knew in St Andrews, had first discovered this group of sandstone vernacular buildings. It was she who had turned a couple of cottages, a smithy and a barn into a dwelling, but her private income had dried up with the fall of Singapore and she had been forced to sell. Jim and Mabel had no building work to do straight away: it was complete and very appealing. As J.M. Barrie had discovered, Mabel's character was in many ways the opposite of the 'grande dame' that she was so often taken for. At South Flisk she could be herself: easy, girlish, resourceful, clever with her needle and never happier than when making a home. Soon, printed cretonne hung at the windows and pictures were on the walls. Polished brass fire-irons mounted guard over the little fireplaces. She filled the deep windowsills of her cottage with her collection of Staffordshire figures: Burns in a blue coat; Wallace, looking suitably warlike; and Shakespeare loftily casting his eye over her collection of books about gardening and country lore.

In gumboots and an old tweed skirt she dug and planned her garden, and before long she had a part-time gardener – a man too old to be called up, curiously called Dutch – to help her. The small granddaughter, by then evacuated to Fife from her home in London, followed them round. The wild grounds of nearly ten acres were all that remained of the abandoned eighteenth-century quarry, and to reach this paradise of deep brown pools, meadows and wild cherries, a stair cut out of the rock face had to be navigated: it soon became known as the Burma Road,[30] and Mabel named the close-cropped turf at the bottom 'Mary's Meadow', from a book of her childhood.[31] It was, as Jim said, a great game, and very good for her. It was good too for Nigel who, although far away at sea with destination often unknown to his family, could dream of a place that he would return to and where he would fish. 'I would rather possess a stony acre in Fife than a beautiful estate in any county in Britain,' he wrote to his mother.

Nigel got leave at New Year in 1943, before embarking for Charleston, South Carolina, and he spent his leave at South Flisk, lightheartedly helping his father to chop wood for the fires. Jim's fancy had most uncharacteristically tempted him into wishful thinking, and he was sure that Nigel would be promoted to a desk job. This was not to be; Nigel, who had volunteered for risks, loved his work. At Charleston he supervised the erection of a new radar system on his ship, the *Nigeria*. When he returned that autumn, it was to tell his family that he was engaged to Cecilia Banister. Jim and Mabel had grown to know Cecilia, so it was with happiness that Jim wrote to Nan Wood in America: 'We love the most charming and delightful girl.' Taking advantage of his ship being in port at Chatham, Nigel and Cecilia were married in December 1943 in St Margaret's, Westminster. His father's severe illness prevented Nigel's parents from being present, but in St Andrews, at Jim's bedside, Mabel read the marriage service aloud. Every day Mabel turned to the first of the 'Forms of Prayer to be used at Sea' in the Prayer Book, as Nigel had asked her. They did not know that the leave they had spent with Nigel at South Flisk that autumn would be the last time they would see their son. Nigel drowned in early summer the next year in northern Ceylon. After a bout of fever, he had been sent to a rest home for officers in the northern hills at Diyatalawa Camp and there, while fishing in a pool of unfathomable depth, he accidentally drowned. Mabel and Felicity had decamped from St Andrews to South Flisk, where life was simpler. They went backwards and forwards between St Andrews and Blebo Craigs by bus, but one day Felicity was late home, and when she arrived it was to break the news of Nigel's death to her mother.

Jim was far away on the other side of the Atlantic, engaged in his work for higher education in the West Indies. It was of the utmost importance that he should not receive the news of his loss casually, or from a stranger, and the Colonial Office cabled Eugene Melville, the Irvines' young friend from the early days of St Salvator's Hall, who was at that time posted to the embassy in Washington. It was known that Principal Irvine was going to pay a visit to Washington on his way home, and it was hoped that Eugene, Nigel's friend, would be the one who would break the news to Jim of his son's death. Sadly, the cable reached Eugene's desk on the day after Irvine had left on a convoyed passage home, and convoys were under complete radio silence. Jim docked in Glasgow and took the first train home. Unfortunately, it was at Leuchars station that a porter offered his condolences, not knowing that he was the first to tell Principal Irvine of his grievous loss.[32]

Many friends tried to sustain Jim and Mabel, who were crushed by Nigel's death. Perhaps the good Bishop Herbert Hensley Henson helped them: 'I shall always think of Nigel as a singularly attractive young man:

gifted and generous, who was marked out for great service, entirely worthy of his family and nation,' he wrote.[33] Jim wrote that 'everything he and Mabel would do now would be saturated with thoughts of Nigel'. Nigel's death was devastating to his young wife.

As Nigel had grown into manhood, his father had turned more and more to him for advice. The fact that Jim now wished for, but in vain, Nigel's 'cheery optimism to blow away minor difficulties and his wisdom to show the way to face major troubles' was a testimony to Nigel's qualities. His father would be sorely in need of such advice during the last difficult years of his life.

VE Day came, and on that day both Jim and Mabel grasped hold of all their courage. It was a day of national celebration, but they didn't have it in their hearts to celebrate. It was a day, however, for which Principal Irvine had prepared. The great medieval bells, the Elizabeth of St Leonard's College and the Katherine Bell of St Salvator's, had been dumb for three centuries. Before the war the decision had been taken to have them recast, but when war broke out it was resolved to keep the bells silent until they could ring in the peace. To the original inscription in Latin, on the Katherine Bell – 'I, James Kennedy, caused this bell to be founded, when Bishop of St Andrews in the year 1452, and called her Katherine' – was added, also in Latin, 'and I James Colquhoun Irvine, Principal and Vice-Chancellor, had Katherine repaired during the world war which began in 1939. After more than three centuries when she was broken and dumb, may she sound again to announce victory over evil and to welcome the sons and daughters of the university to which they brought honour by their sacrifice.'[34] The cost was borne by James Prain, a good friend of the university. On 8 May 1945, as a prelude to the service of thanksgiving in College Chapel, the whole university stood reverently in the quadrangle of St Salvator's College as the bells rang out. The Kate Kennedy Bell 'seemed to be joyously welcoming home those of our number who had served their country and were returning to their midst',[35] but the Elizabeth Bell tolled in memory of the fallen of the university, among whose number was Nigel Irvine, Lieutenant RNVR.

Their principal addressed the depleted gathering of his students that afternoon, at their own request, and as one of them. He thanked them for their sacrifice during the war; looking back across fifty years to a time when he too had been a student, he felt proud that his wartime students seemed to feel on equal terms with him. He told them that on that morning in St Andrews they had special reason to rejoice, for they had kept the torch of enlightenment and learning burning through the years of darkness.[36] He gave his consent to a dance that night, and both he and his brave wife went to it. 'I'm right glad we did,' confessed Jim.

Victory was celebrated in Europe in May 1945, but the war with Japan remained a matter of serious concern. Was it as a patriot or, reluctantly, as a scientist that Jim had to admit 'I am strongly in favour of the Atomic Bomb, despite all the ethical arguments against its use'? Reminiscent of his remark about the use of chemical warfare in the First World War, of it being a matter of retaliation or capitulation, he wrote: 'Well, we got our blow in first: it was a case of either our enemies or ourselves who were going to be pulverised. Two nations (Germany and Japan) have deliberately used science for the persecution of war in the past 50 years, and now two nations (USA and GB) have accepted the challenge and beaten them.'[37]

SEVENTEEN

Avise La Fin

Week in, week out, James Colquhoun Irvine took his seat in the Principal's stall in College Chapel close by the tomb of Bishop Kennedy, where he, James Irvine, had long ago vowed to bring Kennedy's university to life again, to rise like a phoenix from the ashes of earlier times.

James Kennedy, Bishop of St Andrews, was not the founder of the university – that had been Henry Wardlaw – but it is not surprising that Principal James Irvine identified romantically with James Kennedy, who gave to posterity St Salvator's College, the tangible presence in the twentieth century of the fifteenth-century university. Bishop Kennedy's family motto, 'Avise La Fin',[1] brings in the concluding years of James Colquhoun Irvine's life of dedication to the same ideals that James Kennedy held.

In 1946, as the university approached the 500th commemoration of Kennedy's foundation of 1450, Irvine celebrated his jubilee as Principal and Vice-Chancellor. He could look back across fifty years of service: fifty years of ambition, vision and achievement for St Andrews, beginning with the science university of the 1911 quincentenary and the development of a world-class school of chemistry. Then, from 1921, there was the exponential growth in student numbers, buildings and faculties; the restoration of the old and the introduction of the new; and the integration of all that a student in that microcosm of academe should have: encouragement of research, teaching of the highest order, well-stocked libraries, fine rooms in which to live, gymnasia and athletic grounds, and generous bursaries. Above all, he demonstrated an imaginative and tenacious approach to university funding. This was James Irvine's endowment, as the College of St Salvator had been James Kennedy's.

It was fortunate that Principal Irvine, business-like in all he did, brought to the post-war affairs of St Andrews the clarity of his trained scientific mind that was still apparently undiminished. He absorbed government white papers and acts of parliament with a degree of relish, and with an eye to extracting from them the maximum advantage for his university. During the passage of war, the coalition government required the leaders of higher education to prepare for the new social order: one that would inevitably bear the stamp of socialist ideals. The Butler Education Act of 1944 addressed the need for a more radical and pervasive system of secondary education in England and Wales; this was followed by the Education (Scotland) Act in 1945. Universal secondary education had, of course, been an established fact of life in Scotland since 1872, and a generous system of bursaries both at this level and in the universities had pertained throughout the twentieth century through the Carnegie Trust and the Scottish county councils' rate precept for education. However, the expansion of secondary education throughout the British Isles would bring, year on year, a greater demand for university places in every tertiary institution. The pressure for places would be universal. Long before the war, the University Court at St Andrews took note that the pattern of growth was an accelerating one, and it fixed an optimum figure for student numbers, which Irvine was not now averse to extending. The universities were, of course, unnaturally swelled in fulfilment of the promise of special degree courses for Britain's returning servicemen and women. Principal Irvine emphasised, however, that the increase in numbers did not take St Andrews University by surprise. Although in St Andrews this enlargement was not merely a transient element imposed by post-war conditions, Irvine responded to the mood of the times:

> Our duty to the soldier-students who fought for us and the public duty imposed on all universities to implement the findings of the Barlow Report have compelled us to exceed that optimum, and although something may have been sacrificed in fulfilling these obligations, we have gained more than we have lost.[2]

Sir Alan Barlow's report of 1946 on 'Scientific Manpower' identified a critical shortage of scientists and recommended an ambitious programme of university expansion, to be funded by the exchequer. It aimed to double the annual output of science graduates. To balance this, there was a recommendation for a substantial increase in the number of students studying humanities; this might mean doubling the entire output at St Andrews.

Irvine doubted whether the recommendations of the Barlow Report would ever be fully realised, but he grasped his opportunity. It was government policy that the highest priority would be given to ensuring that manpower and materials would be available for building the increased faculty accommodation required as a result of expansion: how such large numbers of students would be housed was apparently of secondary consideration, though not for Irvine. The Barlow Report and the Butler Acts created something of a boom in constructing educational buildings. However, Jim Irvine suspected that, unless he outwitted the Treasury, the same hand that offered such largesse might begin robbing the Scottish universities of funds. The first difficulty was that the government's post-war intervention threatened to make some of the original work of the Carnegie Trust redundant, and the Treasury was prone to look jealously at the trust's coffers north of the border. Irvine, who had been careful with his budget, also feared that the Treasury would raid his reserves. He was, however, a deeply respected and long-serving Carnegie trustee, and he could use his guile to effect. He resolved to 'play the Carnegie Trust off against the Treasury, so as to claim the maximum grant' for St Andrews University.[3]

Irvine was furthermore distressed at the directive that 90 per cent of the available university places should be reserved for returning servicemen and women, and that only 10 per cent was to be allotted to students entering straight from school. Well-prepared school leavers were a university's natural matriculation material, and a poor prospect for their pupils' future education could provoke a crisis of morale in the schools. For twenty-five years Irvine had worked hard to develop a trusting relationship between the schools and his university. In order to mitigate the consequences of the government's directive, and so as to take in a better ratio of school leavers to servicemen, in 1945 St Andrews prepared to double the student population within four years, and Irvine embarked on an enormous expansion of residential accommodation as well as new areas of teaching. As he grew older, he increasingly tried to tighten his authority over his colleagues; he alone acted as the university's proctor, with the connivance of the wardens and sub-wardens of the residences, while still placing his old faith in the master–disciple relationship. The new student body was a volatile assemblage of those who had grown up fast in uniform and those who were still very young. In 1947, the university, as Irvine said, 'crossed the boundary'. St Andrews, with just more than 2,000 scholars, was no longer the smallest of the Scottish universities.[4]

The first quinquennial inspection by the University Grants Committee since before 1939 took place over five days at the beginning of June 1946. Ultimately, all of the new post-war developments depended on a successful outcome, and Principal Irvine had some interesting aspirations, one of which gave rise to an amusing example of Irvine in the rôle of actor–manager. He prepared meticulously for the visitation and, having been convinced that the university should build an important department of biochemistry, he stage-managed a subterfuge with which to achieve this end. He enlisted the help of a young protégé of his, working in the biochemical section of the Bute medical laboratories. John Fewster had been Irvine's last PhD candidate, and his father worked for Principal Irvine's son-in-law at the National Physical Laboratory at Teddington; Jim held John in warm regard. On this day, Jim asked Fewster what he was currently working on; when told, he asked him to put it all away and to set up an entirely new procedure according to the scientific Principal's directions and personal devising. Finally, ushering in the members of the University Grants Committee to the laboratory, the Principal, with a pretence at embarrassment, apologised for being called away on urgent business: 'Perhaps I can leave you with my good friend, Dr Fewster,' he said, 'who will show you what he is working on.' The result of this charade was an unusually large Treasury grant, enabling the development of biochemistry in St Andrews.[5]

No, Barlow did not address how the new intake of students would be housed, but already, as 1940 drew to a close, Irvine had formulated his 'long-range' policy for student accommodation, and he embarked on a speedy expansion of men's residences.[6] After the war, there were just as many importunate headmistresses begging St Andrews to take their clever girls, and St Andrews once again needed to attract good male students. The UGC was applied to, and by 1948 the Scottish architect Ian Lindsay had produced some fine drawings for Hepburn Hall. In fact, between 1940 and 1950 all of the existing men's residences were doubled. On the whole, the buildings put up in St Andrews after the war were well-designed, despite Jim and Mabel's complaint about 'what can one do with everything controlled by Government and new building projects impossible.'[7] Finally, the Grand Hotel, a victim of the post-war slump, was put up for sale, and eventually the university acquired it. For fifty years, the hotel, with its view of the eighteenth green of the Old Course, had welcomed princes, peers and all the world's golfing enthusiasts as residents, but in 1947 it sat on the market while the Roman Catholic archdiocese promoted its wish to see a Jesuit college established there. On the issue of the Grand Hotel's future, Irvine could not lose. To show what could be done, Campion Hall, the Jesuit college at Oxford, was by then successfully established, and Irvine was not at all averse to the contribution that a similar college could make to St Andrews University. Sadly for the Jesuits, however, the bigoted town council of St Andrews refused to give a Roman Catholic college planning permission for a change of use, and the proprietors of the Grand Hotel turned to the university, which was able to buy this landmark building advantageously.

The university under Irvine during the years after the war embarked on some notable works of restoration. In 1951, the early sixteenth-century mansion, Deans Court, which had been requisitioned for the Red Cross during the war, was given its final form and embellishments, having attracted funds from ICI. It was launched as the post-graduate hall of residence that Irvine had dreamed of, where guests would be brought to dine and conversation would flourish: a fertile environment for a cross-disciplinary community of scholars. Its first warden was a chemist, Douglas Lloyd, who also played the organ and composed settings to English lyrical verse; the Principal, in appointing him, regarded Lloyd as a great asset. James Irvine's oldest friend from boyhood, John Rogers, by then chairman of ICI, performed the opening ceremony, and David Traill, also a chemist with ICI, presented a seventeenth-century silver salver as a token of gratitude and goodwill. David Traill had been a research student of Irvine's in the 1920s, and he went on to write Irvine's entry for the *Dictionary of National Biography*. Russell Kirk, a young American post-graduate student studying in St Andrews between 1948 and 1953, was one of the first residents of the reborn Deans Court. He became an important philosopher of conservatism, but he is a player in this story because he fell heir to the same affection for St Andrews that had inspired Principal Irvine. Russell Kirk's book *St Andrews* (1954), in the Batsford series, is arguably the best book on the town and university of St Andrews; Kirk, who lived in St Andrews for such a short space of time, was unwittingly a true disciple of James Colquhoun Irvine.[8]

It would be false to suggest that James Irvine's defence at committee level of the needs of his own university was unique. The Attlee government opened the gates of enlargement to every form of higher education in the country, and all of the senior administrators vied for funding for their own institutions. However, Irvine attracted much admiration from the government for being ahead of the game in providing enough residential accommodation for the enlarged post-war university.

There was one final important development in higher education in which Irvine took the lead. The Workers' Educational Association was something to which he had lent his support during the war. As chairman of the Adult Education Committee of Scotland, his sympathies for the WEA were bound up with the fact that the organisation could give a diploma-level education to those to whom this opportunity had otherwise been denied. It was but another arm of his work in higher education.

In 1937 Lord Lothian handed over the ancient and historical abbey of Newbattle, under the trust of the principals of the four Scottish universities, to become a Scottish college of adult education. Jim and Mabel took greatly to Lord Lothian, and Jim approached the prospect with his usual blend of idealism and interest in the budget. He promised, with Thomas Jones, secretary of The Pilgrim Trust, to put a strong case to the trust for finance to convert Newbattle. Lord Lothian left in the abbey the remarkable library, a large number of interesting and historical pictures, fitments and furniture, so that the abbey would not assume an institutional appearance. Prior to the outbreak of war, the college was in full swing and proving of lasting benefit to students from all social classes. Its situation near the Dalkeith coalfields was, however, unfortunate, and after the war the Coal Board determined to utilise part of the grounds for the excavation of coal and the accommodation of miners. The Coal Board was famously no respecter of fine country houses. Jim was incensed; learned legal advice was sought, and they were told that the action, although highhanded and unscrupulous, was legal. In a limited way, and lacking the beauty of the original idea, in 1949 Newbattle prepared to reopen as a residential unit for the Scottish Youth Leadership Training Association. In yet another instance, Jim and Mabel's view of the gracious world they had once known was blunted by the war.

The post-war Labour government forced owners of fine country houses to take drastic measures that might relieve them of some of the penalties of ownership. Many took the roofs off their properties; others sought rescue in trusts of many kinds. Perhaps Lord Lothian's trust for Newbattle did not live up to all of their high hopes, but in 1947 Irvine heard from Sir Hector Hetherington, Principal of Glasgow University, that the owner of a another property, The Burn, near Edzell, wanted to hand over his house to serve students in Scotland. To work financially, mainstream university involvement was necessary, and this is where Hetherington and Irvine came in. The solution arrived at was that the Scottish universities should each buy into using the house for a certain number of student weeks: an early form of time-share. This opportunity to enjoy 'reading weekends' in fine surroundings has been an enduring success in exactly the way that the donor hoped.[9]

By the mid-1930s, Irvine was already the senior in office of the four Scottish principals, and he had served for several years as chairman of the Scottish Entrance Board. The Scottish universities, their ordinances and even their statutes were bound to procedures that were more uniform than elsewhere in the United Kingdom. Jim Irvine was the natural president of his fellow principals at all their meetings, at which he would attempt to display some impartiality. In the distribution of funds from the Carnegie Trust for the Universities of Scotland, however, Irvine would fight for St Andrews probably more keenly than the next man. His partisanship nothwithstanding, he often extended his support to the whole system of the Scottish universities. Nowhere was this more apparent than with the advent of the National Health Service. The four Scottish universities, acting in accord and directed by Irvine, secured an arrangement with the Scottish Hospital Service that was more satisfactory than the pact that pertained in England. Irvine stood up for Scotland as well as for St Andrews.

The National Health Service (Scotland) Bill was published on 29 November 1946. Irvine went through it carefully, and promptly wrote to the Secretary of State for Scotland to say that its terms fell in line with existing medical management in St Andrews University. Clinical medicine had always been taught in Dundee. The St Andrews Medical School and Dundee Royal Infirmary had long observed a mutual respect that ensured both the allocation of beds and the supply of specialists, but it was universally the case that many of Britain's hospitals were specialist hospitals – in orthopaedics, dentistry, paediatrics and so on – which were owned and managed by non-governmental boards of directors. Irvine set about negotiating the necessary amalgamations and financial settlements that would ultimately produce an enormous university hospital in Dundee. During the war, St Andrews University worked closely with the Ministry of Health and the Department of Health for Scotland in preparation for a seismic reorganisation in the professional training of doctors and dentists. Principal Irvine was proud of his record with dentistry, and he was determined to keep ahead of the other Scottish dental schools that would spring up in response to the recommendations of the post-war Teviot committee on dentistry. Since before the war, dentistry in St Andrews had enjoyed the foundation of a chair and a fully staffed department: it was the first university in Scotland to grant dental degrees.[10]

In July 1947, the top specialist hospital architects in the country, Adams, Holden and Pearson, were brought up from London to look at a large site to the west of Dundee, and to draw up plans for the teaching hospital. The large teaching hospital, now known as Ninewells Hospital, and still on the western side of the city, was completed in 1973. It belongs to Dundee University, which by that time had been made independent of St Andrews by the Robbins Report, and Adams, Holden and Pearson were no longer the architects.

It is worth remarking, however, that it was during this post-war period of phenomenal development that Irvine laid down so much of the physical form of today's universities of St Andrews and Dundee. It was Irvine who had already commissioned a plan for the development of the site in St Andrews bounded by Union Street, North Street and Market Street, to be called University Court.[11] Ten years after Irvine's death, this site was developed as the Buchanan Building for Modern Languages. It was Irvine who brought to Scotland the silver-haired, silver-tongued town planner William Holford, to advise on laying out the North Haugh as a specialist site for new science laboratories – Holford, remember, had advised Irvine on commissioning a plan for the University College of the West Indies. And it was Irvine who, muttering that never again would universities be able to afford to face a building in stone, commissioned College Gate, the fine administrative offices on North Street that bear the subtle imprint of a carved holly leaf from the Irvine crest around the top window in the turret.

It may seem incredible today that one man should get his own way to such an extent and become in effect the sole administrator of St Andrews, in command of every committee. His fellow principal, Hector Hetherington of Glasgow, explained the secret about Irvine in this way: 'He was a very attractive person: he was an advocate and a negotiator of uncommon persuasiveness and resource, and above all he worked. He knew his case in compelling detail – problem, facts, precedents and implications. I suppose most of us felt that when, as often happened, the decision ran rather to his view than to ours, it was the just reward of more than painstaking preparation.'[12]

The biochemist John Fewster was right: 'It didn't matter *what* you thought about him; everyone thought about him.'

Unfortunately, some people had begun to think ill of him. The attack was a personal one, and it first arose from Dundee during the 1930s, when Irvine was at the height of his powers and popularity. Since the beginning of the century, University College Dundee's badly drawn deed of incorporation with St Andrews had given an opening to a vociferous band of separatists. Irvine warned Kipling of this when, rather innocently, the author, as Rector, chose to speak on 'Independence' in 1923: 'Today I am sending you copies of the *Dundee Advertiser* and the *Courier*, the former because it contains the Dundee speech in extenso, the latter to show the "separist" policy at work.'[13]

Dundee, once Scotland's third city, had been an important port. In the nineteenth century its pride depended, rather riskily, on its existence as a one-industry city, but it never fully recovered from the Reformation, and the Great Depression was the final blow to the jute industry that drove Dundee. Its loss of confidence was not helped by the view across the Tay, which showed St Andrews basking in an apparently new glory. The Thomson Press of Dundee, a populist publishing empire of newspapers and magazines, caught hold of the city's mood and, under the banner of separatism from St Andrews University, sought to give Dundee new status by means of possessing its own university. The Second World War brought Dundee the further impoverishment of loss of industry, bombing, social neglect and unemployment. Smallpox was endemic, and rickets was evident amongst the children of the condemned tenements. The city's commercial interest, from which the governors of University College Dundee were drawn, again took up the refrain of separatism. Irvine was quite clear in his own mind that this was nothing more than the propagandist policy of the local press, 'which, in complacent ignorance of university affairs, takes up a dictatorial attitude in fostering artificially what to outsiders may appear to be a reflection of public opinion'. It was apparent that the senior members of the whole university felt nothing but distaste for the campaign that had been imposed on them by the Dundee newspapers. Rather, the council of UCD, but not its governors, still believed that the day would soon come when their union with the university would be redrafted.

The press took up a bullying and provocative position. It was easy for the *Dundee Courier* to spread misleading statements in order to argue the case for separation: it chose to ignore the reality that the medical and dental schools formed no part of UCD and were under the sole management and financial control of the University Court of St Andrews; that the teacher training college, with its chair in education, was an institution under the Scottish Education Department; and that the School of Economics and the Duncan of Jordanstone School of Art had no connection whatsoever with University College,[14] despite the undoubted fact that they did, however, share some buildings and facilities with the college.

During the last quarter of the nineteenth century, no other contemporary Dundonians came forward to add endowments to Mary Ann Baxter's College of Dundee, despite the visible wealth of the 'jute barons' in their fine houses overlooking the estuary. Dundee was slow to attract gifts that could compare with the ones that Irvine had obtained for the alma mater. Harkness had refused point-blank to give to a city that he thought lacked any interest in helping itself,[15] but the Harkness benefaction at work in St Andrews did much, as we have seen, to arouse feelings in Dundee, where folk were convinced that Irvine had done everything to glorify St Andrews at the same time as treating Dundee as a poor relation. It was an emotion, however, not entirely borne out by fact, because Dundee, where the applied disciplines were taught, was funded and developed as the essential partner of the ancient University of St Andrews.[16] Irvine's skill had gained large capital grants from the Treasury for Dundee, even in the difficult early 1930s.

In 1930 Irvine persuaded himself that, by agreeing to take on the vacant and part-time job of Principal of University College Dundee, he could bring matters under control. He would not, of course, be resident in Dundee, and he gave the city's agitators their first legitimate complaint: at a stroke, by combining the principalship of the United College with that of the smaller Dundee College in one person, one of Dundee's three seats on the University Court was removed and their power was weakened. With his usual self-confidence he set before himself 'two ideals: the one to improve the relationship between the College and the University, the other to make University College a more efficient unit in the University'. His colleagues felt he was starting to achieve these ideals, and Irvine thought he could begin to solve the Dundee problem.[17] He became a deputy lieutenant of Dundee. He was a regular passenger on the train that shunted between the twin towns of his university. He was forced by the campaign against him to resign the principalship of UCD in 1939 at a time when many felt he had begun to bring the force of his wide vision to bear on Dundee's future, and when he was laying the foundation for classes leading to a law degree.

More than fifty years on, the attacks on him in the Dundee press can now be seen more clearly for what they were. Some commentaries have suggested that his supporters within University College Dundee were merely his toadies. The evidence does not bear this out: many letters, not just of support but of deep appreciation of all that he achieved in Dundee, came to Principal Irvine at the time of his resignation from the UCD principalship. Those who knew the truth were, however, afraid of speaking out. Many wrote privately in this wise:

I read the *Courier* leader in vain for any reference to all the good work you have done in Dundee – to your kindness towards the staff & the students – to your unfailing readiness to go out of your way to help us – to your kindness in coming over to meetings of societies (Town & Gown, Public lectures, WEA, Chemistry Society etc) – & to your financial & administrative genius in a difficult & complex situation. These are things that should be said, or said publicly. The gratitude

of the Dundee staff should be publicly expressed. But, so far, we have
been afraid lest, in coming publicly to your defence, we should play
into the hands of a newspaper whose vast circulation & lack of taste
& lack of generosity and lack of the ordinary notions of fair play gave
it an overwhelming advantage over ordinary people. We were afraid
really of doing you and the College a disservice.[18]

Nigel Irvine warned his father in 1939 of the danger of failing to stem the
poison that was spreading not only through the city of Dundee but also
through the junior ranks of the university. It was only after the war that Jim
felt driven to defend his university publicly. Walter Moberley, chairman of
the UGC, was soon apprised of Jim's firm analysis of the 'Dundee Racket',
as he would refer to it. Dundee town council had 'started a hare and we
must chase it'.

Irvine was vilified in print, and he hit back at the Thomson Press. In a
letter originally intended for the editor of the *Sunday Times* but redrafted
as a 'Memorandum for the University Grants Committee', he pointed out
that the Thomson Press had already attracted deep opprobrium for abuse
of its powers: in 1946 and again in 1948 it came under investigation by the
Press Commission for, amongst other things, using its columns to spread
falsehoods about the true state of the relationship between Dundee and St
Andrews.[19]

Irvine's line was entirely rational – it was the product of fifty years'
knowledge of these affairs – but he was unyielding. Had something of his
old diplomatic skill and charm disappeared? In these years after the death
of his son, he sought to submerge his grief in long hours of work at his desk.
To his friend David Russell, he allowed the mask to slip, and he wrote of 'our
academic poor relation', but in public Irvine's justification of his approach
to Dundee was that throughout his reign he had ensured that money was
poured into Dundee: the disciplines taught there were more expensive to
profess, and there had been no stinting in adding to the professoriate. St
Andrews had every reason to be proud of the departments on the other side
of the Tay estuary.

The turmoil that led to the commissioning from Lord Cooper of an
examination of the deteriorating relations between Dundee and St Andrews
was made worse in Irvine's eyes by the college governors' appointment of
Major-General Wimberley as Principal of UCD in 1946.[20] He was 'a fatuous
man', Irvine felt, with no previous experience of university administration.
Certainly, poor Wimberley found himself up against Irvine's prodigious

memory for facts. Wimberley's rather innocent but forthright attempt to make something of his job only served to arouse Irvine's scorn. Wimberley found Irvine slippery and Machiavellian in committee.[21]

Irvine was never going to form a trusting relationship with Douglas Wimberley, who was not cast in the same academic mould as the long line of medical and scientific men who had preceded him in post. In Court meetings, Wimberley showed a dangerous determination not to recognise the primacy of the university and the Court over the college in Dundee, and he failed to demonstrate that he was in control of his budget. (Irvine was not only principal of one of the university's colleges – the United College of St Salvator and St Leonard – but he was also Principal and Vice-Chancellor of the University.) Wimberley's attempts to enlarge University College Dundee's departments in order to offer a social science diploma course came up against a brick wall; as long as he pushed for more teaching in the arts, so Irvine, chairing the University Court, would gravely point out that he had tried to stamp out such duplication between the United College and Dundee as uneconomic. Irvine not only feared the idea of allowing Dundee to grow in this way, but he was confident that his grasp of the politics involved in the funding of higher education after the war was second to none, and he knew that the Treasury would not be willing to back any of UCD's aspirations. Irvine's frequent cry, 'What is wanted in Scotland is not more Universities but better Universities', never more applied than it did in 1946.[22]

When Charlie Warr, Dean of the Thistle, spoke at Irvine's memorial service, he must have thought of the struggles in Dundee when he said: 'He would fight to the last for his convictions, whether with others or alone. A mind so clear, and a personality so strong and forceful inevitably encountered, and even invited criticism.'[23]

Thomas Mackay Cooper, Lord President of the Court of Session, was appointed by the Secretary of State in February 1949 to conduct an investigation and to report with recommendations. At first Principal Irvine felt confident of Lord Cooper's sympathy and wise advice. Nevertheless, Irvine and the University Court prepared themselves for a fight. They retained Sir Ernest Wedderburn as solicitor and 'Jock' Cameron, Dean of the Faculty of Advocates, as counsel. So 'the bonnie wark gangs merrily on,' ironically noted Jim Irvine, confiding in David Russell: 'My days and nights are consumed with preparation for the Dundee Racket Inquiry. Morally and educationally the Court's case is impregnable but nevertheless I have an uneasy mind and am far from satisfied with the technique adopted by Lord Cooper. He proposes to limit personal evidence to elucidation of doubtful points in the printed documents and there will be no opportunity to contest the lies and ignorance which make up Wimberley's case . . . the Dundee case is a fraud – but we are not to be allowed a chance to expose it so far as I can see.'[24]

To the casual observer in those days, Principal Irvine seemed frail and ill: he had never fully recovered from his serious illness of the winter of 1943–4. His marginal notes on the draft Cooper Report and his subsequent memoranda and papers, however, suggest that his mental powers were as penetrating as ever. Irvine resolved to maintain a stony silence, and he refused to meet Lord Cooper after the draft report was issued. There was nothing to say to a man who indicated no real interest in the structure of the university, nor in the truth surrounding the development of Dundee during the previous decades. Cooper continued to interpret Irvine's current development of the Dundee Medical School and its acquisition of a mace as wilful defiance of the report's recommendation against the perpetuation of the collegiate system. All that Cooper could think of was his wish to see Sir James Irvine and D.C. Thomson 'disappear'.[25]

The Cooper Report was published late in 1949,[26] while Jim and Mabel Irvine were preparing to go to Jamaica for the installation of Princess Alice as Chancellor of the University College of the West Indies. The recommendations in the report shook the University of St Andrews. Lord Cooper strongly urged the abolition of St Andrews' historic and cherished collegiate system in order to achieve a more integrated university, stripped of the causes of jealousy and friction.[27] He mistakenly thought that colleges were outside the Scottish academic tradition. The supreme governing body of UCD, representing the Dundee town interest, was then flooded by a large number of additional votes purchased by D.C. Thomson, at a price of £1,000, and Dundee town council came right out and declared its wish to see the elevation of their college to the status of an independent university – a proposal rejected by the Cooper Report. The report was unacceptable to all parties except the management council and the Principal of University College Dundee, and when UCD refused to meet with the university authorities it was inevitable that a royal commission would take the matter over. Lord Cooper had thought he could bring a happy ending to an episode for which there would be no happy ending for quite some time. It was too late to expect that Irvine would offer any olive branch to Dundee, as some thought he should.

The verdict of Malcom Knox, who would succeed Irvine as Principal and Vice-Chancellor of St Andrews University and who was, during the Cooper débacle, Irvine's deputy, was probably right: 'The [Cooper] Inquiry should have been a Royal Commission. Peace could only come from reorganizing the constitutional relationship between St Andrews and Dundee and that meant legislation, which could only come from a Royal Commission and not an Inquiry.'[28]

Irvine was intensely conscious of the indignity and even disgrace that a royal commission, with its public discussion and parliamentary debate, would bring on his university, but he was obliged to bow to this – the only – way that might find a solution to the central problem of the unsuitability of the UCD constitution. In May 1951, the prime minister announced the establishment of a royal commission under the chairmanship of Lord Tedder, 'to inquire into the organization of university education in Dundee and its relationship with St Andrews University'.

In June 1951, while Lord Tedder commenced the business of taking evidence from witnesses, Irvine, a lifelong smoker who was by then seventy-four years of age and who had never sought lengthy escapes from his stressful life, suffered a major heart attack. His recovery was slow, but by the late autumn he was allowed to return to work for half the day. His chauffeur would bring the car round to the front door at University House, and then drive him slowly to his office overlooking the quadrangle of St Salvator's College. His evidence to Tedder was, for this reason, kept until last.

The findings of the royal commission were published a year later, and at a special meeting on 14 May 1952 the Senatus Academicus agreed to accept the general conclusions of the Tedder Report. It was clear that weeks of lobbying both houses of parliament lay ahead, and that there was room for modifications and changes in the report, before it was enacted by parliament. This was a process that Irvine, when younger, would have thrown himself into with his compelling power of argument.

'The Dundee Racket' may have been Irvine's Achilles heel, but it should be noted that, after the war, there was also a marked sense of a fresh beginning, and of optimism. Distinguished additions to the university's staff were made; Cedric Thorpe Davie, a composer of considerable standing, was appointed to the lectureship in music.[29]

In January 1950, Jim made his New Year's resolutions with the same forthright spirit that had followed him all his life:[30]

1 Follow Napoleon's rule of finishing one task before beginning another.
2 Follow Wellington's method of replying to letters in a single sentence.
3 Follow the rule of Charles Dickens never to leave a paper on your desk over-night.

4 Follow Lander's rule [a fellow chemical research worker with Purdie]
   to start work not later than 9.30 am.
5 Scorn the example of W. Raleigh, Esq. and don't smoke too much.
6 Remember the Sermon on the Mount.

There were parties again, with full evening dress, medals, and furs brought
out of mothballs. With the rooms of University House free of dust sheets,
Mabel embarked on a programme of redecoration. Rationing was still the
order of the day, but in 1905 Mabel's father, the manufacturer of high-class
cotton goods, had provided her with dozens of damask tablecloths: these
were now sent away to be dyed a pretty shade of pale blue and used to
reupholster the drawing room furniture. The choice of new curtains was
made from bolts of silk sent over from Dundee. Mabel wanted the curtains
to be of the same blue as the sea, but since the colour of the sea changed
every day she had a very difficult task. Everyone who came to call was asked
for their advice.

There were several events during these years that were occasions of
supremely happy resolution. With the installation of Olympic medallist
Lord Burghley as rector there was a return to the type of rector that Principal
Irvine could feel comfortable with. Jim and Mabel would make scrambled
eggs in the University House kitchen late at night for Lord Burghley and
his wife, enthusing them with their stories about old St Andrews, where
with every step the present forges links with the past. Lord Burghley was
later seen at the ceremony of planting an offshoot of the Glastonbury Thorn
in St Mary's Quad, to commemorate the year spent by the Principal of St
Mary's College as Moderator of the General Assembly of the Church of
Scotland.[31] In 1911 young Professor Irvine had vowed to 'put St Andrews
on the map', and over the passage of forty years a long succession of these
graceful ceremonies, great and small, had served his larger purpose.

Domestically, there was great rejoicing at the birth of a boy to Veronica,
who had decided to be confined in St Andrews, where she would have many
comforts. During the 'worst winter in living memory' of 1947, four generations of Jim and Mabel's family lived in University House – Mabel's Irish
aunt, Miss Allan, having come to St Andrews to make her home. Plump,
gentle, sociable and deaf, 'Aunt Lizabee' and her Pekinese certainly drew on
Jim's slender reserves of patience, and the poorly house-trained little dog
did not get on with the Irvines' dachshund, but Jim and Mabel belonged
to an age when families would embrace every generation under one roof.
Felicity, the glamorous younger daughter, took up a job at Buckingham

Palace as personal assistant to the King's private secretary, to the great pride of her father, who had always enjoyed playing the courtier in his role as vice-chancellor. With this, Felicity became the last of their children to leave home.

Perhaps the greatest compensation for post-war troubles, whether large or small, lay in the Irvines' other life at the cottage out at Blebo Craigs, where more land was purchased, and a barn converted to provide a study for the Principal. At first Jim would put himself in charge of his household, shooing Mabel off for afternoon rests while he busied himself in the little kitchen making 'utility' soap with the addition of a cocktail from the chemistry laboratory. Early in the morning, or at four o'clock in the afternoon, his ritual was to bring his wife tea on a tray, 'daintily laid' (a favourite phrase of his), with a posy of fresh flowers to complete his offering. Mabel had begun to suffer from glaucoma. After the war, she visited Harry Edwards, the faith healer, at his establishment at Shere in Surrey, because both Jim and Mabel believed that Edwards could effect some improvement to the blindness that had come upon her with the shock of Nigel's death. As Jim listened to a sermon on faith in chapel one Sunday, he thought of all he believed that a faith healer could do for his poor wife, who was at that moment putting herself in the hands of Harry Edwards.

Jim's science served to broaden his consciousness of the metaphysical, and never was he inclined to dismiss the mysteries of the unknown. His Christian faith sharpened the scientific interest of his later years, which lay in the science of life and in the application of his knowledge of carbohydrates to the furtherance of biochemistry. This was, for him, a new usage of the abused nineteenth-century term vitalism, which long before had been a proscriptive force in the advancement of experimental chemistry. 'It was characteristic of Irvine that only a few days before his death he was busy propounding long-term schemes of research on possible developments of carbohydrate derivatives for use in chemotherapy,' wrote his former student, Professor E.L. Hirst.[32]

Fifty years ago, 'South Flisk', the cottage at Blebo Craigs, was detached enough from St Andrews to provide the perfect place of recuperation from illness, and during the last twelve months of his life the Principal was a sick man. Throughout the late summer of 1951, on his release from hospital, Jim rested at the cottage before easing himself back into some of his work. On one occasion his old friend Hector Hetherington drove over from Glasgow to this corner of Fife to conduct the business of the universities of Scotland in Jim's holiday home, rather than incommode his elderly friend.

It was Mabel's turn to nurse Jim, and she watched her husband like a hawk. Once out of sight of his wife, and with a wink and a smile, he resumed those boyish games with which he liked to amuse his grandchildren. Somewhere in Blebo Woods there was a great beech tree on which he had carved the grandchildren's initials, so that year after year they could measure not just their own growth but the growth of the tree; under the tree the children were amazed to be shown the ecology of Blebo Woods. How like a metaphor for the story of Irvine's life was this game! In thirty years the weak sapling university of 1921 had grown to a tree of large and spreading proportions which, like the beech tree, sheltered a complex growth of inter-dependent forms of education under its branches.

Irvine received all the homage he deserved in his final years. The prestigious Gunning Victoria Prize was awarded to him for his chemistry; with this award, the Royal Society of Edinburgh honoured the way in which, long ago, as a scientist he had broken away from his professor's research, and with great courage and ingenuity embarked on elucidating the carbohydrates, adding insight to the utilisation of these forms in plants.[33] There was justice in this acknowledgement of his life in science, but being Scotland's premier learned society the Royal Society of Edinburgh broke with tradition, and this scientific medal became additionally the occasion for marking a great Scotsman's life in education.

If James Colquhoun Irvine could write his own farewell, he would have said that his crowning joy was that bright autumn day in 1950 when the celebratory pageant of the quincentenary of St Salvator's College unfolded. Against the background of the sparkling sea and fluttering heraldic banners, a noble academic procession made its way along North Street from the college's service of thanksgiving in the fifteenth-century chapel of St Salvator. The Queen, in her red LLD gown, was prominent in their midst, and in St Salvator's Hall, the twentieth-century reincarnation of the old college, she made a speech of great relevance:

> This College has endured many trials during the past five centuries
> . . . for these escapes we must be grateful, remembering that it is easier
> to destroy than to build up . . . The university system of Scotland has
> undergone many changes in the past 150 years, but the individuality
> of St Andrews as a collegiate university remains unaltered, and our
> societies of masters and scholars flourish beyond the dreams of their
> founders.[34]

Representatives of Paris, Oxford, Cambridge and Glasgow – all ancient collegiate foundations – received honorary degrees. A quincentenary medal was struck, and three St Andrews University publications were issued: Dr Annie Dunlop's *Life and Times of James Kennedy, Bishop of St Andrews*; *The College of St Salvator* by Ronald Cant; and *Veterum Laudes*, edited by Dr J.B. Salmond.

The Earl of Crawford and Balcarres gave a commemorative oration which brought the participants' thoughts to the present day and to Master John Almare's thirty-fourth successor – the mid-twentieth-century Principal, who in presiding 'over the destinies of our University adds lustre to a great inheritance and will hand to posterity a tradition which he has so much enriched'.

Before his death, James Irvine had one more task to complete. The year of his birth was significant to him for one thing: it was the year that the lands of the sixteenth-century college of St Leonard were sold by the university – only the ruins of the chapel remained with the university. Harkness had been touched by this pathetic ruin, and he was keen to restore it, but in 1930 he withdrew his offer when Sir Robert Lorimer gave the chapel a negative structural report. The matter lay dormant until 1948, when Irvine, never one to give up, took up the matter afresh as his personal mission, with this indignant endorsement of the records: 'The Chapel belongs to the University: being the only part of St L's College 1527, when the two Colleges were amalgamated in 1747.'[35] That constant friend of St Andrews, Sir David Russell, came forward with a proposal for its restoration in the care of the architect Ian Lindsay, whose report was the converse of Lorimer's: he believed that the building was basically sound. David Russell offered to defray some of the initial costs, including work to the sacristy, which had once been used so scandalously as a wine cellar by Principal Sir David Brewster.

On 8 November 1949 Irvine took Lindsay's plans and drawings to a meeting of The Pilgrim Trust. The costs of restoring the chapel were too great for one benefactor, and the trust, in Harkness's stead, gave £7,000 for the restoration of the building's fabric. Sir David and Lady Russell gave all the chapel furnishings in memory of their son Pat, who was Irvine's godson, and who had been killed on active service in Italy. The University Court would pay for the improvement of the chapel environs: restoration of the pend, its archway, the flagstones and the approach from South Street. On a bitterly cold, late-winter afternoon early in 1952, Jim and Mabel drove round to view the completed St Leonard's Chapel with Lord and Lady Crawford, friends of their old age. James Colquhoun Irvine's work was done.

The Chapel Address that he gave at the end of that academic year of 1952 was in effect his last testament. It was his last opportunity to state his belief that the spiritual and the scientific in man are reconciled by faith in God. Finally, wishing to give his students – soon to graduate – a message to take away with them, he quoted Sir Francis Drake: 'There must be a beginning of any great matter but the continuing to the end until it be thoroughly finished yields the true glory.'[36]

Principal Sir James Irvine was old and ill: each day he grew just a little more tired. Thomas Jones recounted that, after the last meeting of The Pilgrim Trust attended by 'Sir James', three weeks before his death, he and Irvine had talked in the club before retiring. Irvine recalled a confession made by Lord Baldwin in the same place and in similar circumstances: 'I am now ready to go.'[37] So it was with Jim: he was ready to go. He was content.

Sir James Colquhoun Irvine died in the Principal's house, St Andrews, in the early hours of 12 June 1952, at the age of seventy-five. The day before had been a day not unlike so many in his life: some business in college, tea in the garden and a pleasant evening spent quietly at home. That night he suffered another heart attack; his wife was at his side, but this time the attack was fatal. On the evening of that day, a BBC news broadcast paid tribute to the life of a remarkable man. At the same time, Mabel Irvine sent a message to Principal Wimberley of University College Dundee, to the effect that if he were to write a letter of condolence to her she would refuse to receive it. With the disarming modesty that perhaps only a soldier could have, Wimberley remarked in his autobiography that he could only guess at her motives; but if it was because she believed that his arrival in Dundee had triggered everything that led to her husband's death, he could only agree with her.[38]

The flags of all the public buildings in St Andrews flew at half-mast on the day of his funeral, 14 June. The national and international press, and all the scientific journals, followed with obituaries and tributes. Full of honour, he was laid to rest in the cathedral burying ground to the east of the old city that he had loved so well. His memorial service was held on 19 June in the parish church of the Holy Trinity, St Andrews, of which he had been an elder. His humanity had touched the inner recesses of the human heart; his imaginative spirit had brought beauty and enduring qualities to those whose lives he had served to better. The Very Reverend Dr Charles Warr,

Dean of the Thistle, spoke at his memorial service of the dreamer of great dreams to whom St Andrews University owed more than it had done to anyone since Bishop Kennedy founded St Salvator's College five centuries earlier.

The memory of their close and happy marriage was too raw to permit his widow to continue to live in St Andrews. Mabel moved from the intrusiveness of the grey university city to the bustle of Mayfair: like St Andrews, it was essentially a village, but it lay in the middle of metropolitan London, where she shared a mews cottage with Felicity. Friends from her former life, students reluctant to forget their 'Princ', and colleagues of Jim's flocked to her London home, and every summer she and Felicity returned to Fife, where they would be joined by Veronica and her family at South Flisk in Blebo Craigs. Her widowhood lasted for fifteen years. During these years she wrote a beautiful memoir of her life with Jim: *The Avenue of Years*. She had finally to bear alone the tragedy of their daughter Felicity's early death.

In the April 1953 edition of the *Journal of the Chemical Society of St Andrews University*, Professor Read's valedictory leading article on Sir James Irvine harkened back to Sir James's own words:

> I find myself – a twentieth-century scientist – gazing across the chasm of five hundred years to a strange remote world and am conscious afresh of a feeling which never entirely escapes me that, as the thirty-fourth Principal of St Salvator's College, I am privileged to share in the inheritance of a solemn trust; at once I am brought face to face with the question if the duty committed to that long succession of Masters has been faithfully discharged.

Professor Read left his readers with the remark: 'The answer is clear to us and will be even clearer to posterity.'[39]

We, at the time of the 600th year of the University of St Andrews, are that posterity, and we can give thanks for the life of James Colquhoun Irvine. The twenty-first century University of St Andrews, in all its vitality and beauty, essentially owes its present-day form to the vision and talents of the scientist and educationalist who fought for its survival, and who fleshed out the elements of the ancient university with all that a twentieth-century institution of higher education required.

Sir James Colquhoun Irvine:
Honours, Honorary Degrees and Medals

James Colquhoun Irvine was elected FRS in 1918. He was appointed CBE in 1920 and knighted in 1925; in 1948 he became a Knight Commander of the British Empire, and in this year his arms were matriculated at the Court of the Lord Lyon. He was a Vice-President of the Royal Society of Edinburgh, of which he was also a Fellow. He was elected a Fellow of the Educational Institute of Scotland (1933), and was an Honorary Fellow of the Institute of Scottish Architects (1921).

In chemistry, he was Davy medallist of the Royal Society (1925), Willard Gibbs medallist of the American Chemical Society (1926), Elliot Cresson medallist of the Franklin Institute of Pennsylvania (1929) and Longstaff medallist of the Chemical Society (1933). He was awarded the Gunning Victoria Jubilee Prize of the Royal Society of Edinburgh in 1941, for his life's work in chemistry.

He was an Honorary Member of the American Chemical Society and the American Philosophical Society, and an Honorary Fellow of the Franklin Institute of Philadelphia. He was offered the presidency of the Chemical Society in 1924, but he declined in January 1925 because of pressure of work. He was President of the Lancastrian Frankland Society.

His honorary degrees included:

Glasgow (Hon. LLD 1921); Liverpool (Hon. DSc 1925); Penn. University USA (Hon. DSc 1926); Yale (Hon. DSc 1927); Princeton (Hon. DSc 1929); Cambridge (Hon. DSc 1930); Aberdeen (Hon. LLD 1931); Durham (DCL 1931); Edinburgh (Hon. LLD 1933, on the occasion of the celebration of the 350th anniversary of the foundation of the university); Union College Schenectady (Hon. DSc 1938); Oxford (Hon. DCL 1938); McGill (Hon. DSc 1944); Aberystwyth (LLD 1947); and also the LLD of Columbia and New York Universities.

As a recognition of his services to Polish and Norwegian forces in Scotland during the Second World War, he was invested with the Order of Polonia Restituta (Officer, Grand Cross), 1944, and the King Haakon Cross of Freedom (First Class), 1947.

He was appointed as a JP and a Deputy Lieutenant for the City of Dundee in 1928.

He received the Jubilee Medal for HM King George V's Silver Jubilee, and the Coronation Medal for the Coronation of King George VI, whose coronation he attended.

He rendered service to the Scottish Universities Entrance Board, the Scottish Education Department, the Department of Scientific and Industrial Research and the Forest Products Research Board. He was a trustee of the Carnegie Trust, The Pilgrim Trust, the Commonwealth Fund and the Ramsay Memorial Fellowship. He was appointed as an 1851 Exhibition Commissioner in 1934. He was a member of the Prime Minister's Committee on the Training of Biologists (1931); and chairman of the Viceroy's Committee on the Indian Institute of Science (1936), chairman of the Committee on Higher Education in the West Indies (1944) and of the Inter-University Committee on Higher Education in the Colonies (1946–51). He was a prime mover in founding the University College of the West Indies, where the scarlet gown of St Andrews is worn in honour of their founding father. He was an ever-welcome guest in the United States, where he gave many lectures and addresses.

Senior (Honorary) Officers of St Andrews University during James Irvine's Principalship

Chancellors

1900–1921	Alexander Hugh Bruce, 6th Lord Balfour of Burleigh
1922–1928	Douglas Haig, 1st Earl Haig of Bemersyde
1928	Richard Burdon Haldane, 1st Viscount Haldane of Cloan
1929–1947	Stanley Baldwin, 1st Earl Baldwin of Bewdley
1948–1973	Douglas Douglas-Hamilton, 14th Duke of Hamilton

Rectors

1919–1922	Sir J.M. Barrie
1922–1925	Rudyard Kipling
1925–1928	Fridtjof Nansen
1928–1931	Sir Wilfred Genfell
1931–1934	Field-Marshal Jan Smuts
1934–1937	Guglielmo Marconi
1937–1938	Robert MacGregor Mitchell
1938–1946	Sir David Munro
1946–1949	Sir George Cunningham
1949–1952	David Cecil, Lord Burghley
1952–1955	David Lindsey, 28th Earl of Crawford

Notes

The two largest sources of primary research material used passim are:

(a) The personal letters, diaries and other papers of James Colquhoun Irvine and of his wife, Mabel Violet Irvine. These are currently in the private possession of his family. They are abbreviated JCI or MVI (MVW before her marriage). The initials JVG are used to indicate the contribution made by Jim and Mabel's elder daughter, Veronica; and

(b) The Special Collections of the University Library of St Andrews University. These are all prefixed UY.

Other abbreviations are to be interpreted as follows:

NLS   National Library of Scotland
NA   National Archives at Kew
PRO   Public Record Office

Unattributed quotes are, unless indicated otherwise by the context, sourced from the Irvine papers, and from family information.

Introduction

1 *Obituary Notices of Fellows of the Royal Society*, vol. 8, November 1953.

2 MVI to her elder daughter, Veronica Gandy, 25 July 1952.

3 Hew Lorimer, 1907–1993, Scottish sculptor, son of Sir Robert Lorimer, architect, and nephew of the painter John Henry Lorimer. Hew Lorimer lived at Kellie Castle in East Fife, close to St Andrews. The Lorimers were friends of the Irvine family.

4 His full matriculation of arms was not granted until 14 December 1948. Until this date, he quite correctly bore the Irvine crest and the Irvine motto – *Sub Sole Sub Umbra Virens* – on his ring.

5 JVG. Queen Elizabeth, 1900–2002, consort of HM King George VI.

6 JCI. Address given to the North British Branch of the Pharmaceutical Society of Great Britain. 24 November 1922. University of St Andrews, Special Collections, UY 875 Box 1/5.

7 In 1943 the Asquith Commission on Higher Education in the Colonies appointed Sir James Irvine as chairman of the West Indies Committee.

8 Haworth, Walter Norman (1883–1950), KB, FRS, chemist; from 1925, Mason Professor of Chemistry at Birmingham University.

9 Hetherington, Hector James Wright (1888–1965), GBE, Principal of Glasgow University (1936–1961).

10 Obituary tribute written by Sir Hector Hetherington and first published in the *Glasgow Herald* on 13 June 1952.

Chapter 1 The Power House of the Empire

1 Records of births, deaths and marriages in Scotland, Register House, Edinburgh.

2 Daniel Defoe, *A Tour through the Whole Island of Great Britain* (1724–6).

3 Records of births, etc, Register House.

4 1841 census return for Maybole.

5 Hugh Douglas, *Roderick Lawson of Maybole – A Remarkable Victorian Minister*, [Ayr]: Ayrshire Archeological and Natural History Society (1978); and Norman Murray, *The Scottish Handloom Weavers 1790–1850: A Social History*, Edinburgh, John Donald (1978).

6 Records of births, etc, Register House.

7 1871 census.

8 Family records.

9 1871 census.

10 Family records.

11 David Stow (1793–1864), Scottish educationalist.

12 Register of births, etc, Register House.

13 Catalogue of MacFarlane's castings, Mitchell Library, Glasgow Collection: GC f672, 2506541443 MCF.

14 Year Book of the General Assembly of the Free Church of Scotland.

15 JVG recollections. Harry Lauder was a popular Scottish music hall entertainer.

Chapter 2 A Victorian Boyhood

1 The Disruption (1843) was a schism within the Established Church of Scotland over the issue of the Church's relationship with the state. It gave rise to the Free Church of Scotland.

2 Address to the annual meeting of the Workers' Educational Association (WEA). UY 875 Box 2.

3 St Andrews University *Alumnus Chronicle*, January 1953.

4 Address to the Greenock Philosophical Society, UY 875 Box 3.

5 Robert Gillespie, *Glasgow and the Clyde*, Glasgow (1876).

6 Minutes of the General Assembly of the Free Church of Scotland, Year Book 1886 Library of New College, Edinburgh University. SLY 50G.

7 JCI, 'Acceptance Speech of the Hon. Fellowship of the Educational Institute of Scotland', 3 July 1933, UY 875 Box 3.

8 'We Twa' hae Rin Aboot the Braes', from Robert Burns' ballad 'Auld Lang Syne'.

9 *Les Expositions Universelles au XIX Siecle*, Henry Lyonnet, *L'Histoire, La Vie et la Curiosité*, vol. 5, chapter 22.

10 Perilla Kinchin and Juliet Kinchin, *Glasgow's Great Exhibitions*, Wendlebury: White Cockade Press (1988).

11 Henry Drummond (1851–1897), Scottish evangelist, explorer and professor of natural science.

12 JCI, 'Address to the WEA: All Roads Lead to Rome', 27 April 1939, published in Irvine's *The Aim and the End*, Edinburgh and London: Oliver and Boyd (1956).

13 Will of Allan Glen, Records of the Glasgow and West of Scotland Technical College, University of Strathclyde Archives. GB 249 OE.

14 JCI: 'Address Delivered at the Unveiling of the Memorial to John G. Kerr in Allan Glen's School', 9 October 1931. UY 875 Box 3. Published in *The Aim and the End*.

15 John Kerr. 'Testimonial for Chair of Chemistry in Dundee', JCI Private Papers.

16 UY 875 Box 2: 'Presentation to Professor G.G. Henderson'. Also, Henderson Papers, University of Strathclyde Archives, M 70/10/3: 'The First Henderson Memorial Lecture of the Royal Institute of Chemistry', 20 January 1947, given by Professor Sir Ian Heilbron.

17 University of Strathclyde Archives. Chemistry Department Student Records – Technical College. OE 11/12/5/4.

18 St Andrews University Special Collections: Appointment to the Chair of Chemistry in Dundee, 1908.

19 JCI, article in the *Alchemist*, 15 September 1937, UY 875 Box 3.

20 University of Strathclyde Archives: Henderson Papers.

21 University of Strathclyde Archives: Henderson Papers.

22 University of Strathclyde Archives, OE 11/12/5/4.

23 Morris W. Travers, *A Life of Sir William Ramsay*, London: Arnold Press (1956).

24 JCI, 'The Memory of William Ramsay', speech given at the Ramsay Chemical Dinner, 3 December 1937. UY 875 Box 2/20.

25 Alfred Nobel's description of Ardeer, 1871. Quoted in, for example, H. Schück and R. Sohlman, *The Life of Alfred Nobel*, London: Heinemann (1929).

26 JCI, article in the *Alchemist*, 15 September 1937, UY 875 Box 3.

Chapter 3 Civis Universitatis Sancti Andreae

1 R.G. Cant, *The University of St Andrews, A Short History*, 4th edn, Edinburgh: Strathmartine Press (2002)

2 JCI, 'Thomas Purdie', *Transactions of the Chemical Society*, 3 (1917).

3 JCI, 'The Chair of Chemistry in the United College of St Salvator and St Leonard', Centenary Lecture delivered to the Chemical Society of the University of St Andrews, 6 December 1940, UY 875 Box 2; published as *The Chair of Chemistry in the United College of St Salvator and St Leonard*, Edinburgh: Oliver and Boyd, 1941.

4 JCI, 'Johannes Wislicenus (1835–1902)', delivered to the St Andrews University Chemical Society, 18 November 1907.

5 JCI, 'Rewards and Fairies', Second Frankland Oration of the Lancastrian Frankland Society, delivered as president, 14 January 1938.

6 JCI, 'The Chair of Chemistry' and 'Thomas Purdie'.

7 JCI, 'The Chair of Chemistry'.

8 Business records of the proceedings of the After Many Days Club [St Andrews' alumni association], 1952.

9 J.M. Anderson (ed.), *The Matriculation Roll of the University of St Andrews 1747–1897*, Edinburgh: Blackwood (1905).

10 JCI, Dow Lecture: 'St Andrews in Transition', 21 September 1950, UY 875 Box 2/29.

11 Ibid.

12 Rev. George Blair's tribute to JCI, *Alumnus Chronicle*, January 1953.

13 Anderson, *Matriculation Roll*; JCI personal papers.

14 A.E. Gunther, *The Life of William Carmichael M'Intosh, MD, FRS, of St Andrews, 1838–1931, A Pioneer in Marine Biology*, Edinburgh: Scottish Academic Press for the University of St Andrews (1977).

15 *College Echoes*, December 1897; also records of the Kate Kennedy Club, Special Collections of St Andrews University Library.

16 Ibid.

17 R.N. Smart, *Biographical Register of the University of St Andrews 1747–1897*, St Andrews (2004).

18 JCI private library.

19 JCI private library.

20 JCI personal papers. St Mungo is the patron saint of the city of Glasgow.

21 JCI, 'The Memory of William Ramsay', Dec. 1937

22 *Obituary Notices of Fellows of the Royal Society*, vol. 8, November 1953.

23 Archive of the Royal Commission for the Exhibition of 1851, ref: 13A-I-130.

24 *Obituary Notices of Fellows of the Royal Society*, vol. 8, November 1953.

25 Archive of the Royal Commission for the Exhibition of 1851.

26 JCI personal papers.

27 Matriculation records of the University of Leipzig.

Chapter 4 A Student in Leipzig, 1899–1901

1 JCI's address in Leipzig was 27 Ferdinand Rhode Strasse-IV, as evidenced in the matriculation rolls of Leipzig University, and on every letter he wrote from Leipzig between October 1899 and May 1901.

2 See series of notebooks kept by Irvine between 1895 and 1916 in the collection of printed and manuscript books presented to the chemistry department of St Andrews University by Lady Irvine after her husband's death. Volume 18: Robert Eustafieff Rose, April 1904–July 1905, 'Experiments on the Action of Benylchloride hydroxl Groups, in the Presence of Silver Oxide'. On deposit in the Special Collections of the university with shelfmark Purdie Papers ms 38620.

3 See notes in the above archive on the effect of silver oxide on a solution of glucose in CH_3OH, made by JCI in his chemical research notebook, 1901: 'The silver oxide turned very black and a distinct mirror was formed. No smell of aldehyde was noticed.'

4 Irvine's accounts of Johannes Wislicenus are sourced from the tribute to Wislicenus that Irvine gave to the St Andrews Chemical Society 18 November 1907, and published in *The Aim and the End*.

5 Donald N. McCloskey (ed.), *Essays on a Mature Economy: Britain after 1840*, London: Methuen (1971).

6 Archives of the Royal Commission for the Exhibition of 1851.

7 Ibid.

8 JCI Personal Papers: correspondence with Mabel Williams, June 1901.

9 *Arbeit*: literally 'work'; in this instance JCI's thesis.

10 UY 875 Irvine Box 3.

11 Personal papers: Mabel Williams to her mother, Jessie Williams, 2 November 1899.

12 Records of the University of Leipzig.

13 Personal papers: Mabel Williams to Jessie Williams.

14 'The Rotatory Powers of Optically Active Methoxy- and Ethoxy-propionic Acids Prepared from Lactic Acid', published jointly with Purdie, *Journal of the Chemical Society*, 75 (1899), 483.

15 St Andrews University Ordinance 48.

16 MVI, *The Avenue of Years: A Memoir of Sir James Irvine, Principal and Vice-Chancellor of the University of St. Andrews, 1921–1952*, Edinburgh: Blackwood (1970).

17 MVI personal papers: to Jessie Williams.

18 Ibid.

19 Personal papers: Robert Williams to Jessie Williams.

20 MVI personal papers: to Jessie Williams.

21 UY 875 Box 3.

22 MVI personal papers: to Jessie Williams.

23 'Optically Active Dimethoxysuccinic Acid and its Derivatives', published jointly with Purdie, *Journal of the Chemical Society*, 79:2 (1901), 957.

24 JCI, 'Johannes Wislicenus (1835–1902)', delivered to the St Andrews University Chemical Society, 18 November 1907.

25 MVI personal papers: Diary.

26 MVI, *Avenue of Years*.

27 *Annalen* (1868), 145, 302.

28 *Journal of the Chemical Society*, 79 (1901), 668.

29 JCI personal papers: to Mabel Williams, 9 December 1900.

30 JCI personal papers: to Mabel Williams.

31 Archives of the Royal Commission for the Exhibition of 1851.

32 JCI personal papers: to Mabel Williams.

33 JCI personal papers: to Mabel Williams.

34 JCI, 'Johannes Wislicenus': see note 4, above.

Chapter 5 Return to St Andrews

1 *Journal of the Chemical Society*, 79:2 (1901) 957; and St Andrews University Special Collections, Purdie Papers ms 38620/1/48, 49.
2 Willard Gibbs Address, given before the Chicago Section of the American Chemical Society, 17 September 1926.
3 JCI personal papers: to MVW, 11 November 1902.
4 JCI, 'The Chair of Chemistry', 1940
5 St Andrews University Special Collections Purdie Papers ms 38620/1/48 etc; and UY 875/Irvine Box 3.
6 JCI personal papers, correspondence with MVW.
7 Personal papers: MVW to JCI, 8 October 1901.
8 Personal papers: MVW to JCI, 1 January 1901.
9 Personal papers: MVW to JCI, 23 November 1902.
10 JCI personal papers, to MVW, 26 July 1902.
11 JCI with T. Purdie, 'The Alkylation of Sugars', Rep. Brit. Ass., Section B (1902).
12 Archives of the Royal Commission for the Exhibition of 1851, 14 October 1902.
13 UY7 sec. 2/1, papers of the Secretary to the University.
14 Carnegie Trust: Appendix to the Reports to the Trustees 26 July 1902, and records of the same.
15 UY7 sec. 2/1.
16 Records of the Carnegie Trust for Scotland.
17 St Andrews University Special Collections UY Purdie papers ms 38620/1/etc.
18 JCI with T. Purdie, 'A Contribution to the Constitution of Disaccharides', Rep. Brit. Ass., Section B (1903).
19 The Wylde, 13 Panmure Terrace, Barnhill, an eastern suburb of Broughty Ferry. Now the Woodlands Hotel. Information from Alison Lowe.
20 JCI with T. Purdie, 'The Alkylation of Sugars', *Journal of the Chemical Society*, 83, (1903) 1021.
21 UY7 sec. 2/1.
22 Minutes of Meetings of the University Court, St Andrews.
23 JCI personal papers.
24 MVI, *Avenue of Years*.
25 MVI, 'Genius at Dinner', *Glasgow Herald*, 7 December 1909.
26 Personal papers: MVI to Jessie Williams, 14 October 1905.
27 Personal papers: MVI to Jessie Williams, 15 October 1905.
28 JCI notebook of research topics among personal papers.
29 UY Special Collections Purdie ms 38620/1/etc.

Chapter 6 The Professor

1 St Andrews University Special Collections 4 UY7 sec. 2/1 1908/2.
2 Records of the University of St Andrews: Appointment to Chair of Chemistry in Dundee.

3 Personal papers: JCI to MVI from Northwestern University, Evanston, USA, 9 August 1928.

4 Personal papers: correspondence with JCI.

5 4 UY7 sec. 2/1 1908/2.

6 Personal papers: MVI to Jessie Williams, 9 March 1909.

7 4 UY7 sec. 2/1.

8 Personal papers: MVI to Jessie Williams.

9 Ibid.

10 Ibid.

11 Ibid.

12 JCI, Inaugural address as Professor of Chemistry, 7 October 1909.

13 JCI, 'The Chair of Chemistry', 1940.

14 JCI personal papers.

15 Papers of the Secretary to the University, 4 UY7 sec. 2/1.

16 John Burnet was Professor of Greek at the University of St Andrews, 1892–1926.

17 Personal papers: MVI to Jessie Williams.

18 Ordinances 16 and 18 of the University of St Andrews.

19 JCI, 'The Chair of Chemistry', 1940.

20 JCI, 'Thomas Purdie', *Transactions of the Chemical Society*, 2:1 (1917).

21 JCI, Inaugural address, 1909.

22 UY7 sec. 2/1; Minutes of the Meetings of University Court; Reports of the Carnegie Trust for the Universities of Scotland.

23 JCI personal papers: letters from William Denham.

24 2 UY7 sec. 2/1 22.

25 MVI, *Avenue of Years*.

26 2 UY7 sec. 2/1.

27 Personal papers: MVI to Jessie Williams.

28 JCI, 'All Roads Lead to Rome', lecture given to WEA, 27 April 1939. UY875 Box 2.

29 Valuation Roll for St Andrews, 1910–11: 1505.

30 Personal papers: MVI to Jessie Williams.

31 MVI to Jessie Williams.

32 Minutes of meetings of the University Court; MVI to Jessie Williams.

33 Special Collections of St Andrews University Library: records of 1911 quincentenary.

34 Limited edition of 150 copies of *Memorial Volume of Scientific Papers*, St Andrews University (1911), for presentation to the distinguished scientific guests of the university.

35 Personal papers: MVI to Jessie Williams.

36 MVI, *Avenue of Years*.

37 Ibid.

Chapter 7 The Great War

1 JCI personal papers: correspondence with his wife.
2 St Andrews Special Collections UY7 sec. 2/1.
3 Royal Society MS/500/12Aa.
4 NA PRO WO 106/341.
5 UY7 sec. 2/1 21.
6 JVG.
7 JCI, 'Chemistry in War Time', address given to the Empire Club of Canada, 18 October 1932.
8 Memorandum written by JCI, 2 December 1915. UY7 sec. 2/1 22.
9 JCI. 'Chemistry and War': address given to the American Chemical Society 13 August 1928.
10 Minutes of the Chemistry Sub-Committee of the War Committee of the Royal Society.
11 JCI personal papers.
12 JCI, 'Chemistry in War Time', address given to the Empire Club of Canada, 18 October 1932.
13 Minutes of the Chemistry Sub-Committee of the War Committee of the Royal Society.
14 Russell Papers UY 385 1/5/69 Special Collections, St Andrews University.
15 JCI, 'Chemistry in War Time', 1932.
16 The term 'novocain' (or Novocain, with an initial capital), although previously the name of a German proprietary drug, was adopted and habitually used by Irvine. Once it began manufacture in the UK during the 1914–18 war, however, it had to acquire a new trade name, and Kerfoots manufactured it as Kerocain. (See E.H. Shields, *Fifty Years at Bardsley Vale: A Record of Pharmaceutical Progress*, Bardsely, Lancs: Thomas Kerfoot and Co. (1946), Foreword by J.C. Irvine.) Today, the anaesthetic is commonly referred to by dentists and other health professionals as 'novocaine', but the spelling current at the time under discussion – 'novocain' – is used throughout this text.
17 UY7 sec. 2/1 21.
18 Irvine Scientific Papers, Special Collections, St Andrews University, from Chemistry Department. Tribute written by Dr Ettie Steele, *Alumnus Chronicle* June 1978.
19 'Cives', plural of *civis*, as in *civis universitatis Sancti Andreae*. Loosely, it is used to mean 'members of the university'.
20 Dr Ettie Steele's recollections: tribute in the *Alumnus Chronicle* June 1978.
21 MVI personal papers.
22 Russell Papers UY 385 1/5/69.
23 UY7 sec. 2/1 21.
24 Royal Society MS/500/1/43.
25 JCI personal papers.
26 NA PRO WO 106/341.

27 Ibid.

28 Ibid.

29 On 28 July 1915, the Committee for Scientific and Industrial Research was established by Order in Council. Reports of the Committee of the Privy Council for Scientific and Industrial Research, 1915–18, Special Collections of the Royal Society.

30 JCI personal papers: letter, 19 August 1915.

31 JCI personal papers: letter, 1 August 1916.

32 JCI personal papers: correspondence.

33 JCI personal papers.

34 Ibid.

35 Ludwig Fritz Haber, *The Poisonous Cloud: Chemical Warfare in the First World War*, Oxford: Clarendon (1986).

36 JCI personal papers: correspondence.

37 NA PRO WO 106/341; and PRO WO M17 B2.

38 JCI personal papers: letter from General Thuillier, director-general of Trench Warfare Supply Department.

39 Ibid.

40 MVI, *Avenue of Years*.

41 JCI personal ephemera. Charles Lamb: Letter to George Dyer, 20 December 1830, published in *The Works of Charles Lamb: Comprising His Most Interesting Letters – Essays of Elia, the Last Essays of Elia, Eliana, Rosamund Gray, Poems, Sonnets, Translations and Final Memorials*, London: Bell and Daldy (1867).

42 Russell papers UY 385 1/5/69.

43 JCI personal papers.

44 William Jackson Pope to Hartley, 20 August 1917, quoted by Ludwig Haber in *The Poisonous Cloud*, p. 124.

45 Royal Society Library.

46 UY7 sec. 2/1 26.

Chapter 8 The Principalship of St Andrews University

1 JCI personal papers.

2 Records of the Royal Society.

3 St Andrews University Special Collections UY7 sec. 2/1 23.

4 JCI personal papers.

5 JCI personal papers: corrrespondence with E.F. Armstrong.

6 *Nature*, 9 May 1931, p. 723.

7 JCI, 'The Chair of Chemistry', 1940.

8 Inaugural lecture on induction to the chair of chemistry at St Andrews.

9 *Obituary Notices of Fellows of the Royal Society*, vol. 8, November 1953.

10 JCI personal papers.

11 Inaugural lecture on induction to the chair of chemistry.

12 UY 875 Box 2/30. 'The Profession of Chemistry', speech given at the Ramsay Chemical Dinner, 7 December 1934.

13 JCI personal papers.

14 Ibid.

15 Ibid.

16 Ibid.

17 Ibid.

18 UY7 sec. 2/1 24.

19 Russell papers, UY 38515/5/69.

20 JCI personal papers.

21 Ibid.

22 UY7 sec. 2/1 25. Question mark in parentheses in original document.

23 UY7 sec. 2/1 22.

24 Russell papers UY 38515/5/69.

25 UY 38515/5/69.

26 UY7 sec. 2/1 21.

27 Ibid.

28 Ibid.

29 Ibid.

30 UY7 sec. 2/1 25.

31 JCI personal papers.

32 UY7 sec. 2/1 26.

33 JCI personal papers; and UY7 sec. 2/1/28.

34 JCI personal papers.

35 Russell papers UY 38515/5/69. Sir William Watson Cheyne was MP for the universities of Edinburgh and St Andrews, and Sir Henry Craik was MP for the Combined Scottish Universities.

36 JCI personal papers.

37 Ibid.

38 Ibid.

39 Ibid.

40 Ibid.

41 Ibid.

42 Ibid.

43 Ibid.

Chapter 9 The Young Principal

1 David Walker, Regius Professor Emeritus of Law in the University of Glasgow, has supplied the legal sources for the nineteenth-century consolidation of the management of St Andrews University: these are in particular the Universities (Scotland) Acts of 1858, c. 83 and 1889, c. 55. The powers of the University Court were defined under the 1858 act, s. 12; the 1889 act, s. 5 and 6; and the 1889 act, s. 21 The role of the Senatus Academicus was defined by the 1885 act s. 5; and by the 1889 act s. 7.

2 See Cant, *University of St Andrews*, 152–5.

3 JCI personal papers.

4 Mabel Irvine used several affectionate names for her husband: 'Jim' becomes 'Jimbo' and then 'Dimbie'. Before their marriage he was 'my dear old fossil'. To him, she was 'Mabs', even 'Queen Mab' and, when very young, 'Mubbles'. Her children and their spouses referred to her as 'Pettikin' or 'Maimie'.

5 UY 875 Dundee.

6 JCI personal correspondence.

7 *College Echoes*, January 1921.

8 Recollections of former student: information from Professor Robert Crawford, Emeritus Professor of Plant Ecology in the University of St Andrews.

9 JCI, inaugural address as Principal, published in *The Aim and the End*.

10 UY 875 Student Residences.

11 *St Andrews Citizen*, 21 January 1921.

12 UY 875 Union.

13 JCI personal papers: MS of speech made by Rudyard Kipling on opening the Union.

14 Papers of Secretary to the University, UY7 sec. 2/1/28.

15 JCI personal papers: correspondence with Rudyard Kipling.

16 JCI personal papers: correspondence with MVI.

17 Papers of the Secretary to the University, UY7 sec. 2/1/28.

18 Minutes of the meetings of the University Court.

19 UY 875 Box B.

20 Ibid.

21 JCI personal papers: correspondence with MVI.

22 Ibid.

23 JCI personal papers: letter from G.K. Menzies, secretary of the Royal Society of Arts.

24 D'Arcy Thompson papers, MS 19243, Special Collections, St Andrews University.

25 JCI correspondence with MVI. The work referred to is Sir D'Arcy Wentworth Thompson's *On Growth and Form*, Cambridge: Cambridge University Press (1917).

26 Minutes of the meetings of the University Court; D'Arcy Thompson Papers MS 19217.

27 D'Arcy Thompson papers; UY 875 Box File Development.

28 JCI personal papers.

29 D'Arcy Thompson Papers, MS 19243.

30 Ibid.

31 MVI, *Avenue of Years*.

32 Family recollections.

33 JCI personal papers: Visitors' Book, University House.

34 Papers of the Secretary to the University UY7 sec. 2/1/28.

35 Mabel Violet Irvine, *From a Nursery Window*, London: Skeffington (1922).

36 JVG recollections.
37 MVI personal papers: Diary, 1923.
38 UY 875 Box 1.
39 Ibid.
40 Whitaker's *Almanack*.
41 MVI personal papers: Diary, 1923.
42 JCI and MVI personal correspondence.
43 JCI personal papers: correspondence with Barrie.
44 University House Visitors Book; papers of the Secretary of the University UY7 sec. 2/1/28.
45 Minutes of the Trustees of the Carnegie Trust; UY 875 St Salvator's Hall. Lord Sands was the judicial title of Christopher N. Johnston, judge of the court of session and a leading churchman (information from Professor David Walker). H.P. Macmillan was a Lord of Appeal in Ordinary in the House of Lords, and author of *A Man of Law's Tale* (1952).
46 JCI personal papers.
47 Ibid.

Chapter 10 A Golden Age

1 JCI personal papers.
2 Rudyard Kipling papers, University of Sussex, shelfmark C4 Honours, property of the National Trust.
3 For a definition of the office of rector, see Universities (Scotland) Acts of 1858 and 1889. The Rector should only be termed 'Lord Rector' if the holder of the office is a member of the Privy Council.
4 UY 875 CR.
5 UY 875 CR and UY 225: 1922 (Barrie).
6 JCI personal papers: correspondence with Barrie, 10 February 1922.
7 JCI personal papers: correspondence with Haig.
8 *St Andrews Citizen*, 6 May 1922.
9 Reported in the *St Andrews Citizen*.
10 UY 875 Box 2, JCI: Address made to the University of Aberystwyth, 24 October 1949.
11 MVI personal papers: Diary, 1922.
12 Reported in the *St Andrews Citizen*.
13 MVI personal papers: correspondence with Barrie.
14 Janet Dunbar, *J.M. Barrie, The Man Behind the Image*, London: Collins (1970); MVI, *Avenue of Years*.
15 J.M. Barrie, *Courage*, London: Hodder and Stoughton, 1922
16 JCI personal papers: correspondence with Barrie.
17 JCI personal papers: correspondence with Haig.
18 Minutes of Meetings of University Court.
19 JCI personal papers.

20 Anecdote of Robert Crawford's mother; information from the Irvine family.
21 MVI personal papers: correspondence with Barrie.
22 MVI personal papers.
23 Lorn MacIntyre, *Sir David Russell: A Biography*, Edinburgh: Canongate, 1994; *St Andrews Citizen*.
24 UY 875 Box CR.
25 JVG recollections.
26 JCI personal papers: correspondence with Kipling.
27 Papers of the Secretary of the University, UY7.
28 *Glasgow Herald*, 10 October 1923.
29 UY 875 Irvine/Chapel.
30 JCI personal papers: correspondence with Kipling.
31 MVI personal papers: correspondence with Kipling.
32 JCI personal papers: correspondence with Barrie.
33 JCI personal papers: correspondence with Mrs Willis Wood, 1 December 1926.
34 MVI personal papers: correspondence with JCI, 25 April 1928.
35 MVI, *Avenue of Years*.
36 JCI personal correspondence with Barrie. Millicent Fawcett (1847–1911) was a leader of the women's suffrage movement; she was largely instrumental in obtaining the vote for British women over thirty years of age under the 1918 Representation of the People Act.
37 JCI personal papers: Visitors Book.
38 Recollections of Dr John Fewster; also recollections of Donald Kennedy.
39 JCI UY 875 Box 2. 'Forward to the Kate Kennedy Annual', April 1948.
40 *St Andrews Citizen*.
41 JCI personal papers: correspondence with Barrie.
42 MVI personal papers: Diary and personal correspondence.
43 JCI personal papers: correspondence with MVI, 2 February 1928. The question of an official car was only fully solved during the last year of Irvine's life, when the university considered that its venerable Principal deserved a chauffeured car, and Smith the chauffeur, on the payroll of the university, joined the staff at University House. Irvine never mastered the art of driving a car, and left it to his children to drive the vehicle that was eventually bought for his young family.
44 JCI personal papers: correspondence with Oswald Birley.
45 JCI personal papers: correspondence with MVI.
46 JCI personal papers.
47 Minutes of the meetings of the University Court; UY 875.
48 JVG recollections.
49 JCI speeches and addresses: 28 June 1929.
50 JCI personal papers: correspondence with Haig.

Chapter 11 A Citizen of a Scientific Age

1 Dr D.J. Bell, 'Some Developments in Carbohydrate Chemistry', paper delivered before the Chemical Society (of London), 27 February 1953.

2 Quoted in correspondence between JCI and Mrs Willis Wood, 23 September 1926.

3 Sir James Irvine, *Citizenship in a Scientific Age*, Sackville, New Brunswick: Mount Allison University [Canada], 1937. Delivered in a reworked form to the Glasgow Royal Philosophical Society, 1945, and published in its *Proceedings*.

4 See the Bibliography included in James Colquhoun Irvine's obituary published in the *Obituary Notices of Fellows of the Royal Society*, vol. 8, November 1953 .

5 MVI personal papers.

6 JCI personal papers.

7 JCI personal papers: W.P. Wynne to JCI, 20 December 1924.

8 JCI personal papers: C.R. Young, Secretary to the DSIR to JCI, 14 December 1920.

9 Letters of Appointment by Order of Council, dated 16 August 1922 and 8 August 1925. JCI was reappointed biennially over a long period.

10 JCI to Rudyard Kipling, 26 October 1932. Kipling Papers 32/28, property of the National Trust, and on deposit at Sussex University. I acknowledge the permission of the National Trust to use this letter.

11 JCI personal papers: correspondence (January 1925), Eric Barnard of DSIR and Sir Frank Heath.

12 JCI, 'The Chair of Chemistry', 1940.

13 *College Echoes*, 1921.

14 Minutes of the University Court.

15 John Read FRS, *Historic St Andrews and its University*, St Andrews: W.C. Henderson & Son (1939).

16 *Report of the Ninetieth Meeting of the British Association for the Advancement of Science*. London: John Murray (1923).

17 JCI: 'log' of American trips.

18 *St Andrews Citizen*, 3 January 1925.

19 JCI: personal papers.

20 JCI: personal papers, correspondence with the Royal Institution.

21 JCI: personal papers.

22 JCI: personal papers, correspondence with MVI.

23 A vast array of American newspapers, including the *New York Times*, *New York Evening Post*, *New York Sun*, *New York Commercial*, *Philadelphia Public Ledger*, *Philadelphia Inquirer*, *Connecticut New Britain*, *Boston Post*, *Rhode Island Tribune* and *Pottsville Morning Paper*.

24 JCI personal papers: correspondence with MVI.

25 MVI, *Avenue of Years*.

26 JCI personal papers: correspondence with MVI.

27 JCI personal papers: correspondence with Willard Connely, 21 July 1932.

28 JCI: 'log' of American trips.

29 JCI's limerick, in letter to his wife.

30 JCI correspondence with MVI.

31 JCI personal papers: T.A. Edison to JCI, 29 July 1928.

32 Rudyard Kipling, 'The Vineyard', published in *Debits and Credits*, London: Macmillan (1926).

33 MVI personal papers.

34 National Archives of Scotland. SC36/48/379: inventory of will of John Irvine, 15 December 1926, and SC36/48/412: inventory of will of Agnes McNeil Colquhoun, 2 August 1929.

35 Information conveyed to MVI by Dr Steele, Irvine's PA, 18 February 1953.

36 Records of the Carnegie Trust for the Universities of Scotland.

37 John Read, FRS: Obituary of Irvine, published in the Royal Society's *Obituary Notices*.

38 A. Pictet and H. Vogel, *Helv. Chim. Acta* 11, 436 (1928) and subsequent papers.

39 Information from John Oldham.

40 JCI, 'The Chair of Chemistry', 1940.

41 JCI personal papers: letter to MVI 27 June 1930.

42 JCI, 25 October 1949, UY 875 Box 3.

Chapter 12 America's Favourite Britisher

1 MVI personal papers: letter from J.M. Barrie.

2 JCI to MVI, 16 May 1938.

3 JCI personal papers: last page of 'log' of 1932 visit to America.

4 Harkness Memorial address, delivered by Irvine to the University of St Andrews 1940; James W. Wooster, *Edward Stephen Harkness 1874–1940*, NYC: privately printed (1949).

5 Information from Max Farrand and William Connoly, as conveyed to John Read, FRS: cf. *Obituary Notices of Fellows of the Royal Society*, vol. 8, November 1953.

6 Obituary addendum contributed to *The Times*, 22 July 1952 by a Harkness Fellow.

7 MVI personal papers: Diary, 26 Feb 1926.

8 Jan Read, *Young Man in Movieland*, Lanham: Scarecrow Press (2004).

9 JCI personal papers: 'log' of 1926 visit to America, 24 August 1926.

10 Papers of the Secretary to the University, UY7 sec. 2/1/28.

11 UY 875 Box 5.

12 UY7 sec. 2/1/28.

13 Wooster, *Edward Stephen Harkness*.

14 JCI personal papers: Harkness correspondence.

15 Ibid.

16 UY 875 Chapel Box File.

17 JCI personal papers: correspondence with Harkness.

18 Ibid.

19 Thomas Jones, *A Diary with Letters, 1931 1950*, Oxford: Oxford University Press (1954), 26 May 1937.

20 UY 875 Harkness Box; and JCI personal papers: 'Address on Presentation of Harkness Portrait', 18 Nov 1933.

21 Black bun: a sweet Scottish delicacy, consisting of currants, other dried fruits and spices preserved within a thin crust of plain pastry, to be served in slices. It is prevalent in bakers' shops during the weeks before Christmas and eaten at Hogmanay. It was invariably given by Mabel as a Christmas present to absent friends and family.

22 JCI personal papers: memorial address delivered to St Andrews University after death of Harkness.

23 Ibid.

24 Macmillan, *A Man of Law's Tale*, London: Macmillan (1953).

25 JCI personal papers: correspondence with MVI.

26 Herbert Hensley Henson, *Retrospect of an Unimportant Life*, 3 vols, Oxford: Oxford University Press (1943), vol. 2, ch. 20.

27 JCI personal papers: letter from Harkness.

28 JCI personal papers: 'log' of 1932 visit to America.

29 JCI personal papers: correspondence with MVI, 24 August 1926.

30 JCI personal papers: letter from Emily de Forrest, September 1926.

31 UY 875 Box 3.

Chapter 13 This Dear Wee Gossipy Place

1 MVI, *Avenue of Years*.

2 JCI personal papers: correspondence with Professor Eric Baly; correspondence with Liverpool University. Printed Order of Graduation Ceremony, Liverpool University 1925.

3 JCI personal papers.

4 JCI to David Russell. UY 38515/5/69.

5 JCI personal papers.

6 JCI personal papers: correspondence with Sir Robert Bruce.

7 JCI personal papers.

8 MVI personal papers.

9 JCI personal papers.

10 MVI personal papers.

11 JCI personal papers: correspondence with an American friend, 19 February 1933.

12 *St Andrews Citizen*.

13 *Saving St Andrews*, The St Andrews Preservation Trust, 2003.

14 JCI personal papers, Oct. 1939.

15 September 1946. Speech to the Tontine Dining Club of Officials of Fife County Council.

16 JCI personal papers.
17 University House Visitors Book.
18 NLS MS 6032 f.9.
19 NLS MS 6033 f.257 .
20 JCI and MVI personal papers.
21 JCI personal papers.
22 Published in *The Aim and the End*.
23 JCI, *Andrew Carnegie Centenary, 1835–1935*, New York: Carnegie Corporation of New York (1935).
24 JCI personal papers: correspondence 30 Oct 1931 with an American friend.
25 UY 875 Box 5.
26 University of St Andrews/ Walker Trust, *Lectures on Leadership*, Oxford University Press (1950).
27 UY 875 Box 3.
28 *College Echoes*, 13 May 1938.
29 Will of Adam, Lord Gifford, 1887.
30 JCI personal papers: correspondence with Herbert Hensley Henson; see also Herbert Hensley Henson, *Retrospect of an Unimportant Life*, 3 vols.
31 JCI personal papers: correspondence with an American friend.
32 MVI personal papers.
33 JCI personal papers.
34 JCI personal papers, 27 October 1938.

Chapter 14 The Residential System

1 For an account of the founding of the Kate Kennedy Procession, see chapter 10.
2 For an authoritative account of the life of Bishop Kennedy, see Annie Dunlop's *Life and Times of James Kennedy, Bishop of St Andrews*, Edinburgh: Oliver and Boyd (1950).
3 *Scotsman*, 3 October 1930.
4 UY 875 Residences.
5 Information from the late Sir Eugene Melville.
6 Records of St Andrews University Court.
7 UY 875 Box 1/8, delivered to the Congress of the Educational Institute of Scotland.
8 Report of University Grants Committee, 3 February 1921.
9 *St Andrews Citizen*.
10 MVI personal papers.
11 UY 875 Box 5.
12 James Beaton, Archbishop of St Andrews, and Cardinal.
13 UY 875 Box 5.
14 MVI personal papers: letter from JCI.
15 MVI Diary, 26 February 1926.
16 To Harkness, UY 875 Box File Chapel.

17 MVI, *Avenue of Years.*
18 Dunlop, *Life and Times of James Kennedy.*
19 JCI personal papers: Graduation Address, 29 June 1926.
20 Matriculation of Arms granted by Thomas Innes of Learney, Lyon King at Arms, to James Colquhoun Irvine, his descendants and all descendants of his grandfather, Alexander Irvine: dated 14 December 1948. 'Argent, a fess engrailed Sable between three holly leaves slipped vert in chief and a gurges Or and of the third enflamed Gules in base; above the Shield is placed an Helmet befitting his degree with Mantling Vert doubled Argent, and on a wreath of these Liveries is set for Crest a cubit arm naked proper, grasping a test-tube filled with liquid Vert enflamed Gules, and in an Escrol over the same this Motto ECCE EGO, MITTE ME.'
21 *College Echoes*, 13 May 1938.
22 UY 875 Box 6.
23 JCI to MVI, 27 May 1952. Rev. Dr George Duncan, Principal of St Mary's College and Malcolm Knox, Professor of Moral Philosophy and Deputy Principal of St Andrews University. Knox would become Irvine's successor as Vice-Chancellor in 1953.
24 UY 875 Residences.
25 'The Compleat Student', delivered before Dundee Rotary Club, 14 April 1938.
26 UY 875 Irvine Box A.
27 JCI personal papers: Address to the Governors of University College Dundee.
28 Bodleian Library MS Eng c. 4793 f. 63, 2 May 1947, Clement Attlee to his brother, Tom. 'I had a good time in St Andrews despite pouring rain. It is quite a fine little town with some good old buildings – the university – the kirk with extremely good modern glass – interesting ruin of the old Cathedral, while its domestic architecture is much superior to that of most Scottish towns. I naturally recalled Andrew Lang's poem seeing the students, boys and girls, in their scarlet gowns. Unlike most northern universities there are residential colleges the result, I gather, of the energetic efforts of the Vice Chancellor Irvine with whom I had much talk at lunch.'
29 Personal papers: JCI to MVI, November 1848.
30 JCI Dow Lecture, 21 September 1950.

Chapter 15 'Here am I, send me': A Traveller in Education

1 James Colquhoun Irvine's personal motto was *Ecce ego, mitte me.*
2 Sir Hector Hetherington, Principal of Glasgow University, made tribute to him in the *Scotsman*, 21 June 1952: 'Through St Andrews, through the University Entrance Board, through the Carnegie Universities Trust, he influenced strongly the whole course of university and secondary school education in Scotland and further afield as well.'
3 JCI personal papers: correspondence with Nan Wood, 22 November 1928.
4 MVI personal papers: Diary.

5 Ibid.
6 Report of the Prime Minister's Economic Advisory Council's Committee on the   Education and Supply of Biologists. Also, JCI personal papers.
7 British Library. IOR V/26/865/3.
8 JCI personal papers: correspondence with MVI, passim.
9 Report on the Indian Institute of Science, Bangalore, by the second Quinquennial Review Committee (1936).
10 Russell Papers, St Andrews University Special Collections, 38515/5/69, 12 May 1936.
11 *Current Science*, January 1937.
12 St Andrews Special Collections, MS 19278 D'Arcy Thompson Papers.
13 Russell Papers. UY 38515.
14 National Archives CO 318/393/1.
15 ICS56 Moyne Papers, Special Collections, London University.
16 JCI personal papers: correspondence with Nan Wood, September 1943.
17 Anecdote of Tam Dalyell, former MP for Linlithgow.
18 'The Dons Go Westward-Ho', incomplete manuscript of Irvine's account of his first visit to the West Indies. Used passim.
19 Perham MSS Rhodes House Library 27/2/25.
20 ICS56 Moyne Papers, Special Collections, London University.
21 Sir Raymond Priestley's tribute to Irvine published in the *Alumnus Chronicle*, January 1953.
22 NA CO 318/459/3.
23 Sir Raymond Priestley's tribute to Irvine, *Alumnus Chronicle*.
24 JCI personal papers: correspondence with MVI, 1 May 1944.
25 NA CO 318/459/3.
26 Ibid.
27 Russell papers, 38515/5/70.
28 *Illustrated London News*, 17 December 1960.
29 NA BW 90/1037.
30 JCI personal papers, correspondence with MVI, March 1948.
31 'Jamaica Revisited', *Alumnus Chronicle*, June 1950: JCI's account of the last of six visits he made to the West Indies on behalf the University College of the West Indies. The Double Dykes is a street in St Andrews.

Chapter 16 The Second World War

1 MVI personal papers: Diary, 1930.
2 UY 875 Box 3.
3 JCI personal papers, 15 March 1935.
4 Bodleian MS SPSL 23/1.
5 Bodleian MS SPSL 17/153.
6 *St Andrews Citizen*.
7 Walter Ledermann, *Encounters of a Mathematician*, based on an interview with Ledermann in 2000, [self-published] (2010).

8 UY 875 Irvine Box File: Development. John Napier of Merchiston (1550–1617), mathematician, was the inventor of logarithms and the decimal point. He entered St Andrews University as a student at the age of thirteen.

9 St Andrews Special Collections, D'Arcy Thompson Papers MS 21081.

10 Right Honorable Lord Eustace Percy PC (1887–1958), president of the Board of Education 1924–9, warden and vice-chancellor of Durham University 1937–52.

11 JCI personal papers: correspondence with MVI.

12 JCI personal papers: correspondence with MVI; MVI, *Avenue of Years*.

13 Minutes of St Andrews University Court. Also UY 875 Carnegie Trust.

14 JCI personal papers: correspondence with an American friend.

15 *St Andrews Citizen*, 23 March 1940.

16 JCI, 'The Academic Burden in a Changing World' (1942), UY 875 Box 2/27.

17 UY 875 Irvine/ Box 2 Chapel Addresses.

18 UY 875 Irvine Papers Box File Series: Adult Education.

19 UY 875 Irvine/Box 2 Chapel Addresses.

20 JCI personal papers: correspondence with an American friend.

21 Senator Burton K. Wheeler and the aviator Charles L. Lindbergh formed the America First Committee (AFC), the most powerful isolationist group in the United States. The AFC was dissolved four days after the attack on Pearl Harbour.

22 JCI personal papers: correspondence with an American friend, 7 September 1941.

23 The account of the Polish battalions in St Andrews is informed passim by the *St Andrews Citizen*.

24 Polish obituary tribute contributed by Stanislav Seliga to the *St Andrews Citizen*, 21 June 1952.

25 *St Andrews: The Handbook of the St Andrews Preservation Trust to the City and its Buildings*. St Andrews: St Andrews Preservation Trust (1975).

26 MVI, *Avenue of Years* and passim.

27 NLS Borthwick MS 10479.

28 Exhibition, 'Recording Scotland', held at St Andrews University Gateway Gallery, 2009.

29 JCI personal papers: various correspondence.

30 Burma Road: a rough and difficult pass linking Burma with China and of significance during the Second World War. Burma had been overrun by the Japanese in 1942.

31 Juliana Horatia Gatty Ewing, *Mary's Meadow* (1896 and 1915).

32 Information from the late Sir Eugene Melville.

33 Personal papers: letters of the Rt Rev. Herbert Hensley Henson to JCI.

34 JCI personal papers: correspondence with an American friend.

35 Account contributed by Gordon Carruthers, President of the Students Representative Council 1945, published in *College Echoes*, 12 June 1945.

36 Address given by Sir James Irvine, Principal and Vice-Chancellor, published by *College Echoes*, 12 June 1945.

37 JCI personal papers, correspondence with an American friend, 4 September 1945.

Chapter 17 Avise La Fin

1 Avise La Fin: motto of the clan Kennedy, which translates as 'Consider the End'.
2 UY 875 Box 2: 'St Andrews in Transition'.
3 Ibid.
4 Rectorial Dinner for Sir George Cunningham, May 1947: reply to the toast to the university.
5 Information from Dr John Fewster.
6 UY 875 Box 5, 30 December 1940.
7 JCI personal papers: to MVI, 17 May 1946.
8 *St Andrews Citizen*; UY 875 Box 5.
9 UY 875 Irvine Box File: Adult Education; also MVI personal papers: Diary.
10 UY 875 Box IV.
11 UY 875 Irvine Box A.
12 Tribute to Irvine made by Sir Hector Hetherington, Principal and Vice-Chancellor of the University of Glasgow, published in the *Alumnus Chronicle*, January 1953.
13 JCI to Rudyard Kipling, 23 October 1923 Rudyard Kipling Papers 32/28, on deposit at Sussex University, but owned by The National Trust.
14 UY 875 Box IV, memorandum sent by JCI to Sir Walter Moberley, chairman of the UGC. Originally drafted as a letter to the editor of the *Sunday Times*, but never sent. 12 November 1946.
15 JCI, evidence given to the Tedder Enquiry, Autumn 1951.
16 UY7 sec. 2/1/28.
17 Minutes of Meeting of the Council of University College, 19 June 1939.
18 JCI personal papers: letter from Dr Clyde, 20 June 1939.
19 UY 875 Box IV passim and Box V. Also, *Hansard* for the evidence against D.C. Thomson laid before the Royal Commission on the Press, 31 March 1948, pp. 13, 17, 18 of the minutes of that date.
20 Douglas Wimberley was a career soldier. He commanded the 51st Highland Division at the Second Battle of El Alamein, and was often jokingly referred to as Tartan Tam. There are numerous references to 51st (Highland) Division in Field-Marshall Montgomery's two books, *El Alamein to the River Sangro* and *Normandy to the Baltic*.
21 The Very Revd Dr Charles Warr, Dean of the Thistle, tribute at James Colquhoun Irvine's memorial service, 19 July 1952.
22 UY 875 Box IV, 12 November 1946.
23 NLS Manuscript Collections Acc.6119, vol. 3, part 5 of 'Scottish Soldier', an autobiography in five volumes by Major-General Douglas Neil Wimberley.
24 Russell Papers, St Andrews University Special Collections, MS 381515/70/1 'The bonnie wark gangs merrily on' refers to W.E. Aytoun's *Lays of the Scottish*

Cavaliers, and Other Poems (1846), and 'The Burial March of Dundee' in particular, the preamble to which recounts how after the Battle of Philiphaugh, the
royalist prisoners were butchered in cold blood, under the superintendence of
a clerical emissary, who stood by rubbing his hands, and exclaiming: 'The wark
gangs bonnily on.' I am much indebted to John Stirling of the Castle House
Museum, Dunoon for this reference.

25 NLS Acc 6188/18 (ii). Papers of Thomas Mackay Cooper.

26 Jim Irvine expressed his fury in a lampoon, which he based on a well-known
student song and sent in a private letter to David Russell. Russell Papers 3851/5/70.

There was a Wee Cooper in Fife
(Traditional Weaver's Song)
Specially composed for The Edinburgh Festival, September 1949
By JC Irvine.

There was a wee Cooper wha cam' tae FIFE
Nickety, nackety, noo, noo, noo
Tae judge the St Andrews-Dundee strife
Hi willy wallity, hi John Houlity, ruik a rackity, roo, roo, roo

He didna' bring his wig an' goon
Nickety, nackety . . .
But he brocht a lad frae Bristol toon
Hi willy wallity, hi . . .

Likewise a chiel frae Aiberdeen
Nickety . . .
The queerest Nobleman ever was seen
Hi . . .

They widna' lippen tae what we said
Nickety . . .
But took our documents a' as read
Hi . . .

For masel' I dinna' gie a damn
For D. C. Thomson or Tartan Tam
Hi . . . .

But in truth St Andrews wud be curst
Nickety . . .
If forced tae mairch wi' the 51st
Hi . . . .

Sae let us jine in a gentle sport
Nickety . . .
An' burn at the stake the Cooper Report
Hi . . .

For if ye wud lead a peacefu' life
Nickety . . .
Hae Naething tae dae wi' a Cooper in FIFE
Hi . . .

27 Described in *The Times* as a 'counsel of despair'.
28 UY 875 Box IV.
29 Papers of Cedric Thorpe Davie, St Andrews Special Collections MS deposit 63/3/338.
30 From 'Sir James Irvine, An Appreciation', recollected by Dr E.S. Steele for the *Alumnus Chronicle*, June 1978.
31 *Alumnus Chronicle*, June 1950.
32 *Obituary Notices of Fellows of the Royal Society*, vol. 8, November 1953.
33 Gunning Victoria Jubilee Prize oration of the Royal Society of Edinburgh.
34 Professor John Read, FRS, *Nature*, vol. 166, p. 541.
35 UY 875 Chapel Box File.
36 JCI personal papers.
37 Thomas Jones, *A Diary with Letters, 1931–1950*, Oxford University Press (1954).
38 NLS Manuscript Collections Acc.6119, vol. 3, part 5 of 'Scottish Soldier', an autobiography in five volumes by Major-General Douglas Neil Wimberley.
39 This obituary appeared, often in slightly different form, in numerous scientific journals over the coming months, among them the *Journal of the Chemical Society* and the proceedings of the Royal Society.

Bibliography

In a book so heavily based on original sources, the printed book has played a secondary part. However, in addition to the printed sources referred to in the footnotes, the following have informed this book more generally.

Chapter 1

Sylvester Bone, *Sir Muirhead Bone: Artist and Patron*. London: Bayham Publishing, 2009.

S.G. Checkland, *The Upas Tree. Glasgow 1875–1975: A Study in Growth and Contraction*. Glasgow: University of Glasgow Press, 1976.

Carol Foreman, *Lost Glasgow: Glasgow's Lost Architectural Heritage*. Edinburgh: Birlinn, 2010.

T. C. Smout, *A Century of the Scottish People 1830–1950*. London: Collins, 1986.

Stephen Terry, *The Glasgow Almanac: An A–Z of the City and its People*. Glasgow: Neil Wilson, 2005.

Chapter 2

John E. Dolan and Miles K. Oglethorpe, *Explosives in the Service of Man: Ardeer and the Nobel Heritage*. Edinburgh: Royal Commission on the Ancient and Historical Monuments of Scotland, 1996.

Perilla Kinchin and Juliet Kinchin, *Glasgow's Great Exhibitions 1888, 1901, 1911, 1938, 1988*. Wendlebury: White Cockade Press, 1988.

Michael Moss and John Hume, *Glasgow as it Was. Vol. I: City Life*. Nelson, Lancs.: Hendon Publishing Co., 1975.

W.J. Reader, *Imperial Chemical Industries: A History. Vol. I: The Forerunners, 1870–1926*. London: Oxford University Press, 1970.

John Tweed, *Tweed's Guide to Glasgow and the Clyde*. Glasgow: J. Tweed, 1872.

Chapter 3

Ronald Gordon Cant, *The University of St Andrews, A Short History*. Edinburgh: The Strathmartine Trust, 2002.

Douglas Lloyd, *Chemistry in St Andrews* [booklet]. St Andrews: University of St Andrews School of Chemistry, 2003. Available in e-book format from the

University of St Andrews' digital repository of research output, at: http://hdl.
handle.net/10023/589.

*St Andrews: The Handbook of the St Andrews Preservation Trust to the City and its
Buildings.* St Andrews: St Andrews Preservation Trust, 1975.

Chapter 4

James Colquhoun Irvine (ed. James B. Salmond), *The Aim and the End. Being
Lectures and Addresses Delivered by Sir J.C. Irvine.* Edinburgh and London:
Oliver and Boyd, 1956.

Chapter 5

John Frew (ed.), *Building for a New Age: The Architects of Victorian and Edwardian
St. Andrews.* St Andrews: Crawford Centre for the Arts, University of St
Andrews, *c.*1966.

Raymond Lamont-Brown, *The Life and Times of St Andrews.* Edinburgh: John
Donald, 1989.

Douglas Cuthbert Colquhoun Young, *St Andrews: Town and Gown, Royal and
Ancient.* London: Cassell, 1969.

Chapter 6

St Andrews University, *Votiva Tabella: A Memorial Volume of St. Andrews University in Connection with its Quincentenary Festival. MCCCCXI–MDCCCCXI.*
Glasgow: Printed for the University by R. Maclehose and Company, 1911.

Chapter 7

Mabel Violet Irvine, *The Avenue of Years: A Memoir of Sir James Irvine, Principal
and Vice-Chancellor of the University of St. Andrews, 1921–1952.* Edinburgh:
Blackwood, 1970.

Michael L.G. Gardner, *The History of Finsbay Lodge, Harris: Life and Fishing on a
Hebridean Isle.* Bradford: Michael Gardner, 2008.

Ludwig Fritz Haber, *The Poisonous Cloud: Chemical Warfare in the First World
War.* Oxford: Clarendon, 1986.

Charles Howard Foulkes. *Gas! The Story of the Special Brigade.* Edinburgh and
London: Blackwood & Sons, 1934.

Winston Churchill, *The World Crisis,* 6 vols. London: Thornton Butterworth,
1923–7, 1929 and 1931.

Chapter 8

Lorn Macintyre, *Sir David Russell: A Biography.* Edinburgh: Canongate, 1995.

Chapter 10

Janet Dunbar, *J.M. Barrie, The Man Behind the Image.* London: Collins, 1970.

Andrew Birkin, *J.M. Barrie and The Lost Boys.* London: Constable, 1979.

Charles Loch Mowat, *Britain between the Wars, 1918–1940.* London: Methuen, 1955.

Chapter 13

University of St Andrews/ Walker Trust, *Walker Trust Lectures on Leadership, Delivered before the University of St Andrews, 1930–49*. Oxford: Oxford University Press, 1950.

Betty Willsher, *St Andrews: Ancient City in the Twentieth Century*. Kinloss: Librario, 2003.

Betty Willsher, *St Andrews Citizens: Their Societies, Past and Present*. Kinloss: Librario, 2003.

Jo Grimond, *Memoirs*. London: Heinemann, 1979.

Chapter 17

J.B. Salmond (ed.), *Veterum Laudes: Being a Tribute to the Achievements of the Members of St. Salvator's College during Five Hundred Years*. Edinburgh: Oliver and Boyd, 1950.

Ronald G. Cant, *The College of St Salvator: Its Foundation and Development*. Edinburgh: Oliver and Boyd, 1950.

Annie I. Dunlop, *The Life and Times of James Kennedy, Bishop of St. Andrews*. Edinburgh: Oliver and Boyd, 1950

Donald Southgate, *University Education in Dundee: A Centenary History*. Edinburgh: Edinburgh University Press, 1982.

Michael Shafe (comp.), *University Education in Dundee, 1881–1981*. Dundee: University of Dundee, 1982.

Index